Mergers, Acquisitions, and Global Empires

Companies that have acquired other enterprises through mergers and acquisitions (M&A) are in essence akin to the global "empires" of history. In this book, the author weaves a unique narrative that looks both at empires of business created by M&A and at global empires from world history, in an attempt to answer the question: why do certain empires endure for long periods while others collapse in a short space of time?

Empires, whether formed by M&A or by conquest, have a hierarchical relationship of control and domination by a single authority or center, the "parent company" or the "mother country," over another group of people on the periphery, the "subsidiary company" or "colony." Given these similarities in development and structure, the author looks at examples of empires in Western and Asian history and at major M&A cases, and argues that long-enduring empires of both kinds have a common cultural trait: their practice of "tolerance" within their organizations/societies.

While there are books on the topic of M&A and others on empires, at present there is no single text that examines the impact of culture on both. This book is intended to fill this void and to provide hints and suggestions to practitioners of M&A; the book will also interest students of business and history who want an accessible, non-technical narrative on what enables empires, whether they are of nations or of M&A, to endure and prosper.

Ko Unoki has been involved with global marketing, corporate strategy formulation, and strategic alliances while working in the electronics and healthcare industries for several decades, and was also a Senior Fellow at the Twenty-First Century Public Policy Institute of the Federation of Japanese Economic Organizations (Keidanren). This is his first published book.

Mergers, Acquisitions, and Global Empires

Tolerance, diversity, and the success of M&A

Ko Unoki

Routledge
Taylor & Francis Group

LONDON AND NEW YORK

First published 2013
by Routledge
2 Park Square, Milton Park, Abingdon, Oxon OX14 4RN

Simultaneously published in the USA and Canada
by Routledge
711 Third Avenue, New York, NY 10017

Routledge is an imprint of the Taylor & Francis Group, an informa business

British Library Cataloguing in Publication Data
A catalogue record for this book is available from the British Library.

Library of Congress Cataloging in Publication Data
Unoki, Ko.
Mergers, acquisitions, and global empires: tolerance, diversity, and the
success of M&A/by Ko Unoki.
  p. cm.
Includes bibliographical references and index.
1. Consolidation and merger of corporations.
2. International business enterprises. I. Title.
HD2746.5.U56 2012
338.8′3–dc23   2012010799

ISBN: 978-0-415-52874-0 (hbk)
ISBN: 978-0-203-09570-6 (ebk)

Typeset in Times New Roman
by Wearset Ltd, Boldon, Tyne and Wear

MIX
Paper from
responsible sources
FSC
www.fsc.org
FSC® C004839

Printed and bound in Great Britain by
TJ International Ltd, Padstow, Cornwall

Contents

Preface

According to the results of a DNA test that I took out of curiosity several years ago to find out my ancestral origins, I have an ancient paternal ancestor who was born during the last Ice Age in the region of the East Asian landmass where contemporary China is located, and a maternal ancestor who came from somewhere in the present-day Middle East.[1] What I found remarkable was that the DNA test revealed that there is someone currently residing in China who most likely has the same common ancestor as I, going back approximately 1,000 years. For some unfathomable reason lost to history, however, a descendant of this Chinese paternal ancestor and a descendant of my Middle Eastern maternal ancestor decided one day to go (or were taken?) to the islands of Japan. And so, some 200,000 years after my ancestors first came into this world on the African continent and after they trekked out of that landmass all the way to the Middle East and East Asia, I was born in the Japanese archipelago to parents of Japanese nationality.

Despite being born in Japan, circumstances were such that from the age of two to twelve I resided in the United States. I lived in neighborhoods in New York City and Chicago that were predominantly white, and went to the local public elementary schools. Most of my friends were Americans of different ethnic backgrounds. English was in effect my "mother" tongue, as I spoke the language even at home with my parents. My understanding of Japanese was extremely rudimentary, and my happy-go-lucky parents were not concerned about this. I grew up on American TV and enjoyed watching *The Brady Bunch* and re-runs of *I Love Lucy*. Occasional vacation trips to Japan with my parents did remind me of my roots, but I felt more at home in Queens, NY, than in my birthplace of Tokyo.

In recalling my days growing up in the US, which was generally a happy time for me, I remember, though, that I encountered at times some tough or humiliating moments. This occurred when schoolmates with whom I was not exactly friendly, or complete strangers, would hurl hostile racist slurs, calling me a "slant," "Jap," "Nip," "Chink," or "Chinaman." (I found that white and black Americans have a hard time distinguishing a Japanese from a Chinese, but then considering the results of my DNA test, this is perhaps not surprising.) At other times some kid would mock me by stretching his eyes in an attempt to imitate my "slit"-shaped eyes and would start acting out the moon-faced Oriental side-kick of the cartoon detective Dick Tracy, or the "inscrutable" Oriental who was always bowing and couldn't get his Ls and Rs right when speaking.

On the other hand, there was the time when an American classmate told me with calm conviction that although I was born in Japan, and despite my insistence that I was Japanese, the fact that I was living in the US made me an American like everyone else in the predominantly Jewish-American classroom. When many years later I told of my experience of having occasionally faced racial taunts while growing up in the US to a white American friend who was thoroughly WASPish in ancestry, he amusingly recounted the "discrimination" and ethnic taunts he had received while growing up in a predominantly Jewish neighborhood of Flushing, NY. Going through such an experience, my American friend said, was part of the baptism of becoming an American.

The cruelty of children, as highlighted in the cartoon *Peanuts* by Charles M. Schulz, is an unfortunate aspect of life, and in retrospect it may have been inevitable that I was on occasion the target of racial taunts from other kids, given the fact that I *did* look different from the other white American students. Indeed, in listening to or reading the accounts of other Asian Americans, I realize that I was not alone in this respect. But what was totally unexpected was the reception I received from Japanese classmates when I returned to Japan. My inability to speak the Japanese language properly was the cause of frequent teasing and mocking from other students, who labeled me a "henna gaijin", or "weird foreigner." My behavior was considered "un-Japanese," and I was often called an "American" or simply a "gaijin" (foreigner), not only by other students but by teachers as well. When being reprimanded for a mischievous prank committed with other classmates, I was singled out when the teacher said, "Well, I guess you can't control your behavior because you're an American!" The way such statements were delivered made it perfectly clear that being called an American was not a compliment.

Even in adulthood and while working for over two decades at the Tokyo-based Sony Corporation, I received snide remarks from certain colleagues calling me a *gaijin* or an American. A supervisor of mine, before meeting me and not knowing that I was proficient in the Japanese language, remarked to another colleague, "Unoki-san doesn't know Japanese? Well, that sure makes him a 'katawa' (a politically incorrect Japanese word that is banned from on-air broadcasts and essentially means a physically incomplete human being)!" At one point, I had pretty much had it, and challenged a colleague who had declared that I was not Japanese by asking him, "Who or what, then, is a typical Japanese?" To my disappointment, all I received in reply was an exasperated rolling of the eyes and a quick change of subject.

Such experiences while residing in both the US and Japan left me with a strong interest in the topic of culture and intercultural communication, which is the *basso continuo* of this narrative on the impact of culture in mergers and acquisitions (M&A) and on global empires in history. As I until recently worked for a major Japanese consumer electronics company, developments in the

Japanese consumer electronics industry have also spurred my desire to write this book.

In December 2009, the Japanese electronics conglomerate, Panasonic Corporation (formerly called the Matsushita Electric Industrial Corporation, or MEI, until 2008), announced that it had acquired the consumer electronics manufacturer Sanyo Electric Corporation (Sanyo). Sanyo had become a full-fledged subsidiary of Panasonic. For several years prior to 2009, various industries in Japan such as banking, steel, paper, and pharmaceuticals had been undergoing restructuring and consolidation through M&A. For the crowded Japanese consumer electronics industry, the acquisition of Sanyo by Panasonic was perhaps the first large-scale M&A deal, which many industry watchers hoped would become the catalyst to spark further necessary consolidation.

As with all M&A deals, the question that arises is: will Panasonic succeed in making this acquisition work? The answer at this writing is that it is still too early to tell. But for this particular acquisition there is an urgent reason to ask this question. Panasonic is renowned for its manufacturing prowess and its ability to deliver high-quality consumer and industrial products. It does have a significant history of undertaking M&A and alliances, but for the most part they involved the acquisition of considerably smaller companies. The only large-scale acquisition that Panasonic had undertaken before the purchase of Sanyo was the acquisition of the Hollywood film studio Universal Studios in 1990, and this ended abruptly in 1995, when MEI divested the business after an acrimonious management struggle between the two companies. It was definitely not an auspicious case to refer to in foretelling the future of Panasonic and Sanyo.

Management struggles notwithstanding, in the case of the acquisition of Universal Studios it could be argued upon closer scrutiny that MEI at the time did not have a well-thought-out business strategy. The acquisition of Sanyo, however, with its superior solar cell technologies, represents a major step for Panasonic towards its strategic goal of becoming a leader in energy products development. There does seem to be, in this case, a coherent strategic goal behind the acquisition, at least from what has been publicly announced. Furthermore, the acquisition of Universal Studios, unlike that of Sanyo, was a cross-border M&A deal. This presented to MEI new international management and cultural challenges that the company had not experienced previously, and which perhaps exceeded the capabilities of its management at the time. In this respect, it is perhaps unfair to Panasonic to prophesize its future with Sanyo by looking at what happened before with Universal Studios. But, there are doubts.

In 2009 a book came out in Japan entitled *Panasonic ga Sanyo o baishu suru honto no riyu* (The Real Reason Why Panasonic Acquired Sanyo), written by Ogi Masamichi. The author, a journalist and observer of the electronics industry, looks at the history of Panasonic and argues that its corporate culture may be a major obstacle to successfully integrating Sanyo.[2] Indeed, with regard to culture, it is interesting to note that back in 1995 when MEI announced at a press conference its divestiture of Universal Studios, the company briefly cited cultural differences between the two companies as a factor that led to its decision to divest.

The impact of culture on M&A has often been discussed, and there is much literature available on this subject. But what is of particular interest to me is what Ogi described as Panasonic's culture: a culture of intolerance, i.e., a culture that is unable to accept different methods and ideas that were not born within the company.[3] This view of Panasonic's culture subsequently brought to mind a book written by law professor Amy Chua of Yale Law School titled *Day of Empire*, in which Chua argues that every society that achieved global domination, such as the Persian, Roman, and Mongol empires, was able to become a hegemonic power because of its tolerant policies such as respecting the different religions, social customs, and languages of its conquered subjects.[4]

Ogi and Chua, in short, share a similar view of the importance of having a tolerant culture and practicing tolerance, which in essence boils down to accepting diversity in its many forms. For Ogi, a tolerant culture is key for Panasonic to realize a smooth integration of Sanyo with the company, while for Chua, a tolerant culture is at the foundation of a long-lasting and stable global empire.

Drawing largely from the arguments of Ogi and Chua, I will attempt to look at the issue of culture and its impact not only on M&A but also on global empires. The endeavor is in part a reflection of my interest not only in management and leadership, but also in International Relations, which I studied as an undergraduate and graduate student. While I do not intend to undertake a detailed retelling of the history of various M&A deals and empires, I will highlight the strong parallels and analogies between M&A and global empire-building. I will also argue that companies that have been able to achieve their strategic objectives through M&A deals, and empires that have become global and have endured for centuries, share a common cultural attribute of practicing tolerance. I hope through this attempt at cross-pollination to attract readers who have a wide interest in business, history, and international affairs. I also hope that this study will be of use to business leaders, who may be able to learn from the successful integration policies of global empires of the past and apply certain lessons to real-world business circumstances surrounding M&A.

Finally, writing this book has also been a cathartic exercise that allowed me to look back on my experiences of having lived in two distinct cultures and fathom the larger meaning of what I had gone through. As I mentioned earlier, I had some bitter moments of being labeled and considered a "foreigner" in my own native country. I hope that this narrative will help to remind my Japanese compatriots in particular of the importance and the benefits of tolerating diversity, which I believe will be a key factor for Japan to embrace in order to survive as a great power in world affairs in the coming years.

(Note: Japanese personal names throughout the text are in the Japanese order, i.e., surname followed by given name.)

Acknowledgments

This book, which is based on a doctoral thesis submitted to the School of International Corporate Strategy of Hitotsubashi University, would not have been possible without the kind support of the school and in particular of my thesis advisor, Professor Tish Robinson, who had been unfailing in giving words of encouragement and support and showing enthusiasm up to the very end of this endeavor. My thanks also go to the staff at my publisher Routledge and in particular to Associate Editor Lam Yong Ling, who was very supportive in getting my book proposal accepted. Thanks also must be extended to Gail Honda who did a marvelous job in proofreading my original draft thesis. Appreciation and gratitude go to my parents who gave me the experience of living in two different cultures, without which I would not have had the inspiration to write this book, and for their tolerance for letting me grow up as an "American" and not forcing me to learn my "native" Japanese tongue. I also extend my gratitude to the memory of Morita Akio, the co-founder of Sony. It was thanks to his advice that I decided to pursue my university studies in the US, which in retrospect became the intellectual foundation that made it possible many years later to write this book. Finally, last but not least, my thanks go to my wife Ritsuko for supporting my endeavors as a graduate student while working full time, and who had to bear with my time away at my PC and my constant preoccupation with the topic of empires.

1 Introduction

There is a way to get the empire: get the people, and the empire is got. There is a way to get to the people: get their hearts, and the people are got. There is a way to get their hearts: it is simply to collect for them what they like and not to lay upon them what they dislike.

Mengzi[1]

When states are acquired in a country differing in language, customs, or laws, there are difficulties, and good fortune and great energy are needed to hold them.

Nicolo Machiavelli[2]

Identifying an empire

Definitions of "empire"

Empires have been in existence since the beginning of recorded human history and have often played a pivotal and central role in the development of human civilization. As the American socialist priest and journalist Irwin St. John Tucker (1905–1969) put it in the first few sentences of his book *A History of Imperialism*:

> Empires are as old as history itself. When the misty curtain first parts for us upon that stage whereon the drama of life is played, emperors occupy the center of the scene. They have held the leading role ever since.[3]

"Empire" is a word that calls forth many images and emotions. For some, the word may evoke images of the magnificent stone temples and buildings built by the plebeians of the Roman Empire. For others, the painting *The Secret of England's Greatness* by the English painter of historical themes, Thomas Jones Barker (1815–1882), which depicts a benevolent-looking Queen Victoria presenting a bible to a submissive African chieftain in the audience chamber of Windsor Castle, may come to mind. For this author, aside from several images recalled from school lessons and reading history books, the word "empire" brings to mind the British composer Edward Elgar's stirring and solemn song

Land of Hope and Glory with its lyrics by Arthur C. Benson: "By Freedom gained, by Truth maintained, Thine Empire shall be strong.... Wider still and wider shall thy bounds be set; God, who made thee mighty, make thee mightier yet,"[4] the music of which is often heard at university graduation ceremonies in the US (perhaps in playing this music some universities subconsciously desire to bring forth empire builders into this world?). The historian Niall Ferguson of Harvard University, in his book *Empire*, recalls listening in admiration to the adventurous tales of his pioneering relatives who set out to all the far corners of the British Empire, which implanted in his adolescent mind a heroic image of the empire on which the sun never sets.[5] To Ferguson and his family, the British Empire represented bright sunlight, and its legacy and importance were never questioned.[6]

To those who were on the side of the dominated, however, the word "empire" may evoke sentiments of anger and outrage associated with memories and events such as the Amritsar Massacre in British India, when British Indian Army soldiers under the command of General R.E.H. Dyer gunned down several hundred unarmed Indians at a gathering without warning. Or it may call forth the massacre perpetrated by British colonial authorities when they indiscriminately opened fire on Irish football spectators in Croke Park on a day during the Irish War of Independence that would be remembered as "Bloody Sunday." Filipinos may recall their American conquerors torturing captured Filipino "rebels" and destroying villages and killing their inhabitants when their islands were invaded. For some Indonesians, the indiscriminate point-blank shooting in the heads of 470 men suspected of being colonial rebels in the Indonesian village of Lawagede at the hands of the Dutch colonial masters may come to mind. To Koreans who lived under the yoke of Japanese imperialism and to their descendants as well, "empire" may prompt memories of the March 1 Movement of 1919 during which the Japanese massacred several thousand Koreans in an effort to keep their contumacious subjects in their place. For the descendants of the Herero of South-West Africa (present-day Namibia), the massacre in 1904 of over 50,000 of their people at the hands of the Germans, who engaged in indiscriminate shooting and the burning alive of men, women, and children as retribution for rebelling against their imperial rule, may come to mind. For those on the receiving end, all too often life in an empire was not a rosy experience and meant massacres, suppression of individual liberty, slavery, and economic exploitation.

While there are various images, perceptions, emotions, and memories associated with "empire," the word itself is derived from the Latin *imperium*, meaning a domain that is ruled by an emperor. The political, economic, and cultural policies of control historically undertaken by such empire builders as the British, Dutch, Spanish, and Romans over their conquered subjects and territories have in effect made the concept of "empire" suggest a group of people or territories under the political, economic, and social domination of a hegemonic nation or people. There seems, however, to be no ready agreement or understanding regarding its definition. Certain political commentators, for example, have used the word "empire" as a label to describe the behavior and intent of the United

States.[7] American historian Paul Schroeder of the University of Illinois has defined "empire" as the political control exercised by one independent, organized political unit over another.[8] Historian Stephen Howe of the University of Bristol presents a definition of "empire" as consisting of a center and a periphery: a large, multiethnic or multidivisional political unit, usually created by conquest, that is divided between a dominant center and subordinate peripheries which are sometimes distantly located from the center.[9] Meanwhile, the International Relations scholar Michael Doyle defines "empire" as a relationship of political control imposed by a political society over the effective sovereignty of another political society.[10]

Alongside the term "empire," there is the concept of "imperialism." While pointing out that "imperialism" originally referred to the policies of Napoleon III of France in the 1860s, Howe specifically identifies imperialism as meaning the actions and attitudes which create or uphold empires.[11] Thomas McCarthy of Northwestern University, on the other hand, does not make a distinction between "empire" and "imperialism." Although he observes that some authors characterize the former as the "colonialism" of the settler and commercial colonies prior to the last quarter of the nineteenth century and the latter as the struggle among competing national powers during the decades immediately preceding World War I, McCarthy broadly uses both words to refer to the domination and exploitation of peripheries by a "center" that is driven by governments, colonists, or private trading companies.[12] In contrast to McCarthy, Michael Hardt of Duke University and Antonio Negri of the University of Padua in their book *Empire* describe "empire" as something altogether different from "imperialism." While to them imperialism was an expansion of the sovereignty of European nation-states beyond their original territories, empire is a regime that is characterized by a lack of fixed territorial boundaries which not only manages a territory and a population, but also aims to condition human nature and create a situation of perpetual peace through violent means. As they put it, although the practice of "empire" has often been bloody, ironically its concept has always been dedicated to the creation of a universal peace.[13]

While there are of course many other interpretations and definitions of "empire," for the purposes of building a hypothesis for this book I will at this point propose a definition which is essentially a synthesis of the various definitions mentioned above; that is, an "empire" is a hierarchical relationship of control and domination by a single authority or a center over another group of people based in a periphery that is distinct from the center. In the next section I will look at the extent to which this definition of empire is applicable to an act which takes place on a stage other than that of world history and international relations: businesses that undertake mergers and acquisitions (M&A).

Businesses as "empires"

In the context of world history, control within an empire emanates from a sovereign state, but Doyle and McCarthy have pointed out that a non-state body such as a corporation or a religious order can also establish control over peoples and nations.[14] Howe supports this observation by stating that while the focus on empire and empire builders by historians has been in the context of the nation-state, there have been times in history when non-state organizations have taken the initiative in empire-building, a major, successful example being the English East India Company (EIC: the English trading enterprise established by royal charter in the seventeenth century) during the eighteenth century and the early nineteenth.[15] Indeed, during its encroachment upon the Indian subcontinent, the EIC in effect became a government, maintaining its own armed forces, imposing taxes, and enforcing laws. Accordingly, I will argue that the word "empire" can also be used in the business world to describe certain companies that have the characteristics of an empire from world history: the existence of a center (in the form of corporate headquarters), a periphery (in the form of subsidiaries or business divisions), and a hierarchical relationship of control and domination by the people of the center over another group of people in the periphery. The term "empire" to portray such a company has in fact been in use for some time. A director of the EIC described his company, which led British efforts at controlling the Indian subcontinent in the eighteenth century, as "an empire within an empire."[16] Even Hollywood has used "empire" to describe a company. In the opening few minutes of Orson Welles's classic movie *Citizen Kane*, the narrator describes the business conglomerate lorded over by the fictional American newspaper tycoon Charles Foster Kane as an "empire upon an empire."[17]

Aside from applying the term "empire" to certain types of companies, I also argue that in the world of business, the act of two or more independent enterprises merging with each other or of one independent company taking over another (sometimes forcibly), i.e., the act of mergers and acquisitions (M&A), is basically equivalent to an act of imperialism or empire-building where one independent country takes over another by force or other means, or where several independent countries or political entities come together to form a new union. Both in M&A and in imperialism, the outcome is the creation of a dominant center consisting of a "parent" company in the former and a "mother" country in the latter, and a periphery consisting of subsidiary companies or divisions in the case of businesses and colonies in the case of empires.

"Successful" and "unsuccessful" global empires

Both in world history and in business, there have been cases of what I consider "successful" and "unsuccessful" empires. While "success" is a subjective term open to many ways of interpretation and measurement, I argue that the definition of a "successful empire" of world history is as follows and contains several critical success factors. A successful empire in world history is one which has lasted for more than a century. Within a successful empire, its people, both at its center and at its periphery, have seen their level of prosperity rise during its duration and have experienced a non-discriminatory distribution of additionally created wealth. A successful empire has also been able to build up the loyalty of its conquered subjects at the periphery so as to support the continuation of the empire.

Conversely, I argue that the meaning of an "unsuccessful" empire is as follows. An unsuccessful empire is an empire that fails to garner loyalty from its conquered/peripheral subjects and instead creates resistance from them against imperial rule. This in turn may result in a heavy-handed response from the imperial master in controlling its subjects, leading possibly to cases of brutal suppression and discrimination. Inability to contain resistance may lead to the implosion and collapse of the empire. In an unsuccessful empire, there may be growth in prosperity as a result of empire-building, but the conquered/peripheral subjects may not be full participants in the sharing of wealth.

"Successful" business empires

Having identified the primary characteristics of "successful" global empires, I argue that they can equally be used to define "successful" business empires that have been created from M&A deals. To better fit the definition to the business world, however, I have changed the wording of some of the elements of a "successful" business empire, as follows. A successful business empire created from an M&A deal is one that lasts for a long period (at least for 10 years). Further, (1) the business empire is able to achieve its corporate objectives through its merger with or acquisition of another company; (2) the shareholder value, revenues, and profitability of the business empire has not declined as a result of acquiring or merging with another company; (3) the business empire has enabled the acquired business enterprise to contribute to the increase of the empire's revenues and profits; (4) the business empire has been successful in building up the loyalty of its acquired employees and has been able to avoid loss of morale and instability of management and organization; and, (5) if the business empire has divested or dissolved its merger with a "conquered" company, it was *not* as a result of detrimental losses or other major problems arising per se from the merger or acquisition.

A hypothesis for this book

The high rate of M&A failures

According to Robert Holthausen of the Wharton School, numerous studies of the long-term results of business mergers show that the rate of failure has been extremely high: 50 to 80 percent.[18] Michael Porter of the Harvard Business School concluded, based on an analysis of acquisitions made by 33 "Fortune 500" firms (the top 500 companies as surveyed by *Fortune* magazine), that over half of these had been unsuccessful with the end result being divestiture.[19] The American Management Association examined 54 big mergers undertaken in the 1980s and found that approximately one half of the mergers led to declines in productivity and/or profits.[20] Management professor Martin Sikora points out that according to accepted data most M&A deals don't succeed.[21] The negative data on M&A does not seem to apply to the US only. According to an analysis by the consultancy the Hay Group of more than 200 major European M&A deals undertaken between 2004 and 2007, just 9 percent of the business leaders felt that they were "completely successful" in meeting their stated objectives for a merger or acquisition.[22] While the reasons for M&A failure are diverse, the high rate of failure suggests that many business leaders have neglected to heed the oft-cited words of the Spanish philosopher George Santayana stating that those who cannot remember the past are condemned to repeat it. In this regard, the core similarity between the acts of M&A and empire-building as I have argued suggests that business leaders involved in M&A may have also something to learn from the success and failures of empire builders in history.

Despite the lackluster performance of M&A, however, its use as a business tactic remains popular among business leaders. The global M&A activity market topped US$4.3 trillion and over 40,000 deals in 2007, up from US$1.2 trillion in 2002.[23] In addition, globalization has increased the market for cross-border M&A, with cross-border transactions reaching US$2.1 trillion in 2007, up from US$256 billion in 1996.[24] In the so-called emerging markets, M&A activity has substantially increased, with annual increases in the number of cases at 300 percent in China and 68 percent in India.[25] Chinese companies have been on a buying spree of natural resources companies and car companies. According to Thomson Reuters data, in 2009 the value of Chinese outbound M&A was US$42.6 billion, which accounted for 7.5 percent of total cross-border M&A.[26] Meanwhile, Japanese companies are reported to have spent a record US$80 billion in 2011 on acquiring 620 foreign companies, breaking the previous record of US$75 billion on 466 M&A deals in 2008.[27]

Indeed, the ever-growing popularity of M&A suggests that M&A initiators are unaware of the supposedly high failure rates, or that they do not care, or that they feel that they will not fail. Bill Pursche of the business advisory firm First Call Advisors has suggested that most data showing high failure rates of M&A deals is simply wrong.[28] Without getting into a debate challenging the conventional wisdom that most M&A deals are doomed to fail, it is safe to assume that M&A will continue to be used as a tactic by business leaders for achieving their corporate objectives. That is, the act of empire-building will continue in the business world. And as it likely, going by past trends, that cross-border M&A activity will increase in the future, barring of course any major global disruptive upheaval, we can also assume that global business empires will continue to rise and fall accordingly.

The impact of culture on M&A

In many cases of M&A, executives have noted the impact of culture on their outcome. According to a transatlantic study of executives involved in M&A deals cited by the consulting services company Mercer, 75 percent of the participants stated that the harmonization of cultures and communication with employees were the most important factors in the post-merger process.[29] In another study undertaken by the Intelligence Unit of the British news magazine *The Economist*, 67 percent of survey respondents cited cultural integration as the most important and the most critical success factor in an M&A deal.[30]

While these studies have been conducted primarily in a Western setting, awareness of the importance and difficulties of cultural adjustment does not seem to be limited to European or American executives. According to a survey of 16 Japan-based M&A advisors and 51 Japanese corporate respondents conducted by the accounting and consulting firm Deloitte, 73 percent believe that differences in management culture present the most serious obstacle to overcome when looking to undertake a Japanese outbound M&A deal. In addition, 68 percent of Japanese corporate respondents pointed out that they experienced cultural/management differences when attempting to integrate with an overseas target.[31]

But what is culture? Culture is a factor that is not as readily measurable as objective data such as profit margins and other management ratios. Attempts to define it have been made by various scholars. Prominent among them and often mentioned in MBA courses on organizational theory, the Dutch anthropologist Geert Hofstede defined culture as "the collective programming of the human mind that distinguishes the members of one human group from others."[32] In a similar vein, Edgar Schein of the Sloan School of Management considered culture to be the "accumulated shared learning of a given group, covering behavioral, emotional, and cognitive elements of the group members' total psychological functioning."[33] For the purpose of building a hypothesis, I will take the liberty of borrowing from Schein and Hofstede and give a definition of culture as follows. Culture is the "glue" that helps to keep together a particular people in an organization such as a nation, tribe, or company by creating a common identity through the sharing of a system of beliefs, values, and behavior that is distinguishable from another system followed by another group of people.

A hypothesis

In her book *Day of Empire*, Yale University law professor Amy Chua argues that for every power in history that achieved global hegemony, its success was due to the pluralistic and tolerant policies which it employed during its rise to preeminence. In every historical case she takes up within her book she finds that tolerance was an indispensible factor. Conversely, she argues that the decline of an empire tended to coincide with the rise of intolerance and xenophobia, often accompanied with calls for racial or religious purity.[34] In short, Chua suggests that cultural factors, especially those concerning tolerance, come into play in the rise and fall of empires. For Chua, tolerance was the "glue" that kept an empire together and prosperous. I have suggested that various businesses that came together through M&A were in essence "empires." The opinions of executives on the impact of culture on M&A suggest that culture is a factor of prime importance not only in the life of an empire but also for the success of M&A initiators and business leaders. As Chua proposes in her examination of successful global empires, I will suggest in the following chapters that given the structural similarity between a global empire and a business empire built by M&A, the practice of "tolerance" is the common critical success factor among successful M&A business empires. For this purpose, I will define "tolerance," or its practice, as having two major characteristics. First, it is the capacity or ability to accept the coexistence of *diverse ideas and values* and recognize their benefits. Second, it is the capacity or ability to accept the coexistence of *people* regardless of their gender, sexual orientation, ethnicity, religious beliefs, culturally based behavior, and national origin. Nations, societies, and organizations that have within them such capacities and abilities exhibit a high level of what I call "tolerance." Hofstede regarded such nations or societies as having a low level of what he called "uncertainty avoidance," that is, having a high level of tolerance towards ambiguity and uncertainty, and hence being more open and accepting of outsiders and different cultures. Conversely, those societies that are said to have a high level of "uncertainty avoidance" have a low level of tolerance towards ambiguity and uncertainty and hence have within them more ethnic prejudice, xenophobia, and exclusionism.[35]

To conclude, I propose the following hypothesis for this book. Companies that have acquired other enterprises through mergers and acquisitions (M&A) share the essential structural attribute of global empires. Both have a hierarchical relationship of control and domination by a single authority or center, the "parent company" or "mother country," over another group of people based in a periphery that is distinct from the center, the "subsidiary company" or "colony." Such companies are in essence "empires." Furthermore, a "successful" business "empire" created by an M&A deal may share a cultural attribute with "successful" empires in world history, namely a high level of "tolerance." The high level of tolerance has in certain instances led the empire builder in business and in world affairs to accept the coexistence of *different ideas and values* within an empire and recognize their benefits, and to likewise accept the coexistence of *people* and recognize their abilities and potential regardless of their gender, sexual orientation, ethnicity, religious beliefs, culturally based behavior, and national origin. This in turn has contributed to the prosperity of the empire, the loyalty of the acquired/conquered employees/subjects, and subsequently the long-term stability and continuity of the empire.

While Chua had examined in her book the role of tolerance in the rise and fall of global empires, to date no one has in one book taken up examples from *both* global empires and empires created from M&A and looked at how tolerance had impacted the lives of both. As such, with the above hypothesis as a foundation and guide for developing a narrative, I will in the following chapters look at various empires in business and in history and examine the role that tolerance has played in maintaining the life of an empire.

The cases to be examined

The first case from business history that will be examined in this book is the Verenigde Oostindische Compagnie (VOC, sometimes called the Dutch East India Company), the seafaring trading company established in the Netherlands in 1602. The goal of the VOC was simple: to corner the lucrative spice trade in Asia and make money using every means available including the force of arms. As the VOC was formed from the mega-merger of six independent trading companies, structurally it was akin to global empires consisting of several different nations and peoples and hence merits a look as an example of an "empire." In my narrative I will argue that it was the practice of tolerance in the governance of the VOC that helped this business empire to survive for 200 years and made it a highly profitable venture for its investors.

Next to be examined from world history is the Mongol Empire established by Genghis Khan in 1206. The Mongol Empire was the largest contiguous land empire the world has ever known. The Mongols managed to sustain this empire with its multicultural and multiethnic subjects for over two centuries. While examining the rise and achievements of the Mongols, I will focus on the role that tolerance played in keeping together a culturally and ethnically variegated empire. To provide some parallels to the Mongols, I will also look at the Roman Empire, which similarly was a pre-modern empire that consisted of peoples of many cultures and ethnicities and lasted for several centuries. A contrasting case that will be examined is the relatively little known American Empire in the Philippines, which lasted for approximately 40 years.

I will next examine the rise and fall of an empire of business undertaken by the Matsushita Electric Industrial Corporation (MEI, known as Panasonic since 2008), whose Hollywood Empire was born in 1990 when the Japanese electronics conglomerate bought the Music Corporation Agency (MCA), the parent company and owner of the Hollywood-based movie studio Universal Studios, and collapsed when MEI divested it to the Canadian liquor distributor, the Seagram Co. (Seagram), in 1995. Founded by Matsushita Konosuke in 1919, MEI had a long and largely successful history of undertaking M&A as a means of growing its business, which we will look at briefly. While weaving together a narrative on MEI's foray in Hollywood, referring extensively to the reporting of events given at the time by the *New York Times*, the *Los Angeles Times*, and *Nikkei Business*, as well as books by Dennis McDougal and Bernard F. Dick, I will examine aspects of MEI's culture, with a focus on the extent to which the factor of tolerance did or did not play a role during the short life of MEI's Hollywood empire, which turned out to be a disaster that ended in divestiture and losses for the company.

I will look next at another Hollywood empire, that of the Japanese consumer electronics company, the Sony Corporation (Sony). Founded by Ibuka Masaru and Morita Akio in 1946, Sony acquired its Hollywood studio, Columbia Pictures, in 1989. In contrast to what happened with MEI and MCA, Sony's movie empire is still intact, defying the predictions of failure by observers who viewed the acquisition as a prodigious disaster. Accordingly, I will focus on the role that tolerance played in the integration and management policies of Sony towards its acquisition and identify some of the differences between MEI and Sony in their approach to practicing tolerance towards an imperial "conquest."

Given all the M&A deals that have appeared over the past several decades, readers may ask: why choose to look at Panasonic and Sony? There are several reasons. First, both cases of acquisition are akin to the phenomenon of global empire-building. The acquisitions of the movie companies by the Japanese electronics conglomerates led to the creation of large cross-border, cross-cultural empires with a distantly located "mother" company and a colonial holding in its periphery, and hence are relevant to our discussion on empires. Second, the births of these movie entertainment empires were historically significant because they represented, for the first time ever, Japanese companies' taking over what were considered major "cultural assets" of the US and were the largest acquisitions undertaken by Japanese companies at that time. Third, Panasonic and Sony are both Japanese in origin, and both took over companies with origins in the US. Both are basically consumer electronics companies, and both acquired companies in the totally different field of Hollywood movie entertainment. These acquisition cases offer a good opportunity to examine what happens when entities of different nationalities, business models, and corporate and national cultures come into play. Fourth and finally, both MEI and Sony at the time were fairly equal in size in terms of revenues and profitability. These similarities between the two companies provide a controlled environment that makes it easier to see what were the divergent factors between them that prompted the fall of one empire five years after its inception and the continuation of the Sony Hollywood Empire. I hope that the reader will find the above four reasons strong enough to allow me to retell the story of these two empires and highlight certain aspects of their experiences and cultures, especially with regard to the role of tolerance, which will support the arguments and hypothesis of this book.

In addition to focusing on the above specific cases, I will briefly touch upon other examples such as the British Empire in India and Hong Kong, the French Empire in Algeria, the Japanese Empire in Korea, MEI's acquisition of the American consumer electronics manufacturer Quasar, Sony's joint venture with the American broadcaster CBS, the American information technology company Hewlett Packard's acquisition of the American personal computer company Compaq, the merger between the German car company Daimler-Benz and the US auto manufacturer Chrysler Corporation, and the acquisition of the Italian firm Nuovo Pignone by the American conglomerate General Electric (GE).

Admittedly, an interest stemming from my personal and academic background has influenced my choices in weaving this narrative, and I recognize that there are perhaps many other worthwhile cases of M&A and imperialism that deserve attention. However, for the purpose of supporting my hypothesis, I feel that each of the cases to be examined will readily show to the reader the impact of tolerance on the post-merger integration process and on the life and duration of a global empire, whether it is of a nation or of business.

2 An overview of empires

The nature of global empires

Introduction

The constant occurrence of wars, conflicts, and struggles for power in human history indicates that one of the behavioral drivers of *Homo sapiens*, from its appearance approximately 200,000 years ago on the African continent to the present, is the desire to dominate one another. Author and political scientist Francis Fukuyama, in his book *The End of History and the Last Man*, interprets the human drive for domination using Hegel's master-slave dialectic, as elaborated in his *Phenomenology of Spirit*, as a struggle to achieve recognition by others through mortal battle which results in the domination of the master over the slave. According to Fukuyama, Hegel saw this primal aspiration of humans, to be recognized by others as having worth and dignity, as a fundamental factor that distinguishes humans from other animals.[1] Karl Marx, in his *Manifesto of the Communist Party*, presented human history as essentially a struggle for domination between different social classes that has been present with human beings from historical times to the present, with each class struggle ending in either a revolutionary reconstruction of society or the ruin of the contending classes.[2] Whether to fulfill the aspiration of recognition by others or to resist class oppression, as Hegel and Marx respectively suggest, the attempts of *Homo sapiens* to dominate one another over the course of human history have been made in parallel with the development and establishment of various social orders and systems such as feudalism, slavery, dictatorships, and absolute monarchies. Along with the establishment of social orders, from time immemorial the human race has witnessed the rise and fall of empires, some of the earliest being in Egypt (3100 BCE), the Indus Valley (2550 BCE), Babylonia (1790 BCE), and the Shang Dynasty in China (1750 BCE). Most of these ancient empires were regional in nature with territory that was largely contiguous. They comprised peoples that were culturally and ethnically close to one another, as the ability of the rulers to maintain communication and control over vast areas was at the time limited by the available technology. Later there arose empires that were global in scale: the empires of Persia, Rome, Tang China, the Mongols, and England. All of these empires have a common feature of having territories and peoples of various eth-nicities and cultures in far-flung areas under the control of a distantly located "mother country." The act of empire-building in world history has often involved the conquering, absorption, and control of a territory or peoples by another nation or people. Many of these acts of imperialism were undertaken and achieved by the use or threat of brute military force. A parallel in the business world to the act of a country taking over another people or nation using coercive means and scare tactics is where a company undertakes a hostile takeover to acquire another inde-pendent company that refuses to submit to its offer for a "friendly" merger. One such hostile method involves the acquiring company making a public offer for the target company that is far above its market price. Another is where acquiring companies engages in a proxy fight by enlisting the support of other shareholders in removing the recalcitrant management of the target company and replacing it with a board that would be friendly to a takeover—a method akin to that of a hegemonic power achieving regime change in another hostile nation by sponsor-ing a coup and putting a friendly regime in its place.

There have, however, been cases when an empire has been created by peaceful, mutual agreement. The political union of the kingdoms of England and Scotland in forming the United Kingdom is a case in point. The two nations had been at each other's throats for centuries during the Wars of Scottish Independence, with the Scottish king Robert the Bruce's defeat of the English at Bannockburn in 1314 marking a high point in the history of the Scots. Several hundred years later and after sharing the same monarchy for a century, an impoverished Scotland agreed to merge with England. Under the terms of the union, the Scots agreed to give up their independence in return for access to English markets both inside and outside of England. Despite the formation of the UK and the creation of an overriding "British" identity as part of the merger process, England and Scotland continued to exist as distinct cultural entities and, of course, in the hearts and minds of the respective peoples. Tolerance on the part of the English allowed the Scots to pre-serve not only their traditions but also much of their education and legal systems.[3] For two full centuries there was no serious political opposition to the union. Full participation by the Scots in the British political process was permitted, eventually giving rise to Scottish prime ministers such as Ramsay MacDonald, Arthur Balfour, Henry Campbell-Bannerman, and more recently Tony Blair and Gordon Brown. In a move to stave off the calls of independence coming recently from some Scottish nationalists, Scotland was given its own parliamentary assembly in 1999 with powers to determine policies on issues ranging from healthcare to education. At this writing, the Scots, unlike the English, do not pay for university tuition, medical pre-scriptions, or home healthcare. Scotland also prospered from the profits made in the British Empire and from the windfall of the industrial revolution which began in England. In return, the English received over the centuries the valuable loyalty of the Scots during its numerous conflicts with its continental neighbors, and their cooperation in the wars that led to the building of an overseas empire. Despite the various ups and downs in the relationship and calls for independence from some Scottish nationalists, the United Kingdom is still in existence.

The creation of empires through mutual consent (of which, aside from the UK, the creation of the United States of America from the original 13 colonies would arguably be another example) is, however, a phenomenon that is not limited to the world of global politics. A parallel in the business world to the creation of an empire through a political union achieved through mutual consent would be a friendly acquisition, merger, or joint venture (JV) between two or more independent companies. The establishment of the Dutch East India Company, which we will look at in detail in the next chapter, was the result of a friendly merger of six independent companies. An example of a JV which will also be examined below is that of the music recording company CBS/Sony, a business entity that was created in Japan by the mutual agreement of the parent companies: the American broadcasting company CBS and the Japanese electronics company Sony.

Drivers of global empires

The question arises: why does the phenomenon of domination through empire-building occur? If we put aside the views that ascribe the struggles for domination to a desire to fulfill universal recognition (Hegel/Fukuyama) or to a result of class conflict (Marx), we may instead take a fatalistic view that *Homo sapiens* is somehow biologically hardwired for attempting to dominate, since it seems that this is what humans have been doing ever since they appeared and since they have remarkably improved their skills at killing each other. Then maybe we can simply blame our genes or biology for the creation of empires and the resulting fallout throughout human history. If our genes are indeed responsible, and as it is the biological impulse of all living creatures to propagate in order to ensure the continuation of the species, or (as nineteenth-century Social Darwinists such as Herbert Spencer would have it) to ensure the "survival of the fittest," this would also perhaps explain a tendency for empire builders to go forth and multiply, whether they are leaders of nations or in business. Syracuse University psychologist John Marshall Townsend, who had studied the sexual behavior of men in power, noted that would-be Hollywood movie moguls, who, it can be argued, are in some respects empire builders, may be driven by the same biological urges as male bulls: that is, to dominate others and to mate with the most desirable women in the world.[4] The following apocryphal comment attributed to Genghis Khan of the Mongol empire certainly suggests that empire-building had quite a bit to do with satiating a desire to dominate all others and to procreate:

> The greatest pleasure is to vanquish your enemies and chase them before you, to rob them of their wealth and see those dear to them bathed in tears, to ride their horses and clasp to your bosom their wives and daughters.[5]

The procreative drive behind empire-building seemed to have also been in the mind and loins of a British army officer in British India many centuries after Genghis Khan. In the book *Ruling Passions: Sex, Race, and Empire*, which chronicles the sexual history of the British Empire through first-hand eyewitness accounts, author Anton Gill mentions the letter of a British officer who upon his arrival in British India rather crudely recorded for posterity that he "commenced a regular course of fucking with native women."[6]

Scientist and author Jarred Diamond, however, observed that relations of adjacent human tribes, similar to groups of chimpanzees and wolves, were traditionally marked by xenophobic hostility. This may come naturally to the human species given that so much of human behavior is culturally rather than genetically specified, and because cultural differences between different populations are great.[7] That is to say, according to Diamond, cultural differences rather than biology are a driver of competition for territory and for wars that lead to the conquest of one group of people by another, resulting in either extermination or subjugation and, by inference and extension, leading in certain cases to the creation of an empire.

During the mid-nineteenth century, while Europeans such as the British and French were extending their imperial tentacles over the globe, Marx saw imperialism as the end result of capitalists' seeking new markets and profits through trade or conquest, due to the saturation of local markets caused by "the epidemic of over production," resulting in "too much civilization, too much means of subsistence, too much industry, too much commerce."[8] Impelled by the "need of a constantly expanding market for its product," the capitalist/bourgeoisie goes to the ends of the earth and with "heavy artillery ... batters down all Chinese walls." The bourgeoisie forces upon all of its conquered nations the capitalist mode of production and "compels them to introduce what it calls civilization into their midst, i.e., to become bourgeois themselves. In one word, it creates a world after its image."[9]

Building upon Marx's view of oversupply as a chief culprit behind imperialism, the English economist John A. Hobson posed the view that countries such as the US and Europe embarked upon imperialism in order to find markets for overproduction which could not be consumed at home, and for goods and investments. As Hobson saw it, improvements in the methods of production and the concentration of ownership and control of businesses had brought about a situation of excessive production and capital in search of investment. In contrast to the view of Marx, however, for Hobson the "taproot" cause of imperialism was not industrial progress as represented by overproduction, but the misdistribution of consumption power, or under-consumption, within a country, leading to excess savings and preventing the adequate absorption of commodities and capital.[10] But along with this economic root cause of imperialism, Hobson also suggested that primal passions of man were involved, taking the form of a desire to control land, a love of travel, and a spirit of adventure including the lust for slaughter and struggle.[11] Thus to Hobson as well, genes seem to play a role in empire-building.

The Russian revolutionary V.I. Lenin was to build upon Marx's observation and present his analysis that imperialism is the monopoly stage of capitalism, whereby the finance capital of a few big banks fuses with the monopolist combines of industrialists (who have forced out small industry) to support their seizure of the sources of raw materials located outside of the capitalist monopoly economies. Colonies would be established for this purpose and the world would be divided up among the capitalists.[12] As imperialism was the monopoly stage of capitalism and thus the final stage of capitalist development, Lenin believed that the collapse of the capitalist-imperial nations was imminent, a belief that may have influenced and shaped the foreign policy of the Soviet Union during its short existence.[13]

In contrast to Marx, Hobson, and Lenin, who saw the drive for empire as being fueled by overproduction, under-consumption, primal desires, monopoly capital, and the relentless pursuit of profit, the Victorian historian Sir John Seeley put forth the oft-quoted "Accidental Empire" point of view: in his best-selling *The Expansion of England*, published in 1883, he writes, "We seem, as it were, to have conquered and peopled half the world in a fit of absence of mind."[14] This statement has developed a life of its own and has to this day been been assumed to express Seeley's take on British imperialism. A more careful reading will, however, show that Seeley was attempting to describe the innocuous sentiments prevalent among British people at the time, who thought of themselves as a race inhabiting some islands off the northern coast of continental Europe, happily oblivious to the fact that it had colonies where white English-speaking people had displaced indigenous peoples in places such as Canada and Australia. Seeley was aware that a conventional look at the history of Britain and its "parliamentary wrangling and agitations about liberty" may give the impression that the British Empire was created out of absentmindedness. But, as he elaborated, "the history of England was not in England but in America and Asia." That is, the British Empire was the result of a conscious and deliberate effort at overseas expansion.[15]

The British historian W.G. Beasley wrote that the human impetus towards imperialism did not need explaining. As he saw it, humans have always, as individuals or in groups, sought to dominate one another whenever they had the opportunity.[16] Beasley's view is akin to that of Hobson or Townsend. That is, the impulse to dominate one another is something that is ingrained in the human psyche.

In a tone similar to that of Beasley, the political theorist Hans J. Morgenthau, who was regarded as one of the proponents of realist theories in international relations, stated that the creation of empires was essentially a manifestation of achieving power in the international arena of politics. For Morgenthau, who regarded power as the control that men have over other men's minds and actions, all politics was a struggle for power and the aiming for power was something that was natural to humans.[17]

During the early days of the European Age of Exploration, led primarily by the Spanish, Portuguese, Dutch, and English from the fifteenth century to the seventeenth, the search for spices, gold, god, and glory was also a major driver of the empire builders, with traders, soldiers, and priests pursuing their respective conquests literally from the same boat. During the heyday of modern imperialism, from the eighteenth to the early twentieth century, when most of the world was under the imperial domination of European colonial powers including Britain, France, and the Netherlands, imperialism was often justified for economic reasons such as securing markets, trade, and natural resources. Great power rivalry was also a driver of imperialism, with colonial powers pursuing hegemony over one another and engaging in wars over territories and markets. For US president William McKinley, it would seem that the Almighty made him decide to take over the Philippines and save his "little brown brothers" from Spain and savagery: one night, after days of prayer, "Almighty God," according to McKinley, came to him and convinced him that as the Filipinos were a bunch of savages who were unfit for self rule, there was nothing more for the Americans to do than to educate, uplift, civilize, and Christianize these people. After receiving this profound message, McKinley went soundly back to sleep.[18]

To conclude, the drivers behind the building of empires have historically been many and varied. And alongside these, another factor came into play which was to have a profound influence on the fate of modern imperialism: racism.

Empire-building and racism

Racism, or the act of discriminating against a person based on that person's color, ethnicity, national culture, origins and so on, is a subject that is often seen as difficult or politically incorrect to talk about, and the reader may wonder what is the point of presenting a brief discourse on this subject in a book whose main focus is on M&A. Racism is, however, a manifestation of intolerance that I argue is central to the story of the eventual fall of certain empires, and therefore deserves an overview. While such drivers as economics, prestige, and national rivalry fueled the expansion of European empires, the concept of the superiority of European/Western culture and the development of hierarchies based on race also went hand in hand with the empire builders. The inventions coming from the industrial revolution and the cultural output of the Europeans were proof to the European empire builders of the superiority of the West and the racial and cultural inferiority of all others. Thomas Macaulay, a Scottish graduate of Cambridge, historian, poet, and politician, who was twice elected to the House of Commons before serving in British India and who was the architect of British colonial education policy, had nothing but contempt for 5,000 years of Indian and Arabic civilization, as he expressed in a minute on education delivered to the British House of Commons in 1835. While freely admitting that he had no knowledge of either Sanskrit or Arabic, Macaulay claimed, based on knowledge acquired from reading translations of Arabic or Sanskrit works and from the opinions of academics involved with Oriental literature, that the "intrinsic superiority of Western literature" was beyond doubt; that a single shelf of a good European library was "worth the whole native literature of India and Arabia." And when books of fact were compared, the superiority of what Europeans wrote was "absolutely immeasurable."[19]

To some of the empire builders, the "fact" that Western civilization and Europeans were culturally and racially superior to heathen savages was a sign that the Europeans had a destiny to fulfill: "taking up the white man's burden" or pursuing a "*mission civilisatrice*" through the building of empires and the subjugation of these people. In the mid-eighteenth century, the German philosopher Immanuel Kant, in his *Idea of a Universal History on a Cosmopolitical Plan*, envisioned that Europe, which has seen through history "a regular gradation of improvement in civil society ... is in all probability destined to give laws to all the rest" of the globe.[20] The same Macaulay that belittled 5,000 years of Indian and Arabic civilization saw it as the duty of the British to lift up the people of India from the "lowest depths of slavery and superstition," and asserted that the day when the Indians would demand European-style political institutions would be the "proudest day in English history."[21] In the late nineteenth century, US President Theodore Roosevelt believed as well that the "superior" Western man had a duty to look after a people who were unfit to rule themselves. He put this quite succinctly when referring to the brutal US subjugation of the Philippines (about which more below), describing its peoples as "half-caste and native Christians, warlike Moslems, and wild pagans" who were "utterly unfit" for self-rule. For Roosevelt, the US had driven out the tyranny of the Spanish. If the Filipinos were now left to themselves, the islands would fall under "savage anarchy."[22]

Granted, the fact that many of the empire builders of ancient and pre-modern times also considered their native culture superior to "barbarians" shows that the empire builders of modern times were not exceptional in their condescending attitude. The Romans considered anyone outside of the sphere of the Roman Empire a barbarian. The Chinese as well considered all those not part of the majority Han race, especially the nomads of the steppe such as the Mongols, to be barbarians, and it was their conflicts with such people that shaped the Chinese sense of cultural superiority.[23] According to the Japanese Shinto scholar Hirata Atsutane, as the Japanese were the descendant of the gods, they were thus superior to the peoples of all other countries of the world.[24] Hirata claimed that the essential superiority of the Japanese over other peoples came from their practice since ancient times of the cardinal principles governing the proper conduct of man, including humanity and righteousness.[25]

But in contrast to the racism practiced by the Europeans towards their colonial subjects, which was often based on differences in skin color and other outward physical characteristics as well as on cultural differences, the Romans seem to have had no such qualms about skin color or different cultures, being ready to accept a physically different Goth, African, or Spaniard and make him emperor. The Chinese believed that "barbarians" could be reclassified as civilized through their assimilation with Chinese culture.[26] The Tang Dynasty was noted for allowing the "barbaric" and physically different-looking people from Turkish tribes to participate in the Tang government and military, giving them Chinese titles and names.[27] The Tang emperor Taizong married the daughter of a Japanese court noble, Fujiwara Kamatari, at a time when the Tang considered the Japanese as a little above "barbarians" and culturally far behind the Tang. The Empires founded in China by the "barbarian" Mongols and Manchus became assimilated with Chinese culture and were accepted by the Han Chinese as essentially "Chinese" dynasties with the names of Yuan and Qing respectively. To pre-modern imperialists including both the Romans and the Chinese, barbarians could be transformed and treated effectively as more or less equals regardless of ethnicity and origin; the Chinese elite measured the degree of assimilation with Chinese culture based on barbarians' distance from following Chinese ways.[28] Physical differences or the initial absence of culture was not a barrier to assimilation.[29] That is to say, while notions of cultural superiority may have existed since ancient times, a distinction between European attitudes of superiority and those held by the pre-modern empire builders is the attempt of the former to empirically or logically associate racial and cultural superiority with a certain biological determinism based on perceived physical differences such as skin color, skull shape, or facial features. Thus, while for the Chinese it was possible for a "barbarian" to be transformed by accepting Chinese culture, for the European a person who was born black was doomed to be racially inferior in terms of physical appearance and intelligence. The French Enlightenment philosopher Jean Jacques Montesquieu, in *The Spirit of Laws*, summed up the views of those Europeans advocating the slavery of Africans when he wrote that the Africans were "creatures" who were "all over black, and with such a flat nose that they can scarcely be pitied," and were so ugly that it was beyond understanding how God, "who is a wise Being, should place a soul, especially a good soul, in such a black ugly body." Montesquieu goes on to say that the ugliness of Africans and their lack of common sense made it impossible for Europeans to "suppose these creatures to be men, because, allowing them to be men, a suspicion would follow that we ourselves are not Christians."[30] The Scottish philosopher David Hume, after encountering African slaves dispersed all over Europe, wrote with unequivocal conviction in a footnote to his essay *Of National Characters* published in 1742 that:

> negroes and in general all other species of men (for there are four or five different kinds) [are] naturally inferior to the whites. There never was a civilized nation of any other complexion than white nor even any individual eminent either in action or speculation. No ingenious manufactures amongst them, no arts, no sciences.[31]

What is remarkable from today's perspective is that such views imbued with racism, or the belief that there are distinct biologically defined races among humans that can be hierarchically classified based on certain physical and mental attributes, were considered respectable and even academically sound; by the mid-nineteenth century, "scientific" race theory was gaining ground. In 1839, *Crania Americana*, a comparative study of human skulls undertaken by a Philadelphia physician Samuel George Morton, was published. The book explains Morton's views, based on his comparative study of more than 800 skulls, on the distinct differences and unequal aspects of human races. He came to the conclusion that the Caucasian had "the highest intellectual endowments" while the Mongol was "ingenuous, imitative, and highly susceptible of cultivation."[32] In 1850, the British anatomist Robert Knox published *The Races of Man*, in which he attempted to prove the superiority of the white race over all others of color, especially the "despised race" of Negroes.[33] Josiah C. Nott, an American physician and widely-read expert of ethnology, wrote with George R. Gliddon in 1854 a book titled *Types of Mankind* in which he expounds on the "scientific truth" that Caucasians emerged as the most superior of all races and blacks as the most inferior. According to Nott, the "Negro" had never raised or borrowed a single civilization, while the Mongolian had achieved only a "prolonged semi-civilization."[34] The anthropologist Paul Broca and the sociologist Gustav Le Bon argued from the study of skulls that the white race was the most superior, followed by the Mongol race, and finally the blacks, who had the smallest brain.[35] William McGee, an anthropologist and geologist who was president of the National Geographic Society, concluded that "white" and "strong" were synonymous terms, and that because it was the duty of the strong white man to conquer nature and "extirpate the bad and cultivate the good among living things," it was his destiny to enslave the world for the sake of humanity and to increase human intelligence.[36]

Such notions of racial superiority were used as justification for empire that was cloaked in humanitarian rhetoric. In effect, racist views dominated the thinking of the European and American elite during the nineteenth century, and aside from rationalizing empire-building, it influenced the behavior of the colonial masters to the detriment of many of those conquered.[37]

Racist thought also became the basis for policies and actions bordering on genocide. Theodore Roosevelt, in reflecting upon the ferocious wars between white settlers and Native Americans, stated that,

> All men of sane and wholesome thought must dismiss with impatient contempt the plea that these continents should be reserved for the use of scattered savage tribes, whose life was but a few degrees less meaningless, squalid, and ferocious than that of the wild beasts with whom they held joint ownership.[38]

To Roosevelt, war against Native Americans was "for the benefit of civilization and in the interests of mankind," and he asserted that "it is of incalculable importance that America, Australia, and Siberia should pass out of their red, black, and yellow aboriginal owners, and become the heritage of the dominant world races."[39] The Nobel-Peace-Prize-winning Roosevelt on another occasion said with morbid humor, "I don't go so far as to think that the only good Indians are the dead Indians, but I believe that nine out of ten are, and I shouldn't like to inquire closely in the case of the tenth."[40] For Roosevelt, whose face adorns Mount Rushmore in South Dakota and whose heroically posed statue greets visitors daily at the entrance of the American Museum of Natural History in New

York City, the Native Americans deserved nothing short of a "final solution" to their "meaningless" and "squalid" life.

Eventually, the concept of racism and the *mission civilisatrice* as a driver of empire-building was exported from the West to non-western societies. In Japan, the first country in Asia to embark upon modernization and the road to empire, the concept of race was unknown until Western scholars from societies such as the US, Britain, and Germany that were deeply interested in racial matters introduced it in the Meiji period.[41] Japanese–English dictionaries published in 1867 had entries for *jiyu* and *byodo* (freedom, equality) but not for *jinshu* (race) or the more nationalistic-sounding *minzoku* (roughly corresponding to the German *Volk*).[42] As professor of Japanese history at Stanford University Peter Duus notes, the concept of race and the acceptance of racism spread quickly in Japan after its introduction by the Europeans and Americans, with Japanese scholars and liberal-minded journalists such as Taguchi Ukichi (1855–1905) and Takeyoshi Yosaburo (1865–1950) pointing out the Aryan roots of Japanese civilization and suggesting the racial superiority of the Japanese over other peoples, particularly the Chinese and Koreans.[43] In China, the Chinese Revolution leader Sun Yatsen wrote in tones that clearly showed the influence of Western ideas of race, claiming that mankind was divided into five races, with the yellow and white races relatively strong and intelligent, while other races, as they were "feeble and stupid," were being exterminated by the white race.[44] The influence of racism spread far beyond its European and American areas of origin. The political and intellectual elites of Japan, China, and India became obsessed with concepts of racial purity, which led to concerns about racial contamination, and movements towards expulsion or segregation of alien elements represented by different religions or ethnicities.[45] The combination of racism with modern "science," such as phrenology and biology, gave it an air of intellectual respectability that appealed to those Chinese and Japanese who were intent upon catching up with the economically and technologically advanced West. Acceptance of racism, in short, was deemed part of modernity by the intelligentsia and leaders of both countries, and hence a means of being recognized as "civilized" by the West.

Along with being introduced to the European concepts of race, the Japanese leaders of the Meiji era (1861–1912) discovered that Europeans and Americans considered having an empire a badge of greatness and a mark of civilization. While historians have pointed out that the quest for national security, markets, natural resources, and an outlet for surplus population were some of the major drivers of Japanese imperialism, another major driver seems to have been the quest for recognition, a factor we have mentioned earlier as being behind the human urge to dominate one another, as pointed out by Hegel and Fukuyama. The Japanese, who during their 260 years of semi-isolation under the Tokugawa regime (1603–1867) kept their foreign relations limited to a few countries such as China, the Netherlands, and Korea for the purpose of trade, were taught by the "civilized" West that superior races were meant to conquer inferior peoples. Charles LeGendre (1830–1899), a former US army general, US civil war veteran and diplomat employed by the Japanese Foreign Ministry as an advisor and who had close connections with key Meiji leaders including the Emperor Mutsuhito (posthumously Meiji), coaxed the Japanese into taking action to become the protector of the various nations of Asia against European expansion and to bring civilization to a "barbarous" and "primitive" Asia.[46] In cases where attempts to civilize barbarous and primitive people did not bring these people to a civilized stage, LeGendre encouraged the new imperialists to do the civilized thing and, as Roosevelt suggested doing with Native Americans, "exterminate" the people, dealing with them as the Americans and British had dealt with "barbarians."[47] Accordingly, when a number of sailors from the Ryukyu Islands were shipwrecked off the island of Formosa and were subsequently slaughtered by its aboriginal inhabitants, LeGendre urged his Japanese pupils to wrest Formosa away from the decaying Qing Empire of China, which laid claim to the island, and avenge the murders using brutal means.[48] As he saw it, the Japanese needed to act courageously in order to become the protector of the various nations of Asia and to take measures to stop European expansion in Japan's backyard.[49] In addition to the egging on from LeGendre, the US Minister to Japan, Charles DeLong, gave assurance to the Japanese that the US would be partial to them if they desired to occupy other lands such as Formosa for the purpose of expanding their territory.[50] With such advice coming from the "civilized" US, the mission of empire-building by violent means if necessary became a *fait accompli* to the Meiji government leaders, who were eager, to paraphrase the scholar Fukuzawa Yukichi, to "leave Asia and enter Europe" and be recognized as "civilized." Later, both US presidents Theodore Roosevelt and William Howard Taft provided much moral support to Japan's hostile takeover of Korea at gunpoint by looking the other way and ignoring pleas for help from the Koreans.[51]

Despite their entry to the club of imperial powers with the defeat of the Qing Empire and Czarist Russia, the Japanese were not considered racially or culturally equal by the white European and American powers. The Meiji government elder statesman Yamagata Aritomo was well aware of this unflattering perception, citing with resigned indignation the anti-Japanese discrimination in the state of California that flared up after the Russo-Japanese war.[52] Attempts by Japan to insert a "racial equality" clause, calling for the just and equal treatment of all peoples, into the Covenant of the newly formed League of Nations in 1919 were rebuffed primarily by the US, Britain, and Australia. As recently as the 1930s, racial contempt for the Japanese was rampant at every level of the British and American governments. One British naval attaché stationed in Tokyo reported to his superiors in England that the Japanese have "peculiarly slow brains."[53] Winston Churchill was convinced that the Japanese were mentally and physically incapable of going on the warpath for conquest.[54]

Although the people of Japan were certainly aware at the time that Europeans and Americans viewed them as racially inferior, they failed to develop any sense of racial solidarity with their culturally and ethnically close Chinese neighbors that might have challenged Western views of racial superiority. The unsuccessful Japanese attempt to have a "racial equality" clause included in the League of

Nations Covenant was roundly supported by the Chinese. But, hypocritically, the Japanese, who have for much of their history considered China as the source of much of their civilization in the way that Europeans trace their civilization to ancient Rome and Greece, from around the time of the Sino-Japanese War (1894–1895) began to consider the Chinese as an inferior people, calling them "Chankoro" or "Chinks." The writer Naka Kansuke recalled that after that war broke out, he and his friends would talk of the "brave Japanese" and the cowardly "Chinks." Such talk and racist labeling of the Chinese was, according to Naka, encouraged by his school teachers, who urged them on like a mother dog looking after her puppies.[55] By the twentieth century, condescending racist views of the Chinese were widespread in Japan. Kondo Hajime, a former soldier in the Japanese Imperial Army during World War II, recalled being taught over and over that the Chinese were a people of an inferior race.[56]

Impact of intolerance and the end of empire

The late nineteenth century and the early twentieth saw the zenith of European empires, with more than 80 percent of the land mass of the world and hundreds of millions of colonial subjects under their political domination. Japan, Ethiopia, and Thailand were about the only countries in Asia or Africa that were able to maintain most of their political sovereignty in the early twentieth century. Yet by the late 1960s, most of the European empires had disappeared entirely. The last major jewel of British imperialism, Hong Kong, reverted back to China in 1997. While it is beyond the scope of this book to go into the details of the history behind the fall of each empire, it can be argued that a general root cause for the demise of a number of these empires was the racial and cultural intolerance practiced by the colonial masters, leading to discrimination, exploitation, and the persecution of indigenous peoples. Such behavior, and the arrogant attitudes of the imperial overlords, tended to alienate the colonial subjects and, instead of creating loyalty to the mother country, fostered disobedience, resentment, and aspirations for independence. Some examples follow.

British India

The British advance into the Indian subcontinent was spearheaded by the East India Company (EIC) in its pursuit of cotton, silk, tea, and profits. Within the increasing number of Indian territories that came under the EIC's control through military conquest or annexation, the British, inspired by ideas of utilitarianism and social reform which were prevalent at the beginning of the nineteenth century, banned certain native Indian practices that they considered barbaric. This effort went hand in hand with aggressive proselytizing of Christianity by British missionaries in India who joined the traders and soldiers of the EIC. The tensions caused by these developments, combined with racist views towards the Indians and the British insouciance and condescencion toward Indian culture (of which Thomas Macaulay's statements on Indian literature are perhaps typical), were inflamed by the insensitive distribution of rifle cartridges to the sepoy (private soldiers in the EIC infantry) that were greased by certain species of animal fat that were considered taboo to both Hindus and Muslims. This lit the fuse to the sepoy uprising in the Great Mutiny (or First Indian War of Independence) of 1857. Fueled by racial hatred and raging sentiments of revenge, the uprising resulted in massacres and atrocities committed by both the British and the Indians. While the British public was outraged by reports of atrocities allegedly committed by the sepoy who had revolted, British officers were writing home boasting in effect of the atrocities they were committing against the natives. One British civil service officer writing from Allahbad wrote gleefully about stringing up every day 10 to 15 non-combatants.[57] Another officer exultantly wrote about holding court-martials on horseback, and stringing up or shooting every "nigger" they met.[58] Some civilians of Peshawar who were caught exploding some gunpowder at a wedding, as was customary in India, were rounded up by the British and flogged.[59] When the British recaptured Delhi after much intense fighting, Lieutenant Hugh Chichester of the Bengal Artillery unit wrote home reporting shooting Indians for three consecutive days, with some 300 or 400 shot on one day. Chichester called the Indians "brutes" with a "stinking religion."[60] After the end of the conflict, which resulted in the establishment of direct rule by the British government and the termination of the quasi-colonial government of the EIC, the British issued a declaration stating that they would respect India's religions and cultures. According to Queen Victoria's proclamation of 1858 to the Indian princes, chiefs, and peoples, all faiths would "enjoy the equal and impartial protection of the law" and any interference with the religious beliefs of the Indians would be met with the "highest displeasure." Furthermore, the British promised not to discriminate against the Indians and affirmed that "of "whatever race or creed," they would be "freely and impartially admitted to offices in our service, the duties of which they may be qualified, by their education, ability, and integrity, duly to discharge."[61] These are stirring and noble words indeed. However, an underlying and continuous current of racism and contempt among the British towards the Indians prevented a complete closure of the rift between the two, which became a point of contention for such Indians as Mohandas Gandhi and contributed to the eventual demise of British India less than a century after its official founding in 1858. Gandhi began his career of public protest against the British only after becoming increasingly frustrated by the refusal of British colonial authorities to take his complaints of discrimination against Asians seriously.[62] While Churchill is largely regarded by the British as the man who saved Britain against the might of Hitler and is often portrayed in movies as an avuncular if slightly irascible character with superb oratory skills, towards his Indian subjects Churchill was quoted by Leo Amery, the Secretary of State for India, as saying very bluntly that he hated Indians and called them and their religion "beastly."[63] When a famine broke out in Bengal in 1943 which has since been largely attributed to British mismanagement, Churchill put the blame on the Indians for "breeding like rabbits" and refused to provide any aid, while many Indians died of starvation.[64] Indians under Churchill's watch were also discriminated against in the workforce, often getting lower pay than their British counterparts even during the twilight years of the British Raj. In the 1940s, a British railroad driver earned about 300 rupees a month, while Indian drivers were paid only 100 rupees.[65] Aside from the contempt of the elite members of British society such as Churchill, the British regularly referred to the Indians as "niggers." The Prince of Wales on a visit to India was shocked by the "rude and rough manner" with which English public servants and officers dealt with the Indians, and their habit of calling them "niggers."[66] The public protests started by Gandhi against discrimination led to the buildup of a mass independence movement and the departure of the British from India in 1947. While Indian intellectuals today often debate about the legacy of the British, with some of them looking at it in a favorable light especially in regard to the introduction of the English language, railroads, and modern political institutions, an Indian colleague of mine provided some anecdotal evidence of how some educated Indians feel today about the British legacy when he told me several years ago over drinks in a bar in Delhi, "Nothing good came from the British.... The British came, they treated us like dung and stole from us, and when they left, they left the country in a mess."

The British in Hong Kong

In the pre-World War II British Crown Colony of Hong Kong, the British minority routinely discriminated against the native Cantonese Chinese. Chinese were restricted from entering prestigious European hotels and clubs as well as attending European schools. The Chinese also did not have the right of residence in premium residential areas such as Victoria Peak on Hong Kong Island. Instead, the Chinese were given housing akin to rabbit warrens located in a maze of dimly lit narrow streets.[67] Western historians have often written about the mistreatment of the Chinese in Hong Kong at the hands of the Japanese Imperial Army after they routed the British and took it over in December 1941, but few have highlighted the many years of indifference and contempt of the British leading to mistreatment and misrule of their colonial subjects, which is perhaps surprising given the general image of prosperity and Oriental exoticism Hong Kong showed to the world in the postwar years.

Indeed, having lived in Hong Kong for several years during the late 1980s and witnessed the prosperity of the colony, I learned with surprise of the discrimination toward the Chinese and the bleak poverty ascribed to the place in the prewar years, as I had the preconceived notion that Hong Kong was a success story for British imperialism from the start, when the British took over Hong Kong island after it had been ceded by the Chinese following their defeat in the First Opium War of 1842. A Hong Kong native and friend reinforced this view for me when he told me, "Sure, the British were our colonial masters, but at least under them we got rich and in our daily lives they pretty much stayed out of our way." But according to Lucien Brunet, a French Canadian born in Montreal, upon arriving in Hong Kong in November 1941 he noted with "unbelieving eyes" the widespread poverty of the colony, a large number of people without shoes, and women doing the same physical work as men. He concluded that all of the Chinese were "treated as non human."[68] Hunger and diseases such as beri-beri, cholera, smallpox, and tuberculosis were common and widespread in the Hong Kong of the 1930s.[69] The Chinese were shut out from the highest levels of political decision-making and were without an effective means for voicing their discontent. According to Kenneth Andrew, a Hong Kong policeman who served from 1912 to 1938, Europeans in the colony considered the Chinese to be the lowest form of animal life. Andrew mentions several occasions where he witnessed a European rickshaw passenger throw his fare to the ground in order to avoid touching the rickshaw-coolie.[70] The British banned miscegenation between Europeans and Chinese, although this did not prevent European men mating with Chinese women and British soldiers consorting with Chinese prostitutes, another example of empire-building going hand in hand with procreation.[71]

As Churchill professed to hate the Indians, so too did some prominent Britons have a hatred of the Chinese, which in its expression bordered on the genocidal. The author of *The White Man's Burden*, Rudyard Kipling, wrote in his *Sea to Sea: Letters of Travel*,

> I hated the Chinaman before, I hated him doubly as I choked for breath in his seething streets where nothing short of the pestilence could clear the way.... Now I understand why the civilized European of Irish extraction kills the Chinaman in America. It is justifiable to kill him. It would be quite right to wipe the city of Canton off the face of the earth and to exterminate all the people who ran away from the shelling. The Chinaman ought not to count.[72]

The end result of British intolerance, hatred, and indifference towards the Chinese can perhaps be seen in how quickly, in 18 days, Hong Kong fell to the Japanese when the latter invaded the colony in December 1941. While in Hong Kong there were insufficient soldiers and war material to deter a full-scale assault, the British could at least have made a spirited defense had they called upon the Chinese to assist in fighting. But this they did not do. For one thing, the reliability of the Chinese was questioned by the British, who knew that the Chinese resented them and were suspicious of any Chinese carrying weapons.[73] And, as one New Zealander who was living in Hong Kong at the time put it, how could the British call upon the Chinese to fight when British soldiers refused to bathe in the same pool with the Chinese?[74] Moreover, a considerable number of Chinese collaborated with the Japanese owing to the bitter experience of racism they had received at the hands of the British.[75] Once the Japanese had occupied Hong Kong, they had little difficulty in recruiting Chinese collaborators to fill the ranks of the new Japanese colonial government.[76] According to one account, an American pilot who was downed near Hong Kong somehow crawled his way to ask for help from a Chinese peasant, thinking that all Chinese were loyal to the British. Unfortunately for the pilot, the peasant turned him over to the Japanese authorities.[77] After the war, when the Japanese surrendered and the British returned, one journalist estimated that at least 75 percent of the people of Hong Kong could be considered as war criminals for having collaborated with the Japanese.[78]

The French in Algeria

After Thomas Bugeaud and his French troops conquered Algeria in 1830 under the command of the king of France, Louis Philippe I, the French instituted a harsh and discriminatory form of colonial rule over the Algerians that in essence marginalized the native population. In the process of making Algeria an integral administrative part of the nation of France, much in the way that the US had made Hawaii a state of the union, the French forcibly took away land and buildings from the natives. French settlers obtained control over natural resources such as mineral deposits and forests. French colonists and other Europeans gradually displaced Algerians by expropriating their land in cities such as Bone and villages such as Mondovi, where the world-renowned author Albert Camus, the son of French and Spanish colonists, was born in 1913. Although the Algerians were offered the right to apply for French citizenship and demand the full rights of French citizens, few did, as it entailed giving up certain religious practices observed by Muslims. As a means of showing the natives their place and of making them sure that they knew who their new masters were, Bugeaud frequently undertook brutal raids on Algerian homes, harvests, and villages. According to Bugeaud, the Arabs "must be prevented from sowing, from harvesting, and from pasturing their flocks."[79] In one of these raids, hundreds of Arabs were smoked to death.[80] The French political thinker Alexis de Tocqueville defended inflicting such cruelty on the Muslim Algerians as a necessity for the advancement of European civilization. Furthermore, Tocqueville proposed using "all means" for "desolating" the nomadic tribes of Algeria.[81] The racial theories of French sociologists such as Joseph Arthur de Gobineau and Gustav Le Bon, who asserted that the existence of hierarchies among human races was "scientifically" demonstrable, were used as justification for discriminating against and ill-treating the natives.[82] As the British had referred to their Indian colonial subjects as "niggers," so too did the French refer to the Algerian Muslims in derogatory terms, calling them "ratons" (rats).[83] Marginalization of the Algerians continued right into the twentieth century. In 1938, the French Minister Chautemps declared Arabic to be a foreign language in Algeria. The French furthermore forbade the use of Arabic for instruction and administration.[84] In a notorious incident in 1945, approximately 50,000 Algerians were killed through the burning of villages, bombardment of coastal towns, and indiscriminate killings organized by French civilian commandos, all done as reprisal against a riot in the town of Setif which had resulted in the killing of 103 French people.[85] The end result of so many years of discriminatory treatment of the Algerians was the formation of the revolutionary political party the Algerian National Liberation Front, and the start of an insurrection under their leadership against French rule in 1954. After several years of bloody battles that saw atrocities committed by both sides, France retreated from Algeria in 1962. This empire may have lasted for more than a century, but most of the native Algerians under the French did not prosper, and as the Algerians' fight for independence has shown, the French ultimately did not win the loyalty of its conquered subjects necessary for the empire to endure.

The Japanese in Korea

The takeover of Korea by Japan, which started with the establishment of a protectorate in 1905 and was completed with annexation in 1910, was the culmination of Japan's attempt over several decades to wrest control over the peninsula from China and Russia. Japan perceived the peninsula as geopolitically vital to its national security and as a base to extend political and economic influence in northeast China.[86] Along with national interest, one of the goals of the Japanese colonial masters in Korea before and after annexation had been, as the Meiji statesman Ito Hirobumi put it, to bring the "blessings of civilization" to the Koreans and to bring about the institutional and economic reforms necessary to make this happen, reforms which were hampered by an inept and corrupt Korean government.[87] While attempting to bring the fruits of civilization to Korea, the Japanese, like the British and the French in their colonies, pursued similar policies of discrimination and exploitation and held condescending attitudes towards the native population. Large areas of land in Korea were confiscated by the Japanese from 1910 to 1918, creating a class of landless Koreans who became laborers in Japan, earning only meager pay and facing racial taunts and abuse.[88] Chang T'u-sik, who was born in Korea but brought over to Japan at the age of six, recalls the racial taunts of other Japanese children which continued into adulthood with contemptuous remarks reminding him of his station as a Korean.[89] An intimidating Japanese military presence inteneded to control the Korean people was evident as Japan established a large military base at Yongsan, outside of Seoul. Furthermore, every Japanese governor-general of Korea was from the military.[90] While most of the colonial government bureaucracy were civilians, even these civil servants wore uniforms with swords at their side, which accentuated the military color of the colonization and perhaps reflected the wariness of the Japanese towards their colonial subjects.[91] Koreans were not represented in the Japanese Diet and for that matter were barred from even the higher levels of colonial government, as former Korean scholar-officials were replaced by Japanese.[92] As the British did in India, through administrative measures, education, and the media, the Japanese patronizingly encouraged the Koreans to give up "barbaric" customs and mannerisms in order to be considered as Japanese.[93] Arakawa Goro, a Japanese member of parliament and a newspaper editor from Hiroshima, after a visit to the peninsula described the Koreans as appearing to be "vacant," with open mouths and dull-looking eyes. The Koreans, according to Arakawa, with their loose sanitation and sickness, were more akin to wild beasts than humans, a view similar to that held by Theodore Roosevelt of

Native Americans.[94] Koreans, regardless of their personal religious beliefs, were encouraged and sometimes forced to pay their respects at one of the 69 Shinto shrines built by the Japanese.[95] Japan's education system, with Japanese as the language of instruction, was introduced into the peninsula, but the schools that were established were virtually segregated, with Koreans attending schools that were of lower quality.[96] Certain liberal statesmen such as Hara Takashi (1856–1921), however, did work towards establishing a more equal relationship. Hara called for equal opportunity in education and an end to discriminatory practices towards Koreans, which he saw as impediments towards the assimilation of Koreans with Japan. To this end, the colonial government went about enacting reforms to eliminate discrimination in the civil service, the peerage, and the judiciary, and publicly stated that its aim was to realize equal treatment for both the Japanese and Koreans.[97] Hara's assassination at the hands of a right-wing fanatic in 1921, however, and the lack of leadership devoted to such liberal causes after his death, led to only half-hearted implementation of the reforms he had proposed. Despite efforts to unify school systems and personal names, the Japanese authorities refused to allow Koreans to forget that they were indeed Korean, and not Japanese. Government bureaucrats stamped "Chosen-jin" (Korean) over Japanese-sounding surnames on official documents. The police devised identification tests that focused on the supposedly obvious characteristics of Koreans.[98] An especially egregious crime was the massacre of over 6,000 Koreans by Japanese vigilantes and hoodlums committed in the wake of the Great Kanto earthquake of 1923.[99]

Changes in the civil law of Korea in 1940 encouraged the Koreans to adopt a Japanese surname, and although coercion was not used, there was clearly pressure from Japanese authorities which Korean poet Kim Shi Jyong called a "polite threat."[100] During the war years, Koreans were often mobilized for industrial production at extremely low wages or for nothing. A former factory worker from a farming village in Chollanam recalls putting in 12-hour days and never getting paid for work.[101] Young girls from Korea were organized as the Korean women's volunteer labor corps or *kinro teishintai* and conscripted to work in factories for no wages.[102] More notoriously, the Imperial Japanese Army ordered Korean businessmen to procure Korean "comfort women" who were in effect sex slaves and to operate "comfort houses" to be used by Japanese soldiers.[103]

Unlike the British in India or the French in Algeria, Japanese domination of Korea was abruptly terminated by Japan's defeat by the US, and not by any independence movement on the part of the native population. Most Koreans, however, never saw Japanese rule as anything but illegitimate and humiliating.[104] Any mention that the Japanese had somehow "modernized" Korea would bring forth vehement and emotional denials from both North and South Koreans.[105] Recently, however, a reassessment of Korea's colonial experience has led Korean scholars such as Lee Yong Hoon of Seoul University to argue that Korea's current strong economic performance has its roots in the colonial period when the Koreans learned from the Japanese.[106] Indeed, studies have shown that during the colonial period of 1911–1938, annual economic growth rates in Korea was at 3.57 percent, outstripping that of Japan which was at 3.36 percent.[107] Agricultural output in Korea substantially increased, while growth rates in manufacturing averaged more than 10 percent annually. Industry in Korea expanded at double to triple the rate in Japan's other colony of Taiwan.[108] Whatever economic gains the Koreans may have made under the Japanese, demands for independence, which continued right up to Japan's defeat, suggests that the Japanese, in the words of Mengzi, failed to get to the hearts of the Korean people.[109] In the passive Korean resistance movement of March 1, 1919, half a million Koreans took part, calling for independence. The Japanese responded with brutal military and police suppression which resulted in over 7,500 Koreans dead, 15,000 injured, and 46,000 arrested.[110] After this brutal suppression, the Koreans continued to work clandestinely for independence as well as engaging in guerrilla warfare against Japan in Manchuria. This is in stark contrast to the situation in the United Kingdom, where there was no Scottish uprising against the union for more than 200 years after the merger between England and Scotland. A study on Japanese assimilation policies in colonial Korea written by Rikkyo University scholar Mark Caprio concluded that the prime obstacle towards a more equal relationship was essentially the arrogance of the Japanese in their dealings with the Koreans, and that had the Japanese been less arrogant, they would have had a better chance of encouraging Koreans to accept the merits of Japanese culture while getting greater support for Japan's assimilation efforts.[111]

With such condescending, racist attitudes and egregious acts of discrimination meted out by the various imperial masters of Europe, the US, and Japan on their colonial subjects, it is not surprising that the latter (except for a few collaborators) were not sad to see their imperial overlords leave when they did. Conversely, if these empire builders had done away with their racism and arrogance and treated their peripheral imperial subjects as equal to their own citizens, some of their empires might have earned the loyalty of enough colonial subjects to support the colonial masters and to keep independence movements in check. Of course, there is no way to prove this. However, the successful case of the UK, as well as empires such as those of the Mongols and Romans which we will examine below, suggest that having a more tolerant approach that includes respecting the cultures of the colonial subjects and treating them equally with the citizens of the mother country may affect the outcome for the imperial powers.

The impact of racism in business

It is not only in the history of certain empires that intolerance in the form of racism has had an impact. Going by the countless cases of discrimination that are reported from workplaces in all parts of the world, racism is also undeniably a factor that exists in the business world. An especially egregious example of systematic racism used to condone discrimination in the workplace was the Apartheid system of South Africa, which denied equal employment opportunities to blacks and other non-white peoples. Another case where racism may have shown its face in business was when certain sections of the US went wild over the Sony Corporation's acquisition of the American film studio Columbia Pictures in 1989. Politicians such as congresswoman Helen Delich Bentley characterized the purchase as an "invasion" and demanded that the US attorney general investigate the takeover. Peter G. Peterson of the Blackstone Group, who was involved in the deal, suggested that part of the reason that the US media treated the takeover attempt of the film studio MGM/UA by an Australian company as a minor event while putting full coverage on the Sony deal was because of a sensationalist approach that catered to sentiments of xenophobia and racism.[112] Racism in business may have prevented the productive use of new and superior technologies by a company. In his book *The Reckoning*, a chronicle of the changing fates of the Japanese and US auto industries, author and journalist David Halberstam mentions that Ford Motor Company chairman Henry Ford II at one time exploded at the then president Lee Iacocca for having the effrontery to suggest the use of Japanese-made car engines from the Honda company, snarling, "No Jap engine is going under the hood of a car with my name on it."[113] And as in those empires which we have just discussed that practiced racial discrimination and collapsed, racism may have played a role in the demise of certain M&A business empires which we will examine below.

Empires of business

Now that we have briefly examined the development of certain empires from world history, let us look at how business empires have developed over the centuries, while keeping in mind the parallels between the two. As with global empires, various drivers are behind the empires of business created from mergers or acquisitions (M&A) that lead to their establishment and propel their development and growth. To do an in-depth analysis on each of these drivers would, however, only replicate the content of countless business books that deal with this topic. Instead, I will focus on the historical development of these drivers and will present a brief narrative on the development of business, as its scale and nature evolved from simple and modest organizations dealing primarily with the transactions of commodities in limited areas, to vast entities with permanent and complex management structures dealing with transactions of goods and services covering a wide geographic area.

The birth of the company

The earliest records of recognizable business transactions have been preserved for posterity on clay tablets from Mesopotamia dating from around 3000 BCE. The people involved in these business deals at the dawn of history were already making loans to each other. Mesopotamian lenders recorded the repayments of commodities that had been loaned, the amount due, and the planned date of repayment.[114] As we mentioned earlier, the acts of empire-building or of conquering other peoples have been with us since the earliest recorded history, but along with this propensity for going out to dominate one another, humans have also had from an early stage the inclination to buy, sell, or loan goods among one another. And most likely, assuming that human nature hasn't changed much, there was the process of haggling for a better deal as well. Later the Phoenicians, Athenians, and other peoples organized themselves for the purpose of conducting business transactions consisting primarily of the buying and selling of commodities. But the scale of these organizations was small, with the largest one employing about a hundred slaves.[115]

Several centuries later, entities bearing resemblance to a modern-day company, with a permanent management overseeing and managing business transactions, came into existence in several parts of the world, especially in Europe and Asia. Karl Moore and David Lewis, in their book *Foundations of Corporate Empire*, describe how around the time of the Second Punic War (218–202 BCE), certain nobles in Rome organized themselves into entities called publicani, with each of the investing partners or socii obtaining a share of the entity. The publicani, corresponding to modern-day public contractors, provided goods and services for the upkeep and defense of the empire, including shields, spears, swords, and other weapons for use by the Roman armies. The publicani were essentially large partnerships with a legal existence of their own, and in this respect were the first recorded examples of what would today be closest to limited-liability companies.[116] In terms of structure they had features that would be recognizable today: aside from limited liability, they had managers or magister who were entrusted by the socii to run the business, and promagistri or branch managers. The eighteenth-century jurist William Blackstone credits the Romans as having invented the concept of the company.[117] Whether the socii established the publicani from a desire to lower or eliminate transaction costs, which the British economist and Nobel laureate Ronald Coase argued was the driver behind the formation of modern-day companies, is difficult to ascertain. Nevertheless, some of the transactional activities of the publicani that were based in Rome were widespread and conducted through agents based in other cities such as Delos, Athens, and Alexandria, and having agents within the publicani may have contributed to lowering transaction costs. One such publicani based in Rome was reported to have supervised over 10,000 employees and conducted business in Europe and Asia. A notable branch manager or promagistri for this publicani was a certain Terentius Hispo, who was a close friend of the philosopher Cicero.[118] Craftsmen and merchants of the Roman Empire also came together to form guilds which had managers elected by their members.[119]

In East Asia, the Kongo-gumi was founded in 578 CE by immigrants from the Korean kingdom of Pakeche who specialized in the construction and maintenance of shrines and temples throughout Japan. Although the oldest company in the world still in existence is the Aberdeen Harbour Board, set up in 1136, and the oldest continuing private-sector company in Europe is probably Stora Enso of Sweden, which began as a copper mine and started trading its wares in 1288,[120] the honor for the world's oldest "continuous operating" family-based company[121] would undoubtedly have gone to the Kongo-gumi had it not been acquired by another company in 2006.

With the collapse of the Western Roman Empire in 476 CE, much commercial activity shifted to outside of Europe, especially to the Middle East, where Muslim merchants were engaged in a thriving trade with China centuries before Marco Polo arrived in the Yuan China of the Mongols. In China paper money began to be used for some business transactions, and its use was later accelerated with the advent of the Mongol Empire in the thirteenth century. Chinese merchants developed increasingly complex partnerships for the conduct of business, which eventually funded some of the voyages that seafarers such as Admiral Zheng-He undertook to pursue trade opportunities. In industry, China developed capacities for steel production which from the eleventh century outclassed those of Europe for another seven centuries.[122]

While it seems that business in Europe was being eclipsed by all of these developments after the collapse of Rome, Roman business practices were nevertheless passed down by adventurous European traders. These helped to ensure that in the Middle Ages the organization of the company would revive itself in Europe, with the appearance of maritime firms in Italian towns such as Venice in the ninth century. These entities were often partnerships that came together for a specific sea voyage and allowed the landlubber investor to finance a certain trade opportunity without actually participating in the voyage, thereby ensuring some dispersion of risk. Over the next couple of centuries, with the discovery of new lands and development of new sea routes leading to an increase in trade opportunities, these partnerships grew more complex and soon developed ownership schemes that involved the issuance of shares to the investors. More on this follows.

Along with the development of maritime companies, authors John Micklethwait and Adrian Wooldridge describe in their book *The Company* a new form of organization to appear in Florence in the twelfth century from which the word "company" is derived: the compagnia.[123] The word itself, derived from the Latin *com* and *panis*, means the "breaking of bread together." Similar in concept to the Roman publicani, the compagnia were initially small family-based organizations that operated on the basis of limited liability. The impact of the compagnia on modern businesses comes primarily from their introduction of new business tools such as the double-entry bookkeeping method and the use of letters of exchange, which was devised as a practical alternative to coins for transactions undertaken over long distances and of large amounts. With the development and use of these business tools, the compagnia became closely associated with a group of moneylenders known as the banchi (which describes the bench on which the Italian moneylenders sat and is the forerunner of the English word for "bank").[124] The significance of the banchi was that as they developed more sophisticated operations and capital accumulation, thanks in part to the use of new business tools developed by the compagnia, the banchi began to play a role that extended outside of their simple moneylending activities. They started to fund not only voyages and compagnia, but also kings, princes, and states.

This was not, however, the first time in Europe that such an institution engaged in moneylending to royalty and used innovative transaction tools such as letters of exchange. That honor probably goes to the Knights of the Temple or Knights Templar, which was a semi-religious military order of knights appointed by King Baldwin of Jerusalem in 1118 whose original function was to protect European pilgrims on their way to the Holy Land after the first Crusade expedition captured Jerusalem in 1095. The Knights Templar has the distinction of developing the concept of credit for business expansion. They essentially undertook almost all the functions of a twentieth-century bank, including the charging of interest on loans, which at the time was a practice that was forbidden for Christians.[125] For pilgrims to the Holy Land and other travelers, the Templars developed a system of funds transfer by note, whereby the traveler could deposit funds at a local Templar temple to cover travel expenses and receive a coded credit receipt which could be redeemed at any Templar temple at the end of the journey; the traveler would get a cash refund of his account balance or a bill to cover any overdraft. It was a system that resembled both the modern bank check and the credit card.[126] Notwithstanding the Templars' contributions to financial innovation, however, the king of France, Philip IV, envious of the power and wealth of the Templars and heavily indebted to them at the time due to numerous misadventures on his part, decided one day to unilaterally cancel his obligations; he confiscated the Templar's accumulated wealth from moneylending activities to the rich and famous of Europe, and had the knights arrested, tortured, and then burned to death in 1307.

Ninety years after the demise of the Templars, the Medici bank was established by Giovanni di Bicci de' Medici. The Medici bank was certainly a bank, but its interest for us is that it was one of the earliest examples of an "empire of business;" not forged from an M&A deal, but nevertheless an empire that comprised other businesses besides banking. The bank diversified into the wool trade and later went into cloth-making. It also entered the textile-dyeing market and gained control of it by cornering the supply of alum, a chemical that was crucial to the dyeing process.[127]

The drivers behind the formation of M&A business empires

We can only speculate as to why the Medici diversified and branched out from its core banking business, but a modern interpretation of their behavior might be that the bank was trying to reduce the risk attached to engaging in only one field of business. That is, the driver of *risk mitigation* through business diversification, the rationale behind several M&A deals of the modern age (the case of Sony's acquisition of Columbia Pictures is one example we will later examine), was at work. Another aspect of the Medici bank that would qualify it as an empire was that whenever it opened a branch, the bank would organize the branch as a partnership with other investors and provide them with financial incentives to maximize returns by offering schemes such as profit-sharing.[128] It was an empire that was based on an alliance of willing investors who agreed to put in their money for the enrichment of what became their empire as well. For the Medici, the inclusion of investment partners represented a practical method of mitigating risk as well as introducing new blood that could provide new ideas on how to grow the business.

The development of new business organizations such as the compagnia and the banchi in Italy, and techniques for managing business such as double-entry bookkeeping, eventually had an impact on the rest of Europe, leading to the rise of companies outside of Italy, particularly in northern Europe. In many cases the development of such companies was in step with the emergence of the nation-states of Europe.

During the sixteenth and seventeenth centuries, seafaring enterprises with sophisticated professional management bureaucracies backed by groups of investors appeared across Europe. Such a company would be formed when the governing authority in the respective country granted a charter for a monopoly of trade in spices and other goods to a group of merchants who got together for the sole purpose of making money from trade (of course, the granting of charters by the governing authorities was done not out of altruism but with the intent of making money). These companies were not only trading organizations with sophisticated management bureaucracies; as they pursued their trade, some of the companies eventually became de facto governments that ruled over their overseas possessions and trading outposts, with formidable military arms to protect their interests.

Given the scale and scope of their operations alone, which spanned several continents and oceans, the Dutch (established 1600) and English (established 1602) East India enterprises formed as chartered companies were indeed empires in every sense of the word. Yet despite their subjugation of peoples and colonial territories, the main driver for the development and expansion of these business empires was the pursuit of profit. And for many of their ambitious employees, the opportunity for world travel and accumulating great wealth and power was a powerful incentive to work for these companies. Here then is another driver, in addition to risk mitigation though business diversification, behind the formation of business empires that is also the rationale for the creation of some modern-day M&A deals: *the pursuit of gold and glory mixed with hubris.* Siri Terjesen of the Kelley School of Business at Indiana University observed that as managers believe that bigger is better, hubris leads to M&A deals as managers overestimate their own abilities and mimic the strategies of leading companies in their industry.[129] It is also undeniable from the history of these two seafaring enterprises that their drive for profit was closely intertwined with the drive for empire by Britain and the Netherlands in the form of acquiring territory and political control. The companies became in essence the spearhead to the global expansion of trade and played a pivotal role in laying the foundations of the British and Dutch empires in India and Asia. In the case of the Verenigde Oostindische Compagnie (VOC) or Dutch East India Company (which we will later examine in detail), its significance in the history of business is clear: it was the world's first conglomerate and business empire to be born from the mega-merger of six independent trading companies and the world's first joint-stock company.

Behind the formation of the VOC, we can also identity other drivers of M&A that a modern business empire builder might recognize. One of those drivers was the desire to increase profits by decreasing the number of competing trading companies, in effect causing a consolidation of the industry. This driver of *industry consolidation* has been prevalent over time and in many industries since the birth of the VOC. In a modern context, industry consolidation has occurred in instances where a predatory company acquires or merges with other companies in the same field of business, which results in fewer players in the business and less price competition. The predatory company subsequently achieves more market share, and possibly more profits.

Another driver behind the mega-merger of the VOC was the desire to acquire and control internally the necessary economic resources to compete effectively against other competitors. The VOC (like the English East India Company, or EIC) built its own boats, prepared its own docks, and procured and sold spices using its own controlled distribution network. The VOC essentially undertook *vertical integration,* an organizational and intra-company transactional phenomenon seen in the modern-day business world where companies, instead of relying upon uncertain market transactions, utilize internal resources (whether internally created or acquired from outside) to undertake distinct value-adding activities such as designing, producing, marketing, delivering, and supporting its products. However, such large-scale vertically-integrated operations at the time of the VOC and the EIC were the exception. Indeed, until around 1840 business activity around the globe was limited in scale due to the lack of infrastructure for mass transportation and modern communications technology. In the US before 1850, most American businesses were family-run affairs not requiring a full-time administrative staff or a management structure.[130] The lack of technology in communications and transportation made it difficult to gain accurate and timely information on market developments in distant places, which in turn raised the risk for business people in making long-term investments in production or distribution. Hence, most companies or enterprises engaged in business up until the mid-nineteenth century were still small and informally organized. According to the French historian Fernand Braudel, even the biggest bank in Paris on the eve of the French Revolution in 1789 employed only 30 people.[131]

But the development of railroads, large canals, and the telegraph in the mid-nineteenth century, coupled later with the technology of refrigeration, was to greatly change the business environment (especially in the US) by allowing businesses to engage with new customers in distance places and to gain access to production inputs located in a wider geographic area. These technologies of transportation and communications also enabled businesses to shorten production and delivery lead times and improved their access to capital and credit. In short, new infrastructure and technologies helped to bring about the birth of a mass consumer market in the US and later in Europe. As the number of consumers began to increase, so too did the scale of businesses as they worked towards increasing production and reducing costs.

By the early twentieth century, the vertical integration of industries began to appear in such sectors as steel, oil, chemicals, machinery, and automobiles. Companies in these industries began to see the need to alleviate their vulnerability to possible mishaps in the supply chain of raw materials and distribution. They continued to work towards achieving economies of scale in order to increase production and reduce costs, as competition intensified with new players coming into the market.[132] A case in point is the Standard Oil Company of Ohio, which moved into the production of crude oil primarily in order to secure itself a source of supply of the oil that it distributed.[133] Vertical integration was achieved in many cases through M&A. Some companies also bought out other direct competitors in order to acquire their resources and gain more scale as well as to reduce competition.[134] The first major wave of M&A activity in the US occurred between 1898 and 1904. Prior to 1898 the normal level of enterprise mergers was around 70 per year. The number of mergers jumped to 303 in 1898, peaking at 1,208 in 1899 and then leveling off to more than 300 every year until 1903.[135]

Along with all this M&A activity leading to the creation of the first modern business "empires," a consequence that arose was the growing demand for a professional, hierarchical, managerial class that was separate from the owners and who focused on managing the enterprise. To support this demand, the Harvard Business School was established in 1908; although it was not the world's first business school, it was the first in the world to offer a degree called an "MBA."[136] And to fill in the courses being taught at business schools as well as to further the know-how of managers in improving manufacturing productivity, new theories on "scientific management" were developed by Fredrick W. Taylor, Harrington Emerson and others.[137]

While the vertically integrated empires may have on the one hand helped to meet the demands of a growing mass consumer market, on the other hand, their creation may have inadvertently led to the raising of the barriers to entry of an industry. This was a result of the higher hurdles coming from lower market prices as a result of the greater economies of scale of the incumbent vertically integrated empires, and was also due to the greater difficulty for newcomers to access the sources of production inputs, which had been put under the control of the vertically integrated empires. Indeed, fears of declining competition, or the rise of monopolies, and less leverage for the consumer as a result of the raising of barriers to industry entry by vertically integrated empires, led the US government under the leadership of Theodore Roosevelt to break up perceived antitrust activities and alleged national monopolies—an irony considering that Roosevelt was, as we have seen, an unapologetic builder of the American Empire intent on monopolizing the American continent for the white man. Among the major antitrust cases during this time were those involving Standard Oil (1911), American Tobacco (1911), DuPont (1912), International Harvester (1918), and Eastman Kodak (1920).[138]

Along with the rise of the modern vertically integrated business empire, in the early twentieth century a new innovation of corporate organization was developed, leading to the creation of a type of company that emerged first in the US and then in Europe and Japan which we still have today: the vertically integrated *and* horizontally expanded *multidivisional* corporation such as DuPont, GM, and Alcoa in the US and Matsushita Electric (Panasonic) in Japan. These companies undertook large-scale investments in mass manufacturing and distribution for a wide range of products and had a management structure that, aside from certain key corporate functions such as finance and research and development, decentralized central authority and empowered managers who were responsible for the performance of a particular segment of business or of certain product lines.[139] And as we shall see in the example of Matsushita Electric, some of these "M-form" multidivisional companies achieved vertical integration and horizontal expansion through considerable M&A activity. The multidivisional conglomerate was the predominant structure of industrial companies up until the 1970s. An example of this is the US consumer electronics manufacturer RCA (Radio Corporation of America, founded 1919), which at one time was one of the largest companies (in terms of revenues) in the US and during the 1960s and 1970s owned companies such as a broadcasting company (NBC), a publishing firm (Random House), a carpet company, a rent-a-car company (Hertz), and a frozen foods company.

In the late twentieth century, however, the ardor for such multidivisional vertically-integrated, horizontally-expanded conglomerate empires died down in favor of creating companies that were adept at achieving *horizontal specialization*. This meant in some cases the creation of a product supply chain based on the maintenance of a tight network of independent and specialized suppliers and original design/original equipment manufacturers (ODM/OEM) using advanced tools of communication such as the Internet. Horizontal specialization has led in certain instances to the creation of an "informal" empire based on alliances with other third-party partners—the advantage to such an arrangement being that it would enable a company to reduce its overhead assets, allow greater flexibility and speed in operations, and reduce costs in the process. The PC company Dell and the consumer electronics company Vizio are examples of "asset-light" enterprises that use third party ODM/OEM companies to assemble and supply products for sale under their brand names.

Another driver behind the mega-merger that led to the formation of the VOC was the need to obtain skills, personnel, technologies, or resources. This has been a driver for various technology-related companies such as Cisco, Philips, and GE. The latter two companies developed their medical businesses largely through the acquisition of medical technology and services companies.

As mentioned earlier, Marx and Hobson theorized that imperialism was caused by oversupply or under-consumption of goods and services which in each case resulted in declining profits and capitalists searching for new markets. Likewise, in the business world, a driver of *market expansion* exists behind the creation of business empires through the act of M&A, in that companies in search of new markets for increasing revenues may enter into a new territory or country by merging with or acquiring a locally-based player. Yanai Tadashi, the chairman of the Japanese clothing company Fast Retailing known for its Uniqlo brand clothes, justified his company's overseas expansion through M&A by pointing out the limits of the Japanese domestic market, commenting that the company would not be able to survive by simply staying in Japan.[140] An example of market expansion as a driver of M&A which we will look at below is the joint venture of the music recording company Columbia Records with Sony, which for the former served to increase its presence in the rapidly growing Japanese music market.

In addition to the drivers we have mentioned up to now, another driver behind the formation of the VOC was the desire to achieve what is the holy grail of many businesses today: *synergy*, or the acceleration of output, revenues, and profits, and the creation of new businesses as a result of combining or rationalizing the resources and operations of several merging companies. Simply stated, the idea behind synergy would be to achieve $1 + 1 = 3$ or 4 instead of the usual 2. At the time of the acquisition of Columbia Pictures by the Sony Corporation, which we will review in depth, the company initially touted synergy as the justification for the deal: the synergy of hardware and software would further accelerate and expand Sony's presence in the electronics and entertainment business sectors.

As we identify the drivers behind the formation of business empires starting with the VOC, the reader may note parallels with the drivers behind the establishment of global empires: the desire to achieve glory and wealth, to undertake expansion of markets and territory, to obtain various resources. This is another indication of the similarities, aside from their structure, between business and global empires. One may also note the commonalities of drivers between a business empire that was formed in 1602 (the VOC) with the business empires of modern times formed through M&A, such as the desire to achieve vertical integration and industry consolidation, and the desire to obtain skills and personnel. The commonalities of drivers suggest that the VOC was in many ways an empire that acted with a business mindset that modern-day business people can relate to; most importantly, it was a "successful" multinational business empire formed from a mega-merger that lasted for two centuries and provided high rates of returns for its investors for most of its life. For these reasons I have decided in the following chapter to give a narrative of the company's life which will highlight its history and development and focus on the cultural aspect of tolerance that contributed to maintaining the VOC afloat for two centuries.

3   A seafaring empire

The rise of the Dutch East India Company

Introduction

In 1602, a group of trading companies based in the territories known as the Low Countries of Europe in the Middle Ages, which today encompass modern Belgium, Luxembourg, northwest France, and the Netherlands, merged to create what arguably became the most successful trading company of the seventeenth and eighteenth centuries. At its zenith, the Verenigde Oostindische Compagnie (the United East India Company, or VOC) established a commercial empire in Asia which allowed them to challenge and roll back Spanish and Portuguese dominance of the Asian spice trade, hold the English at bay, and monopolize the lucrative export trade in cloves, nutmeg, and mace. Through its "regional head-quarters" in Batavia (present-day Jakarta, Indonesia), which served as the hub for VOC trading posts in Asia, the company engaged in a profitable inter-Asia trade, exchanging Japanese silver and copper, Chinese gold and silk, and Indian textiles. The VOC launched 1,700 ships in the seventeenth century and 3,000 in the eighteenth.[1] Between 1602 and 1700, more than 300,000 people sailed from Europe on these ships; from 1700 to 1795, the number of people traveling on VOC ships exceeded 650,000.[2]

Eventually, with changing consumer demand and the subsequent demise of the spice trade, the Anglo-Dutch wars, the growth of English sea power, and the rise of the English East India Company (EIC), the VOC went into a gradual decline and finally disbanded in 1799. Despite its end, however, the company's performance spanning two centuries was impressive. The gross margin of the VOC from 1640 to 1700 was 64 percent, declining to a still respectable 59 percent from 1700 to 1795.[3] From the year of its founding, the VOC was paying dividends to its investors that averaged 18 percent per year, with a standard minimum rate set at 12.5 percent.[4] Total dividend payments up to 1650 were reported to be eight times the original investment amount, and the annual rate of return to a shareholder up to 1650 was 27 percent.[5] Over the entire period, an incredible 99 percent of the VOC's net profits was distributed to shareholders.[6] In 1670, the VOC was arguably the richest company in the world, paying its shareholders dividends of 40 percent on their investments, employing over 80,000 people of various nationalities including 30,000 soldiers, and possessing a fleet of 200 trading ships.[7] Between 1602 and 1733, the stock price of the VOC rose gradually from par (100) to a peak of 786.[8] Such rises in stock value combined with generous dividends helped to make major shareholders such as the Dutch citizen and mayor of Amsterdam, Dirck Bas, very wealthy.[9] Financially, the VOC was powerful enough to provide intermediary financial services to other Europeans engaged in trade in Asia and to arrange loans for the provinces of the Netherlands.

The company had several sources of competitive advantage. One was a large capital base and the ability to reinvest profits from voyages. This allowed it to make substantial long-term investments for ships, their maintenance, and infrastructure such as docks and overseas forts or factories. In comparison, the EIC had a much smaller capital base, and its company structure was such that it had to return all profits gained to shareholders after each voyage.[10] Another aspect of financing in which the VOC had a competitive advantage over the EIC was the access to low interest rates on loans available in the Netherlands. Reputable borrowers in England paid 10 percent interest, while their counterparts in the Netherlands, which included the government-backed VOC, paid rates of 4 percent.[11] One major development behind the difference in interest rates was that many public works that were going on at the time in the Netherlands, such as land reclamation projects, were stimulating the construction of expensive windmills and dikes. These facilitated the growth of lending and investment by a wide segment of Dutch society including local churches, municipal councils, merchants, aristocrats, and peasants.[12] Competition in lending may have led to a decline in interest rates.

Another source of competitive advantage was the ability of the VOC to command a monopoly on trade, which was guaranteed by a charter granted by the Dutch government and supported by the VOC's ruthless activities, which we will touch upon below, that allowed it to gain a monopoly on the nutmeg and mace trade. Its regional headquarters in Batavia was also a source of competitive advantage. It allowed the VOC to develop a network of information so as to monitor prices in the region while keeping an eye on the activities of its competitors, including the English and Portuguese.

The company also had a technical competitive advantage from the use of a type of freighter ship called the fluyt. Compared to the English trading ships of the time, the fluyt were lightly armed, with usually 12 to 15 cannons, and had a narrow deck area which allowed for a larger cargo bay and economized on fleet manpower. The larger cargo bay enabled the Dutch to engage in bulk trade and keep freight costs low. This construction gave the body of the fluyt a distinctive shape akin to a bulbous pear. The ships had two to three square-rigged masts that were placed much higher than those of the ships of the EIC, which allowed for greater speed. As the fluyt were lightly armed, these ships were often accompanied by Dutch navy warships in dangerous waters, which gave the Dutch the ability to enforce or protect (depending on the point of view) its trade.

Clearly, the VOC's performance in high shareholder returns, profitability, and duration would classify it as an example of an M&A arrangement that turned out to be a "success" as defined earlier. While there are of course limits in seeking parallels with modern M&A examples, I will argue that the success of the VOC has several relevant lessons for the modern aspiring M&A empire builder. These will be outlined in the following narrative.

The rise of the Netherlands

During the thirteenth and fourteenth centuries, most of the towns of the Low Countries were politically independent of each other. Commerce flourished from an early period, with towns such as Antwerp, Bruges, and Ghent attracting merchants from all over Europe. From the fourteenth century the Dukes of Burgundy began to bring some of these independent-minded cities under their control, but it was to fall upon the House of Hapsburg to unite the 17 quasi-independent provinces of the Low Countries under one rule. In 1500, the population of the group of provinces numbered about one million.[13]

In 1506 the king of Spain, Charles I, inherited the territories of the Low Countries. The mother of Charles I was Joanna ("the Mad") of Castile, who was the daughter of King Ferdinand and Queen Isabella of Spain. His father was Philip the Handsome, who was heir of territories held by the Hapsburgs and also of control of the title of Duke of Burgundy. As a result of this blood lineage, Charles I became the first Hapsburg king of Spain upon the death of his grandfather Ferdinand. In 1519 Charles I became the Holy Roman Emperor Charles V in addition to being the archduke of Austria and the ruler of the Low Countries. Continuing the work of the previous Dukes of Burgundy, Charles V was successful in persuading the 17 territories of the Netherlands to unite as a state under his rule in 1543. Charles V was known to have been friendly to the Dutch and gave the Low Countries unrestricted rights to trade. Consequently, the Low Countries further thrived and prospered through trade under his protection.

With the rise and spread of the Protestant Reformation sparked by Martin Luther in 1517, the lowland provinces came under the influence of the teachings of the French Protestant theologian John Calvin. Unfortunately for the Netherlands, Charles V abdicated his rule in 1556 in order to enter a monastery. He handed his rule of the Netherlands to his son Philip II, who became ruler and Catholic king of the Spanish kingdoms, Portugal and the 17 provinces of The Netherlands. Philip II was a devout and zealous Catholic who spoke no Dutch, viewed the growth of Protestantism with alarm, and believed that his mission was to stop Protestant expansion, which was dividing the Netherlands into a predominantly Protestant north and Catholic south. Clearly there was a streak of intolerance within him. His first step in stopping the forces of Protestantism was to appoint Catholic non-Dutch-speaking governors all over the Netherlands and to unleash religious inquisitions and capital punishments for religious heretics. These actions met with a response from the chief of the Dutch nobility, William the Silent of the House of Orange, who started agitating against the Spanish by

submitting a petition to Philip II requesting the termination of religious persecution. Philip II reacted by sending 10,000 troops under the command of the
Spanish Duke of Alva to the Low Countries to crush the Dutch agitators. Along
with the stationing of troops, the Spanish set up tribunals which led to the
imprisonment and execution of many prominent Dutch citizens. They also confiscated the property of many Dutch citizens. The Duke of Alva initiated a
program to forcibly convert the Dutch population to Catholicism in an attempt to
suppress the reformation movement. As if this weren't enough for the Dutch,
Phillip II also ordered the Duke to increase taxes as punishment.

By 1572, the Dutch had had enough. Popular revolts against the Spanish
erupted in the northern Netherlands. In retaliation, the Duke of Alva razed the
city of Haarlem and slaughtered many of the townspeople in Mechelen, Naardan,
and Zutphen.[14] Further atrocities were to follow. In 1576, in an incident which
came to be known as the "Spanish Fury," discontented Spanish soldiers, diso-
beying their orders, left their positions in the north Netherlands and went to the
south to initiate a wild orgy of plunder in the city of Antwerp, where 7,000 city
inhabitants were indiscriminately killed.[15] Although the massacre happened in
the south, the incident was to have a lasting impact on the north and led to the
signing of the Pacification of Ghent, whereby the northern and southern Netherlands declared their intent to unite and drive the Spanish out of the Netherlands.
The union between north and south, however, did not last long. In 1579, the city
elders of the southern Netherlands, having a change in heart and greatly intimi-
dated by the atrocities of the Spanish and the thought of further violence,
declared their loyalty to Philip II and to the Catholic Church. The northern seven
Dutch provinces led by Holland and Zeeland, on the other hand, proclaimed their
autonomy and rights to religious freedom in the Union of Utrecht, which banded
the Northern Dutch provinces into the United Provinces, or what is now known
as the nation of the Netherlands. According to the treaty, all people were to
enjoy freedom of religion and no one was to be persecuted or investigated
because of their beliefs.[16] In contrast to the Spanish, the leaders of the United
Provinces made it a point that the government would not compel conformity of
religion or its forcible imposition upon its peoples.

In 1581, in words and tone that would foreshadow the American Declaration
of Independence of 1776, the United Provinces declared their independence from
the Kingdom of Spain in the Act of Abjuration, which claimed that if a prince
does not defend his people from oppression and violence and instead oppresses
them and infringes their ancient customs and privileges, he is no longer a prince
but a tyrant, and under the circumstances by the law of nature, his subjects, "for
the defense of liberty" have the right to not only disallow his authority, but to
choose another prince "even at the hazard" of their lives.[17]

Although the United Provinces became an independent Republic, its only
governing body was the States General, a representative political body akin to a
parliament that met in The Hague and deliberated on military and foreign affairs,
along with the Stadtholder (or governor), who was a hereditary prince of the
House of Orange. The newly born Netherlands was in essence a loose federation

consisting of provinces that were largely self-governing. Each province had its own laws and regulations.

While a war of independence against the Spanish was going on, shipping and trade, which had been important pillars of the Dutch economy since the European Middle Ages, were continuing and expanding. It may seem surprising given that a war was going on, but the affluence of the Dutch was increasingly leading to growing demand for products such as spices, wines, and silk. To the detriment of the Dutch, however, for much of the sixteenth century, Spain and Portugal controlled most of the spice trade. Especially with regard to cloves, the Portuguese virtually cornered the supply in Europe. Despite what would seem an adverse situation, the Dutch were nevertheless able to participate in the trade of cloves for some period, as the Portuguese appointed them distributors in northern and western Europe. When Philip II and the Spanish took over Portugal in 1580 and subsequently tightened control over the supply of cloves, the Dutch were effectively shut out of the market. This development led to a growing conviction among the Dutch that they had to step up their efforts to gain control of the spice trade.[18] From the 1590s, large-scale trading companies formed by merchants banding together began to appear in some of the Dutch provinces.

The rise of Dutch trading companies

In 1594, Reiner Pauw, the son of a grain trader based in Amsterdam, and others including merchants from Amsterdam and Antwerp such as Dirk van Os and Jean Corel, came together to form the Compagnie van Verre (Company of Far Lands, CFL). The following year, the newly founded company sent four ships with 249 sailors to India in search of spices and other products.[19] Having encountered almost every imaginable hardship during its travels, the much reduced fleet and decimated crew of sailors returned to Amsterdam in 1597, nonetheless earning profits for its merchant investors. Stimulated by the success of the CFL voyage, in the same year Vincent van Bronkhorst, Cornelis van Campen and others formed a rival trading company named the Nieuwe Compagnie te Amsterdam (New Company).[20] These two companies later "merged" to form a company called the Oude Compagnie (Old Company), which was later renamed the Expert Compagnie in recognition of the success of Dutch naval officer Jacob van Neck's voyage to the East Indies (Indonesia) that resulted in high profits for investors.[21] Meanwhile, in the province of Zeeland, the merchant Van De Moucheron established the Veerse Compagnie in 1597 and in the following year the Middelburgse Compagnie was founded.[22] These two Zeelander companies merged in 1600 to form the Verengide Zeeuwse Compagnie (VZC).[23] In 1598 the four trading companies of Magellaanse Rotterdamse Compagnie (MRC), the Moucheron Van der Hagen & Compagnie (HC), the Een andere Rotterdamse Compagnie (RC) and the Delftse Vennooteschappe (DV) were founded in Rotterdam and Delft respectively.[24]

By 1598, no fewer than six proto-VOC companies including CFL were competing with each other for trade with Asia; in that year, 22 ships were sent to

Asia. In August 1599, Issac Le Maire, a well-to-do merchant and grocer who was born in Tournai (located in the lowlands of Belgium) and who lived for sometime in Antwerp before coming to Amsterdam, founded the Nieuwe Brabantse Compagnie (NBC).[25] Along with Le Maire, Jacques de Velaer, who was also from the southern Netherlands, and other Brabantines such as Louis de la Beeque were involved in the founding of the NBC and in the management of the company as directors.[26] Upon its establishment, the burgomasters of Amsterdam granted the NBC a charter for trade with China.[27] In December 1600, with the blessing of the burgomasters, the NBC was able to merge with the Expert Compagnie, thereby creating the Verenigde Compagnie te Amsterdam (United Amsterdam Company, UAS). The new company counted eight sailing vessels as part of its assets. Jacques van Heemskerck was appointed commander of the fleet.[28]

Before the establishment of the VOC, each European seafaring enterprise was usually created for a single journey by a group of ships sent to the East Indies. The life of the company was not to be continuous or semi-permanent as it is with the modern concept of corporations. After the ships returned from their voyages and the company's goods were sold and its profits distributed to its shareholders, the company was dissolved by its directors.[29] However, with the proto-VOC companies, the foundations had been laid for the concept of a corporation with a semi-permanent life. For example, while in principle the proto-VOC companies were formed to oversee single voyages, in some cases a single voyage was actually part of a series of voyages for which the States General and other authorities issued a single comprehensive charter. Consequently, in several instances a proto-VOC company was not dissolved after just a single voyage.[30] Another semi-permanent character of these companies was in most cases a permanency in the composition of the board of directors and shareholders, which on the whole did not change for the duration of several voyages.[31] Furthermore, for those companies whose voyages were complete, the capital returned to investors was usually re-invested via the same directors for the next voyages, which often used the same fleet of ships.[32] Several of the proto-VOC companies also set up outposts for trade in Asia, which further boosted their semi-permanent character.[33]

Within the proto-VOC companies there was only one layer of management: that is, the board of directors (bewindhebbers), who were small in number. Unlike most modern multinational corporations, the proto-VOC companies had no clear separation between the directors and executive officers or managers. Most often the board of directors managed the companies by organizing themselves into departments such as human resources, the rigging of ships, food supplies, and products.[34] The directors in essence monopolized the management of the companies. They determined by themselves such issues as the amount of spices to be bought in Asia and the proceeds to be distributed to themselves after a voyage and the dissolution of the company. Upon dissolving the companies, the directors often made sure to enrich themselves with more than 1 percent of the total value of goods purchased in Asia, on top of the dividends from their investments.[35]

Another feature of these proto-VOC companies was that while there were numerous shareholders (participanten) backing these enterprises, the shareholders usually invested their money via the individual directors and not directly in the company itself.[36] Each director of course knew the identities of the investors he received money from. However, in principle the investments were made anonymously, and the directors did not know the identity of the investors who had invested their money with other directors in the same company. Consequently, the investors were in no position to collectively influence or participate in the management of the company by holding a shareholders' meeting, as is in the case with modern corporations, and thus were passive investors. An exception was the Middelburgse Compagnie, where shareholders who invested beyond a certain required amount of capital were called Major Investors (hoofdparticipanten) and were given limited rights that allowed them to demand the board of directors to disclose information on the operations of the company and the use of its funds. This can perhaps be considered a precursor of the modern shareholders' meeting.[37]

By 1601, trade with the East Indies had grown to the extent that in that year alone, the six proto-VOC trading companies of the Netherlands sent out 14 expeditions consisting of 65 ships that traveled around the Cape of Good Hope in a rush to get their hands on spices. Unsurprisingly, the competition between the companies was causing serious problems price-wise, as they were bidding up the purchasing prices of spices in Indonesia and at the same time price-cutting on the streets of Amsterdam. Naturally, this led to a squeezing of profit margins for everyone. Viewing the situation with concern, the fledgling Dutch government felt that if there were to be any profits left, trade had to be regulated. Furthermore, there was a growing belief among the Dutch rulers that the scale and extensiveness of Spanish and Portuguese trade was such that a united and aggressive effort would be needed to counter the competition. Hence, the idea arose that it would be better to merge the disparate resources of the six trading companies into one entity.

On March 20, 1602, perhaps for the first time in modern business history, a "mega-merger" of sorts took place that would have historically significant repercussions: the Vereenigde Nederlandsche Geoctroyeerde Oostindische Compagnie (United Dutch Chartered East India Company, VOC) was formed by the merger of the six companies of the UAS, VZC, MRC, HC, DV, and RC, with the participation of traders from the northern cities of Hoorn and Enkhuizen (Vennontschappe van Noorder quatiere).[38] According to the charter of the VOC, the company was to continue as an enterprise for 21 years, with a general audit to be undertaken once every 10 years.[39]

Before the merger, each province had regulated its own merchants and championed its own trading companies in the States General. Each of the enterprises had its own board of directors and shareholders and respective sources of financing.[40] And every one of the companies had been competing fiercely against the others as well as against the Portuguese and Spanish. Aside from the jealousy of Zeeland towards Amsterdam's stronger economic position, the free-spirited

Dutch merchants had a strong ingrained dislike towards anything that smelled of a monopoly. In addition, some of the directors of the proto-VOC companies such as Issac Le Maire and Van De Moucheron reportedly had explosive personalities that could be compared with those of modern-day opera stars.[41] Thus we can reasonably assume that the mega-merger that led to the creation of the VOC did not come from a mutual outpouring of goodwill or feelings of altruism from the individual companies. In fact, much of the impetus behind this mega-merger came from Johan van Oldenbarnvelt, the leader of the States General, and Maurice of Nassau, Prince of the House of Orange and the Stadtholder of the United Provinces of the Netherlands. The latter, through patient diplomacy, was able to persuade the companies to put aside their rivalry for the greater good of the Netherlands and to cajole the provinces into accepting a single combined monopoly organization to handle all commerce to the Indies.[42] As stated in the VOC charter, the companies were to be united for the service and profit of the United Provinces, and the VOC was to be managed and expanded for all who would like to participate in the venture.[43]

Although industry consolidation in order to reduce competition and achieve monopoly profits was a major driver behind this mega-merger, there was also the threat of increasing and strengthening foreign competition. As one company, the Dutch merchants and investors were now able to achieve economies of scale, lower transaction costs through the vertical integration of their seafaring operations, and the creation of an extensive network of information exchange that would enable them to compete effectively against the Iberians and the English. In addition to these drivers, there was an economic factor behind the mega-merger: the Netherlands needed and hoped to secure a steady source of revenue through the lucrative spice trade to finance its war against the Spanish and to compete effectively against the Portuguese and English simultaneously. In short, not only was the VOC one of the earliest examples of an M&A arrangement, but its formation is also a result of what we would recognize as aggressive government leadership and intervention in consolidating an industry sector for promoting economic efficiency and competitiveness: a precursor to what we have seen happen in Japan since World War II.

A total of 1,143 investors provided the VOC with 6.45 million guilders in financing (US$100 million in today's money) to hire men, purchase ships, and acquire silver and other products to be exchanged for spices. In comparison, the EIC of England which was formed in 1600 had capital of only 820,000 guilders (US$13 million today) and 219 investors.[44] Furthermore, as the capital of the VOC was permanent, profit brought home from a voyage was used to invest in the further expansion of the VOC's business. In contrast, the capital of the EIC was not permanent; paid-in capital and profits had to be returned to investors once the company's ships returned to England and its products were sold.[45]

Ownership or shares of the VOC was divided into multiple partijen, or "action."[46] The VOC did not give out "action" or share certificates to investors in the modern sense of the word. Instead, investors had their names registered in the VOC stock ledger at the time of purchase. The money of the investors was deposited with the company, upon which receipts were issued. Payment for shares was initially determined to be made in three allotments, but in fact they were completed in 12, with the last payment completed in 1606.[47] The principle of limited liability, while not clearly stated in the VOC charter, was implied; investors were protected from financial ruin as they would lose only their investment in the company if it failed.[48] On the other hand, the charter stated clearly that only when five percent of a return cargo had been cashed would there be returns distributed to investors.[49] When a shareholder sold his "stock," it was transferred to the name of the stock buyer in the presence of two directors of the company.[50] In principle, the VOC welcomed as shareholders anyone resident within the United Provinces. In reality, however, the company was owned by a few wealthy shareholders, with 40 percent of shareholder capital coming from exiles originating from the southern Netherlands.[51] The refugees included famous Antwerp merchant-banking families such as the Bartolottis, Coymans, DeScots, and DeVogelaers.[52] Few foreigners, except for three German immigrants and two Italians, invested substantial amounts. Large investors included the magnate Jan Poppen, whose family by 1631 was the richest in all of Amsterdam, followed by the Antwerp merchant-banking families of the Bartolotti and the Coyman.[53] The largest individual shareholder at the time of the VOC's inception was none other than Issac Le Maire, founder of the NBC. Le Maire invested up to 85,000 guilders.[54] Along with Le Maire, immigrants from Antwerp were the largest investors who funneled their money into the Amsterdam chamber. In this chamber there were more than a thousand initial investors. Out of this group there were 81 "chief investors," of which roughly half were wealthy Protestant refugees who had fled Spanish persecution, and roughly half were native Hollanders.[55] The less wealthy native Hollanders included Gerrit Bicker, son of a brewer; Reinier Pauw, son of a grain trader mentioned earlier; and Gerrit Reynst, son of a soap boiler. Although Holland's towns were typically 10 to 20 percent Catholic, all the chief investors of the VOC were Protestant.[56]

As in the case of the proto-VOC companies, even the larger shareholders of the VOC had very little power. Shareholders initially had no influence as to the choice of directors. Later they were allowed the right to present a list of nominees, which seems to have been theoretical. When company directors petitioned the government to release the VOC from its obligation to publish 10-year accounts in 1612, as stipulated in its charter, which was also the year the company was to allow investors to withdraw their capital if they chose to do so, the government gave permission, and both the publishing of accounts and the repayment of capital were postponed.[57] In a further affront to shareholders, the VOC announced in the same year that it would not liquidate the company in 1623 as originally planned. As a result, shareholders had to sell their shares to other investors if they needed cash, a development leading to the birth of the modern stock market.[58]

There would be little disagreement that shareholders of the VOC had a lot to complain about. However, in contrast to the EIC, which had to return the capital of the company to its investors after a voyage was made and the acquired products sold, the VOC was able to accumulate a permanent stock of capital, which allowed the management of the company the necessary corporate stability and continuity to engage in mid- to long-term planning. Furthermore, stability of capital allowed the company to reinvest for the future, something which was not possible for EIC management. Thus, the argument could be made that while transparency in the rights of shareholders was wanting, the capital arrangements of the VOC enabled the managers to make long-term business plans. In essence, it can be argued that the foundation and practice of what we know today as corporate planning had been established.

The management structure of the VOC

The chambers

While the VOC operated as one company, it had a decentralized organizational structure that reflected its origin. Each of the original six companies based in Amsterdam, Zeeland, Enkhuizen, Delft, Hoorn, and Rotterdam was given its own regional office or chamber. According to the charter of the VOC, each chamber had its own directors (beiwindhebbers) who were also directors in the VOC. Amsterdam and Zeeland had 23 and 14 directors in the company respectively. The chamber of Delft and Enkhusen each had 11 directors, while the chambers of Rotterdam had nine and Hoorn had four. From these directors, members of a general management board for the VOC were to be selected. The VZC of Zeeland initially demanded that each chamber have an equal number of votes, allowing each chamber an equal voice on the board.[59] This, however, proved unfeasible in practice. A compromise situation was worked out when the chambers agreed to select a total of 17 board members, the Heeren XVII, and the number of directors appointed from each chamber was determined and apportioned according to its respective population. Thus, Amsterdam had eight, Zeeland four, Meuse two, and North Holland two. The seventeenth director was to be nominated in turns by the chambers of Zeeland, the Meuse, and North Holland and elected by majority vote.[60] The significance of this arrangement is that even though Amsterdam accounted for more than half the total capital invested in VOC (57.4 percent) as required by the company charter, the Amsterdam chamber was prevented from commanding an absolute majority during board voting. Furthermore, although the Amsterdam chamber initially assumed that the board would perpetually sit in the city of Amsterdam due to its preponderance, Amsterdam nevertheless agreed after deliberation with the other chambers to introduce an eight-year cycle for the board meeting place, whereby for the first six years the board would meet in Amsterdam and the Amsterdam chamber would function as the President of the chambers, after which Middelburg would be the next seat, followed by Zeeland.[61]

The Heeren XVII

The management board of the VOC, the Heeren XVII, is reported to have initially met three times a year, later twice a year.[62] The board discussed a wide range of topics at these meetings. The Heeren XVII engaged in deliberations on what kind of purchases were to be made in Asia and preparations for the sale of goods brought back by returning ships. It made decisions on the building, rigging, provisioning, and manning of ships. The board also took up mundane issues such as the request of a company staff member to have his family accompany him to Asia or the drunken behavior of a staff member.[63] Topics that were considered vital in nature were discussed in advance in subcommittees consisting of members drawn from each chamber. Such an arrangement ensured that each chamber was fully informed and involved in the decision-making process.[64] The Heeren XVII made decisions that were binding on the chambers. As each chamber was represented in the Heeren XVII, the directors ensured that their respective chambers would execute whatever decision was made by the board.

The main Heeren XVII board meeting of the year lasted three to four weeks in the autumn, the timing of which was to coincide with the return of ships from Asia. At this meeting, issues such as the equipping of the next round of outgoing ships, the target quantity of products from Asia, and the allocation of precious metals for the purchases were discussed and determined. The manner in which auctions should be held for the products from Asia was also settled. At another meeting in the spring, financial plans based on the results of the auction of goods from Asia were drawn up. At the summer meeting, the Heeren XVII reviewed the correspondence from Asia and directives were accordingly sent out to the VOC Asia headquarters in Batavia. Both the meetings of the chambers and the Heeren XVII worked their way through an agenda, which was known beforehand so that the chambers could instruct their delegates to the Heeren XVII board accordingly.[65]

As the Amsterdam chamber had the largest number of directors, it was usually involved in the drafting of resolutions within the Heeren XVII. Its size often led the other chambers to delegate decisions to Amsterdam on issues that were not decided upon immediately. In effect, Amsterdam became the dominant player in the VOC board and the merged company. The directives of the VOC were hence often based on the direction given by Amsterdam.[66] If during the meetings the other chambers criticized a position taken by the Amsterdam chamber, the Amsterdam delegates in the Heeren XVII would go back to consult its other directors in the chamber instead of attempting to forcibly push through its decision.[67]

From what we know from various studies, generally speaking, the management of the Heeren XVII board was poorly executed. The members of the board were constantly changing and incredibly had no permanent administrative staff to support the delegates, although they were assisted initially by the secretary of the Amsterdam chamber and later by two advocaten or permanent counsels.[68] The members or directors who made up the Heeren XVII had lifetime membership. Despite records of meetings held twice or thrice per year, the Heeren XVII was not required to have permanent sessions; a general meeting would be held "as often as would be needed."[69] In addition, there was an issue of opaqueness with regard to the selection of the directors from Amsterdam and Zeeland as well as from other chambers.[70] This ambiguity was perhaps an outcome of the founders' insistence on respecting the selection practices of each chamber; there is no mention of this subject in the charter of the VOC.

Understandably, criticism was aimed at the management practices of the VOC. A short book written anonymously entitled *Nootwendich Discours* (The Necessary Discourse) was published in 1622, in which the author castigates some of the directors of the company. In the book they are accused of leaving everything in "darkness" and of feeding the accounting books of the company to the dogs after rubbing them with bacon fat.[71] Other vocal critics of the VOC argued that directorships should be for fixed terms and not for life and that all of the major shareholders should have the right to appoint directors.[72]

To the credit of the Heeren XVII, in 1622 they initiated a reform of the corporate governance practices of the VOC with a renewal of the company charter, which resulted in several changes. One was the establishment of a limited tenure of three years for a director, instead of life. Another was the granting of rights to major shareholders of each chamber who had as many shares as the directors of the Heeren XVII to nominate "Nine Men" from among themselves (four from Amsterdam, two from Zeeland, one each from Rotterdam, Delft, and the northern provinces) with whom the Heeren XVII were obligated to consult on important matters concerning the company. The Nine Men were also empowered to review the annual accounting records of the six chambers, inspect warehouses and the rigging and loading of the outgoing ships, and with the Heeren XVII were given the right to jointly nominate candidates for future directorships in the Heeren XVII.[73] Further reforms allowed the Nine Men to attend board meetings of the Heeren XVII (although they were not allowed to vote) and advise the Heeren XVII on the sales of products and other important matters, review annual purchasing accounts, and appoint auditors to check accounts submitted to the States General. In short, the Nine Men has a parallel with audit committees established in most modern listed companies to oversee the activities of the corporate board.[74]

Batavia—the organization of the VOC in Asia

Aside from the chambers and the Heeren XVII, there was a third management organization which the foundation of the VOC rested upon: Batavia, at Jakarta in Indonesia. While the charter of the VOC was clear as regards the organization of the VOC in the Netherlands, little in the document was devoted to how the outposts of the VOC should be managed, except to say that the directors of the respective chambers might appoint governors, maintain armed forces, and install judicial officers and officers for maintaining order and promoting trade. Governors, judges, and military officers were required to swear an oath of loyalty to the States General and to the Company. Directors were given the right to dismiss the governors and members of the judiciary if the latter were found to have engaged in corruption or other illegal activities.[75]

The first fleets sent out to the East Indies by the VOC in 1602 adhered to the practices of the proto-VOC companies. That is to say, the admiral of the outgoing fleet was given supreme command and all of the Company's onboard employees were subject to his management. In practice, however, this arrangement proved cumbersome for executing fast action towards taking away trade from the various Portuguese trading outposts scattered about in the East Indies region. Consequently, in imitation of the Portuguese, the VOC in 1609 set about establishing a permanent center of control for the East Indies region, which focused all authority in the hands of a Governor General appointed by the Heeren XVII who was to be assisted by a Raad van Indie (Council of the Indies). The Governor General was essentially first among equals of the Council of the Indies and had supreme control over all VOC trade in Asia. He was not, however, empowered to the extent of making decisions without the consent of the Council.

In 1619, as concerns grew about increasing English encroachments and influence in the East Indies, the VOC overthrew the local Pangeran or prince of Jakarta and established a fort which they renamed Batavia, the ancient Roman name of Holland. Aside from Batavia, the VOC established many outposts in Asia. Among them were those in Ambonia (captured 1605), the Banda islands (captured 1609–1619), Ternate (captured 1605), Tidore (captured 1605), Ceylon (captured 1638–1658), Makassar (captured 1666), Malacca (captured 1641), Taiwan (captured 1623 and named Fort Zeelandia; recaptured by China under the leadership of the half-Chinese, half-Japanese Zheng Chengkong, better known as Koxinga, in 1661),[76] Pulicat (captured 1613), and Cochin (captured 1662). Outside of Asia, the VOC wrested away from the Portuguese in 1622 a strategic foothold on the island of Hormuz, which was situated in the narrow entrance of the Persian Gulf leading into the Arabian Sea.[77] The VOC also established a supply center for the company at the Cape of Good Hope (1652).[78] Each of these outposts was administered by the VOC through an appointed Governor General or a Director and his Council. In breadth and scope of activities Batavia was, however, by far the most important of these outposts.

The responsibilities of Batavia included managing trade and shipping between the various VOC establishments in Asia, keeping and maintaining accounting records of trade in Asia, managing personnel administration such as overseeing the number of VOC staff in Asia, providing maintenance and repair works for VOC ships, and providing the seat for the highest law court of the Netherlands in Asia. All communication between the various VOC outposts and the Directors in the Dutch Republic was conducted through the Batavia Governor General and the Council.

As the functions and responsibilities of the Governor General in Batavia and the pecking order between Batavia and other outposts of the VOC indicate, the establishment of Batavia as the seat of the Governor General of the VOC has a strong parallel with modern multinational corporations that have established a hub-and-spoke type of layout consisting of a regional headquarters (RHQ) or hub which is empowered to manage and coordinate the business activities of various branches or spokes within a continent or a region.

The fall of the VOC

In 1799, after a run of 200 years, the VOC collapsed. As with many other stories of companies that have gone out of business, there is no single reason that explains the demise of the VOC. Some of the factors commonly cited by historians include the VOC's inability to adjust its trade to changing consumer tastes, and its inability to maintain its monopoly over the spice trade against the British and the French. Another factor cited is the decline in the quality of the employees of the VOC, as the company increasingly tended to rely upon uneducated young lads from Germany who were no match for the more able employees of the EIC.[79] There is also the issue of the lack of corporate governance, which allowed for widespread corruption among the officers and employees of the VOC, including sailors and governor generals who regularly siphoned off the purchased and plundered treasures of the various voyages for themselves. Despite efforts on the part of the VOC management to counter corruption by implementing a compensation system which linked remuneration to investment and sales rather than placing emphasis on profits,[80] the miserly treatment of the sailors, together with the ability of those higher up such as the governor generals to create their own personal fiefdoms mostly beyond the reach of their masters in the Netherlands, no doubt encouraged corruption. Indeed, the extent of corruption was such that after its demise, the VOC logo came to be read as Vergaan Onder Corruptie—perished by corruption.[81] Along with corruption, low morale of the sailors from miserly pay and a high mortality rate did not help to foster company loyalty within the lower rungs of the company. Political factors also contributed to the demise of the VOC. On-and-off wars between the Netherlands and Britain in the eighteenth century made it increasingly difficult for the VOC to manage its trade between the Netherlands and Asia, leading to declining incomes, rising costs, and increasing debts. By the end of the 1790s, the revenues of the VOC had fallen to the extent that the company was forced to request a moratorium on its debt payments.

The end came when the Dutch government dissolved the VOC and took over its assets, including its imperial outposts, on the last day of the eighteenth century. Perhaps it is worth noting that despite its decline, to the very end of the life of the VOC, the six chambers that were originally six separate companies did not go their separate ways but remained together.

The culture of the VOC: tolerance and intolerance at work

The tolerant culture of the VOC

By the measure of longevity (200 years), increase in shareholder value (from a par 100 in 1602 to 786 in 1733), and returns to shareholders (an average of 18 percent dividends per year on investments), the VOC is arguably an example of an M&A arrangement that turned out to be "successful." Of course, on the one hand its insouciance towards shareholders, its indifference to the plight of the working conditions of its sailors, and its opaque management practices as shown in the selection of its management board would be far from acceptable in modern corporate governance practices. Corruption was also an unworthy feature that would plague the VOC. On the other hand, as the earliest known example of a joint stock company, the VOC was nevertheless a trailblazer and pioneer of the corporation. Its span and scale of operations, from ship building to the final sales of a product, would also qualify the VOC as one of the earliest examples of a vertically integrated company that competed on the basis of achieving economies of scale, lower transaction costs, and establishing an extensive information and distribution network. Its capital structure enabled the stability necessary for management to engage in long-term corporate planning. The VOC was also one of the pioneers of the multinational corporation, with regional headquarters in Batavia empowered with a high degree of local autonomy managing inter-regional trade and the business affairs of subordinate trading outposts in Asia. Many of its employees, especially those on the ships, were of various nationalities.

The question arises: what were the factors that helped to contribute to the maintenance of the VOC mega-merger for two centuries? No doubt, the high returns to the venture and the sharing of risk was a strong incentive for the respective chambers or proto-VOC companies to stick together rather than go their separate ways. There was also political pressure from the powers-that-be to remain united to attain hegemony over the Spanish, Portuguese, and other competitors. In this regard, not only did the members of the VOC pledge allegiance to the company, but they also had to swear their loyalty to the States General of the United Provinces.

I argue that there were also cultural factors that contributed to the longevity of the merger that resulted in the VOC. First and foremost was the common view shared by the investors of the respective companies, whether they were from Amsterdam or Zeeland, that—in contrast to the Portuguese view—the pursuit of profit was to hold precedence over the propagation of the Christian faith. Unlike the Catholic Portuguese, the Calvinist Dutch were substantially less preoccupied with saving heathen souls than with making a profit.[82] This outlook was shaped by the liberal and largely urban environment of the Netherlands existent at the time, where although there was a strict Calvinist clergy, a tolerant civil elite (while committed to the Protestant cause) dominated the political and social life of the people at large, which allowed a great diversity of beliefs to coexist. As the Dutch physician and author of *The Fable of the Bees* Bernard Mandeville suggested, the Dutch had the perspicacity to put everything aside for merchandise, navigation, and unlimited liberty of conscience, which allowed the Netherlands, "that contemptible spot of earth," to become a considerable power of Europe.[83]

In a wealthy society as the Netherlands where literacy and general education levels were high, there was a ready audience for and sympathy towards the teachings of openness and tolerance as espoused by the Dutch Renaissance humanist Desiderius Erasmus and other independent-minded thinkers. Large sections of the Dutch people simply did not believe in strict Church structures, with only 10 percent of the Dutch population enrolled as members of the Reformed Church.[84] However, at the same time, the common Calvinist outlook of the founders of the VOC helped them to be united in their view of their Portuguese opponents as the followers of the Anti-Christ.[85] Indeed, in contrast to the hedonism practiced by the majority of VOC members, there were also among them ardent Calvinists such as the admiral Piet Heyn and Governor General of Batavia, Jan Coen, who complained constantly about the lack of piety among Dutch expatriates in Asia.[86]

The tolerance evident in the Dutch culture of the time, which was shared by the members of the six proto-VOC companies and which extended into the VOC management structure and governance system, extended beyond religion to a more general tolerance. I argue that it was thanks to a tolerant attitude that all of the companies could agree to have every proto-VOC company participate in the governance of the VOC, no matter what their origin or how small the company. This manifestation of tolerance has a parallel among global empires in the United Kingdom, with the Welsh and the Scottish fully participating along with the English in its governance. As in the United Kingdom, the toleration of full participation not only arguably led to the creation of a superseding identity for the proto-VOC companies, but also created for them undeniable incentives to stay together for 200 years, in the form of power and gold (or spices). Tolerance helped the companies to agree on a governance system that prevented voting in the Heeren XVII board meetings from being completely dominated by the largest of the six proto-VOC companies (the UAS of Amsterdam), and allowed decision-making to be determined by the majority vote of all the Heeren XVII delegate members. It can be argued that this show of tolerance helped to keep this merger together by assuaging the fears of the smaller proto-VOC companies of being bullied by Amsterdam. Indeed, it should be noted that out of a fear that Amsterdam would have too much power in a united company, Zeeland had initially little enthusiasm for a merger.[87] Tolerance was also evident in the method of apportioning the provision of services and equipment, when the six companies decided that the Amsterdam chamber would provide one half of all investment, while the chamber of Zeeland would provide 25 percent and the other chambers 12.5 percent each. This was much to the relief of the Zeelanders, who had feared that had the Amsterdam chamber (which provided more than half the capital of the VOC) had their way, they would have gained control over more than half of all operations undertaken by the VOC.[88] In the employment practices of the VOC at management and employee levels, the factor of tolerance was at work as well. Many of the founders of the original pre-VOC companies such as Le Maire came from Antwerp in the southern province of Brabant. Le Maire himself did not become a citizen of the United Provinces until 1601.[89] Along with other directors of the UAS, after the mega-merger he obtained a seat as a director of the Amsterdam chamber and an administrative function within the VOC.[90] Aside from diversity in the composition of the management, in principle, the VOC welcomed investors of all nationalities. As for lower-level employees, here as well the VOC was indifferent to the issue of national origin, as the relatively small population of the Netherlands forced the VOC to look for able-bodied men beyond their borders to man their ships for what turned out to be a one-way trip for many. The high rates of mortality among VOC employees, with about one quarter of the men dying during the outbound journey alone, forced the VOC to look for a constant stream of employees.[91] Manpower requirements became so great that from the mid-seventeenth century most of the soldiers and sailors of the VOC came from outside of the Netherlands. In one recruitment effort, the VOC formed a specialized corps of women who targeted foreign men, mainly from Germany, who flooded into Dutch cities looking for jobs. In return for a cut of their signing and advance and future pay from the Company, the women duped the men with room, board, and entertainment.[92] By 1650, most of the soldiers and sailors of the VOC were Germans, Scandinavians, French, and English.[93]

The duality of VOC culture: coexistence of tolerance and intolerance

In contrast to the tolerance and spirit of compromise which was at the foundation of the management and employment practices of the VOC, there was, however, a dark, intolerant side to the history of the company which needs to be examined and somehow reconciled with its tolerant side. The ambitious Governor General of Batavia, Jan Coen believed first and foremost that a monopoly over the trade of cloves, nutmeg, and mace must be established by the VOC. He also believed, as his actions were to demonstrate, that the ends justified the means, even if it meant the ruthless use of force and the exploitation and massacre of local inhabitants and workers. As he wrote to his superiors in the VOC in 1614, Asia had to be defended with weapons and the weapons must be paid for by profits raised from trade. He concluded simply that the VOC could not carry on trade without war nor war without trade.[94] In 1619, with a force of 19 ships at his command, Coen seized a fortified fishing village called Jakarta and drove out the native people. The VOC conquered 12,000 square kilometers of land and established the newly named Batavia as the regional headquarters of the VOC. Subsequently in the same year, the VOC appointed Coen as Governor General of Batavia. With Batavia as regional headquarters, the VOC embarked upon expanding its trade with countries in Asia including India, China, and Japan. This led to further growth for the company and more riches not only for its investors but for the fledgling Dutch Republic as well. Along the way, Coen and his men were responsible for the death by starvation of virtually the entire native population of the Banda islands, a major source of nutmeg and mace, when they attempted, unsuccessfully, to establish plantations for growing cloves and nutmeg for export.

Coen tried to get his message across to the hapless Bandanese of his intent to monopolize the spice trade by having his men hack to pieces every male

Bandanese above the age of 15.[95] The Bandanese population was also constantly forced by the Dutch overlords to plant, harvest, and destroy trees on the islands to adjust production of spices to demand and maintain market prices at a constant level. To further intimidate the local population and have them understand that he was *really* serious about business, Coen had village leaders tortured, decapitated, and if that weren't enough, displayed their heads impaled on long poles.[96] When the VOC first arrived, the population of the Banda archipelago was estimated to be 15,000; 15 years of VOC rule reduced the population to 600.[97] The Dutch subsequently imported slaves and indentured laborers into the islands. Meanwhile, a few of the Bandanese survivors dispersed throughout the nutmeg groves of the Banda islands, leading a discreet life as plantation laborers and teaching the Dutch the fine art of growing nutmeg.[98] Other Bandanese were caught and shipped to Batavia as slaves. Certainly after the thorough genocide committed against the Bandanese, Coen and the Dutch had no need to worry of any obstreperous Bandanese rising up to seek revenge.

What kind of person would commit such atrocities all for the sake of profits? From what we know from various sources, contemporaries of Coen described him as a pious and strict Calvinist who was demanding and severe with his subordinates and would not hesitate to mete out cruel punishments towards those who misbehaved or rebelled against him.[99] Pieter Both, the first Governor General of Batavia, described Coen as a "delightful" and "God-fearing" man who was modest in his habits, chaste, did not drink, was not self-centered, and was very capable in business.[100] Coen was strict with himself and expected others to behave exemplarily as well. In this regard, Coen was known to often criticize the Heeren XVII and their policies and governance, and he was often scornful of the corruption that he observed in the various Dutch trading outposts in Asia.

Born on January 8, 1587 in the northern Dutch town of Hoorn, Coen spent his early years as an apprentice in the branch of a Dutch trade office in Rome, where he learned the art of double-entry bookkeeping. In 1607, he went out on his first voyage to Indonesia, and in 1612 he went on his second journey, during which he commanded two ships as a senior merchant. The Heeren XVII recognized Coen's abilities and promoted him to the position of Accountant General of all VOC outposts in Indonesia and President of the head office in Bantam and Jakarta in 1613. The next year, Coen was promoted to Director General, the second in command to the Governor General. While on his way up the promotion ladder, Coen wrote a thesis which caught the attention of the Heeren XVII. In his *Discoers Touscherende den Nederlandtsche Indischen Staet*, he discoursed upon the need to monopolize the supply of nutmeg, mace, and cloves so as to raise the profit margins of the company. He also expounded the view that the monopoly of trade should be realized at any cost, including the exploitation of local workers and the importation of Dutch colonists and slave labor.[101] In 1617, the Heeren XVII promoted Coen to Governor General in the East Indies.

Coen, in short, was an incorruptible, efficient, and ruthless businessman with an intolerant and impatient streak towards those who would not conform to him.

He was self-righteous, delivering such famous remarks as, "Despair not, spare your enemies not, for God is with us."[102] He was also a bit of a sadist, as exemplified by his extermination of the Bandanese and his personal mistreatment of a 12-year-old girl, Saartje Specx, who had a Dutch father and Japanese mother. Specx was caught having sex with a 15-year-old man, Pieter Cortenhoeff, whom she was to marry. For her carnal sins, she was publicly whipped in Batavia and Coen had the man decapitated.[103] Sadly for Specx, she only lived on to the age of 19.

Coen was a product of his times in Europe, where piety existed alongside with great intolerance, and cruelty along with humanitarianism. Putting aside the actions against Specx and her lover, apologists for Coen and the VOC may argue that the acts which they instigated on the Bandanese were simply an extreme form of punishment for not observing the sanctity of the trade contracts agreed between them. These agreements stipulated that: (1) the Dutch would be able to exclusively purchase nutmeg and mace from the Bandanese at a price that was lower than that offered to anyone else; (2) the Dutch would be able to sell rice to the Bandanese that was not of the type desired by them and at above market rate prices; and (3) the Dutch would be able to sell to the Bandanese woolen and velvet cloth manufactured in Europe. The Bandanese, however, living as they did in tropical climes, did not find Dutch cloth attractive compared to the Indian cotton weave they preferred.[104] Nor were they particularly fond of the type of rice being sold to them, the Dutch rigidity on pricing, or the VOC's insistence on a monopoly on the supply of spices. It was a fairly one-sided contract much in favor of the Dutch. Furthermore, the Bandanese could not read the contract, as it was in the Dutch language.[105] Accordingly, it is most likely that the Bandanese did not fully understand the implications of the fine print of the contract before agreeing to it. In addition, the Bandanese did not want to be locked in to a dependency relationship with the Dutch and preferred to continue dealing with Chinese, Javanese, and Arab traders who at the least offered goods that the Bandanese wanted, such as rice (of the type the Bandanese preferred), porcelain, and medicines.[106] In this respect, even the English were preferable to the Dutch. Thus the Bandanese defied their agreements with the Dutch and surreptitiously continued to trade with non-Dutch traders. Unfortunately for them, they got caught, and in the eyes of the VOC they deserved the consequences. As their treatment of the Bandanese suggests, for Coen and his cohorts, if the Bandanese could not barter the products they purchased from the Dutch in order to get their own food supplies, and happened to starve to death as a result, well, that was just tough luck; and anyway, it was their fault for not having the necessary marketing ingenuity to barter away the Dutch goods. A contract was a contract. In the eyes of the Dutch, trading with people other than the VOC just to avoid starvation was not a good enough reason to justify a breach of contract that would lead to a loss of profit for them.

In fairness, it should be mentioned that not all of the Dutch were pleased with the brutal actions taken by the sailors and soldiers of the VOC. One major investor of the VOC, Pieter Lijntjens, a Mennonite, withdrew his investment in protest at the warlike conduct of the company.[107] Coen was also at odds with his pre-decessors, Governor General Laurens Reael, a doctor of laws, and his assistant Steven van der Hagen, who both believed in the primacy of negotiation and con-tracts when engaging in trade in Asia.[108] These voices of objection to the geno-cidal acts of Coen have largely been forgotten by the present-day Dutch, however, who have erected a statue in memory of the "Butcher of Banda" in the town of Hoorn.[109]

After the atrocities and genocide inflicted upon the Bandanese, Coen and the VOC trained their sights upon the island of Ambon, where cloves were grown and which had strategic access to the central and northern Moluccas. The end result of their endeavors in monopolizing the supply of cloves was the utter destruction of Ambonese society through massacres, forced famines, and prompt execution of all Ambonese who attempted to raise cloves in areas outside of the control of the VOC. So thorough were the Dutch in their genocidal ways that the Ambonese offered no resistance until 1817.[110] The men of the VOC also tortured and executed 10 Englishmen, 10 Japanese, and a Portuguese who all happened at the time to be in the way of the Dutch in Ambon. According to one account, each of the Japanese and English who were arrested was individually subjected to torture using water and other tools. For over a week the Dutch torturers poured filthy water into cones that were placed above the mouth and nose of the prisoners, who were forced to gulp down the water. Aside from choking them, the excess water caused severe swelling of tissues which further exacerbated their pain. The Dutch supplemented this water torture with the burning of armpits, feet, and hands with a candle and the pulling out of fingernails.[111] As we will see later on, the use of water as a tool of torture would be popular over the course of centuries with other empire builders such as the Americans and the Japanese.

The VOC also massacred a community of Chinese in Batavia in October of 1740, when the talents of the Chinese for business and trade became insupport-able to the jealous Dutch, who pounded and hacked to death an estimated 10,000 Chinese men, women, and children, and destroyed their homes and shops in an orgy of violence lasting three days.[112] Injured or sick Chinese who were in hos-pitals or those chained in prisons were spared no mercy and hacked to death as well.[113] A Dutch apprentice carpenter by the name of Georg Schwarz took advantage of the massacre to steal his Chinese neighbor's pig. When his superior saw this, Schwarz recalled being slapped and scolded by him for not killing the Chinese first and then proceeding to plunder! Accordingly, Schwarz took a rice-pounder and beat to death his neighbor, with whom he had frequently drunk and dined.[114] During this time, the Dutch posted a bounty for the heads of decapitated Chinese, while a Dutch preacher declared that the killing of Chinese was in accordance with the will of God.[115] The leader of this massacre was the VOC Governor General Adriaan Valckenier.

The heinous actions of the VOC during their relentless pursuit of profit are in stark contrast to the tolerance noted in the company's internal employment and managerial practices, as well as to the behavior of the Dutch in general exhibited in the Netherlands at the time. Such acts, amounting to genocide committed against non-European peoples, would suggest that the VOC had little regard for the peoples and cultures of the territories they subjugated. And it would seem that racism, or notions of racial superiority or racial determinism as understood in the later Western European and American sense that justified the subjugation or extermination of inferior races, was already prevalent. However, as certain historians have pointed out, the fact that the VOC entered into contracts (albeit clearly disadvantageous ones to the Bandanese) with the Bandanese and that the VOC expected them to live up to the consequences indicates that the Dutch did not treat the Bandanese as children or inferiors.[116] There is also the example of Johan Maetsuyker, the Governor General of Batavia from 1645 to 1650, who encouraged the Dutch settlers to marry with Asian women with the argument that the offspring would be better capable of tolerating the Asian environment than those born from European parents. Maetsuyker even offered a bonus to any Dutch sailor or soldier who would take a local wife. Maetsuyker's endeavor failed, owing largely to the inability of the Germans, French, English, and Scandinavians to adapt to colonial life. The few that did settle down, such as those in Sri Lanka, mostly became tavern keepers, as heavy drinking was a notable feature of colonial life for the Dutch.[117]

Some historians suggest that during the seventeenth century, notions of "white" superiority were beyond the imagination of the Europeans, and that people such as the English did not bring along any baggage of cultural superiority.[118] Records from the Dutch outposts in Deshima and Hirado in Kyushu, Japan, mention the overall good fit the Dutch had with the Japanese, both groups enjoying strong drink and carousing.[119] Earlier we mentioned that empire builders have had a proclivity for procreation and spreading their genes. The Dutch were no exception and were well known to engage with Japanese concubines, to such an extent that Pieter Nuyts, the VOC governor of Taiwan, remarked that there was as many Dutch "mestizos" as there were full-blooded Japanese living in Hirado, which to him was "an intolerable and ignominious" state of affairs.[120] A case in point was the VOC resident general of Hirado, Albert Wouterson, who fathered three children with a Japanese consort.[121] Batavia issued an ordinance against having concubines in 1621, only to have it ignored, and by the 1630s the ordinance was repealed by the Council of the Indies.[122]

Thus, anecdotes from the time show a mixed picture as regards the VOC's attitude to other cultures, with atrocities and genocide committed against the Bandanese and Chinese and quite a bit of fraternal activity with the Japanese. From this, it is perhaps right to conclude that the VOC as an organization was not racist in its culture. But the people on the forefront working for the VOC such as Coen behaved badly enough, all in the single-minded pursuit of profit. Life and work in the Indies did not bring out the best in people, especially considering that the VOC recruited from the bottom of Dutch and German society.[123] For these people, despite its blindness to national origin, the company was known to be extremely parsimonious, which, along with the atrocious conditions on the ships and in the tropics, further contributed to low morale and probably encouraged outrageous behavior on the part of VOC employees towards other peoples. Mortality rates were high. While the history of each ship within the VOC was different, on average it seems that 10 to 15 percent of all who travelled on VOC ships died of accident or illness before reaching their destinations in Asia.[124] This is not to say that the Heeren XVII was completely indifferent to the health of its employees. Indeed, the company made provisions for medical care and for surgeons and medical chests to be on board each ship.[125] Yet the cramped, fetid, and unsanitary living quarters on the ships led to most of the lower-level crew members suffering from ill health and from diseases such as scurvy and typhus for much of their journey. Once the crew reached their destination in Asia, many were also stricken with malaria, beriberi and other diseases.[126] Sailors were cruelly treated by officers: even the smallest of infractions would lead to punishments such as pounding a surgeon's knife through an offender's hand into the mast.[127] In short, it was a miserable life for most sailors, who were considered by their officers as no better than dogs. Even slaves, who were at least worth money, were in most cases reported to have been better treated than the sailors of the VOC.[128]

How does one go about in explaining the dual nature of the corporate culture of the VOC, exemplified by its show of tolerance in many areas concerning management and employment practices, and at the same time the vicious, intolerant streak that led to the egregious acts of genocide committed upon the Bandanese and massacre of Chinese for the pursuit of profits? One explanation that I propose is that the dual nature of the VOC's behavior reflected the larger national culture of the Low Countries that existed at the time. In comparison to the Spanish who persecuted non-Catholics relentlessly, the Netherlands was a haven for many non-Catholics including Protestants and Jews who were fleeing religious persecution. The openness of the Dutch to other peoples and their tolerance of other religions was indeed a feature of Dutch national life that many people in Europe found attractive. Thus, on the one hand, as a result of their acceptance of outside talent regardless of national origin or religion including Germans, French, English, Scots, Turks, and Armenians, the influx of skilled labor enabled the Low Countries to develop trade, commerce, towns, and a wide range of industries from sugar refining to chemical production. This led to the attainment of the highest living standards in Europe during the sixteenth and seventeenth centuries.[129] Aside from religious tolerance, there was a profound tendency among the Dutch to look kindly upon the accumulation of wealth. On the other hand, while the Netherlands were under the Spanish yoke, the peoples of the Low Countries witnessed great cruelty committed by the Spanish to those would not conform and submit. The "Spanish Fury" entailed thousands of deaths, which shook the will of the Low Countries. The Spanish held inquisitions which resulted in the deaths of many who would not renounce their Protestant faiths. The Spanish in effect practiced the art of "total war" on the Dutch; that is, the inflicting of crushing casualties intended to eliminate all opposition and completely demoralize any survivors. Not only the Spanish, but the Portuguese, French, and English as well undertook this method in dominating local people in Europe at the time.[130] It was an age in which religious piety often coexisted with great violence, sadism, and terror. The Spanish theologian and physician Michael Servetus was just one victim of the religious intolerance of the followers of Calvin when he was burned to death as a heretic in Geneva in 1553.[131] I argue that the cruel actions and behavior of the Spanish while in the Low Countries left a deep scar upon the psyche of the Dutch people, including the founding members and leaders of the VOC (some of whom had fled the Spanish), that subconsciously crept into the recesses of the dominant and traditional Dutch culture of tolerance. Hence, a duality was created in the Dutch national culture, which encompassed a tolerant side on the one hand and a dark streak of cruelty and intolerance on the other hand towards those whom the Dutch considered "alien outsiders" who would not bow their heads to the authority of the Dutch. And it was the extension of this dual-natured national culture into the leadership of the VOC, including people such as Coen, and through them into the corporate culture of the VOC, that helped to maintain this mega-merger while at the same time allowing the company to inflict atrocities and genocide towards those who would get in its way.

Conclusion

Much in the way the United Kingdom came into existence as an empire when England and Scotland agreed to merge with each other, the VOC was also born an "empire" when six independent companies agreed to form one company. Despite its ultimate demise, the VOC was an example of a "successful" empire. It was arguably the world's first joint stock company, provided high returns to its shareholders, delivered profits, and lasted for two centuries with the six companies remaining together until the VOC was ordered to disband. As I have attempted to show in the preceding narrative, the practice of tolerance within the company played a major role in contributing to the longevity and prosperity of the company. The tolerance of the Heeren XVII allowed them to be flexible and pragmatic enough to accept diversity in management and employees and welcome people from all over the Low Countries and Europe within their fold. Tolerance ensured that all of the six proto-VOC companies would participate in the management of the mega-merger. The practice of tolerance also helped to realize equality, as in the Heeren XVII's voting structure laid out in the charter of the company, which ensured that the most powerful party in the mega-merger would not dictate policy unilaterally and that the directives of the company would be established in consultation and through dialogue with other parties to the mega-merger.

Other factors contributing to the success of the VOC

In addition to the practice of tolerance, there were also other factors that contributed to the "success" of the mega-merged VOC, which I have identified as follows.

Showing of results: The profitability of the VOC venture and its high returns to shareholders were strong incentives for the six companies/chambers of the VOC to maintain their merger. That is to say, the showing of results proved to be an important glue that stuck the six companies together.

Agreement on strategy: The six companies shared a common goal and strategy of making money by expanding trade with the East Indies, although there were some objections within with regard to the methods of Jan Coen.

Cultural similarity or the existence of a common overriding culture: The maintenance of the solidarity of the mega-merger was also helped by a cultural factor as well. As the respective managements of the six companies were composed mostly of people from the Low Countries, we can assume that they all shared an outlook prevalent at the time in the Netherlands that was more concerned with making money than with saving souls or spreading the Christian religion. We can also assume that they all shared to a certain extent a willingness to take risks, in that they were willing to put their money into voyages for which there was no sure outcome. They also likely shared a long-term orientation in perspective that allowed them to wait for years for their boats to return.

The presence of strong leadership: Tolerance, on the one hand, played a large part in developing a governance system that ensured the rights of the smaller-sized partners and prevented the largest partner from establishing a dictatorship over the others. This would have certainly helped in placating the fears of the smaller partners of being subsumed by the larger partners, and thus helped to maintain the organizational stability of the merger. On the other hand, this system of governance or corporate culture, which encouraged decisions to be made by achieving consensus or compromise, did not result in an extreme situation in which the Heeren XVII might have become a debating chamber unable to easily and quickly make decisions and undertake their execution. As noted previously, the decision and execution behind most directives and policies were referred to the largest Amsterdam Chamber. Clearly, Amsterdam played a leadership role within the Heeren XVII, which was accepted by the other partners partly because of the concessions to voting and funding given by Amsterdam, and which no doubt helped to resolve deadlocks and speed up decisions.

Lessons for the empire builder

Finally, while the historical environment surrounding the VOC would make it difficult to make an apple-to-apple comparison with modern multinational corporations, there are certain lessons for present-day companies that can be derived from the example of the VOC as a successful case of M&A, particularly pertaining to how to make it last. They are: (1) when merging with others, be sure that your objectives, goals, values, and strategies are aligned and shared with your partners; (2) be tolerant and flexible enough to listen to and accept the opinions of your partners; (3) be tolerant and flexible enough to employ people based on ability and necessity, not on origin; (4) implement a system of corporate governance and organizational structure that will ensure the observance of flexible and tolerant management practices; (5) ensure that risks and rewards are shared and distributed equitably; and (6) ensure there is a leading partner or viable leadership that is able to provide overall direction and develop consensus.

Too bad, however, for the Dutch that they did not have the perspicacity to apply the principles of tolerance and compromise practiced internally by the VOC and within the Netherlands to their imperial possessions in the East Indies and other areas, instead of undertaking and unleashing genocide, massacres, and discriminatory policies towards the local peoples. When the Japanese overran the Dutch East Indies in 1942 and humiliated the Dutch in front of their colonial subjects, Queen Wilhelmina of the Netherlands admitted to the practice of racial discrimination by the Dutch and stated the need to eliminate it, in the process undertaking to reconstruct the Dutch Empire "on the solid foundation of complete partnership."[132] Unfortunately her recommendation came too late. Immediately after the Japanese surrendered, the Indonesian nationalist Achmed Sukarno led a fierce campaign of guerilla warfare in order to gain independence from the Dutch, who initially had no intention of giving up on their empire. After several defeats at the hands of the Indonesians, fruitless battles, atrocities committed by the Dutch against the Indonesians, and growing hostility in world opinion, the Dutch reluctantly granted independence to Indonesia in 1949, thereby ending an empire founded by the VOC. While the Indonesians were certainly happy to achieve independence, a more tolerant approach in colonial rule that included the fair and equal treatment of colonial subjects might have allowed the development of a stronger sense of loyalty among the inhabitants of Indonesia towards the "mother" country, which might have led to a different outcome than the complete fall of the Dutch East Indies empire.

4   The Mongols and the practice of tolerance

The origin of the Mongols

Introduction

From the windswept, grass-covered plains of Mongolia where the sky seems to stretch endlessly, 200,000 horse-riding Mongols burst upon the stage of history in 1206 and fought their way to create within 80 years the largest contiguous land empire in history, spanning approximately 34 million square kilometers and comprising an estimated 100 million subjects.[1] The empire of the Mongols established by their leader Genghis (or Chinggis) Khan stretched at its zenith from the Korean peninsula in northeast Asia all the way to Hungary in the west, and encompassed large areas of the Eurasian continent including present-day Siberia, China, Vietnam, Tibet, Afghanistan, Iran, Iraq, and parts of present-day Russia and Eastern Europe. This was an empire of unprecedented geographic scale more than seven times the size of what the Romans had established in four centuries. But like most empires in history, the Mongol Empire eventually came to an end: internal strife, disease, and other factors such as the assimilation of the Mongols with the local populations led to the dissolution and fading away of the empire. Today, the nation of Mongolia, with a land area three times that of France but a population of only about three million, sandwiched between the two superpowers of China and Russia, is a far cry from what Genghis Khan and his descendants built. The bloodline of the founders of the Empire, however, continued to survive until the mid-nineteenth century on the Indian subcontinent in the Mughal Empire established by Babur, who traced his ancestry back to Chaghatai, the second son of Genghis Khan. If we accept the view that the Mughal Empire was a direct descendant of the Mongol Empire founded by Genghis Khan, it can be argued that the Mongol Empire lasted for a little over 650 years from its inception in 1206 to its demise in 1858, when the British dissolved the Mughal Empire in the aftermath of the First Indian War of Independence (or Sepoy Uprising). And, if we were allowed to stretch our view even further, we could argue that as the last remaining Mongol ruler was the Emir of Bukhara (in present-day Uzbekistan), a descendant of Genghis Khan who ruled until 1920 when he was disposed by the Soviets, the rule of the descendants of Genghis Khan had a life of 714 years.[2]

The DNA of Genghis Khan

The Secret History of the Mongols (*SHM*) is the oldest text on the history of the rise of the Mongol Empire in the Mongolian language. It was written by anonymous scribes of the Mongol court under the supervision of Genghis Khan's half-brother Shigi sometime in the mid-thirteenth century, a couple of decades after the death of Genghis Khan. According to *SHM*, the Mongols were descendants of a blue-grey wolf and a white fallow deer.[3] Several generations of descendants later, Bodonchar, the founder of the Borjigin clan and Genghis's ancestor, was born. As with all creation epics passed down over centuries, the *SHM* is not without controversial aspects. Bodonchar is described as an illegitimate offspring, the father, whose complexion was "as yellow as the sun" having impregnated his mother, Alan the Fair, by rubbing her belly and sending a beam of light into her womb.[4] Such a portrayal may have been an attempt by Mongol scholars to attribute a holy or supernatural origin to Genghis's family. The German sinologist and scholar, Paul Ratchnevsky, however, suggests that this legend alludes to a foreign, non-Mongol origin of the father and hence to Genghis having non-Mongol paternal genes. He also proposes a hypothesis that the Borjigin clan was of Kirghiz descent, given its contemporary description as being tall, red-haired, and having blue-green eyes.[5] If this were true, Hollywood could claim some praise for historical accuracy by having the blue-eyed American actor John Wayne portray the conqueror in a forgettable movie on Genghis Khan.

Recent advances in the study of human genetics, however, have increased our understanding of the origins of the Mongols as well as our appreciation of the possible genetic impact that Genghis Khan in particular had on the modern world. Through DNA testing, we know that genetically the Mongols primarily carry the Y-chromosome (which is a portion of DNA that is passed down basically unchanged for generations from father to son, except for some random mutations) with the genetic marker classified as Haplogroup C3 (M217). Many present-day northern Chinese, and quite a few other Asians such as the Ainu of Japan and the Koreans, also carry this particular marker, the earliest known instance of which is among East Asians born around 20,000 years ago. Within this marker, however, geneticists have identified a particular haplotype variation whose origin goes back to a common ancestor in existence some 1,000 years ago. Genetic studies of more than 40 different populations living in and around the area of the former Mongol Empire have found that nearly 8 percent of the men carry this particular haplotype variation. The spread of this variation could be the result of natural selection. But according to the authors of this research, this is unlikely. Rather, given the time frame of the origin of this genetic lineage and the geographic dispersion of the marker and its link with the Mongols, the National Geographic Society (NGS), which conducted this research, believes that 0.5 percent of the entire male population in the world, or about 16 million men, have a high likelihood of being the descendants of Genghis Khan. Of course, we could never be sure of this unless we actually found the remains of Genghis and extracted his DNA for testing. But according to geneticist Spencer

Wells, a coauthor of this study, this was the first documented case where human culture was apparently responsible for causing a single genetic variation to increase substantially in just a few centuries.[6] Who else at the time, and in the area controlled by the Mongol Empire, could be responsible for this but Genghis Khan and his male progeny? For the researchers at the NGS, the answer to this rhetorical question was quite obvious. The NGS, in a press announcement released appropriately on Valentine's Day, suggested that aside from being the ruler of the largest empire in the world, the DNA data alludes to the possibility that Genghis Khan was a "prolific" lover who helped populate the world—a superb example of empire-building going hand-in-hand, so to speak, with pro-creation and propagation.[7] Various contemporary accounts given by Europeans and Persians seem to back up the DNA data. According to one report, Genghis had a harem of 500 wives and concubines, while another account mentions that the most beautiful women of the empire were selected for Genghis and presented to him.[8] The Venetian adventurer, trader, and explorer Marco Polo left an account of Kublai Khan, a grandson of Genghis, saying that the ruler had four or five hundred of the most beautiful women brought to him from all over the empire each year for his pleasure.[9] Subsequent testing on the mitochondrial DNA (which is passed from mother to daughter) of 201 unrelated individuals from various regions of the former Mongol Empire also suggests that the Mongol Empire played an important role in contributing to the maternal mixture of Mongolians and their conquered subjects.[10] Recent studies have also sug-gested that there is a genetic link between present-day Russians and the Mongols, with as many as 50 percent of Muscovites having Mongol genes.[11]

In effect, DNA research suggests that the descendants of Genghis Khan and the Mongol Empire did not die out, but continue to live on in the blood of those 16 million "sons" and "daughters" of Genghis living all over the world today. The tests also indicate that the suggestion put forward by Ratchnevsky that Genghis had non-Mongol paternal genes is most likely incorrect.[12] Not only do the DNA tests indicate the origins of the Mongols and their impact on the human race, but they indicate the attitudes of the Mongols towards the races of their conquered subjects. In contrast to other imperialists such as the British in India or the Dutch in South Africa, who in their imperial heyday practiced racial seg-regation and generally abhorred the thought of miscegenation, considering it unnatural, the Mongol leaders had a relatively inclusive and tolerant view of coexisting and intermingling with other peoples which, as we shall later see, was also reflected in their policies and practices within their empire.

The changing image of the Mongols

Various contemporary descriptions of the Mongols have come down over the centuries. The Franciscan monk and Vatican envoy to the Mongol Empire, Friar Giovanni Di Plano Carpini, describes the appearance of the Mongols as people of middle height, with eyes and cheeks widely placed apart, flat noses, high cheeks, and small eyes. The Mongols cut the hair on the top of their heads in the manner of the European monks.[13] As for their temperament, Carpini praises the Mongols, saying that they seldom insult one another and that there are no wars, thievery, or murders among them.[14] The Persian poet Amir Khosrow (1253–1324) mentions the Mongols had heads with narrow and piercing eyes, wide, flat noses, and bodies that seemed to have no neck.[15] The Franciscan Friar William of Rubruck who traveled to the court of the Great Khan Mongke between 1253 and 1255 mentioned that the women of the Mongols were "wonderfully" fat, and those with the smallest nose were considered the most beautiful.[16] One of the most extensive accounts of the Mongols and their rulers is given by the Venetian explorer Marco Polo, who traveled widely in the Mongol Empire and was employed in the services of Kublai Khan and the Mongols. He described Kublai as a person of middle height with well-formed limbs, fair complexion, handsome eyes, and a prominently shaped nose.[17] As for the Mongols, Marco Polo praised them for their courtesy, cleanliness, and good manners, and found it worthy to note in his travelogue that the women of the Mongols did not use offensive language, perhaps an indication that this was not necessarily the case in contemporary Europe.[18] Marco Polo also mentioned that the Great Khan of the Mongols prohibited all forms of gambling. Carpini, on the other hand, recorded that the Mongol women were prone to telling coarse and vulgar jokes and becoming drunk, but not to the extent of exchanging words or blows.[19] He added that the Mongol women rode horses as skillfully as the men and were capable of making everything from skin clothes to shoes, and surprisingly to him, all of the women, like men, wore trousers and shot arrows.[20] The medieval English poet Geoffrey Chaucer, who it is certain never visited the Mongol Empire or met either Genghis or Kublai Khan, had nothing but praise for the great Khan of the Mongols, describing him in his *The Canterbury Tales* a noble lord who excelled in all things, upheld the law, and was "piteous and just," "young, fresh, and strong."[21]

Unlike Marco Polo and Chaucer, who saw the Mongols as highly civilized and honorable, some of the Muslims of Central Asia had a negative view of the Mongols. This is unsurprising given that the Mongols under Genghis Khan had thoroughly destroyed the Muslim Khwarizmian Empire and massacred its people, and later under Hulegu, a grandson of Genghis, sacked Baghdad, which was the seat of the Sunni Abbasid caliphate from where the successor caliphs to the Prophet Muhammad ruled. The Kurdish historian Ibn Al-Athir (1160–1233) sums up the sentiments of the Muslims towards the "Tatars," describing them as bloodthirsty barbarians with no respect for life, sparing no one who opposed them, and slaying indiscriminately men, women, children, and even the unborn.[22] Moreover, the Japanese, who had twice fought against and successfully repelled an invading Mongol force in 1274 and 1281, apparently did not have fond memories of them, as indicated by the Japanese word for cruel, brutal, or merciless— *mugoi*—whose root is the Japanese word for Mongol, *moko*. As the contrasting perspectives of Ibn Al-Athir, the Japanese, and Marco Polo suggest, and as it was the case with many empires in history, the contemporary views people had towards an empire varied largely depending on who they were and what kind of relationship they had with the empire builders.

The reputation of the Mongols and their empire changed over time. During the European enlightenment, when the idea of the racial and cultural superiority of the West was gaining support and acceptance in Europe as we have seen above, the idea of a non-white people such as the Mongols administering justice and spreading civilization was an absurd thought. The French philosopher Voltaire in his play *The Orphan of China* described Genghis Khan as "the great destroyer," a "dire scourge," a "wild Scythian soldier; bred to arms and practiced in the trade of blood."[23] Meanwhile, the French political thinker Montesquieu condemned the Mongols in his *Spirit of Laws* as "cruel conquerors" who have "destroyed Asia, even to the Mediterranean; and all the countries which form the east of Persia they have rendered a desert."[24] He further takes a sweepingly condescending view of Asian civilization in general, which he claims has nothing but a "servile spirit," and asserts that "it is impossible to find in all the histories of that country a single passage which discovers a freedom of spirit; we shall never see anything there but the excess of slavery."[25]

From the twentieth century, however, the view of the Mongols has become somewhat mixed, with some historians recognizing the achievements of Genghis Khan and the Mongols in a positive light, pointing out the material and cultural exchanges between East and West under Mongol rule.[26] Historian Jack Weatherford credits Genghis Khan for leading the world into the modern age, while journalist Strobe Talbott calls the Mongols the agents of globalization.[27] Astrophysicist Michael H. Hart put Genghis Khan at number 29 on his list of the most influential figures in history, while the *Washington Post* newspaper selected Genghis as the "Man of the Millennium" in an article published on December 31, 1995. Since 2006, the Chinese have been celebrating Genghis Khan as one of their national heroes, although previously he was dismissed by the great helmsman Mao Zedong as an uncultured nomad.[28] Russian historians during the Soviet era stressed the destructive aspects of the Mongols, and for many decades the Soviets banned their Mongol client state from remembering Genghis Khan.[29] Many Russians perceived the era of Mongol domination under the Golden Horde led by Batu, a grandson of Genghis, as the worst of times and did not hesitate to blame the Mongols for many of the ills facing them, including their national character and their tendency for easily getting drunk and becoming alcoholics.[30] Interestingly, however, there are signs that even in Russia the view towards the Mongol may be changing. The movie *Mongol* released in 2007, which depicts the rise of Genghis Khan (portrayed by a Japanese actor) and was directed by a Russian with a multinational cast and crew consisting of Russians, Mongolians, Chinese, Germans, and Japanese, gives a historically accurate and sympathetic account of the conqueror as a brave warrior devoted to his family who is often forced to deal with vicious enemies using violent means. Much of the reputed cruelty of the Mongols is omitted from this picture, which was nominated for an Academy Award for best foreign picture by the American Academy of Motion Picture Arts and Sciences.

As the comments of Marco Polo, Ibn Al-Athir, Voltaire, Montesquieu, modern historians, moviemakers, and journalists suggest, there are many views

and interpretations of the impact of the Mongol Empire. While it would be difficult to prove, anecdotal evidence from movies, video games, and recently published books suggest the growing prevalence of a more positive view on the
legacy of the Mongols that is a far cry from their traditional image as barbaric
destroyers of civilization. Indeed, even in the field of business, Genghis Khan
and his Mongols are becoming a source of inspiration, as shown in the publication of articles such as "Management and Genghis Khan: Lessons for Multinational Business Enterprises" by John D. Forsyth of Duke University, and in a
comic dialogue printed in *Fortune* magazine that has business humorist Stanley
Bing interviewing a fictional businessman who rates the Sheriff of Nottingham
as superior to anyone in handling tax issues and Genghis Khan as second to none
in undertaking post-merger integration![31]

Granted, though there may have been exaggeration in contemporary accounts
of the Mongols, it is difficult to deny the fact the Mongols destroyed cities and
enslaved and indiscriminately massacred peoples regardless of their age, sex,
ethnicity, or religion. Like the Dutch in the Banda Islands and Ambon, the
Mongols committed acts which would probably constitute genocide today. The
Mongols were indeed ruthless towards their enemies and merciless in warfare.
At the Russian principality of Riazan, the Mongols slaughtered the ruling Prince
Yuri, his family, and all courtiers. The Mongols set churches on fire and raped
all the young women of the city including nuns.[32] In the city of Kozelsk, the soldiers of Genghis so thoroughly punished and exterminated the inhabitants for
resisting them that even the merciless Mongols named it the "City of Sorrow."[33]
During their assault on Eastern and Central Europe, the Mongols relentlessly
burned down towns in Transylvania and southeastern Hungary. They destroyed
churches, slaughtered town inhabitants and raped the women. At one town,
Varadin, located in present-day Croatia, the stench coming from rotting corpses
was so great that even the Mongols were forced to abandon it.[34] The Mongols
almost entirely destroyed the Polish city of Krakow on several occasions, starting with their invasion of Europe in 1241. The Mongols totally wiped off from
the face of the earth some of the cities which they besieged. They so completely
destroyed the Bulgar Kingdom of the middle Volga that its city was never rebuilt
and its population of over 50,000 were killed.[35] When the Mongols invaded the
Japanese island of Tsushima off the island of Kyushu, along with the Chinese
and Korean troops under their command, not only did they mercilessly kill non-
combatants including women and children, which came as a shock to the Japanese samurai, but the few inhabitants of the island who did manage to survive
were rounded up and tied together by ropes passed through holes that the
Mongols drilled through the palms of the captives.[36]

Despite their relentless ferocity, the Mongols, however, spared those peoples
and cities that submitted to them without resistance. A case in point is the
Russian city of Novgorod, which was left untouched when its rulers submitted to
the Mongols without a fight. In addition to this show of mercy, compared to contemporary Europe the Mongols were tolerant on matters of religion, and upright
and lenient in the administration of justice. In their empire, the Mongols

abolished by law the use of torture. Executions for offenses were rare. Within a period of 40 years only 2,743 executions took place in the Mongol Empire, which compares favorably with the execution rate in present-day China, where it is reported that there were around 8,000 executions in 2007 alone.[37] Fines were often substituted for physical forms of punishment. The Mongols also freely put into positions of responsibility in their army, and in the cities under their control, people selected on the basis of ability, regardless of origin. The Mongols, while destroying cultures on the one hand, facilitated the fusion of different cultures through various forms of exchange leading to the further enrichment of those within the empire.

The image and legacy of the Mongols is complicated and full of contradictions. But it is a fact that the empire created by Genghis Khan was a multinational, multiethnic, and global empire spanning several continents that lasted for at least more than two centuries. Going by the definition of what constitutes a "successful empire" stated earlier in this book, I will present a narrative that shows the Mongol Empire as an example of a successful empire and identifies lessons to be learned from the empire-building experience of the Mongols. As with the case of the VOC, where I showed how the attitude of tolerance was realized in policies that helped to maintain the mega-merger of the six proto-VOC companies for two centuries, I will show how the policies of tolerance worked for the Mongols in maintaining their empire. In doing so, I will not go through the entire history of the Mongol Empire but will focus on the its formation process and highlight the factors of structural, organizational and cultural policies that contributed to maintaining the stability and cohesion of Mongol rule.

The birth and rise of the Mongol Empire

Introduction

The core group of the Mongol Empire came into being as the result of a merger of fiercely independent nomadic tribes residing in the area of northeast Asian steppe now known as Mongolia. They included the Tatars who lived in the eastern part of the Mongolian plateau; the Naimans who resided in the west; the Mongols and Keraits in the center; Oirots and Buryats who lived in the west north of the Naimans; Tayichiuds who lived in the far northeast; and the Merkits who lived north of the Keraits and Oirots and south of the Buryats. Some of these tribes engaged in the herding of sheep and animal husbandry in the steppe, while others including the ancestors of Genghis were hunters living in the forests of Mongolia. Before the rise of Genghis Khan, these tribes were generally known collectively as "Tatars" because the Tatars were the most powerful among them. It was only after Genghis came to power that they became known collectively as the "Mongols," although the term Tatar continued to be used by Europeans who often conveniently spelled the word as Tartar, derived from Tartarus, or Hell, suggesting that the Mongols had come from (where else but) Hell.[38]

Ethnically and linguistically there seems to have been little distinction among the tribes, although the *SHM* describes them as the people of nine languages.[39] The various steppe tribes shared a common identity of being the people of "the felt-walled tents." They also shared several religious beliefs such as shamanism and Nestorian Christianity. The Mongols also claimed the Huns as their ancestors, who ruled an empire from the steppes of Asia to Rome and terrified all those whom they conquered or who got in their way.[40]

Much of the early history of the Mongols before the establishment of the empire is characterized by strife and wars. As described by the Persian historian Juvaini, the Mongols had no ruler or leader. Tribes lived apart and there was widespread poverty, which compelled them to pay tribute to the emperor of the Jin dynasty which was based in northern China. The people wore for their clothes the skins of dogs and mice.[41] To further compound this bleak picture, the Mongols were living in an area that was marked by great environmental challenges, with extreme temperatures and fickle weather conditions. Carpini mentioned in his memoirs great wind and hailstorms with frequent lightening and thunder killing many people, and of extreme heat and sudden cold temperatures during a summer in the Mongolian plains.[42] Such an environment made it necessary for those nomads living on the steppe to constantly migrate in search of water and new grass for feeding. Agriculture was as a result limited. From this beginning in a harsh environment, Genghis Khan, or Temujin, as he was known before his ascent as the Great Khan, undertook the unification of the nomadic tribes of the Mongols, defeated the sedentary civilizations of north China and central Asia, and built an empire that eventually encompassed most of the known world from China to Eastern Europe.

An uncertain beginning

Unlike certain other warlords or conquerors in history such as Alexander the Great or Julius Caesar, Genghis Khan did not have a privileged childhood, and his rise to absolute power was anything but guaranteed and smooth. Of the many tribes of the steppe, his was seen by other more powerful tribes such as the Tayichiuds as a small and insignificant group of scavengers who had no claim to a glorious past.[43] In an early period in Temujin's life, his father, Yesugei, was poisoned by his enemies, the Tatars, while on the way back from choosing a bride for Temujin. The tribal elders of Yesugei's clan, feeling no obligation towards Yesugei's family and considering them a burden, expelled Temujin, with his mother and siblings, from the clan, forcing them to fend for themselves. In the harsh wilderness of the Mongol steppe, Temujin and his family barely avoided starvation by living on whatever they could find such as wild plants, vegetables, fish, birds, and rats. The threat of starvation was not the only danger that Temujin faced. In anger and from feelings of being treated unfairly, Temujin with his younger brother one day killed his elder half-brother. This not only brought about an angry scolding from his mother, Hoelun, but also caught the attention of the Tayichiuds, who captured Temujin and made him a prisoner, ostensibly as punishment. Temujin somehow managed to escape captivity with the help of a certain serf of the Tayichiuds, Sorkan-Shira, and returned to his mother and siblings, whose situation of eking out a hand-to-mouth existence had not improved since he was captured.

The rise of an empire through partnerships

After his escape from the Tayichiuds, Temujin forged an alliance with Toghrul, or Ong Khan, leader of the Keraits, a powerful Mongol tribe of the steppe who followed a variant of Nestorian Christianity. Temujin was able to do this by evoking the blood-brother (anda) relationship that his father had with Toghrul. Temujin in essence became Toghrul's vassal, which thereby allowed him to receive the protection of the Keraits. In this capacity, Temujin was able to demonstrate his leadership capabilities, which in turn attracted the attention of an Urianghai forest herdsman who presented his son Jelme as a servant to Temujin. Later another son, Subotai, joined Temujin's growing clan. Subotai himself left his mark in history not only as Genghis Khan's trustworthy subordinate, but also as one of history's greatest generals, whose campaigns were been studied by the Soviets, the Nazis, and military thinkers such as the British Sir Liddell B. Hart. Temujin also established an alliance of equals with the anda of his youth, Jamuka, and together with Ong Khan they rescued the wife of Temujin, Borte. Borte had been abducted by the Merkits in revenge for the abduction of Temujin's mother Hoelun, a member of the Onggirat tribe, by Temujin's father Yesugei. Allied with Ong Khan and Jamuka, Temujin continued to forge alliances and attract followers of his own. Those who joined him, such as the Ungirad, were left unharmed and free to conduct their own tribal affairs.[44] Those who refused to join his alliance were conquered and absorbed by military force.

The reorganization of the Mongol army and society

The process of empire-building through partnerships or conquest initiated by Genghis Khan was accompanied by the reorganization of Mongol tribal society. Essentially, Genghis integrated the Mongol tribes through the creation of a national army. The army was organized on a decimal system which was traditionally used by the tribes. The smallest unit was an arban, which consisted of 10 soldiers under the command of one officer called a Bagatur. Ten arban made up a unit called a djaghoun, 10 djaghoun made up a mingan, and 10 mingan made up a touman, comprising 10,000 soldiers. By reorganizing the army and society, Genghis solidified the "merger" of the highly individualistic tribes and transformed tribal loyalties into loyalty towards the unit leaders that ultimately funneled up to Genghis Khan and his successor Mongol leaders.

The implementation of a decimal system in the national Mongol Army was in keeping with Mongol tradition and enabled Genghis to maintain continuity with past practices, which may have satisfied more conservative elements in his new nation. What was, however, innovative on the part of Genghis Khan was his appointments to key positions of command that did not consider tribal origin or loyalty. In the early days of the Mongol Empire, officers were elected as a concession to tribal loyalties. This practice, however, was later limited to the arban level, while appointments to the highest levels of command became based on actual achievements on the battlefield and military competence.[45] According to the *SHM*, in choosing his elite personal guard of 80 night guards and 70 day guards selected from the army, Genghis Khan, after inspecting the sons and relations of all his captains and soldiers, selected those most capable, fit, and pleasant in looks.[46] Mukali, a former servant of Genghis, became a commander of the Mongol army. Further evidence that Genghis Khan selected his officers on the basis of competency and ability is shown in his appointment of Jebe, Khubilai (Noyan), Jelme, and Subotai, the so-called "four dogs" of Genghis who later on chased down Jamuka when the two had clashed over attaining the leadership of the Mongols. Jamuka described them as ferocious and effective commanders with snouts like chisels who rode on the wind and fed on the flesh of their enemies.[47] None of these "four dogs" was from the same tribe of Genghis. Jebe was a Tayichiud warrior who offered his services to Genghis after their defeat. Khubilai was a prince from another tribe, and Jelme and Subotai were from the Urianghai tribe. Later, the Mongols assigned other non-Mongols such as Chinese and Muslims to positions of command in the Mongol army.[48] From a historic perspective, the assignment of talented individuals to positions of command in the field, based on the principle of having the right person for the right task rather than on tribal loyalty, was an extraordinary and even revolutionary accomplishment that helped to provide the Mongols with the best generals, who outwitted the powers of the day in China, Central Asia, Russia, the Middle East, and Europe. Their Chinese, Central Asian, or Western counterparts were often held down in their abilities by rivalry and a detrimental streak of independence.[49]

The drivers of Mongol expansion

It is not hard to imagine that for some of the chiefs of the tribes and clans who voluntarily joined Genghis, it was difficult to accept the measures put in place by Genghis that directly impacted their prerogatives as leaders, such as the creation of a national army and the appointment of field commanders. But history shows that they did acquiesce to the rule of Genghis, and in all likelihood it was the promise of booty, power, and prestige that kept the merger together and individual tribal loyalties submerged under a comprehensive Mongol identity. This incentive worked not only for tribal chiefs but also for others such as Muslim merchants, who entered into the service of Genghis with the hopes of gaining favorable trade terms with the Mongols and the Chinese.[50] The incentive of gaining riches and power, however, presented a dilemma as well: Genghis had to provide continuous victories and show the money, so to speak, to his followers to maintain his authority and his alliance of unruly and independent-minded tribal chiefs. In other words, for the merger to stick, booty had to be provided, and to provide booty, conquests had to take place, and an empire that would be a permanent source of riches had to be created. Thus, the establishment and structure of the Mongol Empire preordained the never-ending quest for new riches through conquests. War, which entailed constant raiding, plundering, slaughtering, abduction, and the celebratory copious consumption of alcohol after the battle, became a way of life for the Mongols.[51] A parallel in modern business would be an instance where in order to maintain a merger of companies, the acquiring or lead company would have to continuously expand and grow the business to keep its merger partners satisfied with the merger through the delivery of profits and higher salaries.

Another possible driver behind the expansion of the Mongol Empire was the environment. Carpini mentions the harsh climate in his account on the Mongols, but according to recent studies there was a particular point in time when the inhabitants of the Mongol steppe faced an especially severe situation. From around 1180 to 1220, the area of Mongolia faced a drop in the mean annual temperature which resulted in a shorter growing season for grass and posed a consequential threat to the livelihood of the animals of the region. This may have pressured the Mongols to move out of their traditional homelands.[52]

Whether it was the need to keep his troops happy with riches or to feed his people in an increasingly adverse environment, the Mongols under Genghis were now to make their mark in global history. After a series of battles with the various Mongol tribes including the Merkits in 1198, the Tayichiuds in 1200, the Tartars in 1202, and the Naimans in 1204, all of whom were defeated and exterminated by Temujin, the Mongols witnessed a final showdown with Ong Khan, the Keraits (whom the Mongols did not destroy), and Jamuka together going into battle against Temujin over what was in essence a final struggle for ultimate leadership of the remaining Mongol tribes. Temujin emerged victorious, as Ong Khan was killed while fleeing Temujin and Jamuka was captured and executed by Temujin. As a result, the Mongols recognized Temujin as the supreme leader or Great Khan of all the Mongol tribes at a gathering of the Mongol clans or quriltai called together by him in 1206. And with his ascension to Great Khan, the Mongols bestowed upon Temujin the title Genghis (or Chinggis) Khan, which had been interpreted by some scholars as meaning "King of the Oceans."[53]

It should be mentioned that the battles with other tribes leading to unification were not without their respective *casus belli*. Genghis destroyed the Merkits for having kidnapped his wife. He exterminated the Tayichiuds for having imprisoned and humiliated him in his youth. He eliminated the Tatars for killing his father. He also wiped out the Turkic Naimans for having dominated the Mongol tribes from the twelfth century and for protecting Jamuka, who had fled to them after being defeated and pursued by Temujin. Revenge, or the thought of getting more than even and settling old scores, was a major driver for Genghis, who never forgot any slight. In this regard, his behavior was no different from that of the other steppe tribes, for whom getting revenge for old slights was a way of life. Thus during the early stage of the Mongol Empire, the unification of the Mongols was not driven by any master plan for world domination. One might assume, then, that once old scores had been settled, the tribal wars would come to an end. In reality, the ascension of Temujin as the great Khan of all the Mongols marked not the end but the beginning of war as a way of life for the Mongols, for the reasons previously discussed. But from henceforth, the wars would be against outside rivals and enemies, starting with the Tanguts of the Xi-Xia whom the Mongols attacked in 1209.

The global expansion of the Mongol Empire

The Tanguts, a people of Tibetan origin who had established a Chinese-style dynasty known as the Xi-Xia in northwest China, became involved in a trade dispute with the Mongols when they refused the Mongol request to lower tariffs on Mongol traded products. This became the *casus belli* for the Mongols, who resolved the issue in their favor by the use of force and succeeded in making the Tanguts lower the tariffs. While this would have been an opportunity to conquer the Tanguts for good, Genghis instead returned to his native grasslands after the Tangut emperor acknowledged Genghis as his overlord and it was certain that the Tanguts no longer posed a threat on the flank. The Mongols then preyed on their next target, the Nuzhen (or Jurchen) of the Jin dynasty, which controlled China down to the Yangtze River.

In several protracted battles, the Mongols drew some hard lessons on the importance of using siege technologies in attacking walled cities. But they ultimately prevailed, with the help of disgruntled Chinese and Khitan (a Mongolian nomadic people) soldiers and siege engineers who defected from the Jin with grievances of their own against their Manchurian Nuzhen overlords. Genghis defeated the Nuzhen in 1215 and seized the Jin capital of Yanjing located in the area of present-day Beijing. The city was reported to have ended up in total ruins with its inhabitants slaughtered.[54] The Jin emperor Xuan Zong was forced to move their capital south to Kaifeng. But as in the war with the Tanguts, Genghis withdrew to the Mongol steppe once he was able to extract the trade terms he demanded. Again, instead of a permanent empire, acquiring trade and loot seemed to have been the major *casus belli*.

In 1218, Genghis Khan and his Mongol horde attacked and defeated the Kara–Khitan Empire. This empire had been formed by a group of Khitans who were dissatisfied with their Nuzhen overlords of the Jin, who had conquered their Khitan Empire (known as the Liao Dynasty or the Western Liao). At the time of its downfall, the Kara–Khitan Empire was under the control of Kulchug, a Naiman, who had earlier usurped power from the Khitan. The *casus belli* for the Mongols in this case was a settling of old scores with the Naimans, who although defeated in an earlier encounter with the Mongols still clung to power within the Kara–Khitan Empire under the leadership of Kulchug. Kulchug, like many of the other Naimans, was a Nestorian Christian when he established his rule over the Kara–Khitan. Later, however, he converted to Buddhism, and upon his conversion began to severely persecute the majority Kara–Khitans, who were Muslims. His behavior suggests that he lacked understanding of the doctrines of tolerance within Buddhism. Be that as it may, the Mongols did not fail to notice the persecution of Kulchug's Muslim subjects and may have seen this as an opportunity to intervene and take over the Kara–Khitans. Whatever the ultimate reason for war, the Mongols defeated Kulchug and deposed him, which resulted in the ending of the religious persecution of Muslims and the restoration of religious freedom in the Kara–Khitan lands. The people of Kara–Khitan understandably welcomed the Mongols. Their empire came under the domination of the Mongols intact and with the added windfall of numerous gifted Kara–Khitan officials, who provided the Mongols with valuable advice on imperial administration. It has been argued that the Mongol Empire in effect became a successor state to the Kara–Khitan Empire.[55]

With the takeover of the Kara–Khitan empire, the Mongols were next-door neighbors with the powerful Muslim Khwarizmian Empire, which under the leadership of the Shah Ala al-Din Muhammad had established its capital at Samarkand, located in territory seized from the Kara–Khitan. Genghis is reported to have viewed in awe the vast empire of Khwarizmia and its Shah, whose realm included the territories of central Asia, Afghanistan, and Iran. In a missive to the Shah, Genghis, while declaring himself the ruler of the sunrise, politely acknowledged and addressed the Shah as the sovereign of the sunset.[56] The Mongols, well aware of the power of this vast empire, most likely did not have thoughts of conquest and were more interested in the prospects of lucrative trade. A trade mission was dispatched by Genghis. To his later regret, the Khwarizmian Shah rebuffed the Mongol request for trade and executed and humiliated the Mongol ambassadors to boot. The Mongols in their anger began a punitive mission against the Khwarizmia and hunted down the Shah (who died in hiding on an island in the Caspian Sea). The Mongols destroyed the Muslim empire of Khwarizmia in 1221. During their conquest, the fury of Genghis Khan and his horde of Mongols knew no bounds. Upon capturing the Khwarizmian city of Ottrar, the Mongols executed many of the inhabitants including its governor, Inalchuq, whom they put to death by pouring molten silver into his eyes and ears as retribution for his attack on Mongol trade caravans and the killing of Mongol traders and envoys.[57] According to the Muslim historian Juvaini, Genghis is reported to have made a threatening speech to a select audience in Bukhara, telling them that they had sinned greatly, and that for their sins, he, Genghis, was being sent from heaven as the punishment of God.[58] Despite this ominous message, however, Muslim historians mention that there was no rampant plunder or destruction of that city, and that the Mongols merely demanded and received provisions for their army.[59]

While the people of Bukhara may have been relieved, so intense was the anger of Genghis Khan towards the acts of defiance by Khwarizmia that he ordered his troops to divert a river so that it would completely erase the birthplace of the Shah. The conquest of the Khwarizmian Empire is notable among the campaigns led by Genghis for its catastrophic proportions of death and destruction and the particularly vindictive nature of its execution. Mongol troops spread throughout the area of Khorasan, the cultural capital of Khwarizmia, destroying cities and slaughtering entire populations in campaigns that have been compared by modern-day historians as rivaling only Hitler in the immensity of atrocities.[60] In contrast with the campaigns against the Tanguts of the Xi-Xia and the Nuzhen of the Jin, which had clear economic rationales, the war against the Khwarizmian Empire was clearly an act of revenge similar in spirit to the campaigns against the Tatars and the Merkits. The Mongol propensity for getting revenge for slights and insults was alive and well.

The conquest of the Khwarizmian Empire was the first major westward thrust of the Mongols. Further wars included those with the Xi-Xia, which was triggered by Mongol anger at their failure to provide troops for the Mongols; the conquest of Russia; and the defeat of the Teutonic Knights and Knights Templar in Liegnitz (in present-day Poland) in 1241. Genghis was by then dead and his mantle was picked up by his sons and grandsons.

Eventually, the Mongols conquered the Song Empire of southern China and Persia as well. The ultimate boundaries of the empire were established in the west by 1260 with the seizure of Baghdad and the destruction of the Assassins and the Caliph, and in the east by 1279 with the fall of the Song. Both of these limits were marked respectively when the Mongols faced rare defeats: in Egypt, where the Mongols were repelled by the Mamluks, and in Japan, where two invasion attempts ended in catastrophic failure. In the west, after the routing of the Teutonic Knights at Liegnitz, the Mongols were poised to invade Western Europe, but luckily for Europe the Great Khan Ogdei died, most likely a victim of alcoholism. It could be argued that if Ogdei had not died when he did, the Mongol Empire would have expanded right up to the Atlantic Ocean and the history of Western Europe would have developed quite differently.

By this time the empire had become too big for a single ruler, and the Mongols divided their imperial holdings into the Ilkhanate (Ilkhan meaning "lesser khan"), established by Hulegu (a grandson of Genghis), which oversaw the remains of the Khwarizmian Empire and Persia; the Golden Horde, established by Batu (another grandson of Genghis and son of Jochi, the eldest son of Genghis), which ruled Russia; the Yuan Dynasty, established by the Great Khan, Kublai (a grandson of Genghis), in China; and the Chaghatai Empire, established by Chaghatai (a son of Genghis), which ruled over Central Asia. With this division, the "conglomerate empire" became a loosely organized "holding company" with the Yuan Dynasty as the nominal "parent company." Each of the "subsidiary" empires evolved in their own distinctive ways with regards to policies of administration and religion, with little or no mutual interference. Rivalry and battles over turf sometimes erupted among the empires, which may perhaps have contributed to the eventual weakening of the Mongol Empire. But a thread bonded these empires together and kept the whole empire from completely falling apart: the common kinship with Genghis Khan.

At its entirety, the four parts of the empire constituted the largest land-based empire the world had ever seen. The Mongol Empire, which started out from a merger of unruly and independent-minded nomadic tribes, was in essence a family "business" founded and led by a powerful and charismatic leader that became in less than 80 years a multinational empire. And in the formation and consolidation of the empire, the Mongols undertook various measures that led to the development of the modern world.

The contribution of the Mongols to the modern world

The Mongols did more than conquer land and peoples. As a result of their conquests, the Mongols facilitated and encouraged a major cross-fertilization of peoples, ideas, technology, and the arts. Some of the achievements and by-products of this event left their impact on future generations or were later rediscovered, as described next.

A nation of laws: religious tolerance codified

For those who have an image of the Mongols as uncouth barbarians, it may come as a surprise that in addition to reorganizing the army and society, Genghis Khan implemented a body of laws called the *Yasa*. No complete document of the *Yasa* has come down to us and there have been arguments over whether such a coherent codified body of laws ever existed.[61] But we do have bits and pieces of laws and statements of Genghis that have been recorded by various scholars employed by the Mongols. These fragments indicate that the laws of the *Yasa* were aimed at eliminating those practices of robbery, abduction, and revenge which Genghis felt would be detrimental towards maintaining the unity of the merger and which had previously kept the Mongols in a state of perpetual poverty and discord. The *Yasa* in effect had the objective of breaking down individual tribal loyalty and creating in its place a collective identity of the "people of the felt-walled tents." Hence, the *Yasa* outlawed adultery, horse theft, and kidnapping. The *Yasa* tolerated inebriation but within defined limits. People were not to hurt each other and were to forget offenses. They were also told not to give false witness. The people were to respect the elderly and beggars. Treachery was banned. In a nod towards protecting consumers against unscrupulous merchants, whoever became bankrupt three times after taking goods on credit was executed. Those who disobeyed these laws were to be put to death. Interestingly, in cases of murder, the person who had committed a murder could escape the penalty of death by paying a fine. The *Yasa* also covered the practices of the Mongols towards other peoples. The Mongols were to spare nations, peoples, and cities which submitted voluntarily to Mongol rule. The Kirghiz, Oirats, Karluks, and Uighurs are some of the tribes that submitted to Mongol suzerainty and later prospered as members of the Mongol Empire. The towns that had capitulated to the Mongols on their way from Bukhara to Samarkand, such as Herat, were left alone.[62] According to the Syrian scholar al-Umari (1301–1349), Genghis bestowed honors and distinction upon those who surrendered peacefully, and in the process increased his reputation throughout the various lands.[63]

The *Yasa* dictated that no religion was to be shown any preference and each was to be respected. The Mongols augmented this early example of the separation of church and state by exempting all religious institutions from taxes. Marco Polo noted that Kublai Khan, the grandson of Genghis, observed the principal festivals of Christians, Jews, Muslims, and idol worshippers. Upon being asked by Marco Polo why he did this, Kublai replied that he did this to show respect to all of the "four great prophets" of mankind and invoke the aid of whoever of the prophets reigned supreme in heaven.[64] There may of course have been a bit of cynical pragmatism on the part of the Mongols, as they most likely saw that the respect of all religions would ensure some obedience on the part of their conquered subjects. However, considering that this was a period in world history during which Muslims and Christians were at each others' throats in so called "holy wars" and that European Christians were massacring, forcibly converting, or expelling communities of Jews from their towns, the Mongol approach to religion was nothing short of enlightened and worthy of praise rather than condemnation from "enlightened" European philosophers such as Voltaire and Montesquieu.

A paper money economy

Within their empire, the Mongols established a money economy that allowed the use of paper currency instead of heavy gold and silver coins. This facilitated the exchange of goods all over the empire. The extensive use of paper money also increased opportunities for the expansion of loans to merchants. While paper money was first developed and used in China long before the Mongols came to power, it was the Mongols who unified various currencies, controlled the supply of paper currency and spread its use and concept over vast areas from Persia to China. In essence, the Mongols made the concept of paper money actually work. It is not for nothing that, in grudging recognition by the present-day Chinese of the contribution of the Mongols, the current Chinese currency unit is called "yuan," the name of Kublai Khan's dynasty.[65] The Mongol government was also the central banker to the empire. Marco Polo was impressed enough by the novelty of paper money to devote an entire chapter in his travelogue to its use throughout the Mongol empire.[66]

A global communications infrastructure

A major key to successfully keeping together a widely spread empire was to have a communications infrastructure that allowed the speedy transmission of messages from the imperial center to the peripheral areas of the empire. Under Ogdei Khan, the establishment of a "pony express" postal system allowed messages to be relayed from one end of the empire to another in a couple of days, using a relay system of horse riders and foot runners positioned at postal stations located at fixed intervals. A sizable network of roads was also built to support this system. As to how it actually worked, Marco Polo mentioned that messengers girdled with bells would ride on horses at full speed for as much as 250 miles in a day. Several miles before their arrival at the next post, the sound of the bells notified the next relay messenger to get his horse ready to pick up the dispatch and depart without any loss in time, much as a relay runner passes his baton to the next runner in a foot race.[67] Clearly this was a communications network that involved not only much individual effort but also close teamwork.

The Mongol postal network in effect provided the communications backbone of the empire and allowed the Mongols to maintain political control over vast distances from China to Persia. It showed the Mongols' understanding of the importance of speedy transmission of information and logistics in peace and war, which was ably demonstrated in the support of many well-coordinated pincer campaigns against their enemies carried out over considerable distances and geographic obstacles. Despite the lack of modern technology for communications, the advanced nature of the Mongol communications system is apparent when one considers that a similar postal system using horses and relay stations, which became known as the Pony Express, appeared in the US in the 1860s, approximately 600 years after Marco Polo's account was written.

A passport and credit card system

By carrying a paiza or tablet of authority that was issued by the Mongol government, described by Marco Polo as a golden tablet displaying the seal of the Great Khan,[68] a trader could travel to various nations within the empire freely and without hindrance, and with the protection of the Mongols. The paiza could be considered equivalent to a modern traveler's passport, but it was more than that. The holder of the paiza was entitled not only to safe passage throughout the empire, but also to the use of the postal stations and their provisions, the use of accommodations in any city or village, and the accompaniment of escorts or bodyguards on their journey. The tablet also allowed travelers to have all their expenses defrayed. In this respect, it can be argued that the paiza was not only a passport but also the precursor of the modern credit card.

Trade associations

Within their empire the Mongols established merchant associations called Ortogh through which merchants pulled together their resources such as men, camels, horses, and food for undertaking a trade caravan. The Ortogh provided a means of spreading the risk for the individual merchant participating in a trade venture. While the Ortogh was not in any sense a joint-stock corporation as was the VOC, the concept of concentrating resources for the purpose of spreading the risk of trade journeys resembles the motives behind the formation of the VOC as described above. Both the VOC and the Ortogh received full government support and backing. The Mongols supported individual merchants with loans if they belonged to an Ortogh. The Mongol elite and government gave loans to the Ortogh at a rate of 0.8 percent monthly interest, which compared favorably with the rate of 3 percent charged to most borrowers at the time. With these loans, the Ortogh financed their caravans or loaned money to other Chinese merchants at higher interest rates. Such support of trade associations encouraged the expansion of commercial transactions.[69]

Promotion of free trade

Under the Mongols, taxes and tariffs, and other impediments to trade imposed on merchants and products, were either greatly reduced or eliminated altogether. The Mongols reduced taxes on commercial transactions, or what would correspond to the modern Value-Added Tax (VAT) or consumption tax, to a level of only 3.3 percent.[70] This was an early example of supply-side economics in action that stimulated commercial activity and which in effect also contributed to what some historians claim to be the largest free trade zone to exist in history.[71] An indication of the economic activity in the Mongol Empire spurred on by the promotion of free trade can be seen in the travelogue of Marco Polo, where he mentions the huge daily traffic of trade caravans carrying precious stones, pearls, drugs, silks, gold tissues, and spices going to and from China and to other parts of the empire.[72]

Promotion of printing and the creation of a "universal" alphabet

While Genghis Khan was illiterate, with the establishment of the empire the Mongols employed the large-scale use of printing with moveable type for the administration of government. The Chinese had invented the technology for moveable type. However, it was the Mongols who promoted the expansion of its use by establishing printing facilities all over northern China. This development facilitated the publishing not only of government documents but also of books including novels, medical treatises, songs, and poetry. The widespread use of printing by the Mongols reduced the price of books and increased literacy during the Mongol era.[73] To promote literacy throughout the empire as well as to simplify the administrative task of ruling over a multitude of people of various languages, the Mongols created under the guidance of the Tibetan lama Phagspa what they hoped would be a universal alphabet that could write out all the languages of their subject peoples. This was a precursor to the attempt to create a universal language, Esperanto, in the late nineteenth century. The new script, however, was not widely used, due partly to the fact that in true Mongol fashion it was never forced upon the various peoples of the empire, who were attached to their native writing systems.

The use of gunpowder and the development of cannons and other weapons

The Mongols demonstrated ingenuity by synthesizing and cross-fertilizing various ideas and technologies developed by Chinese, Persian, and European engineers employed in the service of the empire. A conspicuous example was the weapons development that provided firepower for the Mongols. They combined

Chinese gunpowder with Persian flame-throwers and European bell-casting technology to create the cannon. This in turn led to the development of other weapons such as the missile and pistols.[74] The Mongols used siege weapons such as the trebuchet, which threw fire and smoke bombs in the campaigns against the Jin and the Khwarizmian Empire, and siege engines such as mobile scaling ladders, battering rams, and tripled-bow siege bows which could puncture city walls located a kilometer away.[75] The Mongols also adopted and modified a Chinese siege engine by comparing it with that developed by the Persians, and created a light catapult which was able to launch a two-pound missile over 100 yards and a heavy catapult that could launch a 25-pound missile over 150 yards.[76] While these weapons had been developed by the Chinese and Persians, the Mongols used these weapons to much effectiveness and established a significant competitive advantage over other enemies that contributed to the victories achieved in their sieges against cities. Most of the people that manned the siege weapons were Chinese who had accompanied the Mongol armies, and the combination of cavalry and siege weaponry became a formidable combination never before seen in warfare.[77]

What is interesting about the above innovations is that while many had been invented by other peoples, the Mongols expanded or refined their use. This is not surprising since it would have been difficult for a nomadic people to develop new technologies and other innovations. It is to the credit of the Mongols that they were flexible enough to utilize ideas, innovations, and concepts without any compunction or regard as to where they were invented or who developed them. Certainly there was no NIH (Not Invented Here) syndrome to hold back the Mongols. They were pragmatic realists. They were also, despite their ruthless destruction of those that refused to submit to them, tolerant enough to accept people with the necessary technical skills and talent to support the Mongol war machine regardless of their origin or regardless of whether they were conquered subjects.

The "barbaric" Mongols and the Americans in the Philippines

During the formative period of the empire, the Mongols are reported to have killed millions of people and destroyed many cities that either got in the way or did not subject themselves to Mongol rule. The Mongol armies were models of efficiency on the battlefield and merciless towards those that opposed. As with the Spanish in the Netherlands and the Dutch in the Banda Islands, the Mongol army practiced total warfare, killing indiscriminately all who did not submit and surrender. A case in point is the total destruction of the Khwarizmian Empire. According to contemporary accounts, the Mongols killed all the inhabitants of the Khwarizmian city of Nishapur, which was razed and ploughed over. In the city of Merv, a total of 1.3 million people were slain, and in Urgench over one million were killed at the hands of the Mongols. The historian John Man sees these events as a Muslim holocaust that is comparable to a certain extent to the

Jewish holocaust of the twentieth century; the only, but perhaps significant difference being that the motivation for the Mongols was not based on any religious or racial ideology as was the case with the Nazis.[78]

Indeed, while the VOC and the Mongols practiced what amounted to genocide, in both circumstances the acts of mass killing were committed as punishment and retribution either for not living up to contractual agreements (in the case of the VOC) or for issuing insults or refusing to surrender (in the case of the Mongols). The Dutch and the Mongols did not have any major religious or racial motivation in their mass killings as did the German Nazis, who followed through on committing genocide for no other reason than to satisfy Hitler's insane preoccupation with creating a racially purified world dominated by blond and blue-eyed Aryans. For that matter, neither the VOC nor the Mongols committed genocide as the nineteenth-century European colonizers did in their thorough extermination of the Tasmanian people of Australia for no other reasons than for sport and business. The European colonialists declared a bounty on the Tasmanians that rewarded hunters £500 for killing every adult Tasmanian and £2 for each child captured alive. "Black catching" became a major business that was enthusiastically pursued by private and official parties.[79] By the late nineteenth century the Tasmanian people had disappeared. Scientist and author Jarred Diamond credits the white Australian colonists for solving its problem with natives by outdoing the Germans in achieving the "most nearly final solution."[80]

Furthermore, before making a sweeping condemnation of the Mongols as intolerant, barbaric mass executioners, we should consider the imperialists and empire builders of recent world history with their indiscriminate killings of non-combatants, torture, and large-scale destruction that were often hypocritically carried out in the name of justice and civilization. In this regard, the subjugation of the Philippines and the methods carried out by the US military in the name of civilizing "savages" is one of the most egregious cases and could be considered not simply as a war of conquest but as one of the earliest examples of a holocaust to occur in the twentieth century. The Philippine-American War of 1899–1903 resulted in the deaths of one to three million Filipinos out of a population of eight million, while American casualties were at 4,234.[81] That is, about 13 to 40 percent of the Filipino population died as a result of the war. Although the conflict "officially" came to an end in 1903, it actually continued until 1916, with military resistance against American rule by Muslims in Mindanao and the Sulu Archipelago.

The historical significance of the Philippine-American War cannot be under-estimated. It marked the birth of an American empire outside of the continental United States established by the overt use of force. It led to enormous destruction of villages, towns, and property, indiscriminate killings, egregious acts of racism, the setting up of concentration camps, and the innovative use of water for torture, all of which foreshadowed behavior in the later wars of the twentieth century. The former CIA consultant and University of California professor Chalmers Johnson argued that the Americans in the Philippines, with their racially-fueled atrocities and statements of contempt and hatred of the Filipinos,

even inspired the budding Japanese empire builders, who were at the time emulating other "advanced" imperialists in methods of dealing with "inferiors."[82]
Indeed, despite pleas of help from the Filipinos in the face of the American
onslaught, the Japanese did not respond and even sent a warship to the Philippines during a critical time in the Filipino uprising as a sign of solidarity with
the Americans, which was much applauded by the latter.[83]

The story of the Philippine–American War has been meticulously retold by
historians and scholars such as Paul A. Kramer, Howard Zinn, Stuart Creighton
Miller, James Bradley, Leon Wolff, and Francisco Luzviminda, whose docu-
mentation of eyewitness accounts written by soldiers in the front line of battle
were referred to heavily in creating the following narrative. Despite the retelling
of the war by these scholars, it seems that not all historians wish to deal with the
details of the subject. Yale law professor Amy Chua has even chosen to ignore
the war. In her book *Day of Empire*, which looks at various empires in world
history, she completely and somewhat incredibly passes over the entire American experience in the Philippines and the plight of the Filipinos at the hands of
the Americans, although she devotes an entire chapter to the American empire
and American expansionism. Chua does not, however, fail to devote space to
Japanese atrocities committed in the Philippines during World War II or mention
the underground Filipino movements that fought against Japanese rule using
guerrilla warfare.[84] Historian Niall Ferguson, in his lengthy tome on the decline
and struggles of empires and the role of racism and violence in the twentieth
century, *The War of the World*, prefers to downplay the events of the Philippine–
American War by simply mentioning in his book that the Americans "had ...
seized the Philippines."[85] In contrast, Ferguson devotes several pages in the same
book to describing in detail the atrocities committed by the Japanese against the
Chinese in Nanjing in 1937.[86] British historian Arthur Cotterell, in his book
Western Power in Asia, does mention the war, but curiously describes it as a
struggle for the *Americans*, whose Gatling guns were ineffective in subduing the
Filipinos with their hit-and-run guerilla tactics, without any mention of the huge
number of Filipino casualties or of the atrocities committed by Americans.
Meanwhile Cotterell, like Ferguson, goes into graphic detail about the atrocities
committed by the Imperial Japanese Army in Nanjing, describing Japanese
actions as a massacre; from a Filipino point of view, American behavior in the
Philippine–American War could also be described as such.[87]

Be that as it may, the Philippine–American war was significant enough to
have inspired the imperial poet Rudyard Kipling to pen his poem *The White
Man's Burden*, which cast the Americans as a race with a manifest imperial
destiny to impart civilization upon the conquered Filipinos, who were "half
devil."[88] In a similar vein, Americans such as President Theodore Roosevelt considered the Filipinos at the time to be nothing more than pagan savages, no different from Native Americans, who were incapable of self-rule. Such
condescending views flew in the face of the declaration made by Galiciano
Apacible, a spokesman for the Philippine independence movement, who pleaded
to the American people to believe that the Filipinos "are a civilized, progressive,

and peace-loving people" that "adopted the electric light" and had established schools and universities.[89]

If there ever was a hostile takeover that completely ignored the aspirations of those about to be taken over, this was it. When the new American imperialists bought the Philippines from the Spanish after Spain's defeat in the Spanish–American War for $20 million, they promptly began to stamp out the Philippine independence movement led by the Filipino Emilio Aguinaldo. He had been fighting against the Filipinos' Spanish colonial overlords who had ruled over the archipelago for three centuries. As a compromise, Aguinaldo proposed to the Americans the independence of the Philippines as a US protectorate. While Genghis Khan would most likely have accepted such an arrangement given his propensity to leave people alone so long as they recognized his dominance and engaged in trade with the Mongols, the US rejected Aguinaldo's proposal. Americans such as the US senator Albert Beveridge declared unabashedly, forgetting that the US had fought a war to become independent from the British, that "The Philippines are ours forever" and for good reason: location and natural resources. As he saw it, a foothold in the Philippines would give the US a door to all of Asia including China, which was a "natural customer" for the Americans. Furthermore, the Philippines had plains and valleys that were far more fertile than those in the US and were capable of supplying the US with coffee, sugar, coconuts, hemp, tobacco, coal, and wood which could provide furniture to the world "for a century to come."[90] In true Mongol fashion towards those who resisted, the Americans were intending to plunder the Philippines.

In terms of sheer scale and magnitude, the destruction and deaths in the Philippines could arguably match if not exceed what the "barbaric" Mongols did to some of their conquests. As documented by Miller, Zinn, Luzviminda, Bradley, and Wolff, US soldiers repeatedly committed rape, torture, and mutilation against the Filipino "savages." A soldier from Kingston, New York, wrote home from the Philippines mentioning that he had received orders from General Loyd Wheaton commanding him and others to burn down the town of Titaia and "kill every native in sight." He reported that about 1,000 men, women, and children were killed. The soldier in a tone of triumph concludes his description of this atrocity by stating, "I am probably growing half-hearted, for I am in my glory when I can sight my gun on some dark skin and pull the trigger."[91] A captain from Kansas wrote home saying that after the Twentieth Kansas division had swept through the village of Caloocan which had about 17,000 inhabitants, "Caloocan contains not one living native."[92] Corporal Sam Gillis of the First California Volunteers wrote to his parents mentioning a US curfew imposed upon the Filipinos on leaving their houses after seven in the evening. Not all the natives decided to obey this, and he writes that "We killed over 300 natives the first night."[93] A private solider from the same outfit wrote admitting that with his own hands he had set fire to over 50 houses of the Filipinos in Caloocan, which had wounded women and children.[94] Eyewitnesses (US soldiers) testified that 1,000 Filipino prisoners of war were forced to dig their own graves and then each received a bullet to the head.[95] The American Red Cross reported that the

Americans were "determined to kill every Filipino in sight."[96] In an assault on the Mount Dajo community, American troops killed over 600 men, women, and children. Photographs were taken of heaped bodies of women and children as proof of the killings.[97] Private Jones of the 11th Calvary wrote home that his troop fired into a wedding party killing the bride and two men, and wounding another woman and two children.[98] Americans beat to death the Filipino mayors of San Miguel and San Nicolas using rattan rods.[99] A reporter for the *New York World* wrote that "It is now the custom to avenge the death of an American soldier by burning to the ground all the houses, and killing right and left the natives who are only 'suspects.'"[100] The Manila correspondent for the *Philadelphia Ledger* reported that the Americans, who considered the Filipinos as "little better than a dog," have been "relentless" in their pursuit "to exterminate" men, women, prisoners, active and suspected insurgents, and even children from the age of 10 up. Prisoners who had surrendered peacefully were reported to have been shot one by one on a bridge "to drop in the water below and float down."[101] A Captain Fred McDonald ordered every native in a particular hamlet to be executed except for one mother of mixed descent who was repeatedly raped by the American officers before being turned over to the enlisted men for their turn.[102] An American congressman who visited the Philippines reported gleefully and piously that no longer were there any reports of disturbances in Northern Luzon as "there isn't anybody there to rebel," and that only "the good Lord in Heaven" knew how many Filipinos were killed. The congressman praised the American soldiers for sweeping the country, taking no prisoners in the process, and simply killing a Filipino whenever they could get hold of one.[103] As if to substantiate the report of the congressman, General "Howlin" Jake Smith, who was put in charge of quelling Balangiga and the island of Samar, ordered his subordinate to "kill and burn, the more you kill and the more you burn the more you please me," and to make the village of Samar "a howling wilderness."[104] When Genghis Khan annihilated the Tatars, he ordered that every Tatar man taller than the linchpin on the wheels of a cart was to be killed.[105] In a similar spirit that would probably have made Genghis smile, Smith also ordered that all Filipino males over the age of 10 were to be killed.[106]

In a throwback to the seventeenth century, when the Dutch VOC tortured their English and Japanese enemies using water, Grover Flint of the 35th Infantry, who served in the Philippines from 1899 to 1901, described in detail to a Senate panel the use of water-boarding for torturing Filipinos. The Filipino, according to him, is held down and has water poured down his throat and nose until he becomes unconscious, at which time he is rolled aside. Flint observed that the Filipino undergoing this torture was suffering greatly, adding that it "must be that of a man who is drowning but he can not drown."[107] According to Charles S. Riley, a clerk at a Massachusetts plumbing and steam-fitting company who witnessed the water-boarding of Tobeniano Ealdama, the Filipino president of the town of Igbaras, Ealdama's throat was "held so he could not prevent swallowing the water, so that he had to allow the water to run into his stomach," the water was then "forced out of him by pressing a foot on his stomach or else with the [soldier's] hands."[108] I recall that a Filipino classmate of mine during my university days told me of the water-boarding torture her relative had to endure at the hands of the Japanese during World War II, but it seems that the Americans had set the precedent for this in the Philippines.

The above accounts suggest that water-boarding seemed to have been an accepted American practice in the early twentieth century. In contrast, the "barbaric" Mongols banned the use of torture or at least curtailed its use. The Mongol legal code of 1291 stated that officials must use reason to analyze and surmise when investigating a person suspected of committing a crime, and should not abruptly impose any torture.[109]

The Filipinos were routinely described as "niggers" by the Americans. The journalist Henry Loomis Nelson wrote back to the US that to American troops in the Philippines, all Filipinos were one race, and being of dark complexion were "therefore 'niggers,'" so that they deserved "all the contempt and harsh treatment administered by white overlords to the most inferior races."[110] Sergeant Howard McFarlane of the 43rd Infantry wrote that 18 of his men had killed 75 "nigger bolomen" and 10 "nigger gunners." Those that weren't killed in the carnage were later finished off by bayonets.[111] An Oregon soldier wrote describing an incident of indiscriminate shooting into forests and homes, and into "anything that looked like a place for a nigger to hide."[112] In addition to the widespread use of "nigger," the racist term "gook" as applied to Asians also seems to have had its origins with US soldiers in the Philippines calling the Filipinos "gu-gu" or "goo-goo."[113]

To the Americans, the Filipino was not only a "nigger" but an animal to be hunted. A volunteer from the state of Washington wrote "Our fighting blood was up, and we all wanted to kill 'niggers' … This shooting human beings beats rabbit hunting all to pieces."[114] Private George Osborn of the 6th Infantry wrote home from Negros: "Just back from the fight. Killed 22 niggers … we just shot the niggers like a hunter would rabbits."[115]

In addition to indiscriminately killing and torturing the Filipinos, the Americans herded them into concentration camps where crowded and unsanitary conditions as well as lack of food led to the spread of diseases such as malaria, beriberi, dengue fever, and death for many. One concentration camp was in Marinduque Island, where the entire population of 51,000 was herded into five camps. According to one correspondent, the prisoners in the concentration camp were "a miserable-looking lot of little brown rats."[116]

To the credit of the Americans at the time, unlike some other imperialists in history, they did not try to cover up or deny that such atrocities were taking place, although there was censorship of press reports. William Howard Taft, who became the US governor of the Philippines and later president of the US, admitted that atrocities such as indiscriminate shootings and torture using water had been committed by Americans.[117] Rather egregiously, Senator Albert Beveridge even justified such acts, stating that while the conduct of Americans have been cruel, the US must remember that it was not dealing with Americans or Europeans but with "Orientals."[118] Senator Henry Cabot Lodge, speculating as to why the atrocities took place, blamed it on the "Asiatics" for bringing such misfortunes upon themselves. According to Lodge, the Filipinos were a "semicivilized" people "with all the tendencies and characteristics of Asiatics," that is, indifferent to life, treacherous, and cruel.[119] Theodore Roosevelt defended the hecatomb in the Philippines by declaring it to be the "proper treatment of weaker by stronger races."[120]

After the US had completed their annexation of the Philippines, Americans continued to mistreat the Filipinos. Filipinos were not allowed to freely emigrate and live in the US, nor were Filipinos allowed to become US citizens (naturalization rights came only after independence in 1946). In states such as California, Filipinos were by law not allowed to marry Americans of European descent.[121] Filipino products exported to the US were subjected to customs duties by an act of congress.[122]

The end result of all the atrocities, mistreatment, and racist rhetoric towards the Filipinos was that the Filipinos never opted to remain a part of the US, despite later demonstrations of American goodwill. Calls for independence persisted up to the very day that the Philippines actually won independence from the US in 1946. Prominent Filipinos had even cooperated with the Japanese at the expense of the US when the former invaded the islands in 1942. Emilio Aguinaldo, despite good treatment from the Americans after his capture during the closing days of the Philippine–American War, decided to collaborate with the Japanese invaders in 1942 in order to achieve independence. The politician and jurist Claro M. Recto, who presided over the drafting of the Philippine Constitution in 1934 under US auspices, was another prominent collaborator;[123] so much for the good will and loyalty that the US hoped to cultivate in the Philippines. The US on its part became anxious to dump the Philippines due to racial fears of Filipino immigration.[124] The American empire in the Philippines was a classic case where intolerance, manifested primarily in racial and cultural prejudice leading to acts of wanton violence, discrimination, and mutual hatred, contributed to its demise.

The "barbarity" of modern society and its pretentious tendency to look down upon less sophisticated societies as "barbaric" is an irony that was succinctly captured by the American writer Mark Twain in his satire *A Connecticut Yankee in King Arthur's Court*. In the novel, Hank Morgan, a nineteenth-century American inventor from Connecticut, wakes up to find himself transported to medieval England after being hit on the head. The bewildered Hank is appalled and disgusted by the barbarity and ignorance of the people of the Middle Ages who have awful manners, practice slavery, and don't hesitate to kill and execute people for the smallest infractions. In the end, however, it is Hank, the "civilized" nineteenth-century American technocrat, who destroys the "barbaric" medieval world and commits genocide through the unleashing of forces of mass destruction created by the science and technology of his modern, "civilized" world. Electric wires, minefields, and Gatling guns are used to slaughter the knights of the Middle Ages. As Mark Twain (who was an ardent opponent of the American conquest of the Philippines) suggests, becoming "modern" or technologically sophisticated does not ensure that modern society has become less "barbaric" than the Mongols.

The Mongol culture of tolerance

But for an empire that did commit large-scale atrocities against their enemies and acts akin to genocide, how can the Mongols be considered tolerant? Indeed, in view of the Mongols' persistent extermination of those enemies who opposed them even after they surrendered, the Mongols would be considered anything but tolerant. While I have no intention of undertaking a revisionist view of history, I would like to go back to my definition of what constitutes tolerance stated earlier. That is, tolerance refers to the capacity or ability to accept the coexistence of *people* regardless of their gender, orientation, ethnicity, religious beliefs, culturally-based behavior, and national origin, and to accept the coexistence of *diverse ideas and values* and recognize their benefits. Going with this definition of tolerance, we can find that there is much anecdotal evidence that the Mongols were tolerant. We have seen that Genghis Khan's four generals whom he considered his "attack dogs" were all from tribes that were not Genghis's. The Mongols freely employed Chinese and Persian siege engineers to support their war effort. In their siege of the Song Chinese city of Xiangyang, a general of the Mongol army was Ali-haiya, a Uighur.[125] Bayan, a general under the command of Kublai Khan who played a crucial role in conquering the city of Hangzhou which led to the fall of the Song Kingdom, was a Turk who aside from being a brilliant commander of troops was also an able administrator who spoke the Chinese language.[126] Soldiers in the Yuan Dynasty were recruited from the European Ossetians of the Caucasus Mountains and Turkic tribes residing in southeastern Russia.[127] The Mongols even employed an Englishman by the name of Robert, who was in their services for almost 20 years before being captured by Austrians during a raiding mission in the Vienna Woods.[128] Robert was a former Knight Templar who was expelled from England and later found employment as an interpreter for the Mongols, who found his ability to speak several languages useful.[129] Despite the acts of what would seem to be uncontrollable anger including the massacre of city inhabitants, the destruction of homes, and sadistic forms of execution, the Mongols were level-headed enough to later employ the many Turkic horsemen of Khwarizmia. Similarly, the Mongols often absorbed able-bodied soldiers who were captured from a defeated foe, using them in many cases for cannon fodder in attacks on enemies.

As the conquests of the Mongols progressed and their empire gradually expanded, the use of a defeated foe's resources included the employment of scholars, scribes, artisans, and craftsmen. Special provisions were drawn up to protect and support artisans and under Kublai Khan, organizations were set up to supervise the works of the artisans. Kublai especially valued Chinese ceramics as works of art to be displayed at court and for foreign trade.[130] The Mongols supported the artistic activities of Chinese painters such as Zhao Mengfu and Gao Kokung, and under Kublai both were appointed to administrative positions in the Yuan government, in the Ministry of War and Ministry of Works respectively.[131] Non-Chinese craftsmen such as the Nepalese A-Nege, who designed and constructed Buddhist temples, were also employed and given patronage by the Mongols. Kublai was so much impressed by the Nepalese that he appointed him the Directorate General for the Management of Artisans, making him in effect responsible for the supervision of all craftsmen in China.[132]

In matters pertaining to the tolerance of diverse ideas and values, all religions practiced in the Mongol Empire were protected by law and treated equally (although it should be noted that Genghis Khan made the Chinese Daoist sage Chang Chun his spiritual advisor, hoping to learn the secrets of immortality).[133] This was perhaps a remarkable state of affairs considering that in most of contemporary Europe there were frequent cases of persecution and discrimination against people on the grounds of faith, especially of the Jews.

The Mongols also employed non-Mongols for running their empire. Uighurs and Khitans provided much expertise and guidance to the Mongols in setting up administrative institutions.[134] In the Ilkhanate government, Persians such as Rashid al-Din were employed. At a time when, as we have mentioned, Jews were discriminated against and persecuted in Europe on account of their religion, Jews such as Sa'd al-Dalwa wielded influence in the Mongol government. Overall, the Mongols were fairly content to leave the day-to-day job of government administration in the Ilkhanate to their Persian subjects, so long as their loyalty was not subject to any suspicion and tax revenues continued to come in. In China, much of the lower-level administration and civil service of the former Song Dynasty was left intact and allowed to function as before. However, the Mongols were reluctant to employ Chinese at the highest levels of government; for financial matters, the Mongols employed non-Chinese administrators.[135] Consequently, a large number of non-Chinese including Middle Eastern and Central Asian Muslims, Khitans, Ughurs, and even Europeans such as Marco Polo worked for the Mongols as administrators.

Despite having a tolerant attitude in utilizing people regardless of their origin and religious beliefs and on the basis of their natural talents and skills, the Mongols made it clear to all that ultimate power resided in the Mongol rulers who were the direct descendants of Genghis Khan. This was necessary for the Mongols to wield control over such a large area of land, to maintain their own distinctive identity, and to preserve the memory of their nomadic roots, which was constantly in danger of being eroded by the great cultures they took over. Indeed, as the decades went by, the Mongols became highly assimilated with the local cultures, as shown by the establishment of a Chinese-style dynasty by Kublai Khan and the conversion of the Golden Horde and the Ilkhanate to the Muslim religion. To have the descendants of Genghis Khan ultimately in control of the empire was also required because the Mongols lacked the essential glue of a common identity which the conquered subjects of various areas could relate to and which would allow them to identify with their Mongol overlords. The only adhesives the Mongols could provide was the rule of the Khan and its symbols backed by brute military force, the promise of being able to live and work according to one's calling and ability, religious tolerance, and most importantly, the promise of riches. Exotic products such as silks, porcelain, and medicines from China sold or given to the Muslims made the latter grudgingly accept the Mongols as their overlords, and similarly the Russians and the Chinese were given or were able to buy hard-to-obtain goods from other parts of the vast Mongol empire such as carpets, jewels, and glass, which helped to purchase their loyalty and prevent them from revolting.[136]

The Mongols were in all likelihood not loved by their conquered subjects, although in fairness to them there were instances when the Mongols were greeted as liberators. We have seen an example of this with the Muslims of the Kara–Khitan, who welcomed the Mongols after the latter had liberated them from the Buddhist Kulchug. Slav peasants who were long oppressed by their Bulgar masters openly welcomed the Mongols when the latter had destroyed the Bulgar kingdom of the Volga.[137] Marco Polo was of the opinion that the Mongols knew that they were not liked by their subjects, especially the Chinese, and that this was a major reason that the Mongols employed so many foreign administrators in China.[138] That is to say, according to the Venetian, the use of foreigners such as Marco Polo in the Mongol government was more a result of distrust of the native Chinese rather than any tolerant consideration of employing people regardless of their origin.

The sources of Mongol tolerance

While we can only speculate as to what the sources of Mongol tolerance were, a reading of Mongol history suggests that there were two main points of origin, one of which stemmed from the traditions of Mongol nomadic society. The Mongol tribes themselves in behavior and practices were tolerant to the extent that they would readily accept brides from other clans and tribes, although of course in many cases the brides were abducted. The Mongols also practiced forging blood-brother ties or anda, which were formed in several cases among people that were not related to each other by blood or that were not of the same tribe. An example of this was the anda formed between Genghis and Jamuka or that of Genghis's father Yesugei and the Ong Khan of the Keraits. Such practices suggest that to a certain extent the acceptance of people from outside of the tribe or clan was an ingrained tradition that came about and was shaped over many centuries of life in the Mongol steppe. The Mongol tribes, while fiercely independent, were flexible and tolerant enough to accept new blood from the outside, and to forge friendships that bridged different tribes. Such a tradition helped the Mongols to assimilate the different cultures of their conquered subjects as well as providing the flexibility and tolerance to make use of people's abilities regardless of where they may have come from. It also encouraged the Mongols to freely mix their genes with the local population. Finally, in traditional Mongol society the men were tolerant enough to accept women as their partners in government, in hunting, and in war.

Another source of tolerance arguably comes from the leadership of the Mongols, starting with Genghis Khan. As we have seen, Genghis tolerated the coexistence of various religions and cultures in his empire and did not force the Mongol way of life upon his conquered subjects. He also initiated the practice of using people, starting with his "four dogs," on the basis of talent and ability and not on tribal origin or loyalty. Commanders of his military divisions were selected on the basis of their achievements. Family or tribal relationships likely did not matter to him in getting a task done. Why this was the case can only be speculated, but I suspect that his precarious childhood experience of having to deal with unscrupulous and back-stabbing relatives who left him and his mother out in the cold after his father's death left an impression that even those related by blood or tribe could not always be trusted. Indeed, we should not forget that Genghis had no compunction in killing his older half brother. The experience of leading a desperate life in the harsh climate of the Mongol steppe may have enforced upon Genghis an extremely pragmatic outlook on life that made him believe that the ends justified the means to survival even if it meant killing one's own relatives or being tolerant enough to ally with people from other tribes and clans.

After the death of Genghis, his policy of tolerance was further impressed upon the Mongol leaders by Sorghagtani Beki, who was the wife of Tolui, the youngest son of Genghis, and the mother of four sons: Mongke Khan, the fourth Great Khan of the Mongol Empire; Kublai Khan, the fifth Great Khan and the founder of the Yuan Dynasty; Hulegu Khan, the founder of the Persian Ilkhanate; and Arike Boke. Women in general enjoyed a high status in Mongol society and are known to have participated in battle with their men as well as hunted with them.[139] Mongol women had property rights and controlled the household. Some of the daughters and daughters-in-law of Genghis served as regents for the various parts of the empire. Mongol women who toiled on an equal footing with their men had far more freedom than their Chinese or Persian counterparts; Chinese women, in fact, had their feet bound.[140] Among the Mongol women, Sorghagtani was distinguished by her perspicacity in seeing to it that her sons received a proper education, each learning a foreign language that was used by the subject peoples. To this end, tutors from all over the empire were put into service to instruct her sons. A devout Nestorian Christian from the Kerait tribe, she also saw the importance of understanding the different religions and made sure that her sons, Mongol court retainers, and officials received religious instruction and enforced the policies of religious tolerance as proclaimed by Genghis. Aside from using non-Mongol tutors for her sons and supporting different religions, Sorghagtani also openly protected traditional Chinese society by supporting peasant farmers who worked on her estates.[141]

Sorghagtani's outlook and the education she imparted and provided to her sons cannot be underestimated, as they for the most part followed her example of respecting different religions and local societies, and employing people regardless of where they came from. Mongke Khan (elected Great Khan in 1251), for example, relied heavily on Chinese and Muslim administrators in addition to Mongols. He also employed Chinese and Europeans to decorate his capital city of Karakorum, and even used the skills of a Frenchman to construct huge decorative fountains that would spout wine. Under his reign, Buddhist monasteries, mosques, churches, and synagogues were built. Such policies in turn ensured or at least contributed to the stability, growth of wealth, and longevity of the empire. Another son of Sorghagtani who was famous for his practice of tolerance was Kublai (elected Great Khan in 1260 after the death of Mongke in 1259 and a power struggle with Arike Boke), Emperor of the Yuan Dynasty of China. During his period of rule Kublai was known for cultivating and supporting the Chinese arts, including pottery, painting, and drama, promoting mass education, employing craftsmen and artists of different ethnicities and origin, and hiring capable people originating from all over the empire including Persian and Arab Muslims, Tibetans, Uighurs, Central Asians, and Europeans for government positions including that of resident commissioners (darughachi) and administrators in various parts of the empire. Kublai regularly consulted with an international group of advisors which included the Tibetan lama Phagspa, who was given jurisdiction over Tibet, and Muslims from Central Asia who were trade supervisors and financial administrators. Kublai sought advice from Muslim and Indian doctors and Persian astronomers, relied upon Muslim merchants from Central Asia as intermediaries for trade, and had Turks serve as soldiers and as tutors to the imperial princes. Kublai's capacity for tolerance also extended to food. During his rule the calorie-sufficient but poorly balanced[142] traditional Mongol diet of mutton, lamb, horse meat, and fermented horse milk called koumis changed dramatically, as chefs of various ethnicities including Chinese, Persians, Turks, Arabs, Koreans, and Tibetans began concocting elaborate dishes that included various fowl, fish such as carp, vegetables, spices such as turmeric, noodles, and meat, including camel, deer, monkeys, weasels, badgers, tigers, dogs, boars, foxes, and rhinos.[143] In keeping with the practice of his mother in protecting traditional Chinese society, Kublai respected the existing networks of obligations and responsibilities in Chinese society by not introducing any disruptive social changes.[144] And, continuing the practice of his grandfather as well as in observing the teachings of his mother, Kublai for the most part tolerated the coexistence of different religions, although following his failure to conquer Japan and the death of his favorite wife, Chabi, dementia and senility unfortunately made him into a persecutor of Daoists.

Other cultural attributes of the Mongols

Aside from the tolerant nature of Mongol culture, it can be argued from various anecdotes that there was a strong propensity towards egalitarianism within Mongol society and equality between superiors and subordinates. According to the *Yasa*, Genghis proclaimed that when speaking to him or anyone else "simply his name (i.e., Genghis) was to be used."[145] Genghis disapproved of the pompous and ceremonial forms of addressing people prevalent in other cultures at the time, such as in Xi-Xia or Song China. Within the court of Genghis Khan there were no stuffy court ceremonies. On the battlefield, Genghis implored his generals to empathize with the common soldier and do whatever they could to see that their warriors and horses did not unduly suffer from thirst or starvation.[146] To the Daoist sage Chang Chun, Genghis wrote that he cared for his soldiers as if they were his brothers.[147] Genghis was also noted to be generous in the distribution of booty. Before doing battle with the Tatars, he proclaimed that any booty would belong to all collectively and it was then distributed under his watch, whereas previously it was the prerogative of each tribal chief to freely choose what to do with whatever booty he obtained.[148] Genghis ensured that each participant in battle was guaranteed a share of loot. Aside from the exhortations of Genghis to his generals, historians have noted that the Mongol officers ate the same foods as ordinary soldiers, another indication of relative equality between superiors and subordinates.[149] The relationship between Genghis and his subordinates was also frank and informal, and he permitted them to freely criticize him.[150] He also acted upon their advice and rewarded them greatly. To Bogorchu and Mukali, two trusted commanders, Genghis commended them by saying that both were able to draw out good judgments from him as well as stopping him from making bad decisions. For their achievements, Bogorchu was given rule over "ten thousand people to the south of the Altai," and Muklai was given rule over "ten thousand people to the north."[151] Finally, towards his fellow Mongols at large, Genghis went to great lengths to show his affinity towards them. His life even after his conquests remained simple and frugal. Despite his victories, Genghis claimed to still wear the same clothes and eat the same food as the cowherds and horse-herders.[152] As we have seen, this sense of egalitarianism extended to the roles of males and females which overlapped prominently in Mongol society.

Another cultural attribute of the Mongols was the streak of individualism in their personal behavior. Individual Mongols were inclined to look after themselves on issues of pride or treachery and did not hesitate to take revenge for slights, which was perhaps a reason why the Mongols failed to unite themselves before Genghis came on the scene. On the other hand, this individualism was tempered by an equally strong sense of self-identity with a group. For the individual Mongol, his or her identity was closely associated with membership in a particular tribe. This was a natural outcome given the fierce and unforgiving natural environment in which the Mongols lived, where it was next to impossible for Mongols to survive outside of their tribe. The narrow escape from death that Genghis and his mother experienced after being thrown out of their tribe and told by their tribesmen to fend for themselves substantiates this. After this experience, Genghis realized that he could not survive unless he belonged to a tribe; hence his joining the Keraits after escaping from the Tayichiuds. Mongol society, in short, had a strong collectivist or group-oriented culture which, however, did not inhibit the rise of dynamic, individualistic leaders such as Genghis or Kublai.

The Roman Empire: a comparison

A parallel case with the Mongols is the Roman Empire. At its peak, the Roman Empire covered approximately 4.5 million square kilometers and had 50 million inhabitants. Although the size of the Mongol Empire dwarfed that of the Romans, Rome's impact upon history and particularly on the cultures and the course of events in Europe was to be just as profound as that of the Mongol Empire. Roman law, for example, became the foundation for the civil laws of many European countries and also influenced the development of English common law as well as US mercantile and maritime law.[153] The Latin language of the Romans, although no longer spoken as a mother tongue, influenced the development of modern European languages. Furthermore, in comparison to the Mongol Empire which lasted about 200 years, the Roman Empire had lasted approximately 400 years by the time the Western Roman Empire was destroyed by the Vandals in 476 CE, and continued for 1,000 years until the Eastern Roman Empire in Constantinople fell to the Ottoman Turks in 1453.

Rome started out as a small village on one of the hills by the Tiber, having been founded (according to legend) by Romulus, a descendant of prince Aeneas (who escaped the destruction of Troy during the Trojan War) in 753 BCE. According to legend, the first Roman king, Romulus, established a senate which was initially composed of people close to him and had the task of ratifying requests for laws made by the consuls, who were nominated by the senate. The consuls stood at the pinnacle of Roman society. Under the Roman monarchy they managed the affairs of the city as well as leading armies into war.

Before Rome embarked upon its imperial adventure, the Italian peninsula where the city was located had in it a mixture of independent city-states, tribes, and clans with diverse cultures, from that of the "barbarian" Gauls in the north to that of the Greeks in the south. At various times in its early history, Rome was convulsed with political disorder and crisis. Once Rome had its internal house in order, the city embarked upon empire-building, becoming the dominant power of Italy by 265 BCE when the city-state fought against Carthage in the First Punic War over control of Sicily. By 133 BCE, Rome had subjugated both Carthage and Greece and reigned supreme in the Mediterranean. The Romans later reinforced the process of unification by developing a common system of law, politics, and language. And unification led to all the natives of Italy becoming citizens of Rome from birth. As the English historian Edward Gibbon noted in his monumental tome *The Decline and Fall of the Roman Empire*, distinctions between peoples were obliterated as they all coalesced into one empire that was united by language, manners, and civil institutions.[154]

Like the Mongol Empire, the Roman Empire was built primarily upon military conquest. But as Rome began to expand, in contrast to the Mongols, its reputation as the source of civilization and its cultural attractiveness founded upon on its laws, customs, grandiose architecture, and the arts also attracted non-Romans to the empire. Members of absorbed, subordinate societies agreed with the Roman view of Rome as the source of culture, and aspired to become accepted by the Romans, as shown in the writings of the Greek Polybius and the Jewish Josephus.[155] Gibbon noted that reverence for Rome among barbarian tribes often resulted in the barbarians' asking the Roman emperor to arbitrate the differences among their tribes.[156] It even led to the remarkable situation where certain cities and kingdoms actually gave themselves up to the people of Rome.[157] In doing so they voluntarily entered into a client-patron relationship with Rome and received the protection and prestige of an alliance as well as exemption from all taxes and the conferring of full Roman rights on their citizens.[158]

A similarity in practice between the Mongols and the Romans is the tolerance shown to different religions.[159] It should be added in passing, however, that the Romans put their foot down on religious practices that they considered excessively barbaric or disturbing to the peace of the empire, as shown in their initial response to Christianity and at times to Judaism. Another similarity was the tendency of both empires to readily adopt the practices of other peoples. As it was with the Mongols, who did not suffer from a Not Invented Here (NIH) syndrome, so it was with the Romans, who according to Gibbon had thrown away their vanity and even considered it prudent and honorable to adopt the virtues and merits of others, even those of enemies or barbarians.[160]

When the Roman Empire began to extend into more distant areas, the same principles of government that secured the peace of Italy were applied to the newly conquered areas, including the right of citizenship for the most loyal colonial subjects. The granting of citizenship with equal rights to the citizens of Rome was further extended under the emperor Caracella, who issued an edict, the *Constitutio Antoniniana*, in 212 CE that granted citizenship to all free men of the conquered territories and not just to a few loyal subjects. The legacy of Caracella as an emperor is dubious, as he usurped power by killing his own brother Geta in their mother's apartment and then purged Geta's supporters by slaughtering 20,000 of them. He also showed a touch of narcissistic megalomania from conscientious modeling of himself on Alexander the Great. Nevertheless, his edict enabled the Roman Empire, forged by conquest, to become a community where political differences between the conquerors and conquered were removed by citizenship. Even slaves who were often ethnically different from the Romans were able to attain citizenship by marrying with Roman citizens. This seems to have been a frequent event given that at one point the first emperor of Rome, Augustus (formerly Octavian before he became emperor and was given the name Augustus by the Roman senate), showed some concern over this. Such ex-slaves could find employment in the imperial civil service, and some were known to amass wealth and hold important posts on the administrative staff of Augustus's own household.[161] The consequences of this expansion of citizenship were profound. As Gibbon noted, the descendants of the Gauls, for example, began to command legions and govern provinces, and became Roman senators to boot. Instead of disturbing the tranquility of the state, the advancement of the Gauls became associated with the safety and greatness of the empire.[162] Such developments led in turn to the creation of a Roman world that was uniform, voluntary, and permanent, with all conquered peoples blended together as one people who now scarcely considered their own existence as distinct from the existence of Rome.[163]

While the conquered subjects of the Mongols, regardless of origin were treated equally by the Mongols, they were not, when it came to actually ruling the empire, equal to the Mongols. Granted, there were foreign, non-Mongolian administrators and local rulers within the Mongol Empire. But ultimately, the Mongol Empire was ruled at the top by the descendants of Genghis Khan. In contrast, non-Romans such as the Spanish Trajan; the African Septimius Severus from Lepcis Magna (in modern Libya); Caracella (who was the son of Septimus and Julia Domna, a Syrian); Elagabalus, a Syrian; Aurelian, a peasant from Sirmian (modern-day Serbia); and Alaric, a Roman general of "barbarian" ancestry; all became emperors of Rome. Not only did the Romans further break down the political distinction between Romans and non-Romans, they were successful enough to promote the concept of belonging to a single, highly attractive civilization which non-imperial subjects could only hope to join. Rome was, in effect, more than just a conquering empire. It became to those who were attracted to it an idea, what the Romans called a civitas, a word from which the modern word "civilization" would be derived. As the Roman philosopher Cicero put it, Rome was a community of gods and men.[164]

The concept of civitas created loyalty, which in turn helped to keep down costs of administrative coercion.[165] In the second century CE under the reign of Antonines it was reported that years could go by in provincial towns within the empire before a Roman soldier could be sighted. As Cicero put it, Rome was more a protectorate than a world empire.[166] This lack of need to provide day-to-day military coercion in keeping together the empire was perhaps the prime achievement of the Roman Empire.

In addition to breaking down the distinction between ruling and conquered peoples, the Romans developed their culture and civilization, which was to prove so attractive to non-Romans by building upon the foundations of the Greek and other great Mediterranean cultures that came before them. Their empire was for the most part created through the conquest or voluntary absorption by one settled people over another. Thus, aside from appealing to the greatness of Roman culture, the Romans could also relate to their conquered subjects through a basic commonality of lifestyles and outlook. The Mongols, on the other hand, were nomads who were constantly on the move in search of greener pastures and developed a culture that reflected their nomadic ways, which had little in common with the settled civilizations. They also, as a result of being constantly on the move, did not have the luxury in terms of time, manpower, and economic resources to develop the trappings of civilization that might have proved attractive to their conquered subjects such as the Chinese, Persians, and Russians. Nor did they develop any philosophy of government aside from "conquer or be conquered" or taking revenge for slights incurred. The Mongol tribes did not have a government bureaucracy that would become a model for the conquered societies, which in most cases had the apparatus of a government structure already in place. Hence, while the Mongols could make an appeal for unity by pointing to a common ancestry for their various Mongol tribes (and also, of course, to the promise of booty), they could not make a cultural appeal to their subjects, who lived a vastly different lifestyle and had rich cultures to begin with. Without this appeal of civilization to point to, the only factors that helped the Mongols keep their diverse empire from falling apart were strict but fair rule backed by the military, the promise of riches, and the practice of tolerance.

The fading away of the Mongol Empire

Historians give several reasons for the demise of the Mongol empire, including internal strife and rivalry among the various khanates, as well as disease which weakened the hold of the Mongols. Chua considers the rise of intolerance, especially that of religious intolerance, as a factor that contributed to the empire's downfall.[167] Ratchnevsky concurs with this view, observing that the rise of religious intolerance led to dissension among the Mongols and the fall of the empire in the long run.[168] In a time when people of different faiths were routinely persecuted, tortured, and put to death for their beliefs, the Mongols initially tolerated all religions. But in the later years of the empire, the Mongols became increasingly intolerant. In the Yuan empire, after Kublai converted to Buddhism, the Mongols began to persecute the followers of Daoism, a belief which was originally protected by his grandfather Genghis. Later, Kublai expelled Muslims from his realm. In the Ilkhanate, after the Ilkhan Ghazan converted to Islam around 1295, the Mongols persecuted and massacred the Christians in their realm. The Ilkhanate Mongols also destroyed Buddhist temples and synagogues. They forced those not following the Islamic faith to convert to Islam or leave the Ilkhanate.[169] This unhinging of one of the few adhesives with which the Mongols had united their sprawling empire could only have made the Mongols even more unpopular among their conquered subjects.

On the other hand, there is the view that the Mongols did not disappear but rather simply became assimilated as their nomadic culture became marginalized.[170] That is to say, the Mongols, while unable to impose their nomadic way of life or present any unifying ideal such as the Romans provided, simply were unable to resist the culture with which they came into contact, and in effect succumbed to the people they conquered by surreptitious assimilation.[171] In all of the khanates, the Mongols mixed with the local population and became assimilated with the local cultures. In 1295 the Ilkhan of Persia, Ghazan, became a Muslim and with his conversion, the Mongols became increasingly Persianized through their adoption of speech, habits, and customs. When the Ilkhanate was dissolved in the 1330s, the Mongols were not expelled. The ruling Mongol class of the Golden Horde and the Chaghatai Empire were assimilated with Turkish culture and intermarried with the local population. The Chaghatai Empire was eventually divided into two parts, the western half called Transoxania and based in Samarkand and Bukhara, and the eastern half called Mughulistan. The Chaghatai Empire essentially survived as an Islamic state. Eventually, one of the descendants of the Chaghatai and therefore of Genghis Khan, Babur, became the founder of the Mughal Empire of India. And in China, the Mongols assimilated with the native Chinese population to such an extent that when they were finally expelled, only 60,000 out of a population of 400,000 Mongols living in China at the time returned to their native land. The majority of Mongols preferred to stay in China.[172]

Conclusion

Despite their success at creating a global empire, where the Mongols ultimately failed was in striking the right balance in their practice of tolerance. The Mongols were too tolerant in the respect that their acceptance of and assimilation with local cultures and mixing with peoples simply swamped their original nomadic identity originating with Genghis Khan. They had instead become Persians, Turks, Chinese, central Asians, and Koreans. The Mongols also proved to be not tolerant enough. Their assimilation with certain religions which was a sign of tolerance ironically gave them a streak of intolerance, leading to persecution of different faiths. The preoccupation with having the Great Khan selected only from among the descendants of Genghis immediately shut out prospects of using more capable non-Mongols in that position, a contrasting situation to that of the Romans, who eventually came to choose non-Romans for emperor.

Yet the Mongols created an empire that was the largest in history, spanning from the Pacific Ocean to Eastern Europe and comprising multitudes of different peoples, cultures, languages, and religions, and lasting well over 200 years. It was an empire that provided myriad opportunities for the exchange of goods, ideas, technologies, and arts, and allowed people to live safe lives that would enable them to fulfill their ambitions, practice their religions in peace, and become rich. It was an empire that sparked the imagination and ambitions of the Europeans and became a catalyst for the birth of the Renaissance and the modern world that we know today. It was an empire that despite its fearsome reputation, practiced tolerance—a tolerance towards accepting new ideas and values, welcoming foreigners into their midst, and actively using the best and the brightest people regardless of their origin for the benefit of the empire.

5   Matsushita's movie entertainment empire

The road from Osaka to Hollywood

Introduction

The Japanese electronics conglomerate, the Matsushita Electric Industrial Corporation (MEI), entered the Hollywood movie business through its acquisition of the Music Corporation Agency (MCA), the parent company and owner of the Hollywood-based movie studio Universal Studios, in 1990. Its arch-rival, the Sony Corporation, had the previous year become a major player in the US movie business with its purchase of the movie studio Columbia Pictures from the soft-drink enterprise the Coca-Cola Company. At the time of Sony's purchase there was a certain amount of uproar in the US, with some sections of the media claiming that the Japanese were "invading" Hollywood. Indeed, this was a period when there were considerable trade tensions between Japan and the US. On top of this, the appreciation of the Japanese yen and low interest rates were fueling the Japanese appetite for overseas investments, leading to a shopping spree that included purchases of prime real estate, buildings, and companies in the US. Regardless of the negative publicity surrounding Japan and Sony, MEI also decided to take the plunge into Hollywood, and on November 26, 1990 announced its intention of acquiring MCA for the sum of US$6.59 billion. It was the largest Japanese overseas acquisition to date, surpassing the Sony-Columbia deal.

Before going any further in our narrative, it is perhaps appropriate at this point to step aside and examine MEI's history and culture, in order to understand why, after going through the trouble of buying a movie studio, it abruptly divested just five years after its acquisition.

Side tour: MEI's history and its learning experience with M&A

The early years

In 2008, an AP News reporter covering the plan by Panasonic (MEI was renamed Panasonic in 2008) to acquire a rival consumer electronics manufacturer, Sanyo Electric Co., wrote that Panasonic's history in acquisitions was dismal.[1] Looking only at the history of MEI's acquisition of MCA and its sub-sequent divestiture after only five years, this would seem to be true. But perhaps unknown to this AP reporter, MEI had in fact a long history of undertaking mergers and acquisitions (M&A), most of them successful. As pointed out by Mizuno Hiroyuki, the former head of research and development at MEI, a reason for the unfamiliarity with this aspect of MEI especially among those based outside of Japan may be that most of the M&A deals were done in Japan.[2]

An overview of the history of MEI/Panasonic shows that the development of the company is closely intertwined with M&A activities. The company has at many crucial instances grown on account of M&A. Most of the M&A deals were undertaken in order for the company to acquire new skills, products, and tech-nologies not available at the time within MEI. Achieving economies of scale and entry into new businesses were also motives behind several of the acquisitions.

Business people today who are involved in M&A can consider themselves fortunate to have the luxury of getting advice from highly paid consultants and experts in the field. Many of them are also fortunate enough to have MBA degrees and to have learned about the basics of M&A through case studies in a school environment. During the early history of MEI, such experts on M&A and post-integration were practically nonexistent within Japan. MBA degrees did not exist. The founder of MEI, Matsushita Konosuke, was an amateur at business with no management experience to speak of when with his wife he established his company and began making electric sockets. Because of wrenching poverty, Konosuke could not even finish his six compulsory years of primary school edu-cation. He had to leave school and home at the age of 11 to work and support his family, which had became destitute on account of massive speculation losses incurred by his father. Konosuke recalled in his memoirs that at this age and for the next seven years he worked at a bicycle repair shop, where he would be repairing bicycles from the early hours of the morning to late at night, with no days for rest except for O-Bon (Festival of the Dead) in August and New Year's Day.[3]

Aside from having to work long hours with little respite, poverty also left Konosuke unable to write in the Japanese language. Upon transferring from the bicycle shop to the Osaka Dento Company (an enterprise that made lighting fix-tures), Konosuke had to turn down a promotion to become an office clerk at his new workplace as he could not write. As he put it, since he did not finish primary school and could not attend night school on account of working from early morning to night, the only thing he could write were indecipherable squiggly-shaped characters.[4]

Konosuke's inability to write properly and his demotion back to the position of repairman, for which he was originally hired, turned out in retrospect to be fortunate for him. He left Osaka Dento at the age of 23 and started his own company, Matsushita Electric Housewares Manufacturing Works (Matsushita), in Osaka in 1918 with ¥100 scraped together by pawning his wife's kimono and other sources.[5] His first employees were his wife, his brother-in-law, and two associates. Konosuke used a two-room house as his office. The first product of the company was a double-cluster electric socket for two light bulbs. Like other start-ups, the beginnings of the company and its outlook were challenging and particularly daunting for Konosuke, as he lacked any formal education, special skills, or connections which he could fall back on. Yet, perseverance drove him to build the company and its reputation. What was a company of five employees in 1919 had become by the late 1920s a respectable mid-sized enterprise that was turning out electric sockets, wiring boards, and electric components.

The first acquisition: Hashimoto Denki

A major turning point for Konosuke and his company came with the Great Depression of 1929. Like many businesses of the time, Konosuke's company was hard hit with declining revenues. While Konosuke was desperately finding ways to keep his employees on the payroll, other company employees were being fired as businesses shrank their operations. Many small businesses were going under. Some of these companies and their owners sought out partners for possible mergers. One of them, the founder and owner of Hashimoto Denki (Hashimoto), a company which was manufacturing radio components, approached Konosuke through a third party with the idea of having Matsushita invest in his company or acquire it outright. The company, which was based in Akashi, was developing synthetic resins that could be used in place of kneaded grease or porcelain in making general purpose wiring boards such as were being manufactured by Matsushita. Synthetic resin was not produced by Matsushita, and although its production was still at a developmental stage, Konosuke felt that getting access to synthetic resin would be a good enough reason to purchase Hashimoto.[6]

A preliminary study of Hashimoto which Konosuke ordered indicated that the company had 100 skilled craftsmen and considerable technical skills. But the management of the company was, from Konosuke's standpoint, lax, and his conclusion was that with the worsening of the economy, left to itself for another four or five months, Hashimoto would go bankrupt. Iue Toshio, a brother-in-law of Konosuke who was one of his trusted lieutenants, argued that it would be better to wait for Hashimoto to go under, as this would give better negotiation leverage for their company. Konosuke, however, disagreed, replying that rather than wait for this to happen, which would only increase the losses of that company, acquiring Hashimoto at its current value would instead show goodwill to the management of Hashimoto.[7] As a result of Konosuke's decision to buy the company, Matsushita injected ¥100,000 into Hashimoto and made it into a public company. Along with this capital infusion, Konosuke sent Kameyama Takeo (his nephew) to be president of Hashimoto Denki. The founder of Hashimoto stayed on as a director of the management board of the company and as chief engineer.

The acquisition of Hashimoto allowed Matsushita to establish a new business segment for synthetic resin wiring boards, which led to the development and release of other electrical tools.[8] But while the end result was positive for

Matsushita, the integration process was not a smooth one. Disagreements on management policy erupted between Konosuke and the founder of Hashimoto. Konosuke later recalled in his memoirs that their management methods were basically different, with work practices that were mutually exclusive in nature. Konosuke claims that he made much effort, but to no avail, trying to convince the former owner of Hashimoto "in a sincere and truthful manner" that what he was trying to do was for the good of the company and for all of the employees at Hashimoto.

The situation according to Konosuke at one point resembled that of a time bomb waiting to explode, as the disagreements between Konosuke and the founder of Hashimoto spilled over to bad feelings among the employees and the unions towards the new owners, which almost transpired into acts of violence against Kameyama.[9]

Persistence and a firm resolve, however, paid off for Konosuke. With constant encouragement given to the employees at Hashimoto by Konosuke and his management team, and with the implementation of his reform measures, the company began to show positive signs of revival. Within six months of its acquisition, the company was able to eliminate its losses and began to show profits. The revival of Hashimoto was such that its factory became a "model factory" for Matsushita.[10] The only regret that Konosuke had was that the founder of Hashimoto did not stay on to see the eventual successful revival of the business, as he had left the company disagreeing to the end with Konosuke's management policies.[11]

I have mentioned this early episode of M&A in the history of Matsushita for several reasons. First, it was the very first time that this company undertook an M&A deal. Second, it turned out to be successful, giving Matsushita a new avenue for business and growth despite internal management disagreements and short-term instability. Third, the success of this M&A deal led to further M&A deals undertaken by Matsushita. And fourth, the methods used by Konosuke for post-merger integration served as a template for future M&A activity.

An empire that did not last: the acquisition of Kokudo Denki

While the economies of Japan and the rest of the world continued to flounder in 1930 and 1931, Matsushita was gradually expanding its business domain and revenues with the acquisition of Hashimoto. The company also entered into the radio manufacturing business through the acquisition in August 1930 of a radio manufacturing company, Kokudo Denki (Kokudo). Konosuke was thus able to get his hands on radio technology and manufacturing skills that would enable his company to enter the rapidly growing consumer radio market. Unlike the acquisition of Hashimoto, however, the acquisition of Kokudo did not achieve the results which Konosuke was looking for. Radios at the time were sold primarily through radio distributors. The products of Matsushita, on the other hand, were sold through electric appliance shops. When Matsushita began selling the products of Kokudo through his shops, dealers began to receive a large number of radios returned from irate customers complaining about defects. A close inspection by Konosuke and his team revealed that nothing had changed in terms of the management and execution of production processes or methods since the acquisition. This was not surprising, since Konosuke, as with the acquisition of Hashimoto, had left the pre-acquisition management of Kokudo intact. Instead, the problem of an increasing number of dissatisfied customers was coming from how the radios were distributed. Formerly, Kokudo had sold its radios through radio shops that were staffed by technicians who were usually versed in radio technology. Before a radio was actually delivered to a customer, the radio shop would undertake a quick quality inspection of the radio product delivered by the manufacturer, and would fine-tune and tweak the product as needed. This was necessary at the time, since most deliveries from the manufacturer to the radio shops were done by bicycles, and often the unpaved roads upon which the bicycles traveled upset the delicate structure of the radios, which consisted of vacuum tubes that were highly sensitive to any vibration. In most cases, defects were remedied and potential defects were corrected before the product was actually delivered to the customer's home (where further corrections were made by the radio shop technicians as required). The electric appliance shops which Matsushita used for distributing its products did not have such a pre-delivery inspection process, nor did they in most cases have the technical know-how to fine-tune radios even had such a process been introduced. Consequently, radios sold through Matsushita-affiliated electric appliance shops were returned in numbers not seen in the radio distributor channel. Konosuke in his memoirs relates how he debated with Kokudo's management and argued that the solution would be to aim to produce a defect-free radio. Kokudo's management responded that such a proposal would be impossible to realize and that the solution would be rather to distribute radios using radio distributor shops, as was done before acquisition. With no resolution or consensus, Konosuke instead came to an agreement with Kokudo's management to sell the company back to its owners.[12] Despite Konosuke's tolerance, which led him to keep the management of Kokudo upon its acquisition, differences of opinion in managing the business and the inability of both parties to accept each other's views led to the dissolution of this M&A deal. Interestingly, though, while Konosuke, as the new owner of Kokudo, had had the power to change Kokudo's management in view of their intransigence, this he did not do.

Without the engineers of Kokudo, it looked at first almost impossible for Matsushita to enter the radio market. Nevertheless Konosuke and his research team, led by Nakao Tetsujiro, were able to do so three months after the divestiture of Kokudo through internal research and development. The first Matsushita radio came out on the Japanese market on June 1931 and was sold at ¥40, which was expensive considering that the market price for radios at the time was between ¥25 and ¥30.[13] Amid strong complaints from dealers, who protested that the price was too high, Konosuke blasted the dumping of products by manufacturers that was going on during the deflationary depression as "an unhealthy situation." As he saw it, unless a product is sold with a "proper" profit margin put on top of the "proper" cost of the product, a company cannot be managed well, nor can industry or society develop. Selling a product at a price which did not command a level of profit that reflected its inherent value was a "sin" and went against what Konosuke called the "Way of the Merchant."[14]

Notwithstanding the complaints of dealers, and in vindication of Konosuke's strong belief in the necessity for the selling price to reflect the "proper" cost and profit margin of the product, the sets produced by Matsushita proved resilient enough to be distributed and sold through its electric appliance shops. This enabled the company to justify its relatively high price to customers and to ship out radios in large quantities, as well as to build its reputation as a manufacturer of good-value and high-quality products. Later Matsushita acquired patents developed by third parties, and in a magnanimous gesture intended to build up the industry, the company licensed them to other radio manufacturers at no cost.[15]

An acquisition makes Matsushita a battery empire: Komori Kandenchi

Bicycle lamps manufactured by Matsushita were selling well. In 1930 Matsushita was producing bicycle lamps at the rate of 100,000 units per month. Dry-cell batteries that were used in the lamps were also being sold in large numbers. Monthly production of batteries was at 500,000 pieces per month, but even this was not enough to keep up with demand.[16] Matsushita, however, was not manufacturing batteries. Instead, it was relying on an outside vendor called Okada Kojo to produce batteries for Matsushita with its "National" brand name on them. To keep up with demand, Matsushita expanded its source of batteries by contracting a battery manufacturer based in Osaka called Komori Kandenchi Seisakusho (Komori). Komori was competing with National brand batteries on the market. But Konosuke was able to persuade Komori to enter into a partnership agreement with Matsushita that would have Komori produce batteries exclusively for the National brand.

The popularity of bicycle lamps continued to be translated into ever-increasing demand for batteries. Competition for batteries was heating up, with prices falling rapidly. While urging continuous increases in production, Konosuke also pressed hard for price reductions on batteries. At one point, however, the owner of Komori began to feel trepidation as to where his company was going. In response to the latest pleadings from Konosuke for price reductions, he replied that while it would not be impossible to continue reducing prices by following Konosuke's management directions faithfully, there was the possibility that the economic depression would worsen, leading to a further intensification of competition. As he saw it, to simply increase production output and reduce the per-unit cost was a foolhardy solution. Instead, for Komori to survive and for the interest of all, Komori's owner on this occasion offered to transfer his factory and its production infrastructure lock, stock, and barrel to Konosuke. For Komori's owner, allowing his company to come under the wings of Matsushita was the best bet for survival; he openly admitted that as far as factory management went, Matsushita's methods were superior to his own. Furthermore, this move to Matsushita gave Komori's owner an opportunity to finally retire with his "face" intact.[17] Konosuke was understandably dumbstruck by this proposal, as he did not at this point have any thoughts of entering the battery business. But, having been impressed with the long-term thinking of Komori's owner, Konosuke agreed to buy his company without hesitation. On September 2, 1931, only a couple of days before Japanese forces would invade Manchuria, Matsushita acquired Komori and renamed the company Matsushita Denki Dai Hachi Kojo. As with the acquisition of Hashimoto Denki, the acquisition of Komori also turned out to be a resounding success. The dry battery business became a core business of Matsushita and by 1943, when the company was spun off as the Matsushita Kandenchi Kabushikikaisha, Matsushita had the largest market share of dry batteries in Japan.[18] Its winning streak would continue after the war with a market share exceeding 40 percent.[19]

Like the acquisition of Hashimoto, the acquisition of Komori became a template for certain procedures or principles of M&A integration that were applied in future acquisitions. One principle that Konosuke laid down with the acquisitions of Hashimoto, Kokudo, and Komori was to interfere as little as possible with the management of the acquired company and allow as much autonomy as possible. Konosuke told the employees of Komori that as no one knew more about Komori than its employees, it would be in the best interest for all parties that they should continue to manage its factories. To emphasize this point, Konosuke declared that he would not send in anybody from Matsushita to oversee the company.[20] While reassuring the Komori employees by allowing them autonomy and the continuation of their management, Konosuke also, however, made sure that the management principles espoused by him and followed by his Matsushita employees were also applied to the acquired entity, and that the new employees were treated equally and effectively as Matsushita employees. According to Konosuke, not long after the acquisition of Komori, for two hours per day for a duration of two months, he made it a rule to personally go over to the Komori facilities, view at first hand the management situation, and provide suggestions for improvement or reform where he thought necessary.[21]

The formation of Matsushita's management principles

As the example of Komori suggests, Konosuke in essence espoused an outlook of tolerance when it came to post-merger integration—but a tolerance that was tempered with defined limits. Yes, the former management and employees were allowed to continue to work, and yes, former management methods would be accepted. Good practices, technology, and know-how of the acquired entity would be emulated and cross-fertilized with other businesses and business groups. But the acquired entity at the same time was expected to follow the management principles, or the Matsushita Way of management, and make improvements to its business in accordance with the tried and proven methods of

Matsushita. It was made clear that as far as corporate culture goes, the Matsushita Way was the dominant and overriding culture that was to encompass the entire company. This may smack of intolerance, but what is essential to note from the M&A cases of Hashimoto, Komori, and Kokudo is that Konosuke did not unilaterally ram his principles down the throats of his new acquisitions. Instead, he actively and personally worked towards gaining trust, understanding, support, and acceptance of his methods.

In 1932, Konosuke formally laid down his concept of the mission of the company to his employees: "overcome poverty, relieve society from misery, and bring wealth." As he put it, Matsushita should strive to produce goods as abundantly and cheaply as tap water; when this is realized, poverty will be eradicated, happiness brought about, and a paradise on earth will be created.[22]

In 1935 Konosuke codified his management principles into five points which were later expanded to seven:[23]

Contribution to Society: To provide high-quality goods and services at reasonable prices, thereby contributing to the well-being and happiness of people throughout the world.

Fairness and Honesty: To be fair and honest in all business dealings and personal conduct, always making balanced judgments free of preconception.

Cooperation and Team Spirit: To pool abilities and strength of resolution to accomplish shared objectives in mutual trust and full recognition of individual autonomy.

Untiring Effort for Improvement: To strive constantly for improvement of corporate and personal performance even in the worst adversity, so as to fulfill the firm's mission to realize lasting peace and prosperity.

Courtesy and Humility: To always be cordial and modest and respect the rights and needs of others, thereby helping to enrich the environment and maintain social order.

Adaptability: To abide by the laws of nature and adjust thought and behavior to ever-changing conditions so as to bring about gradual but steady progress and success in all endeavors.

Gratitude: To forever be grateful for all the blessings and kindness received so as to live with peace, joy, and strength and overcome any obstacles encountered in the pursuit of true happiness.

Through such rituals as the daily recitation of the seven principles of the company laid down by Konosuke and the singing of the company song, the idea was that assimilation along with integration would be achieved through the creation of a company-wide mentality that conditioned every employee to keep their heads down, focus on the business basics, avoid wasting time on foolish publicity, and be modest.[24] If such practices such as the singing of the company song and the recitation of the seven principles smack of religious ritual, this is not surprising, given that Konosuke relates that his inspiration for setting down the company principles and of having his employees recite them daily came from his chance encounter with a fervent religious leader and his ecstatic followers in the spring of 1932.[25]

The birth of a mega-empire: Matsushita Electric Industrial Corporation (MEI)

The company continued to grow steadily in the 1930s. In order to cope with the growing size and variety of its businesses as well as to delegate the day-to-day management of operations as much as possible to his managers on account of his poor health,[26] Konosuke introduced the concept of the business division, allocating his 1,400 employees into four major business divisions. The four divisions were responsible for their respective businesses from product development to sales, and each was accountable to headquarters for the profitability of its respective business domain. Although Alfred Sloan at General Motors is usually credited with creating the concept of the autonomous business division, Konosuke's timing of introducing the division system in 1933 was close enough for him to be considered a co-inventor of the idea.[27] In 1935, Matsushita Electric Manufacturing Works became a joint stock company and was named the Matsushita Electric Industrial Co., Ltd (MEI). By this time the company had 3,500 employees and more than 600 product lines.[28] Many relatives of Konosuke were on the board of Matsushita at the time, including his brother-in-law Iue Toshio, his nephew Kameyama Takeo, the husband of his wife's sister Nakao Tetsujiro, and two of Iue's younger brothers.[29]

With the coming of full-scale war to Japan in 1937, MEI like many other companies at the time underwent an experience which was to leave a great impact on its future. The war was a time when MEI flourished as a supplier of military goods to the Japanese war machine, including such products as engines, airplanes, and ships.[30]

MEI's JV with Philips: Matsushita Denshi Kogyo

Defeat in 1945 ushered in a new era for the company. In 1952, after several years of painfully rising out of the ashes of defeat, skirting the almost total collapse of the Japanese economy, enduring the humiliation of being purged from industry, having his Matsushita Group disbanded by US occupation forces, and having his trusted brother-in-law and Matsushita board member Iue Toshio leave the company to form his own company, Sanyo Electric, Konosuke put to use his accumulated knowledge of M&A and made the audacious move of initiating a joint venture (JV) with the Dutch electronics conglomerate Philips. The result was the creation of Matsushita Denshi Kogyo (Matsushita Electron Corporation-MEC), a company which would produce TV tubes, transistors, electronic components, and semiconductors. Although the initial costs of investment for MEI was high, with the company paying to Philips an exorbitantly high percentage of technology license fees and a one-time JV fee amounting to almost half the paid-up capital of Matsushita,[31] the technology acquired through the JV enabled Konosuke to build his company into a major player in the consumer electronics market.

As with almost all JVs, the venture with Philips came to an end in 2001 as part of a comprehensive restructuring plan for the entire Matsushita Group initiated by its president Nakamura Kunio. In that year, MEI bought out Philip's share of the venture. Despite its lifespan of less than 50 years, I argue that the JV could be classified as a success. MEC contributed to the growth of the Matsushita technology base and management skills as well as to the growth of MEI's consumer electronics business, especially for lighting and TVs. Furthermore, as a wholly-owned subsidiary, MEC continues to live on within the Panasonic Group and provides proprietary technologies to the other Panasonic group companies. The JV also turned out to be a successful partnership for Philips.[32] For MEI, aside from technology, the JV allowed it to acquire management know-how from a company that had for several decades been a world-renowned multinational conglomerate. Konosuke freely admitted to using such know-how in MEI when it was possible to adapt it to a Japanese work environment.[33] During the early years of the JV, MEC sent a young engineer, Yamashita Toshihiko, to the Netherlands to study with Philips and acquire the essentials of management from them. Yamashita later became the first president of MEI that was not a relative of Konosuke's.

Konosuke's capacity for tolerance

The name of the joint venture, MEC, with the Matsushita name in it, its location (in Japan), and the nationality of its employees (almost all Japanese) suggest that the Matsushita corporate culture rather than that of Philips was dominant throughout the enterprise. Konosuke's stance, however, reveals an aspect of him that was mentioned earlier: his capacity for tolerance and acceptance of different ideas and methods, as shown in his willingness to take the management practices from Philips which were worthy of emulation and adopt them to other areas of the Matsushita group. As it was with the Mongols, Konosuke did not seem to suffer from a NIH (Not Invented Here) syndrome.

Konosuke's readiness to adopt the practices of other companies also indicates an eagerness to learn from others, a reflection of his hunger for education and knowledge coming from his lack of formal schooling. Such enthusiasm for studying the methods of others and adopting their practices also requires an attitude of respect and humility, essential qualities expected of all Matsushita's employees, as enshrined in the seven management principles of MEI as dictated by Konosuke.

The success which Matsushita had with M&A in its early history, which enabled it to expand horizontally into various new businesses as well as to achieve vertical integration of its business operations, suggests that the company, or Konosuke in particular, understood what was required to make an M&A deal successful, whether it was a Japanese or foreign company to be acquired. I argue that it was the cultural factor of tolerance that Konosuke practiced which made it possible for Matsushita to succeed with its M&A deals. In fact, Konosuke in his various writings stressed the importance of having a tolerant attitude and mindset. In his book *Sunao na kokoro ni narutame ni* ("Developing an Honest Mind") Konosuke stated that the most important factor for people in communities to achieve a better life together is to have the spirit of tolerance, which can help people appreciate the differences in each other and understand that diversity can contribute to improving society. Consequently, according to Konosuke, a person should strive to accept another person's existence and differences and make an effort to live together in harmony.[34]

In short, tolerance as understood and espoused by Konosuke allowed for the retention of the acquired company's management and the acceptance of business practices or elements of its corporate culture. This ensured a measure of long-term organizational stability, as in the acquisition cases of Hashimoto and Komori. It was this attitude of tolerance that ultimately led Konosuke to respect the differing views of Kokudo's management and to divest Kokudo instead of firing the owners and managers of the company. Equally, the spirit of tolerance which was reflected in the acceptance of new technologies and better business practices, as in the case of the JV with Philips, contributed ultimately to the growth of MEI's technological prowess as well as the strengthening of management know-how.

The acquisition of JVC: tolerance at work

Tolerance was also shown in the management of Japan Victor Corporation (JVC), a company that MEI had acquired majority ownership of in 1954. The company, which manufactured audio products, had been a wholly-owned Japanese subsidiary of the US electronics conglomerate RCA which acquired the US-based Victor Talking Machine Company, famous for its "talking machine" phonographs and its "Nipper" ("His Master's Voice") dog logo. In the pre-World War II period, JVC sold phonograph equipment in Japan. RCA's presence in Japan, however, was to come to an end in the late 1930s when ominous signs of war between Japan and the US began to appear, and RCA sold JVC to the company known today as Toshiba. After the war, as corporate finances were in bad shape due to losses incurred during the war, Toshiba decided to dump JVC and sell back its shares to RCA, who were interested in getting back at least the Nipper logo. Konosuke, who got word of the possibility of RCA re-entering the Japanese market at this point, decided to act quickly and buy the company before RCA could make any move. As he put it, if RCA returned to Japan right after the war when the country was still too weak to resist American capital or technology, "chaos" would occur and destroy the prospects of the revival of Japanese industry.[35]

Interestingly, Konosuke claims that before making his decision, he had barely seen the company or its factories.[36] Nevertheless, he was convinced of the "value" which the company had in terms of its technology and brand including its logo.[37] After acquiring the company, Konosuke sent some of his senior management to manage the company, as he felt that the level of management did not match the high level of technology that the company had.[38] He also convinced Nomura Kichisaburo to take the position of president of the company. Nomura was a singular choice as he was neither a JVC nor a Matsushita group employee; nor had he formerly been involved in the business world. Nomura was a former Imperial Japanese Navy admiral and the former ambassador to the US who was involved in the final fateful negotiations that led to Pearl Harbor. After the war he became a member of the Japanese Diet. Several people around Nomura were dead against his taking on a task for which he had no experience.[39] Nomura was reported to have said at a board meeting that he did not know who Misora Hibari (who was at the time probably the most famous and popular singer in Japan) was. For someone heading a company that also had a recording music business such a statement was, to say the least, extremely embarrassing. Konosuke admitted that normally such lack of knowledge of the industry would not be acceptable for a person who was heading a company such as JVC.[40] Konosuke, however, justified and defended his choice by claiming that a virtuous person such as Nomura could become the "spiritual pillar" for the company to rally around and rebuild itself.[41] And so, with Nomura as president and with lieutenants sent in from MEI, the company embarked upon its new life within the Matsushita group and recovered rapidly.[42]

Aside from appointing Nomura and sending in a few managers from MEI, Konosuke left the company as it was and did not erase its identity. Again, it was his tolerant view of management that left the JVC Nipper logo, the name of the company, the company song, and indeed its own management practices intact. No "Matsushita" was added to the company name. Indeed, as it was with the Mongols who held in awe the Chinese empire and preserved and adopted its culture, so it was that Konosuke had great feelings of respect for JVC as a company, which led to his policy of leaving its identity pretty much intact. Konosuke in his memoirs admitted that MEI could not equal the "greatness" of JVC and that rather than teaching JVC a thing or two about technology, the role of MEI was to support JVC in getting its management back to a "normal" state.[43]

In the long term, Konosuke's tolerance allowed JVC to take a development path separate from that of MEI and to make a name for itself as the developer of the VHS home video system, the ultimate winner in the VCR wars against the Betamax video system developed by Sony. As a result, JVC contributed a considerable amount of profit to MEI's coffers.[44] Several decades later, as part of a major corporate restructuring, Panasonic divested its majority shares in JVC.[45] But I argue that its life under the Matsushita Empire was overall a successful one. Without JVC, MEI would never have been able to compete against Sony and dominate the home video (VCR) market. History, in other words, would have been quite different had Konosuke not had the perspicacity to acquire JVC or to have managed the company as he did—that is, leaving it much alone.

Yet, in glaring contrast to the JV with Philips or most of the other early M&A that Matsushita had undertaken, the acquisition of MCA turned out to be a spectacular failure, ending in a money-losing divesture for the company five years after its acquisition. Meanwhile, as of this writing, Panasonic's arch-rival Sony is still holding on to its Hollywood studio and has even managed to attain a market-leader position as well as increase revenues. On the one hand, Onishi Ko, a former executive at MEI and the dean of the company's affiliate think tank, claims that despite the divestiture the company was able to maintain a research lab within MCA, without which the company would not have been able to develop the technical know-how that led to its taking a leading position in the co-development of the Blu-Ray High Definition video disc.[46] Onishi, in a brave attempt to put a good spin on the whole affair, is in effect suggesting that some good to came out of the acquisition, in line with Konosuke's emphasis on learning from an M&A experience. On the other hand, Nakamura Kunio, chairman of Panasonic at this writing, scoffs at the notion of seeing anything good from the acquisition of MCA, bluntly asserting that "it was a complete failure" without there being any learning experience.[47] What happened?

Intolerance at work: the acquisition of Motorola's TV division, Quasar

The M&A activity which MEI undertook from the 1920s to the early 1960s, with some rare exceptions such as the JV with Philips, all involved Japanese companies. An argument can be made that despite the different corporate cultures that were involved, there was nevertheless an underlying national culture that provided some basis for a common outlook with regard to goals (which for most Japanese at the time meant achieving economic recovery). This made it relatively easy to achieve post-merger integration.

It was not until 1974 that MEI undertook its first major acquisition of a non-Japanese enterprise, when it bought the TV manufacturing division of the US company Motorola, which produced TV sets under the brand name of Quasar. Incidentally, in the previous year, Konosuke had retired from his position of chairman due to ill health, and became an advisor to MEI.[48] Takahashi Kotaro, a trusted advisor of Konosuke for many years, became chairman, while Konosuke's adopted son-in-law, Matsushita Masaharu, remained at the helm as president of the company.

Motorola, which produced transistors and electronic equipment, had been manufacturing transistorized color TV sets with the Quasar brand since 1967. In hopes of expanding its presence in the US TV market by having a manufacturing facility in the US (its arch-rival Sony, after all, had had its own TV plant in San

Diego since 1971), MEI purchased Motorola's TV division and incorporated it as Quasar Electronics Inc., a wholly-owned subsidiary of MEI.

For several years MEI continued to produce TV sets with the Quasar brand. Under MEI stewardship, however, sets that were manufactured in the US by Quasar were increasingly being built out of components sourced from Japan, with the result that the quality of the products noticeably improved. Quasar engineers were quick to admit this improvement and were reportedly amazed by the fall in the repair rate of their TV sets.[49]

While the "rescue" and "revival" of Quasar under MEI was celebrated in the US media, grumblings and voices of discontent from the American employees that later became public, culminating in a discrimination lawsuit against Quasar and MEI, suggest that the integration process did not proceed as successfully as it had in the MEI's previous M&A ventures.[50] For one thing, what was in essence a US TV manufacturer became instead a sales and marketing company for MEI-engineered products that were assembled in the US and sold under the Quasar brand. As Trevor Reisz, a former manager with Quasar, stated in a documentary on MEI produced by the US public broadcasting station PBS and aired on its *Frontline* program, Quasar under MEI became a company that did not do engineering. Instead, all the company did was to assemble parts and key components from Japan and put them into TV cabinets. For Reisz, Quasar became a distributor with a final assembly operation.[51] Not surprisingly, talented people and those with technical skills began to leave the company after MEI's takeover; a sign perhaps that the colonial subjects of MEI became demotivated or disillusioned.[52]

On another front where it seemed that post-merger integration was not going smoothly, Almon Clegg, a former general manager of Quasar, recalled seeing a situation where there were two organizations within the company, one Japanese and the other American, with virtually no communication between them. According to Clegg, who was interviewed for *Frontline*, the Japanese had their "own little cultures and their own little thing going on" and one could "walk across the hall for example and it was just as though it was a different company."[53] Jerome Hellmann, another former Quasar manager, mentioned that in meetings with both Japanese and American staff present, the language used in the conversation would suddenly become Japanese, with the Japanese discussing back and forth among themselves, presumably about what he had just been saying.[54]

Not only was there a feeling of a lack of communication between the Americans and their Japanese masters, but there was also a sense among the American Quasar employees that they were not truly accepted by MEI. Reisz recalled with bitterness that even though a number of the Americans had tried to really learn the "rules of the game" and become a part of the "family," it felt as though "it was Japan's goals to make sure we didn't know the rules of the games, so that we could not become part of the family ... and we would constantly be kept outside."[55] If true, this is indeed a startling contrast to previous M&A activity, where as we noted Konosuke worked intently to gain the support for his management methods by actively teaching his newly acquired employees the "rules of the game." In the beginning of the new relationship with MEI, Reisz relates that he would often sit with his new Japanese colleagues in the company cafeteria at lunch time until one day he was told by a Japanese colleague that it would be better for him to sit with his American compatriots. Upon inquiring why he should do this, Reisz says that he was told that the Japanese were discussing things relating to Japan and that he was not part of it.[56] Reisz further mentions a certain Japanese co-worker from MEI who seemed to get along with the Americans to the extent that Reisz struck up a friendship and got to know him well through their common interest of tennis. One day, according to Reisz, the Japanese disappeared from various get-togethers with other Americans. After some period, Reisz called him up inquiring what had happened. The Japanese replied to the effect that he was "becoming too American." When Reisz responded wasn't that the intention while he was in the US, the Japanese answered, yes, but only up to a certain point.[57]

In May 1986, a major restructuring took place at Quasar during which a considerable number of people were laid off. With a recession going on in the US economy, two factories and the company's engineering staff were phased out. According to Reisz and Hellmann, all the people that were fired were American employees, including three-quarters of the American managers of the company. Not a single Japanese employee left the company.[58] For those American managers that remained, their salaries were frozen, while the Japanese managers sent from MEI received increases in pay.[59] It is not hard to imagine that it must have been quite a shock to those Americans who were familiar with MEI's past history and its efforts in keeping its workforce intact, even in times of economic depression, to find themselves all of a sudden out of work.

One could perhaps argue in defense of MEI that Konosuke's proclivity to respect or tolerate the traditions or culture of an acquired company was manifested in the acquisition of Motorola's TV division, as MEI continued to market the Quasar brand name and did not force the use of the Matsushita brand on the new subsidiary. Considering the past efforts that MEI had made to respect the integrity and practices of an acquired company's management and workforce and to treat them essentially as the equals of all other MEI employees, however, the above statements from the American employees of Quasar suggest that the Quasar acquisition stands as a glaring counterexample of an integration process that did not have the factor of tolerance at work. One could argue that had MEI shown more tolerance, it might have allowed them to develop a spirit of solidarity between the Japanese and Americans instead of creating a sense of separateness between the two managements. Tolerance might have allowed the Japanese to treat the Americans as true equals, which would have led to a more fair restructuring program instead of having only American managers and employees fired or their wages frozen. The practice of tolerance might also have led to the opening of advancement opportunities for American Quasar employees within MEI itself. This would have worked towards creating a feeling of belonging to a larger Matsushita family group of companies; instead, a lawsuit was brought by laid-off American workers against the company.[60] Whether having more tolerance would have worked to improve the performance of this M&A arrangement is difficult to say. But it certainly would not have hurt to have had better interaction between the Japanese and American sides. This might have led to more workplace solidarity which would have worked to the benefit of MEI. MEI could have also learned from Quasar, as it had from other partners in the past, had it not consciously held back from becoming "too American."

A counterpoint to the intolerance at Quasar: the acquisition of
Nakagawa Kikai

Aside from the successful M&A examples of Hashimoto, Komori, MEC, and JVC mentioned earlier, another contrasting counterpoint to what happened with Quasar and the conspicuous lack of tolerance shown during its integration with MEI is the acquisition of Nakagawa Kikai by MEI in 1952. Founded by Naka-gawa Yasuharu in 1939, the company began producing refrigeration equipment for US occupation forces after World War II. Not long after it started manufac-turing refrigerators, Nakagawa approached Konosuke offering to sell his company to MEI. Aside from being impressed by the enthusiasm of Nakagawa after meeting with him for the first time, Konosuke relates that what was most memorable was Nakagawa's complete willingness to submit to the authority of Konosuke without any conditions. For Konosuke such total submission con-vinced him that Nakagawa could act decisively and made him intuitively con-vinced that he could work with Nakagawa.[61] Without even looking at Nakagawa's facility, Konosuke immediately bought up Nakagawa Kikai and renamed the company Nakagawa Denki (Electric). The company was to produce refrigerators for MEI and allow MEI to become a major player in the new refrig-erator market, which was to grow rapidly in the postwar recovery years. Later the company was completely absorbed into the Matsushita group and was renamed Matsushita Reiki Kabushiki Kaisha. For Nakagawa, the reward for his submission to the management of MEI and his willingness to learn from them, as well as the contributions he was making to MEI, was to be promoted to vice president of MEI. Nakagawa was now responsible along with other MEI execu-tives for overseeing not just his own company, but the entire Matsushita group. Konosuke treated an outsider as an equal with someone from MEI and judged him on the basis of his achievements rather than his origin. Without knowing it, Konosuke followed the practice of Genghis Khan, who selected his generals on the basis of their ability and achievements and not their origin.

This show of tolerance for outsiders as seen in the case of the acquisition of Nakagawa failed to repeat itself in the case of Quasar. Even though the company submitted itself to the management and manufacturing methods of MEI, and even while its American employees were willing to learn from the Japanese, the treatment which the American employees received made them feel that they were not truly accepted within the Matsushita family. Not a single American Quasar employee was ever promoted within MEI as Nakagawa was. A major change in situation was that by the time Quasar was acquired, Konosuke was already in semi-retirement and no longer managing the day-to-day affairs of the company. Perhaps the principles of tolerance, especially with regard to respecting diversity, that Konosuke espoused did not fully permeate throughout the company. Then again, it could have been simply the case that the management of MEI believed that while implanting the MEI culture onto a Japanese company was not that difficult given that the Japanese employees of both companies grew up in the same national culture, the cultural gap between Japanese and American employees was simply too great for the MEI culture to be understood, let alone accepted, by the Americans. After all, how could the Americans, who had been taught from an early age at school to actively promote and talk about themselves in front of other people through classroom activities such as "Show and Tell," ever be able to relate to the precepts of Konosuke, exhorting one to keep their head down and be modest, which is also considered by many Japanese as a cultural virtue of the Japanese people?[62]

Thirty years after its acquisition, Quasar ceased to exist as a company within the Matsushita group. The brand is no longer used by the company. Interestingly, after the Quasar acquisition there were no further major overseas acquisitions undertaken by MEI until the MCA deal. Perhaps this was an indication that MEI realized the difficulty of integrating non-Japanese companies and was wary of further global M&A. This also suggests in retrospect that MEI should have made more effort to learn how to work with a company and its employees who came from a different national culture. MEI may have had the know-how and factor of tolerance for the post-integration process with Japanese companies, but as the Quasar example suggests, it seems that the MEI employees lacked the tolerance to accept the Americans as equals, and instead considered them inferior subordinates not worthy of being fully accepted in the Matsushita family. When we go on to look into the case of MEI's relationship with MCA, I will argue that it was this factor of intolerance that led to its disruption and ultimate demise.

MEI plunges into Hollywood

The seeds that sprouted into MEI's acquisition of MCA were planted at an early stage, before the top executives of the two companies actually met. Michael Ovitz was a Hollywood-based talent agent who owned the Creative Artists Agency (CAA), a major Hollywood company that represented some of the top movie stars and studio executives including Steven Spielberg, Sylvester Stallone, Madonna, and Barbra Streisand. A UCLA pre-med graduate, Ovitz started his career as a mail boy at the talent and literary representative firm the William Morris Agency, working himself up in the company for several years before founding CAA.[63] Ovitz was not a filmmaker himself, but through his agency he packaged several deals including the actors, directors, and writers he represented for making films such as *GoodFellas*, starring Robert De Niro and directed by Martin Scorsese.[64]

The 43-year-old Ovitz was not only known for brokering movie deals for his illustrious clients. In 1989 he made a name for himself as a skillful deal-maker who helped to realize Sony's acquisition of Columbia Pictures. This likely caught the attention of MEI, for in the autumn of 1989, MEI approached Ovitz and CAA with the proposal of buying a major Hollywood studio.[65] Accordingly, Ovitz made a study of the US entertainment industry for MEI and identified MCA, the parent company of Universal Studios, as a possible target. He discouraged MEI from going after the film entertainment company Paramount Communications or the movie studio Orion Pictures; the latter by that time was almost bankrupt.[66]

The drivers behind the acquisition

Coming on the heels of Sony's acquisition of Columbia, there was speculation that MEI was also looking for a library of films and TV entertainment to augment the sales of its consumer electronics products and to prepare for the advent of High Definition (HD) television broadcasting, with the view that having content would be an integral part of providing home entertainment systems that included electronic hardware and software.[67] There was also the view within MEI that having a movie studio would enable the company to compete effectively on several fronts against Sony in the upcoming HD age. Indeed, one MEI executive stated bluntly that if MEI only concentrated on providing electronic hardware, the company would lose out to Sony.[68]

In addition to gaining valuable entertainment assets to battle against Sony, the senior management of MEI also viewed the acquisition of a movie studio as a means to change the culture at MEI. For several years prior to MEI's acquisition of MCA in 1990, the company was perceived by industry watchers to be losing its mojo, as it failed to produce any hit products even while operating profit margins averaged close to 7 percent.[69] This was not to say that internally the company was standing still. Indeed, since 1983 when Yamashita Toshihiko, who was not related to the Matsushita family, was directly appointed by Konosuke as president of the company, MEI had taken steps to restructure the company. This included such measures as shifting internal resources away from the home electronics business to the rapidly growing information-communications and semiconductor businesses. Such shifting of resources naturally entailed a shift in the centers of power within the company, which in this case meant a weakening of the hold of Konosuke over his company. Yamashita retired some of the key right-hand people who had supported Konosuke over the decades, and replaced them with people who were home-bred professionals in their respective fields. Konosuke was reported to have been displeased with the changes that Yamashita effected.[70] Throughout his tenure, Yamashita was resisting pressure from Konosuke and the chairman Masaharu, the adopted son-in-law of Konosuke, to have Konosuke's grandson Masayuki appointed a member of the board. Eventually, however, Yamashita succumbed and approved Masayuki's appointment. Yamashita was reported to have been bitter about this; after Masayuki was appointed,

Yamashita had let it be known publicly that he felt that it was too early for Masayuki, who was 41 years of age to become a member of the board.[71] Yamashita's opposition to the appointment of Masayuki perhaps also stemmed from what he perceived to be a culture of nepotism growing within MEI. Several years later, when Masayuki became executive vice president of the company (1997), Yamashita, who by this time was an advisor to the company, blurted out, at a party attended by reporters and executives from other companies, that MEI could not be considered to be in a good state when a person (Masayuki) is selected vice president of the company just because he happens to be the grandson of the founder, Konosuke. Yamashita railed further against the company, noting that 80 percent of the board members were the "henchmen" of the chairman, Masaharu, and that despite this "absurd" situation, the younger the generation of the employees, the less criticism he found to exist against such nepotism.[72] This outburst from Yamashita, highly unusual for a Japanese businessman who would normally be reluctant to publicly hang out any of his company's dirty linen, is worth noting as he implies that at the very top of MEI, people (including Morishita Yoichi, who when Yamashita made this statement had been president of MEI) were now being promoted based not on ability but on how close they were with the founder Konosuke and his family members.

In retrospect, it was perhaps a sign of defiance against nepotism that in 1986 Yamashita nominated Tanii Akio as the next president of MEI. Tanii had entered MEI in 1956 after working several years at two companies unrelated to MEI. Tanii was not one of the full-blooded MEI employees who had entered the company right after leaving school. He was not even a university graduate, having graduated from a machinery trade school. What was also unusual for a Japanese "salaryman" was that Tanii did not drink.[73] Tanii caught the eye of Yamashita by successfully leading the company's efforts in developing the VHS home video system.[74] As the successor to Yamashita, Tanii further accelerated the restructuring efforts of his predecessor. This included the creation of horizontal function platforms that worked across the various business divisions, which were essentially vertical silos with little interaction with each other. A restructuring and reorganization of the business divisions established by Konosuke was undertaken, resulting in the creation of "Operations Groups" that were now given the prerogative of freely using internal capital for growing their respective businesses.[75] Tanii also saw to it that the number of layers of management was reduced and the powers of authority were devolved to lower levels to improve operational performance and management efficiency. In 1990, to further strengthen his management support team, Tanii appointed Mizuno Hiroyuki as senior managing director to oversee the semiconductor business and Murase Tsuzo as vice president to oversee the rest of the manufacturing. Along with vice president Sakuma Shoji in charge of sales and Hirata Masahiko, director and vice president in charge of accounting and control, the four formed a senior management board that deliberated on corporate strategic issues. One issue was the proposal to acquire MCA, which according to Tanii was brought to the attention of the board "by a third party" (i.e., Ovitz) right after its establishment.[76]

Tanii also kicked off a company-wide campaign which he called "Break Through" in 1990. The campaign was to encourage initiatives for "breaking the shell" of the current business structure of the company and creating new businesses. As Tanii explained in an interview with the Japanese business magazine *Nikkei Business*, achieving "Break Through" didn't just mean breaking the shell of existing businesses and structures; it also implied creating something new.[77] All of the slogans that MEI had dangled in front of its employees to rev them up in the past were in Japanese, but for the first time, alphabetical letters were used, perhaps intended as a symbolic "breakthrough" from past practice.[78]

Despite the reforms, restructuring program, and the exhortations to "break through," MEI's business performance remained lackluster, with the lowest revenue and profit growth rates among all the major electronics manufacturers, including Sony and Toshiba, between 1985 and 1990. By 1990 MEI's profit margins had declined to almost half the level of 1984. Accordingly, there was a widely held view both within and outside of the company that MEI was not doing enough to change itself, and Tanii in particular was perceived as being too concerned about others and not decisive enough.[79]

Nevertheless, Tanii and his team persevered in 1991 with their "Break Through" campaign, and when the proposal to acquire MCA came up, they saw this as an opportunity to achieve a real breakthrough in changing not only the business structure of the company, by expanding its focus from "monozukuri" (making products) to other new businesses of the coming "multimedia age," but also its culture, which was beginning to be seen both inside and outside the company as a major impediment to radical change.[80] According to Sakuma, Tanii viewed the acquisition of MCA as an opportunity to further boost the changes that were being made to the corporate culture of MEI.[81] Tanii stressed that aside from getting access to software for the multimedia age, he wanted to "change the corporate culture of MEI through its interaction with a different culture."[82] Or perhaps to put Tanii's remark in another way, the acquisition of MCA would be the "gaiatsu" (outside pressure) which the Japanese were fond of using (especially politicians and bureaucrats for going around the "teikoseiryoku," or the entrenched powers of opposition) in order to make radical changes to the corporate culture of MEI.

But what was it exactly in MEI's culture that people such as Tanii wanted to change? Under the leadership of Konosuke, who for all practical purposes was an absolute ruler, all employees of MEI were to act without question upon his orders. The individuality of the MEI employee was subsumed into the larger collective of MEI workers, which to Konosuke became the primal competitive advantage of the company. And indeed this stress on group action as opposed to emphasizing individual initiative was enforced and inculcated through several rituals. All employees of MEI began their work day with the daily singing of the company song and the recitation of Konosuke's seven principles. The company song was broadcasted through intercoms at noon and in the evening. All employees wore the same company uniform, which changed color with the passing of Fall and Spring. One employee admitted that what they did in terms of these rituals was no different from that being practiced by believers of a religion.[83] When I asked another Panasonic employee if all the employees actually sung or just mouthed the words of the company song every morning, he replied that "we all sing. But sometimes I have to admit that I forget the words or mix up the verses." He also added that, "I have been working for Matsushita since graduating from college. Singing the company song every morning and reciting Konosuke's seven principles was something which I took for granted and did not seem strange to me at all."[84] A former MEI employee stated that everyone in the company was to share the same values and same way of thinking, which included being adept at avoiding and minimizing risk.[85] Konosuke eschewed flamboyance and promoted modesty. Indeed, in my own official interactions with employees of MEI/Panasonic, if there is one word I would use to describe their behavior it is that of a pleasant humbleness or low posture. When I pointed out to a friend from MEI what I noticed as the general behavior of MEI employees, he concurred with my observation, adding that this was due to the fact that the employees of Matsushita were taught to be "merchants" in the service of the customer.[86] The company was also known to be frugal to a fault. It was perhaps this corporate culture, emphasizing modesty, frugality, and group action over individual initiative, that led to the company's being more of an imitator, especially of its arch-rival Sony, rather than a creator or pioneer. Indeed, the way that the company competed with its rivals was in keeping with Konosuke's view that if someone had a good idea, then one should go ahead and use it and improve upon it. That way engineering and development risks would be kept to a minimum. While the people at Sony sometimes looked down upon this tendency of Matsushita to copy the efforts of Sony, and derisively called the company "Maneshita Denki" (a play on the company name Matsushita Denki with the unflattering meaning of Copycat Electric Company), the low-risk approach of Konosuke nevertheless helped MEI to successfully grow over the decades and become one of the largest conglomerates in the world.

It was clear to Tanii that to literally achieve the "Break Through" at MEI would require a changing of the Konosuke-Japan-based corporate culture as described so that a new type of Matsushita-Man (and woman) could be created. In an interview with *Nikkei Business*, Tanii admitted that there existed a general view that MEI had a mono-culture which was due to the strong impressions left by the founder and the prevalence of employees who were "kintaro-ame" (a Japanese expression that is used to describe the similarity of people in their looks, thoughts and behavior; "kintaro-ame" is the actual name of sweet pieces of candy cut out from the same dough which are of the same size and in the shape of a small man, i.e., "kintaro"). But, as he saw it, "in this day and age of diversity and internationalization, the company had to be transformed into a company of individuals."[87] Tanii stressed that with this "Break Through" initiative the corporate image of the company must change considerably in five to 10 years. Tanii in essence suggested that a new culture that placed more emphasis on individualism rather than the power of the collective had to be created so that MEI would be able to deal with the dawn of a new age that would require people to think boldly beyond the confines of a Japan-based mentality. MEI was no longer to be a company that produced "kintaro-ame" employees who all behaved and thought alike as Konosuke wanted them to, i.e. always inquiring what top management had to say and behaving passively.[88] No longer, to use a Japanese expression, was the nail that stood out to be hammered in. Instead, the new MEI was to have a dynamic corporate culture that would allow employees to fully stress their respective spirit of individualism and let, to paraphrase Chairman Mao Zedong, creativity bloom. As the *Nikkei Business* observed, the management principles of Konosuke were to be completely disavowed.[89]

What would Konosuke, had he been alive, have made of this opportunity to acquire MCA? One executive of Panasonic stated that if the founder had still been around he would not have made such an acquisition, as the entertainment business field was simply too different from what he was used to.[90] Sakuma, however, believed otherwise. For him, Konosuke was a radical person, and had he listened to the pros and cons of buying MCA, Sakuma is convinced that he would have agreed to the acquisition.[91]

While MEI was thinking up reasons to justify its purchase of MCA, the movie studio on the other hand was not doing well in its movie business. It also had some mishaps, such as the disastrous opening of its studio tour in Orlando, Florida, in 1989 and a failed investment in a Toronto-based theater chain.[92] To resuscitate its movie business, which had not had a major hit since *Jaws*, and to recoup its failed investments, MCA's chairman and president, Lew Wasserman and Sidney Sheinberg, began to consider the possibilities of partnering with a stable and large source of financing that would provide MCA with the capital to expand its business, possibly through acquisitions of record companies, TV networks, and investments in entertainment theme parks. In this respect, there was some strategic fit between MCA and MEI.

The deal

Expanding and diversifying its business through M&A was not a new endeavor for MCA. Indeed, MCA, which was founded in Chicago in 1924 as a booking agency for touring musical bands, became a movie entertainment company through its acquisition of Universal Studios in 1962 when it purchased its parent Decca Records (which had acquired Universal Studios in 1951). After that acquisition the company spent cautiously for some time, but then from 1987 MCA went on a major spending spree on investments and acquisitions, dishing out approximately US$650 million in stock and cash for investments in toy companies, music companies, a television station, and a theater chain.[93] MCA also explored the possibility of a merger with Paramount Communications, but talks did not proceed well and ultimately collapsed due to the clashing egos and the reportedly abrasive personalities of MCA chairman Lew Wasserman and Paramount chairman Martin Davis.[94]

When Ovitz heard of the collapse of talks between MCA and Paramount, he decided to act upon the recommendation he had given to MEI and informed

Felix Rohatyn, of the financial services firm Lazard Freres and Company, of MEI's interest in buying a Hollywood studio. Rohatyn also happened to be a board member of MCA (since 1979) and its financial advisor.[95] Ovitz also contacted Robert Strauss, another MCA board member who represented MEI as a lobbyist in Washington DC. A concern of Ovitz was the possibility of legal repercussions that might result from MEI's acquisition of MCA, and of political backlash on the heels of Sony's earlier purchase of Columbia Pictures, which whipped up a storm of controversy in the US media. Ovitz hoped that with Strauss's legal skills and connections in Washington, he would be able to steer the deal away from any political or legal mishaps.

While Ovitz way laying the groundwork for negotiations between MEI and MCA, the shots on the MEI side at its Osaka headquarters were being called by Matsushita Masaharu, the adopted son of the founder Matsushita Konosuke and chairman of the company. Although Tanii Akio was the president and CEO, the decision to go ahead with the acquisition was Masaharu's.[96] According to *Nikkei Business*, at an annual management conference that was held on January 10, 1991 at the company's gymnasium located in Osaka, Masaharu gave his assembled executives and employees an account of how the idea of buying a movie company came from a "third party." He then mentioned that after deciding to make this flying leap into the movie business he turned around to see that no one was following him, a statement that perhaps emphasized the point that the decision to buy MCA was his and his alone.[97] A senior manager of MEI after hearing the speech was reported to remark that MEI was going to be taking on an enormous risk, and that given the circumstances it was difficult to tell if people were more excited or scared. Other employees were reported to have been mystified as to the exact reasons for the undertaking.[98]

Be that as it may, Tanii, being the good corporate soldier that he was, now had to ensure that the acquisition of MCA would be a success and without trouble. Not knowing anyone in Hollywood and not being a competent speaker of the English language who could deal with the fast-talking executives of the movie studios, Tanii decided to meet with his compatriot Ohga Norio, the president of Sony and the executor of the company's acquisition of Columbia Pictures, to get some ideas on what it meant to own a Hollywood studio and what preparation he needed. To one that might soon become a rival in the field of entertainment, Ohga was understandably reticent about giving any specific advice on how to survive in the industry.[99] In an interview with the *New York Times* Ohga commented that Tanii-san, being such a gentleman, was probably going to require some time to acclimatize himself to a wholly different world that he didn't know about yet.[100]

Tanii could have talked with Ovitz or his soon-to-be partners at MCA in order to better understand what his company was getting into. But Ovitz on his part kept both parties away from each other during the negotiation process, which was said to be a reflection of his negotiation style.[101] At the same time, Ovitz used the services of Strauss as a back-door channel at crucial moments.[102] Tanii consequently did not attend any of the negotiations that were carried out between the two parties in New York.[103]

After several weeks of negotiations conducted through Ovitz and some haggling over the purchase price between Wasserman and MEI, which was eventually resolved thanks to the back door mediation of Strauss, MEI made their tender offer to the owners of MCA, over the US Thanksgiving weekend of 1990, of US$66 per share plus an equity stake in MCA's New York City TV station WWOR, which was worth US$5 a share, making the total acquisition cost for MCA US$6.59 billion.[104] MEI also proposed to shoulder MCA's debt of US$1.36 billion.[105] On December 29, 1990, MEI's tender offer was officially accepted by MCA's owners. MCA as an independent company had ceased to exist. At the time it was the biggest acquisition undertaken by any Japanese company, dwarfing even Sony's earlier purchase of Columbia for US$3.4 billion. The heads of MCA, Wasserman and Sheinberg, were rich before the acquisition but became more so afterwards. They later may have had much to grumble, whine, and complain about concerning life under their Japanese masters, but certainly from a financial standpoint they had little cause for self-pity. According to the *New York Times*, Lew Wasserman signed a new five-year contract with his Japanese masters that included a US$3 million annual salary, considerably more than what Tanii was getting as president of MEI. Wasserman also exchanged his 4.95 million shares of common stock in MCA for tax-free preferred shares with a face value of US$327 million. The shares, while redeemable for several years, were reported to pay annual tax-free dividends of US$28.6 million, at a rate of 8.75 percent.[106] Like Wasserman, Sheinberg also signed a five-year contract with his new masters, his annual salary being US$8.6 million. Sheinberg was reported to have at least 1.293 million shares of stock in MCA, which were valued at US$71 per share or US$66 in cash, plus a share of stock in WWOR TV. The buyout of Sheinberg's shares netted him US$91 million.[107] Like Wasserman, Sheinberg was also offered by MEI the opportunity to exchange his shares for preferred shares of MEI, but he turned down the offer, preferring to receive his money from the share buyout immediately.[108]

Wasserman and Sheinberg were not the only ones to make a hefty amount of money. The investment bankers representing MCA and MEI respectively collected fees for their services amounting to over US$20 million: Felix Rohatyn was able to earn US$16.75 million for Lazard Freres and Company, which represented MCA, and Allen and Company received US$8 million for representing MEI. The Washington law firm of Akin, Gump, Strauss, Hauer and Feld received US$8 million for its legal services to MCA.[109] As for Ovitz, who played a major role in getting the bargaining parties together, his company was reported by the *New York Times* not to have received any fees, as it was presumed that CAA was not a formal financial advisor to any of the parties in the transaction.[110] But according to another source, Ovitz earned US$40 million for his services.[111]

For MEI, which had no experience in running a Hollywood studio, the most important aspect of this acquisition was the retaining of Wasserman and Sheinberg as the heads of MCA. Wasserman had created MCA and with Sheinberg had been at the helm of Universal for several decades, which made them the longest-serving heads of any major movie studio in Hollywood. The two of them would have been irreplaceable for MEI, which had no connections in the Hollywood community and no knowledge of possible replacements. Early on in the negotiation process, MEI in a show of good faith made it clear that they were not interested in buying MCA without Wasserman and Sheinberg.[112] Accordingly, it was MEI through Ovitz that actually invited the two executives to name their salaries, to which MEI readily agreed.[113] MEI extended the contracts of both Wasserman and Sheinberg with the added proviso that in case Wasserman was no longer Chairman, Sheinberg would assume that role. For MEI, it was already apparent that the successor to Wasserman would be Sheinberg.[114] MEI also magnanimously announced that as for overall management within MCA, those MCA board members who wished to remain in their positions could do so, but in keeping with its position as the new owner, the company added that it would be sending in a sufficient number of board members to ensure that it was in the majority.[115]

In late November of 1990, Tanii held a press conference announcing MEI's intent to acquire MCA. After releasing details of the deal, Tanii was asked by a reporter whether his company would be willing to make a World War II movie that was critical of the Japanese Emperor Hirohito (posthumously Emperor Showa). Tanii, taken by surprise by this question, replied awkwardly that he could never imagine such a case, and so never expected to hear such a question. Tanii was clearly uncomfortable. He continued on, however, saying that as MEI's cooperation with MCA was part of a broader Japan-US cooperative framework, no such movie, he believed, would ever be produced.[116] Tanii's comment rang alarm bells among the detractors of Japanese investment, raising the fear that the Japanese were intent upon interfering with the creative aspects of American culture. Fearing a possible backlash just after the negative reporting of Sony's acquisition of Columbia Pictures, MEI issued a statement saying that both MEI and MCA were committed to maintaining the creative independence of the latter and aimed to "produce great works of entertainment" in a stable environment.[117] Just to be sure that MEI's position was fully understood, Tanii later issued a personal statement saying that MEI had no intention of becoming involved in decisions regarding the subject or content of creative products at MCA and that doing so would simply be "inconsistent with sound business practices."[118]

Despite this reassurance given to the American public that MEI would respect the creative integrity of MCA, MEI stumbled badly at the opening gate. Tanii's comment to the press was in stark contrast to those of Morita Akio, co-founder of Sony, who in reply to the same question posed to Tanii responded immediately and unequivocally by saying that Sony would not interfere if its newly acquired movie studio made such a movie criticizing Hirohito, but added that he could not vouch that Japanese distributors would touch the film for distribution in Japan.[119] Whatever the reasons there may have been for the different responses and for better or for worse, MEI's adventure in Hollywood had begun.

MEI the conqueror and MCA the conquered

A low-key start

For most of the first year (1991) at MCA after its acquisition by MEI, life continued pretty much as it had before, with the company remaining the conservatively run kingdom of Wasserman and Sheinberg. Unlike at MEI, where all company employees from the chairman of the company down to the floor employee wore the same ordinary-looking company uniform, old men in dark suits called the shots in the headquarters building of MCA known as the Black Tower, while younger movie-makers dressed in sweatshirts ran around the studio lot attending to the creative side of the movie business.[120] Eventually, however, after the acquisition, the conservative dress code of MCA headquarters gave way to a more casual look, with an increasing number of staff coming to the office in Paisley ties and blazers. Wasserman himself was seen on a Saturday at a labor union negotiation wearing a red sport coat, while Sheinberg once appeared at the office wearing a kimono, which was his lighthearted way of showing respect to his Japanese overlords.[121]

It was not only the dress code at MCA that changed after the acquisition, but also the atmosphere of the workplace. In the early months under MEI, Sheinberg's management team of two dozen senior executives who were responsible for running the day-to-day operations described the place as "actually fun to go to work" for the first time in many years, and described the mood as "collegial."[122] Even Sheinberg himself seemed to have been infected by some new feeling of exuberance. It was reported that each afternoon when going into his office, Sheinberg would peer out and howl like a wolf like some mischievous teenager.[123] All in all, it would seem that MCA genuinely welcomed its takeover by a Japanese company, but then again this would not have been surprising considering how much money Wasserman and Sheinberg had made from being acquired by MEI.

Since the acquisition, the top officers of both companies had met each other only four times.[124] The first face-to-face meeting between Tanii and Wasserman did not in fact happen until January 15, 1991, almost two months after the acquisition of MCA was announced. Interestingly, before this meeting, the first stop the MEI executives made on that day in Hollywood was the CAA office to pay their respects to Ovitz. Later, the executives moved on to Universal City, where they received a VIP studio tour.[125] On the evening of the same day, Tanii had dinner with Wasserman at his Beverly Hills home. According to an account given by executives who were given an after-dinner briefing from Wasserman and Sheinberg, Tanii had told them that MCA was to continue its operations as it had always, "independently and expansively."[126] It is not difficult to imagine that the management of MCA was relieved to hear this.

To help facilitate the mutual learning and integration process, a 25-year veteran of MEI's legal department, Uede Atsuro, was sent over to MCA, where he had an office in MCA's Black Tower building. Uede had the title of "MCA

Liaison" and was expected by MCA to "get the right people" from the studio and the parent company to talk together.[127] Aside from attending some management meetings, his functions were never clearly defined.[128] His command of the English language and his position in the legal department, however, suggest that aside from learning from MCA, another task was to listen in and keep an eye on MCA's management.

Contrary to the initial fears of some MCA executives and in contrast to what was then happening at Columbia Pictures, where Sony was actively revamping and recreating the studio's image more in line with Sony's exuberant image and renaming the company Sony Pictures Entertainment, MEI was playing it low-key—for the moment. In other more subtle ways, however, MEI pushed for its presence in the studio facilities during the first couple of months. A suggestion box was set up by MEI where employees could directly send their views and opinions to senior management, something which MEI had been doing on their facilities for several decades. Sending a complaint or suggestion to Wasserman and Sheinberg, however, was something that the MCA employees would have found intimidating, given the short temper that Sheinberg in particular was famous for.[129] MEI also began to circulate its global newsletter to the MCA facilities, which kept members of the Matsushita group informed on latest product information as well as introducing the MCA employees to the writings and corporate philosophies of Konosuke.

But apart from the introduction of the suggestion box and the distribution of the company newsletter, other cultural trappings of Matsushita were not introduced. Neither the Matsushita company song nor Konosuke's seven management principles were sung or recited by the MCA employees each morning. MCA company spokeswoman Christine Hanson said to the press that Matsushita was not involved in the day-to-day creative aspects of running MCA.[130] A top Hollywood executive who frequently lunched with Wasserman and Sheinberg on the MCA/Universal lot concurred, saying, "Nothing has changed, not even the menu at the commissary."[131] Sheinberg himself was satisfied with his new Japanese masters, who were keeping themselves unobtrusive. He said, "I find no fault with this relationship at all. And I'm too old and too rich to lie to anybody."[132] Indeed, Tanii himself admitted that MEI was intentionally keeping a low profile, saying that the management of MCA was to be left "to the experts."[133] He added, "Wasserman's philosophy is close to our own, so we are very friendly towards each other."[134] Tanii's comments reinforced the view at MCA that MEI was not going to meddle in the affairs of movie-making. Studio chief Tom Pollock commented, "It's our understanding that what Matsushita wishes is for all executives at MCA to use their best judgment as to how to run a software company."[135] For the first couple of months at MCA after the acquisition, the new Japanese masters of MCA were keeping out of the hair of Wasserman and Sheinberg. But this blissful honeymoon period was not to last forever.

Rumblings of discontent

In December of 1991, MEI rejected a proposal from Sheinberg to bid for the record company Virgin Records (Virgin), best known as the label of the British rock group the Rolling Stones, for US$600 million. Going after Virgin was in Sheinberg's view a means to further expand MCA's music business, which had already acquired the recording companies ABC, Infinity, Motown, and Geffen Records.[136] Sheinberg and his executives had been preparing for several months for this acquisition, and its rejection by MEI was a disappointing blow to the MCA executives. David Geffen, who was head of Geffen Records and had sold his record company to MCA before the acquisition by MEI, commented bitterly that "If Matsushita is not helping us become bigger and better, then likely I'm not going to continue because I am interested only in winning."[137]

For MCA executives, using M&A to grow within the entertainment business was nothing new. Geffen Records for example, contributed around US$40 million in operating profits in 1991, more than any other division within MCA.[138] Aside from the potential added revenue, the acquisition of Virgin was also viewed as an opportunity for MCA to strengthen its overseas distribution of music and further expand its global presence and sales, which had increased over 20 percent since 1965. Al Teller, who was the chairman of MCA Music, the music recording division of MCA, said, "What made the deal strategically important was that it provided an overseas operation from which we could build a comprehensive global presence."[139] From an industry standpoint, what MCA was proposing to do was nothing out of the ordinary, as many movie, TV, publishing, and music businesses were undergoing consolidation. For industries such as movies and music, which were at the mercy of a public that was increasingly fickle in its tastes and which were also expanding globally at a rapid rate, M&A was a means to further gain global market share and to spread the risks from hits and misses in movies and music.

The proposal to acquire Virgin was not an idea that arose at the spur of the moment or the result of an instantaneous flicker of inspiration. MCA's management had made intensive studies before putting together their proposal and had contacted Felix Rohatyn of Lazard Freres (who was also an MCA board member) alerting them of their interest. A high-level meeting suggesting the seriousness of intent of both MCA and Virgin was held in September 1991 in Los Angeles. Richard Branson, chairman of Virgin Records, and Ken Berry, president, both flew in from London to attend the meeting. On the MCA side, Wasserman, Sheinberg, Geffen, Teller, and Lazard's Ken Jacobs participated.[140] Interestingly, no one from MEI was in attendance. In addition to this top-level meeting, in what would correspond to a preliminary act of due diligence, MCA had also sent a dozen executives to London to examine the financial books of Virgin and to interview Branson. MCA also hired a law firm to draw up a purchase agreement.[141]

All the intensive preparation, however, came to naught when MEI unilaterally rejected the acquisition proposal without giving an explanation.[142] MEI seems to have been outwardly unconcerned with the depth of disappointment at MCA. Furuichi Mamoru, a member of MEI's board, commented upon hearing of MCA's reaction: "If that disappointment is true, then MCA management can handle it. We have the confidence that they can handle it very smoothly."[143] Furuichi added, speaking through a translator, that MEI's goals were the same as David Geffen's, "to be No. 1 in the world. We have the same target."[144]

Thorne EMI bought Virgin for US$973 million, considerably more than the opening bid price of US$600 million proposed by Sheinberg.[145] Aside from being disappointed, Wasserman and Sheinberg became aware, according to the view of several associates, was that they were no longer running the company. Wasserman commented to the press sometime after the rejection that it was now no longer possible for him to make a business deal without having the Japanese involved.[146] Sheinberg's earlier giddy behavior at headquarters suggests that they both thought that the Japanese would be simply passive investors who occasionally came by to check their property. The fact that this was not to be the case was a revelation that was especially bruising to Wasserman, who was accustomed to calling all the shots and who had micromanaged such details as to what the employees working in the Black Tower MCA headquarters building should be wearing. An associate commented after the rejection of the Virgin acquisition proposal that "This is a real departure from his glorious past. He had been king. Now, he is a lion in winter. It was really sad. Can you imagine Lew Wasserman going to Osaka as a division head?"[147] Wasserman was 23 years old when he joined MCA straight out of high school. After working at a couple of odd jobs as an usher and a nightclub publicist he had built up MCA and had led the company from 1946 until its acquisition by MEI. Under his leadership, the company grew from a talent management and scouting agency to a major film studio in 1962 when it acquired Universal Studios. His long tenure made him the last of the great Hollywood studio moguls. Sheinberg, a Columbia University graduate and lawyer by training, had been managing MCA at Wasserman's side for over 20 years after rising through the ranks of MCA's bureaucracy, becoming vice president of Universal Television in 1968, president in 1970, and chairman of the board and president of MCA in 1973.

At first glance money might appear to have had something to do with MEI's rejection of MCA's acquisition proposal to acquire Virgin Records. MEI may have been put off by the prospect of suddenly dishing out a substantial sum of money for an entity about which they had little knowledge. There may also have been a lack of understanding on MEI's part of the strategic significance that the proposal held for MCA. This may have been due to the lack of communication on the issue between the two sides, in addition to the company's dearth of experience in the entertainment industry. In this regard, both sides were at fault. But from MCA's point of view, time was of the essence in carrying out this acquisition, and they may have felt that they did not have the luxury to take the time to go all the way to Osaka to explain their proposal in detail. They may have believed that MEI would give them a blank check for whatever they proposed. MCA may also have felt that MEI, with its huge bureaucracy, was too slow to come to a decision. An MCA executive recalled that when MEI built a Panasonic consumer store on MCA's property, "It seemed to take a long time, months and months. They seem to have a lot more bureaucracy than we do."[148] A language barrier also existed between the two sides, which made communication difficult as well as hampering efforts in building trust. An MCA executive complained to the *New York Times*, "How can I get to know someone through a translator? How do I even know if I like him?"[149] On the MEI side, executives may have been irritated and resentful of the fact that none of the MEI senior executives were involved in the preliminary talks with the Virgin management. Even though MEI had declared that it would respect the "creative independence" of MCA, they may not have expected that a "subsidiary" would just go out and do an M&A deal on its own. MEI would tolerate MCA's movie-making activities, retain its management and employment policies, and continue its brand and logo without any "Matsushita" name attached (in contrast to Sony, which had renamed the Columbia studios Sony Pictures Entertainment). But undertaking an aspect of corporate strategy that would have a financial impact, albeit relatively small, on MEI's coffers without prior consultation may have been going beyond what was deemed tolerable for MEI's management.

Indeed, as to what was considered within the boundaries of tolerance for MEI, Konosuke had demonstrated a knack for practicing tolerance to ensure a smooth process of integrating acquired companies. But at the same time there was a limitation to that tolerance for some of these acquisitions, as Konosuke insisted upon injecting his management principles into the acquired company. I view this as a means to maintain a subtle form of control by submerging that company in the dominant Matsushita culture. In the case of integrating MCA, however, there was little means to immerse it in the Matsushita culture (even though there were subtle attempts as mentioned above), simply because of MCA's cultural distance from MEI. MCA was a movie studio with a flamboyant, extroverted, and extravagant mindset that practiced profligacy and paid little attention to the bottom line. Industry watchers noted that creative accounting in Hollywood was a permissive art.[150] And in this field Wasserman's team of accountants were known to be highly skilled. MCA's talented lawyers meanwhile drafted contracts that were structured to get as much as possible out of the actors and directors of the industry and were considered templates to be emulated by other players in the movie industry.[151] MCA executives, with their high salaries, traveled in private jets, worked in spacious offices, lived in large luxurious homes in Beverly Hills and other well-to-do neighborhoods, and often hobnobbed with actors and catered to their whims. Senior management at MEI, meanwhile, often lived in modest homes in and around garish Osaka, as did the many other "salarymen" of the country, and in most cases commuted to their workplace by public transportation. It is not difficult to imagine that MCA and MEI management had little in common in terms of work-styles and lifestyles and that it would have been difficult for them to empathize with each other on this account. As technology analyst David M. Benda speculated, for MEI management such a difference in environment would have made it difficult for the Japanese executives to understand why, for example, actors should have personal private jets put at their disposal by a movie studio.[152]

There were also other more mundane issues such as language difficulties and geographic distance which kept the two sides apart. Of the senior management of MEI, including Matsushita Masaharu who was a University of Tokyo law graduate and Tanii who was an engineer by training and education, none was proficient in the English language and none had lived in the US long enough to appreciate its lifestyles, let alone have an awareness of Hollywood's distinctive culture. Daniel Fessler, an assistant professor of anthropology at UCLA, described Hollywood as having a culture of its own with its members using common behavioral markers such as their style of dress, various decorations, and a distinctive dialect. A female originally not of this culture may be allowed in, but only because she represents an opportunity for the male members to mate with her. Males not part of the Hollywood culture, however, are seen as potential competitors for resources. They will not be invited in but instead sought after for their money or for whatever value they have.[153] If Fessler's observation is true, MEI was, as suggested earlier, simply an absentee landlord for MCA, which was going to be milked by the latter for cash.

These differences in culture and the lack of understanding and appreciation for the entertainment business may have, according to this view, created a feeling of uncertainty and fear of losing control among MEI's management. This sentiment was exacerbated by the rapid moves made by MCA towards Virgin, a move which was also too quick for the lumbering and methodical MEI bureaucracy. The attitude of tolerance initially shown towards MCA was shorn away in order for MEI to retain some control over the behavior of the studio that would guarantee a degree of certainty in a very uncertain industry. Thus, for MEI, the unexplained rejection of the Virgin proposal was in effect an indirect message to Wasserman and Sheinberg: yes, the creative life of your studio would go on as before, but actions that would impact us in any way, especially with regard to MEI's coffers, would have to be explained. Wasserman's lament to the press after the Virgin proposal rejection, that he now could not make any decision without the Japanese, indicates that this is how he interpreted the decision of MEI.

Aside from sending indirect messages indicating its intent to have the last word on major strategic decisions, MEI was determined to back up its words by implementing managerial practices and infrastructure for keeping the studio in line. MEI accountants began to increase their requests to MCA for extensive financial data on the studio's operations.[154] MEI also began (some would say rather late) to set up formal management structures that would work towards integrating the two companies. A management board or executive committee was set up between the two companies made up of the top three MEI executives and MCA's chairman and president Wasserman and Sheinberg.[155] In January 1992, MEI set up three subcommittees whose task was to do the grunt-work of the executive committee.[156] One committee was to work on formulating a long-term vision for the next 10 to 15 years for the combined MEI–MCA entity.

Another committee was to work on promoting joint development of hardware, software, and technology. A third committee was to focus on financial and fiscal issues.[157] In March, MEI established an Entertainment and Arts Division with the mission of overseeing MCA. As announced by MEI, "the division will work to support MCA in Japan and to help projects worldwide in the business area, not the creative area" and was to be headed by the same Furuichi Mamoru who had earlier shrugged off MCA's bitter disappointment over the Virgin rejection.[158] An MCA executive described Furuichi after having met him during a visit in the previous month as "more of a creative guy than a hardware guy," which to the people of MCA was a relief.[159] In reaction to the moves towards integration by MEI, Sheinberg was guardedly supportive. The newly established Entertainment & Arts Division in MEI could help smooth relations, he said, if it supported MCA and presented MCA's plans in such a way that MEI could digest them. He warned, however, that if someone at MEI got the idea that this division was to manage MCA in the form of some sort of shadow government, disaster would be the result.[160]

From the timing of these developments, it would seem that MEI's tolerance for respecting the creative independence of MCA was blown away as a result of the latter's audacious attempt at acquiring Virgin. It could thus be argued that the setting up various management control structures was a backlash against a subsidiary that was behaving in an independent manner which was incomprehensible and simply unacceptable to the stodgy electronics manufacturer. Another way to look at MEI's about-face on tolerance was that it was an inevitable development coming largely from its manufacturing-based corporate culture. Manufacturers have a goal of keeping disparities in the quality of output as low as possible during mass production runs. This in effect requires the manufacturer to take an intolerant attitude towards deviations from the standards of quality and processes of production that must be observed and followed in order to eliminate defects. Indeed, having had the opportunity of working alongside Panasonic engineers, I have observed the almost fanatical but dedicated obsession of their engineers in eliminating those elements and factors that do not fit with the Panasonic process or philosophy of manufacturing which is aimed at achieving high levels of product quality. Accordingly, MEI's attempt to control MCA was simply an effort by MEI to ensure a level of quality in the output of its studio by not having it deviate from behavior which to MEI was outside the norm. Indeed, shortly after MEI acquired MCA, MEI executives suggested to MCA that they stop making flops and make more hit movies, as if there was some quality control system, involving "kaizen" or incremental improvement, in making blockbusters.[161] The management of MCA responded by saying that there was no way of telling whether a movie would be successful or not until after it was released.[162] Like all movie companies, MCA had good years and bad years, and nothing but an oracle could change that.[163] But unfortunately for MCA, such explanations did not get through to MEI.[164]

While I concur that there were differences in mindsets which may have led to misunderstandings between the two parties and that a factor of intolerance on the part of MEI may have been an impediment in building closer relations and mutual trust, I believe that there was another element at play which may have influenced MEI's decision towards its Virgin acquisition proposal which had little to do with cultural differences or misunderstandings. In retrospect, it may also have had a serious impact on the long-term nature of the MEI-MCA relationship.

Little known at the time to the executives of MCA was that several months prior to MEI's rejection of MCA's proposal to acquire Virgin, a scandal had embroiled MEI management. During the summer months of 1991, Osaka prosecutors discovered that a subsidiary of MEI, National Lease, had made illegal loans in the form of debentures to the proprietress of a high-class Japanese restaurant in Osaka named Onoue Nui, who had a dubious reputation for accurately predicting stock price movements.[165] For some unfathomable reason, the traditionally penny-pinching accountants of the Matsushita group illegally loaned her approximately ¥50 billion. Onoue was arrested on charges of fraud and breach of trust. At National Lease, the manager in charge of loans was arrested and convicted on similar charges. Aside from the illegal loans made to Onoue, National Lease also made dubious loans to various real-estate and construction companies. The immediate impact on National Lease was that it withdrew from the loan business and became reborn as NLF Finance, a company that was now focused on getting back loan payments.[166]

The financial impact on MEI of the dubious activities of National Lease was reported to be around ¥380 billion.[167] MEI suffered an enormous setback to its reputation which was further compounded at the time by the discovery of 400,000 defective refrigerators being sold in Japan.[168] A total of 700,000 refrigerators had to be recalled to have defective compressors replaced, which cost the company ¥30 billion.[169] To add fuel to the fire, another financial mess was brewing within the Matsushita group as its management discovered that a subsidiary company, Matsushita Kosan, was accumulating huge amounts of unrecoverable loans made to property and tourist-site developers as a result of the swift downturn of the Japanese economy caused by the bursting of the financial bubble in 1991.[170] The company was also forging savings account statements with another company and was making fraudulent credit claims.[171] The chairman of the subsidiary was Konosuke's son-in-law Masaharu and the president of the company was Masaharu's son (and Konosuke's grandson), Masayuki. Under the circumstances, it would have made extremely bad publicity for MEI if this subsidiary headed by Konosuke's son-in-law and grandson went under. Not surprisingly, MEI continued to support the finances of Matsushita Kosan.[172] But the support that MEI management gave to this subsidiary created rumblings of distrust among MEI employees towards its management and to the founding family.[173]

All of these events surrounding MEI in Japan were happening while MCA was putting the finishing touches to its Virgin acquisition proposal. Accordingly, although the rejection of MCA's proposal may have been a means for MEI to show that it was ultimately in control of the relationship, I view the rejection as stemming not from any overt intolerance on MEI's part for MCA's culture or its business practices but rather from extenuating circumstances and simply bad timing. Senior management of MEI may have been badly distracted and in a state of panic as a considerable amount of bad press on the various scandals engulfing the company was printed at the time. People were calling the 1990s the "lost decade of Matsushita Electric" with scandals and quality issues erupting.[174] The scandals and product recall were also having an effect on MEI employees. One senior MEI executive recalled that for the first time in the company's history, its senior management had lost the trust of its employees, and as a result the latter no longer looked to them as a unifying force.[175] Such a situation may have precluded the MEI senior executives from sitting down and calmly deliberating on MCA's proposal; hence their lack of any proper explanation to MCA for their rejection of it. And the scandals were also costing the company a not insignificant amount of money. MEI management may have also perceived it as unfavorable to dish out money in Hollywood while they had to make amends for illegal loans made at home and deal with declining employee morale.

The scandals can also be seen as having long-term repercussions on the MEI-MCA relationship and negatively impacting MEI's initially tolerant attitude towards its Hollywood studio. To take responsibility for the Onoue scandal, vice president Sakuma Shoji, who was responsible for overseeing the management of subsidiary companies of the Matsushita group, resigned in March 1992. Sakuma, who was three years younger than president Tanii, had made a name for himself in sales for several years in Europe and became a member of the board at the relatively young age (for a long-established multinational Japanese company) of 51. While there was little reaction from MCA on Sakuma's resignation in particular, his international background suggests that he had some experience in communicating and working with non-Japanese, which would have been an asset for MEI in its relationship with MCA. After resigning from MEI, Sakuma became president of the Japan-based satellite broadcaster WOWWOW. In this capacity, as the head of a broadcaster that provided entertainment content and software, he registered some success in making inroads in the entertainment industry and established the broadcaster as an alternative to terrestrial broadcasters. Sakuma's performance at WOWWOW suggests that he had, or was flexible enough to develop, an understanding of how the entertainment industry worked. Had he stayed on at MEI and continued to participate in the management of the relationship with MCA, the relationship between the two companies might have not become as acrimonious as it did.

Vice president Hirata Masahiko, who was head of accounting, was demoted to a member of the board. Hirata had made a name for himself within the company by strengthening and centralizing the control of accounting personnel, wresting control away from the human resources department. Ironically, Hirata's purpose in doing this was to ensure the integrity of its accounting personnel.[176] In line with Konosuke's belief that "accountants are the compass of the company," Hirata also sought to create a more aggressive accounting department that would be able to audit the management of the various companies within the Matsushita group.[177] Hirata was one of the few top executives whom MCA management was acquainted with, as it was he who was the main driver of negotiations on the MEI side for the acquisition of MCA. At one point, Hirata's standing within MEI was such that industry analysts considered him as a plausible contender for the position of president after Tanii.[178] Thus, in more than one way the demotion of Hirata was an unfortunate development for MCA. An MCA executive commented, "This is a man we had a relationship with. We spent a lot of time educating him. If he's off the [joint executive] committee, we'll have to educate someone else."[179] In retrospect, had Hirata not been demoted, he might have been able to maneuver his accounting team to accommodate the acquisition proposal coming from Virgin, given his responsibility and his relative familiarity with the MCA team. But by the end of 1991, Hirata's power base was too severely weakened to give any support to an acquisition proposal, especially one that required a substantial amount of money at a time when MEI was plagued with debts from illegal activities.

President Tanii resigned from his position as president of the company in February 1993, taking responsibility for the scandal at National Lease.[180] Morishita Yoichi, an MEI employee since graduating from Kansei Gakuin University in 1957, took over as president. A close friend and ally of Masaharu, Morishita did not speak English and was completely unfamiliar with the entertainment business and with MCA.[181] He had spent most of his time before his ascendancy in sales and marketing, including supervising the Corporate Industry Sales Division for the Japanese market.[182] Morishita was the most junior of the executive vice presidents of MEI at the time; he was never considered by industry analysts a true contender for the top position.[183] Most unfortunate for MCA, however, was that Morishita was reported to have been critical of the deal to purchase MCA.[184]

As soon as Morishita became president, his management team began to scrutinize the activities of the accounting department under Hirata and discredit him. In a rare public acknowledgement, Morishita commented that the accounting group in MEI headquarters was to be blamed for the state of management at MEI subsidiaries which he described as "a mess."[185] Vice president Murase Tsuzo, who with Masaharu was the only one left of the original members who were at the helm of MEI at the time of the acquisition of MCA, had his powers sharply curtailed and left the company in June 1996, becoming an advisor to MEI upon his departure.

Masaharu's credibility was at stake, and while all the scandals were brewing he was pushing the board to have his son Masayuki become a senior director (which he eventually did become in 1992). For these reasons, he could not have supported MCA's plans for business expansion, which to the other board members might have appeared as profligate and ostentatious behavior. But one good thing for Masaharu was that the scandals gave him an excuse to oust Tanii, even though he had already had taken responsibility for the scandal at National Lease by taking a 50 percent pay cut for three months.[186] Masaharu considered

Tanii a thorn in his side, as Tanii constantly attempted to impede the influence of the Matsushita family in his belief that this was necessary for MEI to be a "normal" company.[187] Much to Masaharu's consternation, Tanii at one point even had the audacity to warn Masaharu about his statements to the public and his behavior.[188]

As mentioned above, one of Tanii's objectives in acquiring MCA was to change MEI's culture. Given that it was Masaharu's decision to acquire MCA, Tanii's goal may seem more like an afterthought than a reflection of any well-thought-out vision or strategy. But Tanii's attempt to pick up hints on how to run a movie company from Ohga Norio, his compatriot predecessor and competitor in the movie business, suggests that Tanii and his associates understood that MCA had a different business model, that it involved risks that were difficult or almost impossible to measure, moved at a fast speed, and was entrepreneurial in nature. Tanii and his team wanted that kind of free-thinking, out-of-the-box type of daring to permeate and change the conservative MEI culture put in place by Konosuke, which encouraged the following of others and improving inventions made elsewhere. For them, the creating of new businesses, or the breaking of "shells," could only be possible if they changed the culture, for which they hoped MCA would be the catalyst. As Murase explained, in the past the company had tried many slogans to change the MEI mindset, but nothing could better convey the seriousness of the MEI management about realizing change than the acquisition of MCA, which had brought about an awareness of software among the younger employees of MEI and had given them new "opportunities to dream about and look forward to."[189]

For Masaharu, the son-in-law of Konosuke who was adopted into the Matsushita family, the acquisition of MCA represented an opportunity for him to finally come out of the shadow of his father-in-law, with whom he had had an uneasy relationship over several decades.[190] Even though Masaharu was chairman of the company, as long as Konosuke was around, the employees and indeed people outside of MEI looked upon Konosuke as the final authority figure. This was well proven to be the case in 1964 in a humiliating incident for Masaharu, who was president of the company at the time. At a conference of MEI dealers held in the resort town of Atami, Konosuke, who was chairman, abruptly decided to come out of semi-retirement status and take full charge of reorganizing the company's domestic sales distribution structure and business practices in the face of an unexpected barrage of criticism from dissatisfied dealers, in effect bypassing Masaharu's authority. In 1989, however, Konosuke had passed away and Masaharu was finally free to do what he wanted without Konosuke looking over his shoulder. His decision to do something as radically different and full of risks as to buy a movie studio suggests that he too entertained thoughts of using MCA to change the culture of MEI as molded by Konosuke.

Nevertheless, with the scandals that engulfed MEI in the summer of 1991, the credibility of the MEI management was severely weakened. Most of the people that had been involved with the acquisition of MCA, including Tanii, were pushed out. Along with this changing of the guard, including the appointment of

Morishita as president, the tolerance that Tanii and his team had shown for the management and business practices of MCA was to be blown away for good. Under the new regime of Morishita, who was reported to be hostile to MCA as well as uncomprehending of the original intentions of its role within the Matsushita group,[191] the objective of using the culture of MCA to transform MEI into a more entrepreneurial, risk-taking company was now going to be pushed aside in favor of going back to what Konosuke would have considered the basics: the manufacturing and sales of hardware products.

Further disappointments for MCA

With new management in place at MEI in early 1992, further disappointments for MCA were to follow. A plan put together by MCA to make an equity investment of about US$50 million, or a 20 percent stake, in a Universal Studios theme park in Japan was rejected by MEI in an imperious manner which Wasserman and Sheinberg found insulting.[192] MCA, MEI told them, could manage such a park but not own it. They had to find other investors. For MCA, the theme park business was one area which they felt they could compete with the likes of Disney. Sheinberg explained to the press that theme parks were of special importance to the movie studio.[193] MEI's rejection of MCA's plan was once again a sign that their Japanese masters did not understand MCA's business. In fairness to MEI, however, MCA did get the green light to undertake a US$3 billion expansion over 10 years at its Universal Studios Florida facility, which included the building of a second theme park and five hotels.[194]

In short, given the bursting of the financial bubble in Japan and the scandals which had embroiled MEI, the company was not about to embark upon ventures that were considered by them financially dubious and unfamiliar.[195] As reported by the *New York Times*, MEI vice president Murase explained that:

> Matsushita's main business is electronics and the project is a sideline for us. If the bubble economy had not collapsed, maybe the situation would have been better. In all of Japan, everybody is suffering from diminished asset value. It is not the situation to be aggressively spending money.[196]

Indeed, with Morishita at the helm of MEI, the company was playing a different tune. After taking over, Morishita indirectly disavowed the efforts made by his predecessor to change the culture of MEI, declaring that US-style approaches and radical moves were not in order for transforming the company.[197] Instead, there would be a steady effort to work off the corporate fat taken on in the 1980s, which would include cutting staff, reducing hiring, thinning out management ranks, shifting some production to low-wage countries, and rationalizing R&D programs, product lineups, and distribution channels.[198] Despite the reasoning of MEI for rejecting MCA's theme park proposal, to a bitter Sheinberg who believed that with a relatively low level of investment they could get high returns in a business which MCA was familiar with, MEI was simply stringing MCA along.[199]

MCA may have had bitter feelings towards their parent, but Wasserman and Sheinberg were not to easily give in to what they viewed as MEI's passivity.[200] What may have spurred them on was that fact that after a dismal 1991 and 1992, 1993 was turning out to be record year for MCA, with revenues reaching US$4 billion and operating profits close to US$400 million. *Jurassic Park* had much to do with this success. In contrast, however, while the movie business was doing well, MCA's TV production business had been lackluster, with Universal Television lacking popular programs, notably comedy which could be valuable for syndication.[201] The next pitch Wasserman and Sheinberg made was for MCA to take a 49 percent stake in the US TV broadcaster NBC. MCA may have been encouraged to look at this possibility since rival Viacom had acquired Paramount Communications and another rival TimeWarner had also explored buying NBC. This was a moment when rival companies were aggressively expanding their businesses through M&A. The proposal was immediately rejected.[202] Undeterred, In September 1994, Wasserman and Sheinberg flew to Osaka to make another pitch for acquiring a US broadcaster; this time a 25 percent equity stake in CBS. The idea was to work with the business conglomerate ITT Corporation in a joint bid for CBS.

The meeting held on September 17 between MCA and MEI executives at MEI headquarters turned out to be a disaster. In retrospect it was the first sign that the MEI-MCA relationship was doomed. After the MCA executives were required to do a presentation of their proposal to some junior MEI executives, Morishita, who was late for the meeting by two hours, finally entered the conference room and after the usual exchange of greetings and pleasantries to the American visitors turned to Wasserman and Sheinberg and said, "I see you have been told." Sheinberg was confused. "Told what?" he asked. Morishita turned to his executives and said, "You mean you haven't told them yet?" Apparently, the decision to reject the CBS proposal was already made before the MCA executives had arrived in Japan.[203] According to one MCA executive, Sheinberg was livid and stormed out of the conference room, and "practically said 'Fuck you!'" to his Japanese masters.[204] Later, after returning to the US, Sheinberg told the press, "I did not feel that we had been treated as adults. I felt that we had been treated as children. Our people were totally demoralized. Matsushita doesn't understand as the head of a company I have to keep the troops motivated."[205] Sheinberg added that, "it was not just what they did, but the style. The meeting was not called to hear our presentation but to tell us all the reasons for turning the deal down."[206]

Morishita seems to have been taken by surprise by Sheinberg's public outburst.[207] Here was a manifestation that the two sides viewed each other differently. For Morishita it was unthinkable that a "subsidiary" would air its differences with the parent company out in the open. For Sheinberg and MCA, on the other hand, their bitter reaction to the rejections of their proposals and their public airing of their views indicate that they did not look upon themselves as a subsidiary, nor did they view MEI as their "parent." As some industry observers have suggested, the management of MCA more likely viewed itself as an equal strategic partner to MEI.[208]

In response to the charges that MEI had treated the MCA executives in a dis-respectful manner, MEI officials offered an apology as well as an innocuous explanation, particularly concerning the late arrival of Morishita at the meeting. According to Murase, Morishita was late because he had been attending a special board meeting to consider the "sudden proposal" from MCA and the meeting ran longer than expected.[209] As for the reasons behind the rejection, Murase said that the MEI board rejected the proposal because the future of TV networks was uncertain in an era of shifting entertainment technologies. The board also ques-tioned whether there would be enough profit in TV network production, given that MCA's own television business was far from being its strongest division.[210] MEI also feared a backlash similar to what Sony had earlier experienced when it purchased Columbia Pictures, and told the press that MEI did not want to take action that would cause extra controversy.[211] Given the negative publicity and bashing that MEI had been receiving for several months in Japan over the loan scandals and product recalls, the desire of MEI to avoid any further negative coverage in the US was not difficult to understand. MEI was at least outwardly contrite with regard to its behavior towards the MCA executives. Murase said, "We really hope we can recover the past good relationship. We are thinking about how to recover the mutual trust."[212]

Sheinberg wrote a letter to Morishita upon his return to the US. In it, Shein-berg demanded another opportunity for making a pitch for buying CBS as well as other properties and assets which he felt would be in the interest of MCA's business. While Sheinberg was demanding a rematch, the director Steven Spiel-berg and music producer David Geffen announced that they were teaming up with Jeffrey Katzenberg, the former chairman of the Walt Disney Co. studios, to launch an entertainment company called DreamWorks SKG. Katzenberg had previously quit his job at Disney after he was refused a promotion. Spielberg and Geffen had close ties to MCA. Spielberg had made the hit movies *Jurassic Park* and *Schindler's List* with Universal Studios, and Geffen was head of MCA Records and a board member of MCA. The members of the so-called Dream Team, as the three were dubbed by the Hollywood media, signaled the possibil-ity of teaming up with MCA only on the condition that Wasserman and Shein-berg remain at the helm.[213] Another tentative proposal they had was for DreamWorks to establish their studio facility on a 35-acre site located in Univer-sal's back lot.[214] Suddenly, for Wasserman and Sheinberg the possibility of making more money and gaining their independence from the Japanese loomed large. Not surprisingly for Hollywood, rumors began to fly that the Dream Team, Wasserman, and Sheinberg were looking into buying back MCA from MEI. MEI, on the other hand, issued a terse statement saying that it was unaware of any buyback plan from MCA.[215]

For MEI, however, the announcement of the formation of DreamWorks SKG and the concurrent rumors of Wasserman and Sheinberg attempting to buy back MCA should have been disturbing to say the least if they were paying attention. In effect, MEI was going to lose Hollywood's most financially successful film producer, and on top of that, there was the possibility that its management team at MCA was going to rebel and defect. Yet, despite the potential gravity of the situation, MEI executives seemed relatively unconcerned about a possible confrontation, downplaying the difficulties in the relationship as stemming from what Murase described as "a lack of understanding and common culture."[216] In retrospect, this lackadaisical response from MEI could have been an indication that the company had by this time already given up thoughts of continuing in the movie business.

Be that as it may, as a result of the developments concerning the Dream Team, the agenda of the meeting that Sheinberg had demanded with MEI was to concern substantially more than acquiring a stake in CBS. On October 18, 1994, Wasserman and Sheinberg again met with executives from MEI. This time, Morishita and his staff flew to San Francisco. A sign of MEI's growing concern about MCA was that 82-year-old MEI chairman Masaharu had also flown from Osaka to meet with Wasserman. The two met for 30 minutes. Masaharu did not attend the larger meeting held afterwards at the Mark Hopkins Hotel, at which he had Morishita represent the company. To ensure that both sides accurately conveyed their comments to each other, each side brought their own interpreters.[217] The meeting lasted for over four hours. Immediately afterwards, Wasserman flew back to Los Angeles with the feeling that the meeting had gone badly. Sheinberg, on the other hand, was less dour.[218] According to one MCA executive, the meeting centered on the issue of who was to be in control of MCA's business.[219] Wasserman and Sheinberg had told the MEI executives that unless they were given more control of their business, they would resign. They demanded that MEI sell them back 51 percent of MCA, in effect giving them a controlling interest and theoretically allowing them to pursue the plans of expansion through acquisitions which they had presented to MEI earlier. They most likely also had in mind the possibility of teaming up with Spielberg and his colleagues. In effect an ultimatum was presented to MEI: either give up control of MCA, or lose not only Sheinberg and Wasserman, but also the top movie producer in Hollywood.

The MEI executives did not give their reply at the meeting. In a statement to the press, Murase commented, "Right now, our positions are rather apart, but we are convinced that our policies based on Matsushita tradition are right. We have exchanged our opinions, but we cannot find the compromising point."[220] In retrospect, Murase's comment was revealing of MEI's post-Tanii stance towards MCA. Tolerance towards MCA would continue to be shown by keeping MCA's senior management in place. But, as far their creative independence went, which was originally guaranteed by MEI at the time of the acquisition, this was now to be bounded by Matsushita "tradition" which the company believed was unequivocally for the better—hence deying the possibility of compromise between the two companys' positions. Instead of taking on the risks associated with M&A in a field of which MEI had little understanding, MCA was in effect told to simply turn out money-making movies using strict quality control methods and "kaizen," and keep a close eye on the bottom line—something which all the other businesses within the Matsushita group were doing. Instead of being flamboyant in behavior, MCA was to be a modest and humble studio and its accountants were to be penny-pinching in every respect. Such a practice of keeping the current management of the acquired company but ensuring that the Matsushita culture was dominant was in line with the past methods of integration of MEI's acquired companies. MEI was in effect attempting to apply its past integration practices to MCA. But as far as Wasserman and Sheinberg were concerned, just having them continue as the heads of MCA without giving them the freedom to expand the business as they saw most fit was clearly not a sign of tolerance. As Sheinberg angrily commented to the press, if MEI wanted them to stay, why did they not listen to them?[221]

Despite their lamentations, the two men were not in a position to take unilateral action towards buying back MCA. MCA had made record profits in the previous year of 1993, with an operating profit margin of 10 percent, which exceeded the level achieved by its Japanese parent.[222] Meanwhile, Sumner Redstone, chairman of the media conglomerate Viacom, had acquired Paramount Studios after a bidding war with QVC Television for US$10 billion, or almost 50 percent more than what MEI had dished out for MCA.[223] Wasserman and Sheinberg may have been rich, but the view from Wall Street was that given such developments, MEI would most likely make them pay more than double the amount it had spent purchasing MCA.[224]

For MEI, the October 18 meeting must have been the last straw, as they immediately made moves to sort out MEI's relationship with MCA. The following month, the company publicly announced that it would finally develop a strategy for MCA and that it would hire the investment banker Herbert Allen of Allen & Co. and Michael Ovitz to draw up various strategic options. Apparently, the committees that had been established earlier in 1992 to set up a vision and strategy for the companies were not working. At the first of those meetings, four MCA executives flew to MEI's headquarters in Osaka, where they were met by several MEI officials. The two sides met with each other for nearly six hours, moving boxes around on an organization chart. According to an MCA executive, "Nothing, nothing ever clicked. We learned almost nothing about each other."[225] No further meetings were held.

For this apparently new effort, Matsuda Motoi, the director of accounting, finance, and auditing for MEI, told reporters in Japan that the company would work with MCA to come up with a short- and mid-term business strategy. Motoi frankly blamed the dispute between the two companies on MEI's unfamiliarity with the film industry.[226] Given that the people who were originally involved with MCA from the time of its acquisition, such as Tanii, Hirata, and Sakuma, were now out of the picture, and that Morishita, president of MEI since the start of 1993, had not met with MCA executives until September 1994, this was not surprising. In response to this initiative from MEI, MCA was reported to have been guardedly hopeful, saying that several scenarios could emerge from Allen & Co.'s evaluation but that the critical issue was to give MCA the flexibility to make major strategic moves to grow, such as acquisitions.[227]

Despite what seemed a new effort by MEI to work closely and in a cooperative manner with MCA, for Morishita, who showed no interest in the entertainment business or any desire to familiarize himself with MCA, his conclusion on what to do about MCA was already decided upon immediately after the October 18 meeting.[228] His main goal was to put all focus on rebuilding and strengthening MEI's core electronics business. Restructuring efforts were to be accelerated and MEI's reputation as a solid manufacturer in the wake of the various scandals and product recalls was to be restored. MCA was to be sold off. Instead of advising MEI on future strategy, Allen & Co. and Ovitz were to work on a divestment plan. As if to substantiate this, in a little-publicized announcement, MEI had asked Ovitz and Allen to determine MCA's net worth.[229] Thus, contrary to the impression that MEI's announcement may have given to the public, during their visits to Japan in late 1994, Ovtiz and Allen advised MEI not on future strategy but on the best way for MEI to deal with the management crisis which they had on their hands. The possibilities boiled down to three options: selling MCA, acquiescing to Wasserman and Sheinberg, or replacing the two men.[230] All the talk about establishing new strategies was in fact a cover for MEI's real plans.

The element of uncertainty surrounding its movie business also spurred MEI to divest the movie studio. Only a few hit movies (*Fried Green Tomatoes, Beethoven, Scent of a Woman*) were produced in 1992, which failed to compensate for the flops (*Mr. Baseball, American Me, Dr. Giggles, The Public Eye, Out on a Limb, Leaving Normal*) that Universal turned out. In contrast, 1993 was a banner year for Universal, with hits such as *Jurassic Park, Schindler's List*, and *A Dinosaur's Story*, which put the studio at second place after Warner.[231] On the other hand, 60 percent of its revenues came from just the three hit movies out of a total of 11 releases for the year, which included a slew of forgettable movies such as *Matinee, Splitting Hairs, Heart and Souls*, and *Mad Dogs*, each earning less than US$20 million at the box office.[232]

On the horizon for 1994 was *Waterworld*, starring Kevin Costner, which was being publicized as the most expensive movie made to date and tremendously over its US$100 million budget. In a statement which was sure to irritate MEI, Sheinberg had said that no one should make a picture that cost this much money.[233] Meanwhile, sneak previews were giving the yet-to-be-released film a reputation as the "largest neutron bomb in history."[234] One former confidant of Wasserman suggested that the huge outlay for *Waterworld* was in effect an effort by Wasserman and Sheinberg to wrest financial control of MCA back from the Japanese.[235] Unless the executives of MEI were totally ignorant for some reason, they must have been aware that they had a potential bomb on their hands, and this as well most likely accelerated MEI's efforts to unload its Hollywood studio business. If that was not the final nail hammered into the coffin, pre-tax operating profits of MCA's film business in 1994 fell to US$130 million from US$200 million in the previous year.[236]

Wasserman, however, did not suspect at all what Morishita had in mind and instead ranted against MEI's evaluation of MCA's net worth as an attempt to judge his performance.[237] Sheinberg, upon learning of Ovitz's clandestine visits to Japan, remarked that Ovitz would never betray him.[238] Wasserman and Sheinberg were also incredibly naive and unable to read between the lines to understand what

MEI's latest moves truly implied. Refusing to give up on their demands for more control, the two men flew to Osaka in January 1995 with various project proposals, including the prospect of having DreamWorks establish their headquarters on the Universal Studios lot.[239] Nothing came out of the meeting and the two men flew back to the US. The two men were not, however, reported to have been dejected.[240] Wasserman, whose confidence was built on a half billion dollars in Matsushita stock and on consistently winning against every adversary, felt that he could eventually win in the power politics with MEI, which to him had become a waiting game.[241]

But all those trips to Japan and waiting it out were to be in vain for Wasserman and Sheinberg. By the spring of 1995, MCA was no longer with the Matsushita family. And no one, including Wasserman and Sheinberg, knew that MEI had sold MCA to the Seagram Company until after it had been announced.[242] Al Teller, the head of MCA's music division, confirmed that the MCA executives were notified "after the fact" and then asked to participate in the divesture process, which in his view reflected the "difficulty of the relationship with Matsushita."[243]

On April 9, 1995, MEI announced that it had sold 80 percent of its stake in MCA to the Canadian liquor distributor the Seagram Company (Seagram) headed by Edgar Bronfman Jr. for US$5.7 billion, giving MCA a total value of US$7.1 billion. If MEI had not had preferred stock obligations to Wasserman, the company might have completely unloaded MCA to Seagram instead of having to continue to pay Wasserman an annual 8.5 percent dividend totaling US$28 million per year.[244]

The amount that MEI received was slightly more than the US$6.59 billion that the company had paid in 1990. But as part of the deal, MEI agreed to assume MCA's debt, totaling US$1 billion (including US$200 million for *Waterworld*), so in effect the company was getting only US$6.1 billion.[245] Furthermore, with the yen trading at ¥85 to the dollar in 1995 in contrast to ¥129 to the dollar at the time of acquisition, the company was in fact losing money in yen terms. While revenues at MCA had grown from US$3.4 billion in 1989, with profits of US$192 million, to an estimated US$4.6 billion with profits of US$400 million in 1994 on the eve of its divestiture,[246] for MEI this M&A deal, its biggest one yet, was an undisputable money-losing disaster on an unprecedented scale.

In his announcement to the press, Morishita tried to put a positive spin on the divestment, saying that MCA has grown during the five years under MEI ownership and that both companies had contributed to significant advancements of new digital video standards.[247] Despite divestment, MEI, according to Morishita, was still to play a role in the future of MCA through some retaining interest in the company.[248]

Later, at another news conference, Morishita offered an explanation as to why MEI had pulled out. In 1990 when the company had acquired MCA, there was an expectation that it would provide MEI with packaged movie content for MEI hardware, such as videocassette recorders and future High Definition TV sets.

But Hollywood was rapidly changing. Regulation changes were making it possible for TV broadcasters to go into movie production. In order to deal with these changing circumstances, MEI would have had to consider alliances with communications companies such as those in cable television and broadcasting. It would also have had to move fast. A spokesman for Morishita quoted him as saying, "In order to spread the Hollywood cultural asset via a very broad network, it is necessary to have a large fund and to make timely judgments."[249] In effect, Morishita was saying that the Hollywood environment had changed beyond the expectations of MEI and that to adapt to such changes would have required MEI to change its initial strategy and business model of distributing packaged movie content to help drive sales of its electronic hardware equipment. MEI would also have needed to increase investments so as to build alliances, and to move quickly. For Morishita it was a change in the Hollywood business environment that led him to conclude that holding on to MCA was not necessary for his main task: the revitalization of MEI's core business, which was electronics. Interestingly, Morishita did hint that aside from the changes in the business environment, cultural differences contributed to the decision to divest, but he did not elaborate any further.[250]

For Wasserman and Sheinberg, their journey with the Japanese, which had looked promising in the beginning, ended up with both losing face. MEI had completely disregarded the demand from the two to buy back a controlling portion of MCA. MEI hadn't even bothered to make a courtesy call to Wasserman after the divesture was announced.[251] Their attempts at wresting control and money from mighty Matsushita ended up ignominiously. Like the Americans on the eve of Pearl Harbor, they had far underestimated what the Japanese were capable of pulling off if pushed into a corner. As the *New York Times* suggested, the film *Bridge Over the River Kwai* (made by Sony-owned Columbia Pictures, incidentally) may have given Wasserman and Sheinberg the illusion that the Japanese would respectfully defer to an elderly corporate leader such as Wasserman.[252] If so, they were dead wrong on this. But at least they became enormously rich.

Conclusion: the impact of tolerance, or its lack

Many believed MEI copied Sony's move into Hollywood by buying MCA, and there can be little doubt that MEI wanted a movie library as much as Sony did to drive its hardware electronics business. But it also had the objective of using MCA as a means of "breaking through" the culture of MEI and in the process creating a new type of Matsushita employee and new businesses. MCA was to be the outside force or "gaiatsu" to accelerate initiatives to change MEI's culture from one that emphasized uniformity, humility, and obedience to the group into something more dynamic that would look upon individualism and individual initiative as a merit. During the first four years of Tanii's tenure, the company created a computer division and strengthened its industrial equipment and semiconductor businesses. Tanii also worked to consolidate MEI's sprawling empire of close to 90 companies in Japan alone.[253] MEI was shifting the production of lower-value-added products such as refrigerators and air conditioners to outside of high-cost Japan, thereby freeing the factories in Japan to concentrate on developing high-value-added products. As some industry observers noted, only after Tanii took over as president in 1986 did MEI begin to resemble a true multinational. MEI was establishing partnerships with other non-Japanese companies to acquire new technologies and know-how for building workstations. The engineers of MEI under Tanii were being exposed to a new culture that emphasized individual initiative. Kuninobu Shigeo, a computer engineer, said, "We've learned how to quarrel. Ordinarily it is not something you do here in Japan, so at first we were pretty confused."[254] The interaction with MCA's culture was to further accelerate change and involve more engineers and employees like Kuninobu. In such a climate, MEI might have been expected to respect MCA's culture and the independence of its business, and to leave it alone as they had suggested at the time of the acquisition.

But unfortunately for Tanii and his likeminded associates, the scandals and product recalls that occurred under their watch shattered their vision and strategy for MEI. To compound the problems that occurred, Tanii was also embroiled in a battle against the son-in-law of the founder which ultimately led to his ouster. This was unfortunate because Masaharu himself also wanted to change the company in order to get out of the shadow of his father-in-law. In this respect, both men shared the same goal; by ousting Tanii, Masaharu lost a valuable supporter for changing the culture of the company. But the fallout was not limited to Tanii, as others who were involved in the acquisition of MCA were all pushed out or demoted. This led to the rise out of nowhere of Morishita Yoichi, who was loyal to Masaharu but indifferent or even hostile to MCA. Masaharu, however, was not in a position to go against Morishita, as the scandals had weakened his reputation within the company, and he was also anxious for Morishita's support to promote his son Masayuki up the ranks of the board of directors.

Morishita's main concern in the wake of the scandals and product recalls was to restore the reputation of the company and to refocus the company's efforts on revitalizing its core electronics business. A change in strategy occurred as a result. No longer would MEI be effecting cultural changes that bordered on the esoteric to accommodate the creation and pursuit of new businesses and high-risk ventures such as making movies. US-style approaches to transforming the company would also not be accepted. Instead, the company would go back to the basics and stoically undertake what it always did well: "monozukuri" or making products that were good-quality, lower-cost copies of Sony products. For MEI, this meant reemphasizing the "tap water" philosophy espoused by Konosuke. High-quality, low-cost products were to be mass produced for everyone to enjoy. In the true top-down fashion of Matsushita, corporate management deviations from his philosophy would not be tolerated. This was to be a revolution, but a revolution from the top which signaled a "restoration" of the principles of Konosuke.

These moves by Morishita spelled doom for the relationship between MEI and MCA. Under Morishita, no longer would MEI tolerate the independence of MCA. MEI would no longer consider MCA as an equal partner or as an important catalyst in changing the culture of MEI. Instead, MEI would force its traditions upon MCA. MCA was simply to be one of the many subsidiaries of the Matsushita group. Although there would be no daily recitation of Konosuke's principles of management or singing of the company song, this change in strategy leading to a change in attitude led to rejections of any major proposal that was to come out of MCA, with the comment that MEI knew what was best, namely the infallibe Matsushita "tap water" philosophy. After all, with this philosophy, the company had grown from a mom-and-pop operation to a multi-billion dollar multinational far outclassing MCA in size. Furthermore, it was only under Tanii, when the company had started to go against the Matsushita culture, that the scandals and product recalls began to appear. If MCA was to continue as a member of the Matsushita family, MCA was from now on to make only low-cost movies with the impossible guarantee of having the movies appeal to everyone. MCA was furthermore not to pursue what MEI considered risky ventures such as running theme parks or broadcast networks. In effect, MEI under Morishita was rejecting the high-risk corporate culture of Hollywood and MCA. From MCA's point of view, this was a complete betrayal of what MEI had originally promised to MCA: the maintenance of its creative independence. Under the circumstances, they fought to make MEI keep its word—but to no avail.

In the end, it was the disappearance of tolerance owing to a change in leadership and strategy that led to the demise in the MEI-MCA relationship. The demise of tolerance was accelerated by MEI's return to the basics of making hardware, so that there was nothing for MEI to learn from a US movie software company. In retrospect, despite the streak of intolerance that existed within MEI, the demise of the MEI-MCA relationship may not have been inevitable. The relationship might have continued if the scandals and product defects and the struggle for power with Masaharu had not occured, and if Tanii and his associates including Hirata and Sakuma had not been pushed out of power. There was a prevailing view at the time that if there had been no National Lease scandal, vice president Sakuma would have been the successor to Tanii.[255] If that had happened instead of Morishita becoming president, Sakuma, who eventually became president of a satellite TV broadcaster, might have continued to support MCA in its plans for business expansion, which in turn would have led to the development of a very different relationship.

Tolerance, as preached by Konosuke and practiced in MEI's acquisitions and joint ventures, meant that the good practices of the acquired enterprise were not only accepted, but were also adopted by MEI where applicable. The culture of the acquired entity was respected and largely left alone. The acquisitions of Komori Denki and JVC are cases where this was actually practiced. Tolerance also meant respecting some of the traditions of the acquired company, such as its company name and trademarks. Hence, companies such as JVC and even Quasar saw their names remain in existence after their acquisition. And as the retaining of Wasserman and Sheinberg showed, tolerance also meant respecting the current management of the acquired company as much as possible. To its credit, MEI to the very end of the relationship did not fire a single MCA senior executive, despite all the differences between the two sides.

At the same time, there were to be limits to tolerance. Management and business autonomy, for example, would be allowed, but as the employees of Komori Denki were to find out, this was to be tempered with accepting the management principles of Konosuke, which, it should be added, was not forced but gradually accepted and implemented through the process of dialogue initiated by Konosuke. MCA was also to find out the limits of tolerance when it had its business plans rejected and was told that MEI knew what was best for the movie studio. For MCA, the only way to resolve such a situation was to seek its independence from the Matsushita Empire.

To conclude, the lack of tolerance was a factor that had impacted the relationship between MEI and MCA. As it was with the Mongol Empire and the VOC, leadership also proved to be decisive in determining whether tolerance was to be practiced or not. Under Konosuke, tolerance that allowed for the continuation of the acquired company's brands and management and the acceptance of its management and employees into the larger Matsushita family contributed to the success and continuation of its acquisitions such as Komori Denki, Nakagawa Kikai, and JVC. Under Tanii, his determination to change the hardware-minded group-oriented culture of MEI which was so closely tied to Konosuke led to the tolerance that initially resulted in a "hands off" policy towards MCA. Under Morishita, it was conversely his attempt to restore the company to its manufacturing roots and to the culture of Konosuke that led to the intolerance of the business practices of MCA and ultimately to its divestiture. For Morishita, the revitalization of the hardware electronics business was all that mattered and interested him—not the buying of broadcast companies and other businesses which he didn't understand, or the making of movies which only sucked in money with no guarantee of becoming a hit. But in a subconscious salute to Konosuke, Morishita made no attempt to change the management of MCA. Instead, as with Kokudo Denki, which Konosuke sold off when he could not come to agreement with its management, Morishita simply sold off MCA as well, with its management intact.

Postscript

Despite the divesture of MCA and the attempts of Morishita to revitalize MEI's core electronics, the company for the period of 1995–2000 continued to register low revenue growth and profit margins.[256] In 2000, Nakamura Kunio took over as president of the company. To convey his sense of urgency to his colleagues on the challenges he felt MEI was facing, Nakamura said, "We are in a critical situation, having nowhere to fall back to. If we cannot achieve a quick rebound, Matsushita will become history."[257] Indeed, in the fiscal year of 2001 MEI very much had its back to the wall, with plummeting sales and an operating loss precipitated in part by the bursting of the Internet (dot-com) bubble in 2000. For the next couple of years, until 2006, Nakamura undertook measures such as cutting the workforce by about 26,000 and cutting corporate pension benefits.[258] Structural reforms, including the consolidation and rationalization of businesses and the distribution system, elimination of product lines, and reduction in management layers, helped the company to register a profit in the following fiscal year and maintain further growth in profits, so that by fiscal year 2005, operating profit margins had reached almost 5 percent.[259]

After the divestiture of MCA, MEI continued to make M&A deals, of which the most recent and largest in scale was the acquisition of Sanyo Electric in 2008. At the same time, MEI also divested several of its businesses, the most prominent example being JVC, which had originally been bought by Konosuke. Interestingly enough, while President Otsubo Fumio, the successor to Nakamura, commented that there were duplications of businesses between MEI and JVC which was a factor behind the decision to divest, he also alluded to certain aspects of JVC's "predisposition" which were at odds with MEI, making it necessary to review the nature of their relationship.[260] Otsubo was in effect hinting that one of the reasons that MEI was selling off JVC was its different corporate culture.[261] The tolerance that Konosuke preached, which had allowed JVC to go on with its independent ways under its own management for several decades and retain its own culture, was being disavowed if not totally disapproved of.

While I will refrain from going into detail on Nakamura's reforms,[262] I will mention that under his watch attempts were made to rebuild what has been described by Nakamura as "the stagnated corporate culture" of MEI.[263] In words that echo the efforts of Tanii to create a new Matsushita culture and a man (and woman) who was not a "kintaro-ame," using the culture of MCA as a catalyst, Nishimura Hiroaki, General Manager of the Global Human Resources Team of the Corporate Personnel Group in MEI, stated in 2005,

> To become a truly global company, we must act globally in getting people. To achieve, this, however, will require that we accelerate our efforts at localization and we must also nurture local talent. At the same time, we must train the Japanese executives in being able to deal with business on a global scale. We must also proceed in globalizing the corporate culture.[264]

Although MEI as a global business was expanding its presence in the world, Nishimura admitted that "business for MEI was very much centered on the activities of the Japanese, and especially Japanese men. With such an old model which is based on past practices and experience, new businesses cannot be born."[265]

In 2010, Panasonic issued its Diversity Promotion Vision:

> As a truly global company, we are aiming to create a corporate culture that *respects different values and encourages diversity.* All employees will *freely*

demonstrate their individuality and creativity to enable both the company and themselves to continue to grow with the ultimate goal of becoming the No. 1 Green Innovation Company in the Electronics Industry [italics mine].[266]

In what seemed an almost uncanny repeat of the "Break Through" slogan and its objectives, as stated by Tanii but coming almost 20 years after he was ignominiously ousted, MEI in its new corporate vision expressed its desire to create a new corporate culture that tolerated and accepted diversity and individualism, which parted ways with Konosuke's collectivist ideal. With this new vision, the company was acknowledging that diversity and individualism *are* essential for it to survive and prosper in an increasingly globalized business environment and to grow new businesses. A Japan-centric approach had to be discarded in favor of a global mindset and capabilities. Capable people, regardless of their nationality, were to be put in positions where they could make use of their full potential and contribute to the company. In retrospect, Tanii was a leader too much ahead of his time in his "Break Through" vision for MEI.

Throughout this narrative on MEI's M&A experience with MCA and other companies, I have argued that tolerance was a factor that helped Konosuke and MEI achieve success with its M&A of Japanese companies. Conversely, intolerance led MEI to fail in integrating the American company Quasar by not accepting and treating its non-Japanese employees as truly equal with the Japanese, which frankly was akin to an act of racism. Intolerance also played a part in MCA's divestiture, as MEI after Tanii refused to accept the creative independence of the company as was originally promised, and MCA in turn balked at accepting the "Matsushita tradition" which leaders such as Morishita considered at the time to be the correct and only way to do business.

If MEI is serious this time about its goal to develop a tolerant culture that "respects different values and encourages diversity," and if in its global expansion it considers cross-border M&A as a strategic option, it is to be hoped that it will reflect upon its experience with Quasar and MCA, keeping in mind the tolerance preached by its founder and his approach towards M&A integration, which emphasized building trust, support, and acceptance of the "Matsushita Way" through dialogue with his newly acquired employees.

6   Sony's movie entertainment empire

Introduction

From the moment the Japanese electronics conglomerate Sony Corporation acquired the Hollywood movie entertainment company Columbia Pictures Entertainment (CPE) and its movie studio Columbia Pictures (Columbia) from the Coca-Cola Company in 1989, people of various backgrounds including captains of industry, industry watchers, and journalists were describing the acquisition as a disaster in the making. They predicted that this odd-couple marriage between a Japanese consumer electronics manufacturer and a Hollywood movie studio would not last—that it would sooner or later end ignominiously for Sony. Journalist Edward Klein, in an article for the pop culture magazine *Vanity Fair*, reported that Shima Keiji, chairman of the Japanese public broadcaster NHK, warned Sony chairman Morita Akio when the latter told him of Sony's plans to purchase CPE in 1989, "You don't understand Hollywood. It won't work. You're asking for trouble. You're getting into a business that you won't be able to control. Don't do it!"[1] A couple of years later the *Los Angeles Business Journal* reported in 1994, "Hollywood executives say Japan's power in Hollywood is fading and they expect Sony and Matsushita to sell their studios or partial stakes in them in the near future."[2] Financial analyst Emanuel Gerard concluded that Sony's move to acquire CPE was "an unmitigated debacle."[3] Among the US media in particular, a characteristically un-American *schadenfreude* was at work. Author John Nathan recalls a hostile press that jeered at every mistake and loss that Sony made and continuously predicted the company's exit from the movie business.[4] For those predicting disaster, if ever there were an M&A deal that was *not* meant to be, this was it. As late as 2005, in a book *Deals From Hell: M&A Lessons that Rise Above the Ashes*, business professor Robert F. Bruner of the University of Virginia presented Sony's acquisition of CPE as a failure accompanied by lessons on what to avoid when undertaking an M&A deal. Of course, most of the criticism was not without warrant. The early years of CPE under Sony were indeed tumultuous and included several high-profile and expensive management changes, a massive and costly write-off of US$2.7 billion which wiped out nearly 25 percent of Sony's shareholders' equity, several costly bombs at the box office including *Last*

Action Hero, and a major changing of the guard within Sony's management.[5] Furthermore, the "synergy effect" touted by Sony as a major reason for the acquisition simply did not happen initially as the company envisioned it; that is, people who viewed a movie made by CPE did not necessarily buy Sony hardware equipment. As noted by Dartmouth College professor of leadership and management, Sydney Finkelstein, "Columbia Pictures could never on its own have the market power to dictate market acceptance of Sony hardware products."[6]

Yet, more than 20 years later, CPE, renamed Sony Pictures Entertainment (SPE) shortly after its acquisition, remains within the Sony corporate empire. Even more important, it has for at least a decade (2000–2010) consistently been profitable and has staked out its position as one of the major studios in Hollywood, vying for the top position in market share. Not only has it produced profits and a steady stream of revenues for its parent, it has also helped to diversify the sources of profit for Sony, which had been heavily reliant upon its electronics business. Perhaps because of SPE's steady performance and Sony's tenacity in keeping hold of the studio, criticism of Sony's acquisition has lately (as of 2010) been muted. Indeed, the *New York Times* commented in late 2009 that after bouts of dysfunction and chaos SPE had stabilized with a management team more durable than at some of the other major studios.[7]

Another undeniable benefit from the Sony-CPE union was the establishment of the Blu-Ray High Definition (HD) home video format as the industry-wide standard, which Sony, along with Panasonic, developed and pushed for adoption in the market. A competing format developed by the Japanese electronics manufacturer Toshiba also vied to become the industry standard, but without a major studio guaranteeing support for its format, Toshiba was clearly at a disadvantage. Not only could Sony immediately supply movies and TV shows in the Blu-Ray format, but the fact that it was a major player in Hollywood with a substantial network of allies within the industry ensured support from other major Hollywood studios and influential individuals, support that Toshiba ultimately failed to win. The initial expectations of so-called synergy from the merger of hardware and software, leading to increased sales of Sony hardware products, may not have materialized as imagined, but at least Sony was able to avoid a repeat of the Betamax VCR fiasco and justify its development costs for Blu-Ray. In this respect, software was able to drive the acceptance by consumers of a single new standard platform for video.

It may still be too early to consider Sony's acquisition of CPE a "successful" example of an M&A deal. Furthermore, from a strategic standpoint, critics point out that the acquisition of CPE has failed to produce any synergy to drive the sales of Sony electronics products. Bruner states that the firing in 2007 of the Sony CEO Nobuyuki Idei, who had been president of the company since 1995, was in effect an admittance by Sony's directors of the failure to achieve the originally targeted convergence or synergy between Sony's hardware and software businesses.[8] But I argue that despite the early tumultuous history of the acquisition, its current performance within the Sony group and its contributions to supporting the Sony's electronics business, as in the introduction of the Blu-Ray format, make it a qualified success. Furthermore, Sony's hold over SPE has far exceeded that of MEI's hold over MCA. While MEI opted out of Hollywood after just five years, Sony has held out to the time of this writing.

Several books and articles provide detailed narratives of Sony's foray into Hollywood, of which John Nathan's *Sony: The Private Life* (1999) and journalists Nancy Griffin and Kim Masters's *Hit & Run* (1997) are noteworthy for providing a meticulously researched recounting of the events of the time; both are referred to extensively in this chapter. Countless newspaper and magazine articles, particularly in the *New York Times*, the *Los Angeles Times*, and *Vanity Fair*, also followed Sony's every move into Hollywood. In the sections that follow, I will only briefly highlight Sony's experience in Hollywood and focus primarily on the role of culture in Sony's management of its Hollywood studio. To start off, I will first go back to the roots of Sony and focus on the management principles that the founder Ibuka Masaru established and with co-founder Morita Akio promoted within the company, which came to define Sony's corporate culture.

The origins of Sony's culture

The Sony prospectus

As we saw in the previous chapter, the growing of the company through M&A was an integral part of the history of Matsushita Konosuke's MEI. This stands in stark contrast to the history of Sony, which grew largely from organically driven business development. Immediately after the end of World War II in May 1946, Ibuka Masaru, an engineer, founded what was to become the forerunner of Sony, the Tokyo Telecommunications Company, with a start-up capital of ¥190,000 or approximately US$500. According to the company prospectus drawn up by Ibuka, the company was formed with eight specific purposes of existence in mind:[9] (1) to establish an ideal factory that would stress a spirit of freedom and open-mindedness, and where engineers with sincere motivation could exercise their technological skills to the highest level; (2) to reconstruct Japan and to elevate the nation's culture through dynamic technological and manufacturing activities; (3) to promptly apply highly advanced technologies which were developed in various sectors during the war to common households; (4) to rapidly commercialize superior technological findings from universities and research institutions that are worthy of application in common households; (5) to bring radio communications and similar devices into common households and to promote the use of home electric appliances; (6) to actively participate in the reconstruction of the war-damaged communications network by providing needed technology; (7) to produce high-quality radios and to provide radio services that are appropriate for the coming new era; and (8) to promote the science education among the general public.

With only 20 engineers, with whom he had worked at the Japan Precision Instrument Company during the war, Ibuka sought to create a company that would focus on developing and manufacturing communications equipment such as radios and voltmeters that were demanded by many customers including the Japanese government, scholars, and researchers. As the company prospectus states, Ibuka also had in mind developing products that were going to be demanded by the general public, who for the most part had had their lives devastated by the war and were now on the slow road to rebuilding their lives.

The prospectus also addresses what kind of culture Ibuka had in mind for the company. According to Ibuka's vision, Sony was to be a company where "freedom" and "open-mindedness" were to prevail, where the employees were free to express their opinions and promote their own ideas. The exchange of ideas and debate among peers and between superiors and subordinates was to be encouraged, and engineers were to be allowed to freely sharpen their skills and knowledge. Formalities were to be avoided where possible. As Ibuka stated in the prospectus, "We shall avoid having formal positions for the mere sake of having them."[10] Just emerging from a period during which the Japanese experienced many restrictions on basic liberties such as freedom of speech and thought, the culture that Ibuka sought to establish within his new company was invigorating and refreshing for a war-weary population. Rituals that promoted company unity and produced conformity, such as the daily singing of the company song or the recitation of the company principles as was done at Matsushita Electric (MEI), was to be deliberately eschewed. While Matsushita Konosuke exhorted his MEI employees to "pool abilities and strength of resolution to accomplish shared objectives in mutual trust,"[11] at Ibuka's company the individual efforts and respective abilities of employees were emphasized. As Ibuka put it in his prospectus, "We ... shall place emphasis on a person's ability, performance and character, so that each individual can fully exercise his or her abilities and skills." Despite this stress upon individualism, Ibuka did not, however, take lightly the need for teamwork. In his preface to the prospectus, Ibuka related that while embarking upon setting up the company he "began to conceive of ways for ... motivated individuals to be united on a personal level, to embrace a firm cooperative spirit and unleash their technological capacities without any reserve."[12]

Co-founder Morita Akio, in his memoirs *Made in Japan*, reconfirmed the importance which the company's leadership placed on promoting a vigorous corporate culture of individualism. According to Morita, "At our company we are challenged to bring our ideas out into the open. If they clash with others, so much the better, because out of it may come something good at a higher level."[13] Morita also stressed the importance the leaders of Sony placed from its early history on the "principle of respecting and encouraging one's ability—the right man in the right post—and ... constantly [allowing] him to develop his ability."[14]

Another aspect of the culture of Sony was that it was to be a company where risks and new challenges were to be welcomed and encouraged. The company was to actively take the risks of developing products never made by anyone before. As Ibuka made clear, "We shall welcome technological challenges ...

avoid any formal demarcations between electronics and mechanics and shall create our own unique products ... with a determination that other companies cannot overtake."[15]

The origins of Ibuka's thought

Ibuka was born in 1908 in Nikko, Tochigi Prefecture, located north of Tokyo. Both of his parents were from the northernmost island of Hokkaido. Ibuka was born into well-to-do circumstances. His father, Tasuku, the descendant of an illustrious line of samurai in the service of the Matsudaira clan of Aizu, was an engineer who studied at the Tokyo Institute of Technology and worked for a prestigious copper-mining company, Furukawa Kogyo. His mother, Sawa, was the daughter of a wealthy landowner and, rarely for a female at the time, a university graduate, having studied at the private Japan Women's University in Tokyo.

While Tasuku was working for Furukawa in Nikko, the future founder of Sony was born. Tragedy struck early, as his father died at the age of 30 from tuberculosis when Ibuka was two years old. Several years later, Ibuka's mother remarried, but fortunately for Ibuka he got along well with his stepfather, who seemed to have accepted him as his own son. Ibuka fondly relates that when he took the difficult entrance exams for Kobe Junior High School in the spring of 1921, his stepfather, who accompanied Ibuka to the school grounds to hear the exam results, immediately proceeded to order new shoes and a school uniform once they found out that Ibuka had passed the exams.[16]

During his junior high school days Ibuka encountered wireless technology, which sparked his lifelong interest in radios. Also at this time Ibuka became more closely acquainted with Christianity. Ever since he was born Ibuka had had connections with the religion. His father and other relatives including his older sister were followers. Although it is not clear when Ibuka's father became a Christian, according to Ibuka his father was personally acquainted with Nitobe Inazo, a Meiji-era (1868–1912) scholar, educator, and writer who graduated from Johns Hopkins University in the US and universities in Germany with several doctorate degrees and later served as an official at the secretariat of the League of Nations. Nitobe had done much in his lifetime through writings and public speeches to promote friendship between Japan and the US, and struck up a friendship with president Theodore Roosevelt, who was much impressed with Nitobe's book, *Bushido, the Soul of Japan*. It was partly thanks to Nitobe's rapport with the president that the US became sympathetic to the Japanese cause in the Russo-Japanese War (1904–1905). While deeply patriotic and devoted to elevating Japan's position in the eyes of the world, Nitobe was also a devout Quaker Christian who spent much time and effort promoting Christian principles and humanitarian teachings in Japan. Ibuka suggests his father may have fallen under the influence of Nitobe and hence the teachings of the Christian religion.[17] Ibuka's mother, while not a Christian, was also acquainted with Nitobe, who according to Ibuka treated her with great affection.[18] Interestingly, Ibuka did not receive a baptism at the time of his birth. Rather, according to Ibuka, it was from the time when he was a junior high school student that he started to go to church, which he claims could have been due to sentimental feelings that he had for the hymns that were sung in church which he liked very much.[19]

Ibuka suggests that his initial encounter with Christianity had no special meaning, but later when he was a student at Waseda High School his interest in the religion would become genuine. At one point Ibuka lived in a dormitory near his school that was run by Christians, before leaving in protest at what he considered the lenient and hypocritical attitude of its Baptist minister, who failed in his eyes to follow the Christian precept of "love thy neighbor" and for who tolerated the loose morals of other students.[20]

A certain individual who later became his mentor also influenced Ibuka's feelings for the Christian religion. That person was Yamamoto Tadaoki, a professor and head of the engineering science department at Waseda University. Yamamoto's son and Ibuka went to the same kindergarten in Tokyo, and according to Ibuka, Yamamoto treated him kindly.[21] Ibuka claimed that it was his admiration for Yamamoto that had made him decide to enter Waseda.[22] Yamamoto, a graduate of Tokyo Imperial University (Teidai), was known for having built up the engineering science department at Waseda and for doing research on television technology. Along with Takayanagi Kenjiro, he was one of the first developers of television broadcasting technology in Japan. Cosmopolitan and liberal in outlook, with an affinity for the western lifestyle reflected in his western-style house complete with the latest electric appliances available to only a few affluent people, Yamamoto was also a devout Christian, having been baptized when he was a student at Teidai. Yamamoto was an ardent follower of Uemura Tadahisa, a well-known pastor of the protestant Christian Church of Japan who preached at the Fujimicho church in Iidabashi, Tokyo. His followers included such figures as the writers Shimazaki Toson and Kunikita Doppo. It was at this church, where Yamamoto was a church elder, that Ibuka received his baptism while in his third year of high school. According to Ibuka, it was on account of Yamamoto that he become a Christian.[23]

Another Christian who would have an influence on Ibuka was Maeda Tamon. Maeda had an illustrious career that including being a journalist, a representative at the International Labor Organization of the League of Nations, a member of the House of Peers, governor of Nigata Prefecture, and minister of education in the Higashikuni and Shidehara cabinets. Maeda became Ibuka's father-in-law and the first president of Ibuka's newly established company which eventually became Sony. Maeda was described by his contemporaries as being of amiable character and as holding a view of the world based on his Christian beliefs.[24] Takagi Yatsuka, who worked alongside with Maeda at one point and was later an honorary professor at the University of Tokyo (Todai), described Maeda as a man of unwavering principles with an unlimited capacity for tolerance and sympathy for others.[25] Maeda was also an enthusiastic follower of Nitobe's. Maeda's daughter recalls her father as being strict with himself and with others. But thanks to the influence of Nitobe, whom she described as a warm-hearted tolerant spirit, she had seen her father change into a more tolerant and compassionate person.[26] Ibuka as well recognized the influence of Nitobe on Maeda's beliefs. But more importantly for the development of Ibuka's view of life, he recalled that he was greatly attracted to the way of thinking of his father-in-law and admitted to being heavily influenced by him.[27]

The Japanese Meiji Constitution promulgated in 1890 guaranteed all Japanese the freedom of religion with the proviso that the exercise of this right did not disturb the peace or infringe upon their duties as citizens. Despite this assurance from the state, for a Christian such as Ibuka, it would have been extremely difficult, or required a dual system of belief combined with a leap of faith, to reconcile the nationalistic teachings of the Japanese state education system, which espoused as a matter of fact the divinity of the emperor, with the monotheistic religion of Christianity. As explained unequivocally in pamphlets put out by the Japanese Ministry of Education such as the *Fundamentals of Our National Polity* (Kokutai no hongi), published in 1937, the Japanese emperor was a descendant of the sun goddess Amaterasu Omikami, and to serve the emperor was the rationale for the life of the Japanese and their codes of morality.[28] In an environment that promoted a belief system that held the emperor as divine and the Japanese people as descendants of the gods, the fact that Ibuka remained a Christian and did not conform to the beliefs of the majority of the Japanese is perhaps a manifestation of his individuality. That his Christian mentors such as Yamamoto and Maeda were men of a liberal outlook may have also ingrained in Ibuka's mind an association of Christianity with liberalism, which may have made it difficult for him to accept the growing rejection in Japan during the 1930's of Western philosophical concepts such as individualism and liberalism. As asserted in the *Way of the Subjects* (Shinmin no michi), a pamphlet published by the Education Ministry in 1941, exposure to the Western ideologies of individualism, liberalism, utilitarianism, and materialism was leading to the destruction of customs and traditions passed down by the forefathers of the Japanese. For the Japanese to be rescued, they were to devote their minds and bodies to the service of the emperor, which was the purpose and meaning of life.[29] In effect, Japanese nationalist teachings were calling upon the Japanese to repudiate the concept of a "self" and all forms of pursuits in life that aimed at achieving personal happiness and liberty.

But even before the publication of such pamphlets and the increasingly ultranationalist, anti-individualist, and anti-liberal bent of the government, Ibuka would have most likely been aware that businesses in prewar Japan had been for some time adopting a collectivist philosophy in their management practices that was antithetical to the concept of individualism. This tendency was partly in response to rising labor unrest, the permeation of socialist and radical views in society, and the formation of trade unions. In the late Meiji period, business leaders such as Muto Sanji had promoted the idea of the company as the parent of a "great extended family" (dai kazoku shugi). As he put it, to prevent the rise of labor unions, corporate paternalism that focused on employee satisfaction and the public benefit had to be practiced. Managers were to mold employees into obedient workers by benevolently treating them as if they were children in their care or members of their own family. If managers did this, Muto believed that a natural kind of mutual affection would develop between employers and employees leading to an improvement in the quality of output and returns on expenses paid for the welfare of employees.[30]

While Muto is credited for his efforts to find the model of corporate familism,[31] the long history of isolation that Japan had experienced under the Tokugawa regime may have naturally conditioned the people to easily submerge their identities into various organizations, thereby making it easy for the concept to permeate throughout the Japanese business world and be accepted by the power holders of the country. As explained by the Meiji statesman Ito Hirobumi, the Japanese, being homogenous in race, language, religion, and sentiments, had, as a result of their long seclusion, unconsciously become a vast village community where cold, rational thinking and public decision-making had always become restrained and bogged down by the warm human emotions between men.[32] Consequently, what made Japan different from other countries is that instead of cold and rational calculation, moral and emotional factors often came to the fore in Japanese business transactions. That is to say, while companies would normally go out of business as a result of poor performance, in Japan, by contrast, sturdy businesses would be dragged down for the sake of saving collapsing enterprises from the abyss, which would on one hand lead to a temporary lowering of the general level of prosperity, but on the other hand allow the avoidance of violent shocks to the economy as a whole.[33] It would seem that Ito was presciently describing the situation of post-bubble Japan in the 1990s, when many so-called "zombie" companies that had no chance for survival were kept on life-support systems by banks and other creditors. Perhaps this shows the continuity of some aspects of cultural behavior over long periods of time. While clearly preventing what the Austrian economist Joseph Schumpeter described as the process of "creative destruction" inherent in a capitalist society, which he saw as fundamental to the birth of innovation, this moral and emotional factor was the means, according to Ito, to maintain the bond between patron and protégé and the capitalist employer. Conflicts would be mitigated and the principle of mutual assistance would prevail throughout society. Thus Ito on one hand viewed this form of corporate paternalism, embodying the interplay of moral and emotional factors between the capitalist and the employee, as a way to prevent the advance of "dangerous" socialist ideas. On the other hand, Ito also saw the dangers of too much of this social peculiarity, claiming that unless it is held in restraint, free discussion is apt to be smothered, leading to cases where the transference of power in a village may become an internal family question when it really ought to be considered within the parameters of national or village interest, which includes getting the best and brightest people as leaders. Accordingly, Ito saw free discussion as a prime necessity for the welfare of society.[34]

In contrast to Ito, who saw that the excessive practice of a village-based familism or corporate paternalism could smother free discussion among individuals, Muto, who saw employees to be treated as members of a family and hence in a benevolent manner by their managers, suggested that as "good children," the employees were to do as they were told in accordance with the wishes of their manager-parents. No back-talk would be allowed. Individualistic behavior was to be eschewed. Shibusawa Eiichi, another Meiji entrepreneur who left his mark in history as the founder of many joint stock companies, supported Muto's views of corporate paternalism and viewed it as a positive factor in contrast to the "extreme" individualism practiced in the West. As he rosily described it, within the Japanese corporate family system, not only does the person who is at the head of a family support his family members, but through his warm-heartedness, the employer will begin to love the employee, the employee in turn will respect the employer, and everything will proceed harmoniously.[35] Espousing the views presented by business leaders such as Shibusawa and Muto, managers in the newly emerging industrial sector of prewar Japan invoked the "beautiful" Japanese traditions of obedience, loyalty, and harmony to placate obstreperous laborers and unify all social classes so as to attain Japan's imperial goals.[36]

To promote harmonious employer-labor relations and in support of Muto's concept of the company as an extended family, the Japanese government introduced legislation that in effect acknowledged the "beautiful custom" of paternalism as the basis of a stable social order. Later the government announced that each company was now recognized by law as a "family" (jigyo-ikka).[37] A pre-World War II government bureaucrat responsible for maintaining peaceful labor relations envisioned that the factory of Japan would become one big family, with the factory owner as a benevolent parent looking after the welfare of the employees. In such an arrangement, strikes would become unthinkable, and the productivity of capital would increase, leading to a rise in the nation's wealth and power.[38] The concept of corporate paternalism as first conceived by Muto and later adopted by the Japanese government in an attempt to create a "harmonious society" may have hence become the basis for those well-known management practices of Japanese companies in the postwar period: seniority-based promotion, lifetime employment, and company-based (as opposed to industry-based) trade unions.

Given his independent-mindedness and respect for his liberal mentors such as Yamamoto and Maeda, it is hard to imagine that Ibuka was sympathetic to the nationalistic diatribes raised against individualism and liberalism. An incident also suggests that Ibuka did not think favorably of Japanese militarism and what it stood for. In his junior high school days in Kobe, Ibuka mentions in his memoirs that he along with other students took part in some military training exercises conducted by the army. During one such exercise Ibuka and other students suddenly had their faces slapped by an officer who reprimanded them for horsing around. Ibuka relates that he was extremely surprised at the time by this punishment for a minor childish infraction and that it left a deep impression upon him.[39] Although Ibuka does not say so directly, the fact that he had bothered to mention this incident many years after it happened is perhaps suggestive of the negative feelings he had towards the glorification of the military and its use of violence in silencing those that disobeyed them.

As for the concept of corporate paternalism, it is not clear what Ibuka's views on this were. However, his statement within his prospectus which calls for creating a workplace where a spirit of open-mindedness and freedom would prevail suggests that Ibuka was more interested in having people speak their minds rather than having them behave as obedient sheep who simply followed their shepherd managers. His call for open-mindedness and freedom was in effect a repudiation of the anti-individualistic values of Japanese prewar culture.

Origins of Morita's thought

To Ibuka's credit, his vision of a factory where freedom and open-mindedness would prevail did not end up being only on paper, but was established in his new company from the start, in which Morita Akio, the co-founder of Sony, also played a major role. Morita recalled that when the company had just begun, it was small enough that the entire company could come together and discuss each problem that came up and try different approaches until they were able to come to a solution. Morita credits this atmosphere of free discussion as one of the drivers for the company's remarkable growth.[40]

And as the company grew, differences of opinions continued to be tolerated and respected. At one time in the early history of Sony, Morita, who was deputy president, got into a heated argument with the chairman of the board, Tajima Michiji. Tajima, as described by Morita, was an old-school gentleman who had had a distinguished career as director general of the Imperial Household Agency. The two argued about some matter, with Morita persistently pushing his views and finally angering Tajima to the point where the latter threatened to leave the company, saying that he could not be in a company where he and Morita were sometimes in conflict and did not share the same views. Morita, however, completely took Tajima by surprise by calmly responding that if both had the same ideas on everything there wouldn't be any point for both of them to be in the same company and receive a salary, and that furthermore if he resigned it would be an act of disloyalty to the company.[41] Whether Tajima agreed to Morita's views or not is not known, but in any event he decided to stay on.

Morita was no doubt greatly attracted to the character of Ibuka, whom he described as a person of great leadership qualities that included the ability to take a young group of cocky engineers and mold them into a management team where everyone cooperated and spoke their minds.[42] But Morita's tolerant view on respecting different viewpoints was also a reflection of his upbringing. As the eldest-born son of a sake-brewing family with a history going back hundreds of years, family tradition dictated that Morita would succeed his father as the head of the company business. But since Morita from his early years took an interest in science, his father, Kyuzaemon, showed a high level of appreciation for his son's talent and interests and did not force him to conform to his own beliefs or desires. When Morita joined Ibuka upon the creation of Sony, Kyuzaemon, who by now had likely given up any thought of his eldest son succeeding him in the family business, threw in his full support for his son by providing funds for the start-up venture.

Morita's tolerance for the diversity of viewpoints was also connected with a respect for those who did not fit the mold, or belong to the "mainstream" of Japanese society. Sociologists who focus on Japan often cite the proverb about "the nail that sticks out is hammered in" as representative of the social and psychological constraints that keep individual Japanese people from straying from socially accepted behavior and practices. Morita, however, welcomed to Sony those who did not conform or follow the accepted path laid out for Japanese, and on several occasions put out want ads in newspapers declaring, "We want nails that stick out!" Representative of this policy was that unlike many other large Japanese corporations, Sony made a conscientious effort to hire Japanese who had studied at universities abroad. Morita also published a book titled *Never Mind School Records* which attacked the Japanese attachment to judging people and their abilities by the university they graduated from. While being raised by a tolerant father who accepted his son's aspirations and sacrificed family traditions certainly had an impact on Morita's views, his position within Japanese society at large may have also influenced his outlook. Although born into wealthy circumstances, Morita was from the city of Nagoya which was considered to be unsophisticated compared to cosmopolitan Tokyo. As his wife Yoshiko put it to journalist Edward Klein, "[my husband] was just a country boy from Nagoya. He didn't know how to dress. I'm from Tokyo, and I made him cosmopolitan. I made him everything he is today."[43] As for educational background, although Morita graduated from Osaka Imperial University with a degree in physics, the university was considered by those obsessed with school ranking games considerably farther down the pyramid of Japanese universities which had, of course, Teidai/Todai at its apex. These factors, from his "unsophisticated" Nagoya origins, to his graduating from what was considered a less prestigious university, may have subconsciously impressed upon Morita that he was not part of the "elite," represented by a clique of Teidai/Todai graduates who became high-ranking government bureaucrats or who were working at one of the major keiretsu (conglomerate) companies such as Mitsui or Mitsubishi. All of this worked to make Morita a reactionary who accepted people of his kind—nails that stuck out—into his company as it embarked on a "something new, something different" path, unlike the keiretsu companies.

Sony culture at work

For several decades after its establishment in 1946, Sony used and developed trend-setting technologies and manufactured "world's first" or "world's smallest" products such as the transistor radio, transistor TV, desk-top calculator, videotape recorder, Walkman, Compact Disc (CD), Trinitron color TV, and portable video cameras. These products not only made a name for Sony and earned the commercial tag line "It's a Sony," but also established Sony's reputation as a company that did not follow others, Former Sony employees often regard the achievements of Sony as a result of the corporate culture established by Ibuka and Morita that allowed them the freedom to pursue their ideas. A case in point is the achievements of Kihara Nobutoshi, who was the first university graduate coming straight out of Waseda University to join Sony in 1947. In his many years at Sony, Kihara chalked up a list of significant accomplishments such as the development of the tape recorder in 1950, the transistor radio in 1955, and the world's first home videotape recorder in 1965. It is not an exaggeration to say that if Kihara had not joined Sony, the company would not be where it is today. Aside from his own brilliance, Kihara was known for getting the best and brightest engineers around him but never tightly binding them together as a group. Masuda Sohei, a former executive in charge of product development who had worked under Kihara, recalled that when working for him he did not have the feeling that he was working for someone above him. Rather, Masuda felt that Kihara worked together with his staff. According to Masuda, Kihara was the type of person who believed that the individual who came up with an idea was the person who most understood the idea and allowed his people full freedom in further developing it.[44]

With its unique trend-setting products Sony created for itself an image of being a formidable technology innovator. But the company was also a pioneer in Japanese business history. Under Morita's leadership, Sony became in 1961 the first Japanese company to offer company common stock in the US and in 1970 the first to be listed on the New York stock exchange. Sony was the first Japanese company to sell its own electronic products using its own resources in the US without resorting to the help of a trading company. At a time when all Japanese electronics companies were exporting their products from Japan to the US, Sony was in 1972 the first Japanese company to open a plant in the US to manufacture TV sets. And under the initiative and leadership of Morita, Sony entered the music recording entertainment business with a joint venture (JV) with the American broadcast company CBS, which was the owner of Columbia Records (CR): the first ever JV between a Japanese electronics company and a US broadcast and music-recording company. This took place in 1968, immediately after the Japanese government deregulated restrictions on foreign direct investment (FDI). As I argue that what happened in the management of this joint venture would have an impact on Sony's management direction for Columbia Pictures, I will next examine what took place in this joint venture.

The creation of a new joint venture (JV) empire: CBS/Sony

The setting up of a JV

In March 1968, a help-wanted ad was placed in the national daily newspaper *Asahi Shinbun* that announced, "We are looking for people to build CBS/Sony Records." The ad featured the company logo of the newly announced JV, a combination of the two logos of Sony and CR. The ad invited applications from people who were interested in making "musical dreams come true" and who wanted to "build CBS/Sony into the best record company in Japan."

The placement of the ad represented the first major step in building up a JV from scratch. This was the first time ever that a Japanese electronics hardware manufacturer had formed a 50–50 JV with a major, internationally known American recording company. It came on the heels of the deregulation of FDI in Japan in the previous year, which allowed foreign equity participation of up to 50 percent in certain companies and the setting up of subsidiaries. With no precedent, setting up this JV was going to be in many respects an experiment for Sony.

Prior to the setting up of the JV, CR had been distributing its master recordings through Nippon Columbia (NC), a company established in 1910. At the time of its inception by an American residing in Japan, Fredrick Whitney Horn, the company was known as Nippon Chikuonki Shokai (NCS). It was famous for having produced the first record players in Japan and for essentially starting the record industry in Japan.[45] In 1927, NCS acquired the Columbia name from a capital tie-up with a British record company Columbia Graphophone Company (CGS) and subsequently became known as NC. Meanwhile, CGS had bought its parent, the Columbia Phonograph Company, and was its distributor up to the outbreak of World War II. When the war ended, the US radio broadcaster, Columbia Broadcasting System (CBS), came into possession of the Columbia trademark and the recordings made by the defunct CGS through the acquisition of the American Record Corporation (ARC) which had earlier acquired CGS. While CBS began to issue records worldwide under the Columbia label, it was not able to buy back the Columbia brand name from NC in Japan, and instead entered into a licensing agreement that made NC the distributor of Columbia recordings in Japan.

During the 1950s and 1960s, under the ownership of CBS, CR expanded its business globally with hit recordings by such artists as Frank Sinatra and Tony Bennett. It was known to be a technology pioneer by developing the LP record in 1948 which greatly boosted the industry by improving sound quality, ease of use, and affordability. CR was also the first major recording company to recognize the growing prowess of the Japanese in the field of electronics when they used the C37A, a vacuum-tube-based studio recording microphone made by an up-and-coming company called Sony, for stereo recordings of works by Beethoven, Mozart, Mahler, and Brahms conducted by the renowned Bruno Walter.

Despite growing sales which led to a worldwide market share of 20 percent, management at CR was dissatisfied with its performance in Japan and believed it was being constrained from further expanding the business because of its distribution agreement with NC.[46] In anticipation of deregulation for FDI in Japan, which would then allow foreign ownership of up to 50 percent in certain industries including the music recording business, CR management discussed with NC the possibility of the former buying 50 percent of NC for CBS.[47] These conversations did not get anywhere. In 1967, the Japanese government at last announced the deregulation of FDI. With this new development, CR began to negotiate with several Japanese record companies on setting up a joint venture agreement. But according to Harvey Schein, who was president of CBS International and responsible for CR's joint ventures around the world, he was making no headway and was feeling "thwarted and miserable."[48] No one would give him a straight answer, which caused Schein to presume that not giving a straightforward "yes" or "no" was common business practice in Japan.[49]

Schein had a breakthrough when a former NC employee whom he had hired introduced him to Morita.[50] While Schein was of course acquainted with Sony and Morita, he initially did not seem to have in mind Sony as a partner, and was instead looking for advice.[51] Unknown to Schein, however, Morita had long concluded that having a presence in the music business would naturally complement Sony's electronics business. He may have also been stimulated by the recent entry of JVC (which was a subsidiary of MEI) into the music business.[52] In effect, there was to be a meeting of minds at their first encounter.

Schein and Morita met for lunch near Sony headquarters in Shinagawa, Tokyo, and upon listening to Schein's predicament and his goal of finding a partner, Morita responded with an offer to set up a joint venture with his company. Schein recalled that before even finishing their soup they had the outlines of a 50-50 joint venture. Schein was impressed by the fact that Morita seemed to have a good grasp of English, could understand ideas instantly, and furthermore predicted that in less than a year after the lunch they would see this new venture come into existence.[53] A week after the luncheon meeting between Morita and Schein, executives from CR, including Schein, Goddard Lieberson, president of CBS's Columbia Records Group, and Walter Yetnikoff, a vice president and lawyer by training at CBS who was responsible for international contracts, flew to Japan and visited Sony headquarters to hammer out the guidelines of the joint venture. On Sony's side, those who participated were Morita, Senior Managing Director Iwama Kazuo, Senior Managing Director Kodama Taketoshi, Managing Director Yoshii Noboru, and Director Ohga Norio. Yetnikoff, who later played a major role in Sony's acquisition of CR and Columbia Pictures, had a moment of trepidation when he visited the Sony office and saw "two funny guys" wearing the Sony uniform of short blue jackets coming out to greet them. Yetnikoff recalled saying to himself at the time, "this is ridiculous."[54] Despite this precarious first impression of Yetnikoff, and much to the surprise of Schein and the other CBS executives who had become accustomed to the slow decision-making of Japanese companies, Sony came back with a draft contract proposal in 10 days. To work out the details, Ohga and Schein were designated as the representatives of the two companies.

Tough negotiations followed on the various details of the JV. After it was agreed that the JV was to be set up, a notable stumbling block was the naming of the company. CBS insisted that the joint venture be called CBS/Sony in consideration of CBS's reputation in the international recording industry. Morita, however, was adamant that the company be called Sony/CBS. The company was to be based in Japan, and having the Sony name come first would signify Sony's objective of establishing itself as a major supplier of electronics hardware and music software. Furthermore, the order of the names would reflect Sony's being in charge of the JV's operation in Japan.[55] Fortunately, a face-saving compromise was worked out when both parties agreed that the ordering of the company names for the JV should be done on the basis of alphabetical order. Whether this was ever explained to the public is not known. As Morita had predicted to Schein, CBS/Sony was established less than a year (March 1968) from that initial lunch in October 1967, and a barrel of the Morita family's sake was opened for a celebratory toast between Morita and Schein. With a capital of ¥720 million, the company had the honor of becoming the first foreign-Japanese JV to be established after the set of deregulations on FDI in Japan had gone into effect in 1967. It was another Sony first.

Creating a new culture: anything goes

Sometime after Morita's lunch meeting with Schein back in October 1967, Ohga recalls that he was called into Morita's office and told that he wanted to do a JV with CBS and that he wanted him to head the new company.[56] While Morita became president of the company and was the nominal head of CBS/Sony, Ohga, who was appointed senior managing director, was put in charge of running its day-to-day operations. Previously a director in charge of manufacturing and production at Sony with responsibility for product development and design, public relations, and advertising, Ohga now moved over to the JV as a full-time executive.[57]

As Sony had no prior experience in the music recording business, naturally there was no template for building the new company. Curiously, although CBS owned half of the JV and was technically allowed to staff up to half of the company board with its own people, it did not provide any management executives.[58] Nor did it give any advice or requests to Sony on how to run the company. CBS would of course provide the library of master recordings of its artists for distribution by the JV. But once the JV was established, CBS had other things to do than help run a JV in Japan. In retrospect, this complete reliance upon Sony for running the JV reflected the high level of trust and regard that CBS and Schein in particular had for Morita as an individual and Sony as a company. For all practical purposes, the company was to be run by management supplied by Sony. In addition to Ohga, Sony transferred several executives to assist him in running the company, including Ozawa Toshio, Matsuo Shugo, Inoue Yoshikatsu, and Kanai Hiroshi. All of these executives transferred their employment status from Sony to the JV. Ozawa, who joined Sony from the mining company Furukawa Kogyo, became Ohga's right-hand man. Under Ohga at Sony, Ozawa had distinguished himself in production management and in overseeing restructuring at a major parts supplier for Sony.

With the board members of the JV in place, Ohga assumed the task of staffing the company. True to the spirit of Sony's prospectus, Ohga was given a free hand in hiring people. He seemed, however, to have some trepidation about finding enough people in time to go into business. When Ohga voiced this concern to Morita, Morita simply replied, "Oh, something will work out."[59] No instruction was given by Morita, nominally the president, on what kind of people he wanted. On one point, though, Ohga was adamant: the new JV was not just going to be a record company but was also going to reform and modernize the industry. In his view, the industry was trapped in obsolete practices and relationships between record companies and retailers that were detrimental to the growth potential of both. The widespread practice of consignment, for example, led to rampant distribution of records by the record companies to retailers who did not have to pay for the records until after they were sold, and were allowed to return unsold merchandise. To Ohga, this was "like pouring water through a sieve" and inhibited the creative tension that was needed to focus the efforts of distributors and vendors on identifying and offering appealing music records to consumers.[60] Ohga decided that he needed people who were not constrained or influenced by past industry practices; people who could bring fresh perspectives. Accordingly, the want ad that was placed in the *Asahi Shinbun* mentioned earlier stated that the new company wanted inexperienced and energetic people with fresh ideas and that anyone "regardless of nationality, age, gender, academic attainment, or physical disability" was welcome to apply.[61]

The want ad was meant to catch the eye of the Japanese public. And in many ways it did. There were no restrictions on age. Non-Japanese were welcome. Furthermore, people who had studied at less well-known universities were welcome. To advertise in this way was unheard of, since even as recently as the 1960s the most prestigious Japanese companies, such as the large trading houses of Mitsubishi and Mitsui or steel companies, searched for future candidates of managerial potential largely at the top national universities such as Todai or Hitotsubashi. Graduates of first-rate private universities such as Waseda were considered as second-rate material and options for these companies.[62] Accepting someone who was a graduate of a non-Japanese university would have been unthinkable unless that person had some strong connections. Sano Sumio, a former director of Sony and an alumnus of Waseda, related in his memoirs on Sony that when he applied to a large trading company upon graduation, he found out that graduates of Todai were automatically given a fast track entry plan and required only an interview to enter the company. Graduates of private universities, on the other hand, in addition to the interview, had to take an English language proficiency exam. Although he successfully passed the exam, Sano was told that there was an opening only at a subsidiary of the trading company. Sano promptly refused and went to Sony instead.[63]

But while the explicit disregard for academic achievement as stated in the ad may have caught the attention of interested readers, for those who were aware of the JV's parent Sony and its co-founder Morita, this was nothing new. For several years Morita had publicly stated that school records were not an absolute indicator of success. He even published a book, *Never Mind School Records* (Gakureki muyoron), in which he elaborated on this view and according to one apocryphal story even threatened to burn each employee's school records kept in the company's human resources files. He and Ibuka made it a policy at Sony that candidates for the company would be selected on the basis of their ability and not their school background. Sano recalled that when he applied for the entrance exam for Sony, unlike at other large companies, all of the candidates, whether they were graduates of Todai or Hitotsubashi or private schools such as Waseda, had to take the same exam at the same time in a large assembly hall. Sano thought at the time that Sony would indeed do a fair evaluation of the students.[64]

This is not to say, however, that Morita had an anti-Todai or national university bias. Far from it. According to a former senior managing director of Sony and an alumnus of Hitotsubashi, Morita, who was concerned about getting high-caliber employees in Sony, requested him to go to his alma mater and scout for potential Sony candidates.[65] But Morita, unlike many traditionally-minded Japanese businessmen brought up within the Japanese educational system, simply did not care if someone came from a less than prestigious university, or even if he or she had graduated from a Japanese university or had been educated in the Japanese education system for that matter. At an interview with Morita, which took place when I was 16, for a Sony scholarship to study at an international high school in the UK, he asked me what I was planning to do about university after graduating from the school. After promptly replying that I was intending to go back to Japan and study at a university in Japan, Morita responded in a curious but friendly tone, "Why do you want to go back? It will just be a waste of time. You should continue your studies outside of Japan. You can learn and experience more things at some of the best universities in the world." In retrospect, I believe this comment may have very well reflected Morita's view of the Japanese education system.

After a slow start, the ad started to attract attention and a flood of applications came in. In total 7,000 applied and 80 were accepted, including a candidate who was 70 years of age and well past the traditional retirement age of 55 in Japan at the time. According to Ohga, "only a handful" of the new recruits had any experience in the recording industry.[66] Even Ozawa, Ohga's right-hand man, knew virtually nothing about the industry and owned only 10 LP records.[67]

To his new employees and management colleagues, Ohga emphasized that CBS/Sony was a totally independent company, part of neither Sony nor CBS. They were to have complete freedom and authority in building the company as they wished, so long as they did not do anything that would harm the brand images of the parent companies.[68] New employment practices were to be introduced that would encourage individual initiative, replacing the traditional system of lifetime employment and promotion by seniority.[69] This guideline accorded with Sony's prospectus, especially with regard to its statements stressing freedom and allowing individuals to freely utilize their personal abilities.

Despite the JV's emphasis on freedom, however, discipline, especially in employee behavior, was to be emphasized within the company. Ohga believed that if the JV was to overhaul the industry, it had to set an example of upright behavior in the eyes of its industry partners. To this end, and in recognition of the freewheeling nature of the music industry that gave way to loose controls on spending and the indulging of the temperamental habits of difficult-to-please artists, Ohga enforced certain codes of behavior such as punctuality and strict monitoring of expenses. Quartz watches were given to all employees with the decree that no one would be admitted to a meeting if they were even one minute late. Ohga reviewed all expense reports submitted by the employees.[70]

The JV was a product of both Sony and CBS, but without a doubt Sony's corporate philosophy heavily influenced and dominated its corporate culture. It was a culture that was inclusive and sought to accept people of different backgrounds, but the fact that most of the people in the new company had no experience in the music recording industry must have been unsettling to CBS. Although its old partner NC did not prove to be very good at growing the business in the eyes of CBS, at least it had the experience of many decades in the Japanese music industry. But to CBS's credit, it did not oppose Ohga's hiring policy. CBS was acting in a spirit of tolerance. Had it lacked tolerance, it might very well have sent its own directors into the JV. But it did not.

While CBS was more of a passive investor as regards the day-to-day running of the JV, Sony and CBS did have some differences of opinion. When Sony developed a new tape-based digital audio recording format called DAT (Digital Audio Tape), CBS was not pleased that the new format would allow consumers to make home digital copies of LP records and was reluctant to support the format.[71] Digital audio technology meant that consumers could theoretically make an unlimited number of copies from the original digital copy of the LP without having any sound deterioration (excluding of course the usual pop and crackle surface noise sound of LPs picked up by the digital recording) as was the case with analog-based copies made with cassette tapes. Such activities would crucially cut into sales of LP records. The possible loss in LP music sales would be at the expense of DAT hardware sales. According to Yetnikoff, CBS contended that Sony's technology was allowing people to make free copies of LP records at home and at one point dispatched him to convey CBS's views to Morita.[72]

Other points of contention between the two parents came about when Lawrence Tisch assumed the day-to-day management of CBS. While praising the founders of CBS, William Paley and Frank Stanton, as "two giants who had steered CBS to greatness," Ohga scornfully described Tisch as a "desktop calculator" who wanted to squeeze dividends and funds out of the joint venture.[73] Tisch insisted, for example, on doubling the dividend payout from the JV, and investing the retained earnings of the JV in real estate and in businesses that had nothing to do with the business of CBS/Sony.[74] Instead of fighting it out with Tisch, however, Ohga accommodated his demands with counterproposals of his own, such as having the JV build record plants for CR in the US and acquiring all of CBS's record and CD plants around the world except for one in Korea. Ohga also agreed to have the JV increase its dividend payout on the condition that both parents double their investment in the JV. Such moves, and also the buying of a lemon grove in California using money from CBS/Sony helped to satisfy Tisch for a while.[75]

The result

With the management and employees of the JV in place, Ohga proceeded to establish four goals for the company: (1) become number one in record music sales within 10 years; (2) build a headquarters building as soon as possible; (3) pay out the highest salaries in the Japanese record industry; and (4) build a factory for pressing records in Japan. Under the leadership of Ohga, who became the president of CBS/Sony in April 1970, the JV eventually achieved all four targets, although Ohga admits that it took 11 years to become the largest record company in sales in Japan.[76]

While working towards achieving these goals, the JV also implemented measures desired by Ohga that shook up the Japanese record industry. With substantial help from Simon and Garfunkel's soundtrack album *The Graduate*, which was distributed by CBS/Sony and was a hit worldwide as well as in Japan, the company was able to persuade record-store owners to sign purchasing contracts for buying records.[77] Through such agreements, the JV was not only able to establish its own network of sales outlets but more importantly it established an industry precedent that was counter to the prevalent practice of consignment distribution between record companies and record stores.

CBS/Sony also started up a new genre of Japanese music when it began cultivating new talent, beginning with the singer-actress Yamaguchi Momoe, who was scouted by the company while still a high school student for what Ohga had described as her "idol-like" good looks and "genuine musical talent."[78] This new genre, which Ohga credits as being the brainchild of Sakai Masatoshi, a CBS/Sony employee who formerly worked for NC, was based on the idea of building a marketing package around so-called "idols" who would be distinguished more for being *kawaii* or cute rather than for any genuine musical ability.[79] Whether the creation of this new genre of Japanese pop music helped to realize one of Ibuka's objectives of Sony for "elevating Japan's culture" is open to debate. It must have also been galling for Ohga, who in an earlier life before coming to Sony was a professional opera singer, to indulge in a field that was far from the music of Wagner or Mozart. But Sakai's achievement was certainly in line with Sony's philosophy of doing "something new, something different."

By opening up a new genre in Japanese pop music and through the mass production and cultivation of more female and male "idols" after Yamaguchi, the company became the largest record company in Japan in sales. CBS/Sony became a business entity in its own right with its own management policies and strategies, not just a distributor for its US parent CBS. The JV also branched out and diversified its business portfolio into non-music areas as well, when it set up companies such as CBS/Sony Family Club Inc. (mail-order), CBS/Sony Publishing Inc. (book publishing), and Sony Creative Products Inc. (cosmetics).[80]

To the credit of CR, it did not force its own sense of musical direction and creativity upon its Japanese partner. Even for original master recordings from CR, CBS/Sony was given a free hand in repackaging, such as changing the order of music tracks or the album title, or redesigning the record jacket to suit Japanese sensibilities.

By 1983, the JV, which had been renamed the CBS/Sony Group Inc., was so successful that it was able to build factories on its own without financial help. It was a company without debt and rewarded employees with bonuses three times a year and shareholders with large dividends.[81] Moreover, in an early example of what Sony had defined as "synergy," CBS/Sony became the platform to launch the new technology of the CD, which was co-developed with Philips. The CD became the new industry standard in music playback, which was to replace the LP and drive a whole new range of hardware equipment of which Sony would become a major supplier.

In 1987 Sony acquired its JV partner in CBS/Sony, Columbia Records (CR), from CBS for US$2 billion. This was the first major purchase of an American entertainment company by the Japanese. Walter Yetnikoff, who was at the time CEO of CR, remained in his position. And as was the case with CBS/Sony, and in what was a sign of things to come with Columbia Pictures, Sony stayed out of the management of CR and left the running of the business largely to Yetnikoff and his management team. Yetnikoff stressed to reporters that Sony was a hands-off owner and "a better company and a better caretaker" of the record division than its former parent (i.e., CBS).[82]

Three years after its acquisition, Sony renamed CR as Sony Music Entertainment (SME) and listed 22 percent of its shares on the Tokyo Stock Exchange, raising a sum of US$1.2 billion for the company.[83] In view of the purchase price of US$2 billion paid for CR, the increase in shareholder value of SME since its purchase by Sony suggests that the acquisition of CR could also be considered a success. Another sign that reinforces this view is that 23 years after its acquisition, SME (which subsequently absorbed the music company BMG) is still within the Sony Group, contributing as much as 7 percent of total company revenues in 2010.

The application of tolerance

Much of the spirit of the corporate values held by Sony, such as stressing individual freedom, taking up new challenges, and creating something different which were enshrined in the company prospectus and practiced by Ibuka and Morita, were observed at the JV. People were allowed to create new business models and sectors. A culture of tolerance as manifested in an inclusive employment practice also existed at the record company. Prospective employees of CBS/Sony were chosen on the basis of capabilities, regardless of where they came from or their previous experience. But tolerance was also practiced by CBS when it allowed the JV to go its own way in developing business and allowed Sony to set the tone of corporate culture at the JV. It is not clear why CBS left everything up to Sony in managing the JV and did not send any of their own people to serve as board members. Perhaps CBS felt it did not understand enough about the Japanese market or culture to make any worthwhile contribution. Or it could have simply been that it could not find any executive willing to work and live in Japan at the time. Or maybe the CBS executives genuinely wanted to respect the artistic and creative decisions of their local Japanese partners. Whatever the reasons, judging from the result of the JV, CBS's passive stance on the management of the JV and its tolerance towards accepting Sony as the driver of the JV both contributed to the JV's success.

The JV with CBS was no doubt a valuable learning experience for Sony on how to manage a merger as well as to how to manage and develop a company and business that was profoundly different from its own core business of electronics. Having this prior experience was a major point of difference between Sony and MEI when they each entered the movie entertainment business. Unlike the latter, Sony was in the advantageous position of utilizing its know-how gained during its JV experience when it took on the management of Columbia Pictures Entertainment, which it acquired in 1989. But as we shall see, the use of such an experience would not be without costs.

How to and how not to run a movie company

A studio with a legacy

After the acquisition of CR in 1987, Sony went on to complement its purchase of a music entertainment company with the acquisition of Columbia Pictures Entertainment (CPE) from the soft-drink manufacturer, the Coca-Cola Company. For Sony, the acquisition of CPE along with CR put under its wings a library of music and video software that would theoretically help drive its core electronics business as well as create new business opportunities through synergies of hardware and software.

The studio that was to become Columbia Pictures (Columbia) was founded as the CBC (Cohn–Brandt–Cohn) Film Sales Company by the Cohn brothers, Jack and Harry, and Joe Brandt in 1919. Its output in its early years was the production and distribution of short silent movies or "shorts" that centered on vaudeville acts. This gave the Cohn brothers the reputation of being the "Short Subjects Kings" within the burgeoning movie industry, which came with a derisive acronym for CBC: "corned beef and cabbage."[84] Despite its reliance on shorts, however, the studio was able to transition into the "talkie" era, and from the 1930s the studio (renamed Columbia Pictures in 1924) became a major producer of feature-length films. It also continued to indulge in its tradition of producing shorts, the most famous being the immensely popular short comedy flicks starring *The Three Stooges* which first came out in the 1930s and continued until the 1950s.

As a movie studio Columbia turned out hit Academy-Award-winning movies from the 1930s to present times, such as *It Happened One Night, Bridge Over the River Kwai, A Man for All Seasons*, and *The Last Emperor*. Its golden age as an independent studio was probably the 1960s, when it produced a succession of memorable hits starting with the Academy Award-winning *Lawrence of Arabia* in 1962, followed by *Dr. Strangelove* (1964), *Cat Ballou* (1965), *The Professionals* (1966), *The Silencers* (1966), and *Casino Royale* (1967).

Aside from movie production for distribution in theaters, in the late 1940s the company entered the rapidly developing television broadcast market and set up a subsidiary, Screen Gems, which became a distribution vehicle for Columbia movies to be aired on television. Screen Gems also was devoted to the development of programs for TV, some of which became major hits, such as *Father*

Knows Best, Bewitched, and *I Dream of Jeannie*. Popular game shows such as *Jeopardy!* and *Wheel of Fortune* came under the Columbia umbrella with the studio's acquisition of Merv Griffin Enterprises.

Like many of the other Hollywood studios, Columbia had over the years turned out some costly flops which put the company at times in severe financial difficulties. In contrast to the 1960s, the 1970s began on a difficult note for the studio when it reported the greatest net loss in its history, US$28 million, in 1971, caused primarily by a string of forgettable duds released in 1970.[85] The studio subsequently fired 300 personnel as part of a restructuring. The company was also besieged by a case of managerial impropriety when its chairman, David Begelman, was found to have forged the signature of the actor Cliff Robertson for a US$10,000 check in 1976 and embezzled company funds amounting to approximately US$60,000.[86] The amount, however, paled in comparison to the US$300,000 which a Screen Gems employee embezzled between 1974 and 1978.

Fortunately for the studio, it was able to get back its bearings in movie production in 1975 when it released a succession of hits including *Shampoo, Funny Lady*, and *Tommy*. In 1977, Columbia continued its winning streak with audiences with the release of *Close Encounters of the Third Kind* and *The Deep*. The studio fully recovered from its faltering start at the beginning of the 1970s when it came out with the Academy-Award-winning movie *Kramer vs. Kramer* in 1979.

With the start of the 1980s, things continued to look upbeat at Columbia with the release of *The Blue Lagoon* and *Seems Like Old Times*, both of which were hits in 1980. In addition to movie making and TV production, Columbia was busy entering the newly developing home video market. This market was kicked off by Sony's introduction of its Betamax home video recording and playback machine in 1975 and the subsequent entry of the rival VHS home video recording machine produced by JVC and MEI. In a tie-up with the largest US consumer electronics company at the time, RCA, the two companies formed RCA/Columbia International Video to distribute Columbia's movie and TV production content on RCA-supplied VHS tape. RCA's objective in tying up with Columbia was to accelerate the sale of its VHS machines, while for Columbia the deal represented the opening of another channel of distribution for its motion picture and TV content. In retrospect, the signing up of Columbia with RCA, which was getting its VHS machines from MEI and JVC, was a critical factor in establishing the market dominance of the VHS format over the Betamax. As Morita was to later admit, it was also a factor that influenced his decision to acquire a major movie studio. Columbia also entered into a licensing agreement with the cable TV broadcaster Home Box Office (HBO) which involved having HBO bear 20 percent of the expenses associated with program production in exchange for equity ownership of the film content and exclusive distribution rights.

With its movie business flourishing and its expansion into other areas of movie-content distribution making future prospects for the company even brighter, the soft-drink manufacturer the Coca-Cola Company found Columbia attractive enough to buy it for US$750 million in 1982. Attractive indeed: Coca-Cola paid almost twice the market value for the studio at US$75 per share. Flush with cash, Coca-Cola viewed the acquisition as an opportunity to diversify its business portfolio as well as create new sources of value through synergies obtained by combining different products and businesses.

There had been talk during the 1960s of a takeover of the studio by some third party such as the corporate raider Maurice Clairmont, but this was the first time the takeover actually materialized. To quash any worries of Columbia employees, Coca-Cola stressed to its new colonial subjects that it would not infringe upon the authority of the studio management. It also expressed its approval of Columbia's management by complimenting Frank Price, chairman and president of Columbia Pictures at the time, and his top staff on their "business-like demeanor."[87]

But despite assurances of non-intervention, Coca-Cola practiced the opposite. After acquiring the company, Coca-Cola initiated business expansion measures such as setting up a joint venture with the broadcaster CBS and HBO to form Tri-Star Pictures and buying the Loews Theatre Chain, which gave Columbia a nationwide distribution outlet for its movies. Price was apparently disturbed by such moves, particularly with regard to Tri-Star, as it went against his philosophy of "less, not more."[88] Price had his start in the movie industry in the 1950s and was responsible for producing the hit movies *Kramer vs. Kramer, The Electric Horseman, The Blue Lagoon,* and *Seems Like Old Times* as well as overseeing the production of the hit TV shows *Columbo, Kojak,* and *The Rockford Files* while he was president of Universal Television at MCA. To him, movie making was a fine methodical art which required attention to details from the weaving of a story to its production. Quality, not quantity, mattered. Not so to Coca-Cola. Now Columbia would have a vertically integrated operation where customers would be served Coke while watching a movie produced by its studios in a Columbia-owned movie theater. Elusive synergies would at last be achieved. Or, so the thinking went. To do this, though, Columbia had to increase its output of movies, which had been set at eight films a year under Price.[89] After Price had left the studio in 1983 Coca-Cola installed Guy MacElwaine (who was president of Columbia while Price was still chairman) as his successor and saddled him with a production requirement of 18 movies a year. For Columbia, the new mandate of Coca-Cola was "more, not less," and screw the finer points of quality or art. If a movie turned out to be a dud, it could be replaced by another movie. For Coca-Cola, movies were essentially products in the same league as mass-consumption products such as soft drinks.[90]

Another sign that Coca-Cola had backtracked on its non-interventionist stance was its active participation in selecting management personnel. After the formation of Tri-Star, Coca-Cola shifted Columbia personnel to the new studio, starting with Victor Kaufman who was a protégé of Price. Naturally, Price was not pleased that his second-in-command was now the head of a studio that alongside with Columbia reported directly to Coca-Cola. Coca-Cola later sent in its own former vice president and manager of marketing operations, Peter Sealey, who was given the mandate to apply the company's marketing techniques to Columbia. Sealey was a native of Florida who started his marketing career at Procter & Gamble and moved to Coca-Cola in 1969 to become brand manager for the Sprite brand.[91] Later, as head of marketing at the company, Sealey was involved in the acquisition of Columbia. Sealey had no experience in the movie industry, but that was apparently not an issue for Coca-Cola when it sent him into Columbia. The company considered his marketing expertise in the soft-drink business superior to anything that Columbia could offer. But he found the movie industry a difficult place to be. Years later, in an interview with a Japanese business magazine, Sealey recalled that there were two aspects of difficulty in managing a movie studio. First, the studios considered it a virtue that they were cut off from the outside world, and they clearly differentiated between those working outside of the studios and those who are within. Those on the outside, according to Sealey, were called "civilians," i.e., public servants, non-combatants. After Coca-Cola had acquired Columbia, Sealey on his part made a personal attempt to assimilate himself into Hollywood society by growing a beard and doing away with his three-piece corporate suits.[92] A second major difficulty according to Sealey was that the industry itself had no discipline, as the heads of studios who were fired from one studio usually got hired by another with no interruption in receiving enormous amounts of money. When Sealey was president of marketing at Columbia, the head of the studio was earning more in a year than the CEO of Coca-Cola (Roberto Gozueta) at the time. To Sealey, having a business such as a movie studio, with its Hollywood movie culture idiosyncrasies, within a company like Coca-Cola that had according to Sealey a "normal" business structure, was not an easy thing.[93] Apart from pointing out the closed nature of the movie industry and castigating the behavior and practices of studio executives, the observations by Sealey also suggest the inability of Coca-Cola to accept or tolerate the nature and practices of the industry, which were part of Hollywood culture that had developed over the decades since the industry's inception in the early twentieth century. For Coca-Cola executives such as Sealey, the phrase "That's show business" apparently wasn't well received.

Sealey was appointed as head of marketing, even though Price would have preferred his close friend Marvin Antonowsky to take the position of marketing the film business after Ashley Boone, who was president for marketing and distribution at Columbia, departed to MGM studios. The application of Coca-Cola's marketing techniques as introduced to Columbia by Sealey led to cost-cutting, disregard for traditional Hollywood modes of marketing, and mixed results.[94] Sealey was reported to be indifferent to such standard Hollywood marketing activities as promotional tours associated with the launch of a movie or charity premieres (at which theaters would normally be rented out by the movie studio), so long as they were either curtailed or the associated costs were reduced.[95] Ad budgets were cut. Unfortunately for Sealey, while the production output of movies was doubled upon the orders of Coca-Cola, a substantial number of films failed to be properly promoted due to a shortage of ad money. Under Sealey's watch, *Ishtar*, starring Warren Beatty and Dustin Hoffman, was a huge US$43 million bomb. Quite a few people at the studio who had been working there for many years were no doubt unhappy that a "civilian" was calling the shots only to make a mess of things. And not surprisingly, when Sony took over Columbia, the company, which had stated publicly that it would retain most of Columbia's management, did not offer Sealey a job.[96] After leaving Columbia, Sealey in 2005 had predicted that "Howard Stringer (who became CEO of the Sony Corporation in 2005) will decide within 18 months to sell off Sony's entertainment assets including movies, music, and games,"[97] a prediction perhaps made to defend his record at the studio and emphasize that no one from outside of Hollywood could successfully manage the movie business. Of course, he has so far (at this writing) been proven wrong.

Sealey's appointment and the power he had as president of marketing and distribution at Columbia also reflected the degree to which Coca-Cola curtailed the autonomy of the studio head. In 1983, Frank Price left Columbia after a string of failures (*Annie, Hanky Panky, Things are Tough All Over, Wrong is Right*) which were all released coincidentally in the year Coca-Cola took over in 1982. Although it might appear that bad performance was behind Price's departure, it was actually caused by Sealey's presence.[98] Indeed, the amount of power that Sealey wielded in calling the shots for marketing and the fact that Sealey's presence was due to the whim of Coca-Cola must have made Price dissatisfied with the limits of his authority. Several years later in an interview with the *Los Angeles Times*, when asked if Sony was going to be a stronger and more successful owner of Columbia than Coca-Cola, Price replied, "The record of Columbia during the years Coke owned it was not very good. Clearly, I would anticipate [Sony] being much more successful." When the reporter pressed Price upon where he thought Coca-Cola had fumbled, Price evaded answering, saying "I don't want to comment on Coke. I'd just as soon duck it."[99] While Price does not specify that his dissatisfaction with Coca-Cola came from the limiting of his authority, the fact that he later returned to Columbia when Sony took over with assurances that it would not interfere in the running of the studio clearly indicates the source of his dissatisfaction.

After Price left, Fay Vincent, an entertainment lawyer who had been with Columbia Pictures since 1978, became chairman and CEO. In a move that looks as though Coca-Cola was attempting to co-opt the management at Columbia, Vincent was made executive vice president of Coca-Cola and put in charge of the company's entertainment activities. While the move could be favorably taken as an opening up of new opportunities for Columbia employees within the Coca-Cola Empire and a sign of equal treatment to Columbia management and employees, it also reflected a move on the part of Coca-Cola to further limit the authority of the studio heads and to run the business from its Atlanta headquarters.

Coca-Cola appointed Guy MacElwaine as Price's successor as president of the film division of Columbia; MacElwaine was likely made aware of the limits to his position when he was unilaterally saddled with a movie production budget determined by the parent company, which expected earnings growth.[100] Although Roberto Goizueta, the CEO of Coca-Cola, made it clear to MacElwaine that "There is only one head of the studio, and you are the head of the studio,"[101] MacElwaine commented, "Autonomy ... is a strange word. Everyone likes to use it. I can remember a lot of studio heads going around [saying] 'I have complete autonomy.' Nobody has complete autonomy."[102] MacElwaine left Columbia in 1986, leaving behind a string of forgettable failures including *A Fine Mess*, *Violets are Blue*, *Armed and Dangerous*, *Jo-Jo Dancer*, and *Your Life is Calling*. Immediately after his departure the British movie producer David Puttnam came on board as chairman and CEO of Columbia Pictures, only to leave the company less than a year later in September 1987. He left in his wake only one movie that became a memorable hit and an Academy Award winner: *The Last Emperor*. After Puttnam left, Dawn Steel, former head of production at Paramount, became president of Columbia Pictures. Her legacy in film production was at best mixed: *Casualties of War*, while critically acclaimed, turned out to be a casualty at the box office; box office revenues from *Ghostbusters II* did not generate the revenues Columbia expected. *When Harry Met Sally*, on the other hand, was a hit in 1989. Clearly with the neverending changes in studio heads, Coca-Cola was experiencing some management issues.

In September 1987, Coca-Cola announced a reorganization that would separate its entertainment business sector from its soft drinks operations, forming a new business entity called Columbia Pictures Entertainment (CPE). CPE would be 49 percent owned by Coca-Cola, with the remaining shares held by Coca-Cola shareholders and Tri-Star shareholders. Mediocre results at the box office and poor financial results were major factors that spurred Coca-Cola to partially divest its hold on the studio as a means of reducing financial risk and to retain just a 49 percent share in the firm. In that year, Columbia released the costly *Ishtar*, which, despite a first-rate cast and costly marketing activities promoting the film, bombed at the box office and became the target of scathing reviews and a joke of the industry.

This partial divestiture marked the beginning of the end of Coca-Cola's foray into Hollywood. In the new organization of CPE, the two studios of Columbia and Tri-Star were to operate as business divisions. Along with this corporate reorganization, Columbia announced that it would lay off 500 employees or about 14 percent of its total workforce.[103] Even this restructuring measure, however, would not be able to stem the debt of close to US$1.5 billion that accumulated in 1988 despite an increase in the studio's market share of box office receipts. High costs incurred for getting big-name actors such as Michael Douglas, as well as major box office duds beginning with *Ishtar*, had a big impact on the studio's profitability. The studio's market share had by then dropped consecutively for five years, and went from 19 percent in 1985 to 9 percent in 1988.[104] Restructuring had also impacted morale at the studio, with loyal employees who had been at the company for many years being pushed out into an uncertain job market.[105]

Despite declining performance, Coca-Cola continued its presence in Holly-wood, though since its partial divestiture it was more of an investor than an active player in the industry. But the lackluster performance of the studio in 1989 was the last straw for Coca-Cola and strengthened its view that it had to leave the business for good.[106] Although the summer of that year turned out to be a good time for the Hollywood film industry, Columbia unfortunately again did not do well, turning out such box office underperformers as *Ghostbusters II* and *Casualties of War*.

With a dearth of hit movies, floundering market share, and an accumulated debt totaling close to US$1.5 billion, Columbia would not have been the prime choice for investors thinking of putting their money in a movie studio (although it did have a considerable movie library of 3,000 films and 25,000 TV episodes from 270 television shows, and a distribution channel of 800 screens across the US).[107] Furthermore, in contrast to MCA Universal, which at the time had been profitably run by the autocratic Lew Wasserman and Sidney Sheinberg for several decades, Columbia management was facing frequent changes at the top. At the time of the divestiture of the studio to Sony, Victor Kaufman was the CEO of CPE (having been installed in that position after being moved from Tri-Star just two years before in 1987) and Dawn Steel the president of Columbia Pictures.

Such was the sad state of Columbia on the eve of its divestiture by Coca-Cola. To compound Columbia's financial difficulties, the studio at the time had few movies in the pipeline of development. According to an account related to the *Los Angeles Times* by Alan J. Levine, who joined CPE as president of its film group right after the studio's acquisition by Sony, Levine and the new man-agement "opened the door in the vault, and [found] it was virtually empty ... Columbia made very few pictures."[108]

But for Sony, or rather more specifically for Morita, who was the driving force behind Sony's decision to buy a movie studio, it seemed that such con-cerns were secondary, as it went all out to acquire Columbia, paying Coca-Cola a purchase price of US$3.4 billion, assuming all of its debt, and on top of all this, buying the management team of the Hollywood producers Peter Guber and John Peters for US$200 million, which was estimated to be about US$60 million more than their market value.[109]

Motives of Sony's acquisition

What impelled Morita to go after Columbia? To the general public and investors, Sony executives stated they were creating "a total entertainment business around the synergy of audio and video hardware and software."[110] Software would drive Sony's core electronics business and help the company to reign supreme in con-sumer electronics. In other words, the Betamax fiasco would not be repeated if Sony had a movie studio. As Morita stated, "If I owned a movie studio, Betamax would not have come out second best," referring to the triumph of the JVC-developed VHS home video tape format over the Betamax.[111] Michael (Mickey)

Schulhof, who was the highest-ranking American executive in Sony at the time of the acquisition and who played major roles in the acquisitions of both CR and CPE, elaborated to *Fortune*: "In the late 1970s we began to recognize the need to take Sony beyond hardware. Through our experience with Betamax, we discovered that the compelling motivation for the purchase of hardware is software."[112]

Ohga on his part stated that the "real reason" for purchasing Columbia was High Definition TV (HDTV). Having a movie studio that could produce High Definition (HD) movie and TV content would be a critical element if Sony was to manufacture HD production equipment and spread the HD format into households—so the reasoning went.[113] Indeed, it was for its TV production content that Columbia was notably strong, as its former owner, Coca-Cola, had made some valuable acquisitions. These included the production company of Norman Lear, which had produced such hits as *All in the Family*, *Sanford and Son*, and *Maude*, and Merv Griffin Enterprises, which brought to Columbia the popular game shows *Jeopardy!* and *Wheel of Fortune*, both of which are still (as of this writing) going strong. A show which had been on air for several years, allowing the accumulation of a substantial number of episodes, would prove to be a lucrative source of income in the years to come through its syndication to various television broadcasters. Estimates indicated that with just three shows, *Married ... With Children*, *Designing Women*, and *Who's the Boss*, Columbia would end up earning US$500 million in syndication rights. As Ohga put it, "Movies are a studio's marquee, but the money is made in television."[114]

Another factor that may have driven Morita to go into the movie entertainment business was that the company's leadership believed that the rise of new players in the consumer electronics markets from such countries as Korea would make it increasingly difficult for the Japanese to differentiate themselves, unless they developed niches where it would be difficult for other players to imitate them.[115] Unless the Japanese moved into other market areas and produced higher-value-added products that could differentiate them from the Koreans and other players, they would end up with a fate similar to that of the US electronics conglomerate RCA, which was put out of business partly by competition from Japan. Sony management felt that efforts to diversify, leading to less reliance on the fickle consumer electronics market, needed to be made for its survival. Indeed, in the early 1980s and before Sony's entry into the entertainment business, I recall as a new employee in the company's Broadcast and Professional Products Division that senior management was announcing targets of a 50–50 revenue ratio between consumer electronics and non-consumer businesses (e.g., industrial and broadcast-related products). Considering the current stiff competition from Korean players in the consumer electronics market, such as Samsung and LG, which is giving Sony a run for its money, these views on the need for diversification proved to be highly prescient.

But despite all the reasons later given by Sony for acquiring CPE, the Sony board originally rejected the idea of buying the studio after they weighed the pros and cons surrounding the deal. Some of the objections raised included

Columbia's high asking price, and the fact that no one in Sony knew anything about the Hollywood movie business. The objections sounded logical from a business point of view. It was only after Morita wistfully expressed his regret and disappointment about not having a movie studio that Ohga and his corporate team were galvanized to go after Columbia and fulfill Morita's dream.[116] This suggests that they were other reasons behind Sony's decision for acquiring a movie studio that were not purely based on business factors.

One such factor may have been that which afflicted many empire builders in history and business: an aspiration for power. Although it was Morita who was the primary driver for the Columbia acquisition, Walter Yetnikoff, the CEO of CR, who had been on close personal terms with Ohga since the formation of CBS/Sony, had for some time been lobbying Morita and Ohga to purchase a movie studio. With a studio, Yetnikoff believed that Sony could create various kinds of synergy between music, video, and hardware.[117] It was Yetnikoff who played a major role in the negotiations leading to the acquisition of CPE by Sony and in recommending to Sony the production team of Peter Guber and Jon Peters for heading the studio. Having observed with envy the power that Steve Ross enjoyed as head of Warner Brothers,[118] Yetnikoff said, "I wanted to be Steve Ross. Oh, absolutely. I wanted to have dominion over an empire."[119] An executive who was involved with the acquisition confirmed that "Walter wanted to be Steve Ross, and he said that in front of groups of people as a joke. But he meant it."[120] Yetnikoff believed that Sony would have no problem in managing a movie studio, because, as he put it, "I thought I was going to manage it."[121] Manage, that is, with Guber and Peters as the heads of Columbia. According to a participant in the deal to get the production team, "Walter wanted people in that job whom he could control ... Walter was extremely confident [with Guber and Peters] because of the father-son relationship he had with Jon Peters."[122] Thus the acquisition of a movie studio would not only fulfill Morita's dream but would also satisfy Yetnikoff's aspirations for power and an empire.

Another factor that may have influenced the Japanese Sony executives to buy CPE was hubris. The late 1980s was a time when the Japanese economy was in its so-called bubble stage, with land prices sky-rocketing, and Japanese companies backed by a strong yen and low interest rates were snapping up pricey real estate and companies in the US. It was a time when the US viewed Japan as threatening to overtake the US in economic supremacy. The acquisition of Columbia Pictures and its movie library, an icon of American culture, would be just another "conquest" in the US economy by a Japanese company that had virtually wiped out the US consumer electronics industry and already had a US music entertainment company under its belt.

Hubris, however, is often related to the need to mask a feeling of inferiority, and it may be that the need to dispel an inferiority complex was a subconscious factor behind the acquisition. As we noted earlier, Morita may have felt like an outsider to mainstream Japanese society on account of his origins and background. In a sense, the fact that the company he co-founded did not belong to the mainstream "keiretsu" or network of Japanese conglomerates may have exacerbated these sentiments. The acquisition of an icon of American culture, something which was not attempted before by any Japanese company, may have been his attempt to achieve the status of an accepted "insider" of Japanese society.

The feelings of inferiority may also have come from Morita's dealings with the West, in particular the US. While Morita was seen by many Westerners as the most "internationally minded" Japanese on the public stage, seeming to be at home in New York and comfortable in dealing with foreigners using his heavily Japanese-accented English, he was nevertheless of a generation that had first-hand witnessed the defeat of the Japanese military machine by the US and Allied forces. He had seen and experienced the scorn that Westerners held towards products that were labeled "Made in Japan." Such experiences may have left the patriotic Morita with a nagging sense of inferiority, which may have driven him with a subconscious urge to beat the Americans at their own game. As Idei Nobuyuki, the CEO of Sony who was later handpicked by Ohga, put it to author John Nathan *(Sony: The Private Life)*, the "Japanese of the generation before mine [Idei was born in 1937, Morita in 1921] had an inferiority complex about foreigners. Akio Morita himself was a living inferiority complex."[123] If Idei's observation is correct, what better way for Morita to overcome this sense of inferiority than to buy a symbol of America—a major movie studio and its cultural assets—and overwhelm the descendants of Commodore Perry and the victors of World War II?

Once Morita and his management decided to go into the movie business, the immediate question that naturally came up was: which studio? To answer this question, Yetnikoff contacted Mike Ovitz of CAA who, as we saw in the previous chapter, also played a role in MEI's acquisition of MCA (Universal Studios). Ovitz recommended that Sony purchase MCA. It had sound management led by Lew Wasserman and Sidney Sheinberg and a movie library of 13,000 films, which dwarfed that of Columbia's 3,000.[124] Morita also reportedly admired MCA.[125] If MCA was not for sale, Ovitz next recommended Paramount. According to a Hollywood source, Columbia was not first choice.[126] Given the widely reported troubles that Coca-Cola was having with Columbia's management and the studio's declining performance, this was not all surprising. Despite the recommendations of Ovitz, however, Sony eventually settled upon acquiring Columbia and almost simultaneously went about getting the production team of Peter Guber and Jon Peters to lead the studio.

Various cultural drivers

What followed with Guber and Peters as the heads of the studio has been documented in books and news articles and will not be replicated here in chronological detail. Rather, what will be recounted below are some of the drivers I have identified as being associated with the culture of Sony that simultaneously played through the Guber-Peters era in a polyphonic jumble and would have an impact on the future direction of Sony's management of its movie empire.

Driver no. 1: Sony's obsession with getting the right people for the
right positions

Since the time that Ibuka and Morita created Sony, a fundamental principle of the company was to get the right people in the right positions. Accordingly, Morita stressed to his people that the acquisition of CPE must come with superior management.[127] With this principle in mind and with the advice of Yetnikoff, Sony went out to hire the producers Jon Peters and Peter Guber, who were known for producing such hit movies as *Batman, Rain Man, Gorillas in the Mist, The Color Purple,* and *Witches of Eastwick.* In the new CPE under Sony, the two became cochairmen, with Guber as CEO and both men as senior executive officers and members of the board's executive committee. In contrast to CBS/Sony, which was headed by people such as Ohga who were outsiders to the music industry, it seemed that Sony was playing it safe by hiring people who seemed to be insiders of the movie business.

The two had diverse backgrounds in upbringing and education. Peter Guber, who was 47 at the time of Sony's acquisition of CPE, was a lawyer with two law degrees from New York University and an MBA from the Columbia Business School. He also was a professor of law at UCLA. While still an MBA student Guber had joined Columbia Pictures, and after three years, at the age of 29, he was made head of the studio. After leaving Columbia Pictures and before teaming up with Jon Peters, Guber became an independent producer, producing such hits as *The Deep* and *Midnight Express.*

In contrast to Guber with his elite educational background, Peters came from a broken home in San Fernando Valley with an abusive, alcoholic father; he ran away from home after having been kicked out of reform school at the age of 12. Through hard work, however, Peters was a millionaire by the age of 21, having become a success in the hairdressing business. His salons catered to the Hollywood rich and famous, among them Barbra Streisand, with whom he would carry on a well-publicized relationship and who would support Peters in his production of the movie *A Star is Born,* starring, of course, Barbra Streisand. The movie was panned by the critics but nevertheless grossed US$140 million, making it a huge success and signaling the arrival of Peters the movie producer.

In 1976, Guber and Peters met each other for the first time when Guber was still the studio head at Columbia Pictures. Peters had come to the studio with a proposal for a movie, *The Eyes of Laura Mars.* Guber recalls meeting Peters and being sufficiently impressed with the latter's fire-in-the-eyes enthusiasm to the point of wooing Peters into making a movie. Peters on his part made a counterproposal of becoming Guber's business partner.[128] Guber accepted. Thus, in a nutshell, was born the team of Guber and Peters.

On the surface, with several outstanding hits to their credit and with the endorsement of Yetnikoff, Guber and Peters may have looked to the top Sony executives like the right people to run their newly acquired movie studio, although the two had never actually run a studio together. It seemed so to those that really mattered within the company, starting with Morita, Ohga, Yetnikoff, and Schulhof, who upon meeting Guber for the first time found the chemistry between them "wonderful."[129] Ohga, upon talking about films with Guber, remarked that Guber's eyes sparkled, and that he could feel his passion about films, which impressed Ohga.[130]

Hollywood, however, had different opinions of the two. One Hollywood executive labeled Peters as brilliant but mercurial and described him as having no feelings if a person working for him burned out. The same executive also considered Guber to be a difficult person at times, but said that at least he did not demean the people around him.[131] Sue Mengers, an agent who once managed Barbra Streisand, said of Peters, "He's like trying to withstand a hurricane. If it weren't for Jon, I'd be 20 years younger today. And he gave me a lousy haircut for my wedding."[132] There were also stories going about of Peters's "hair trigger temper, tantrums, fisticuffs."[133] Steve Ross of Warner Bros warned that if Morita knew what he was getting into, he wouldn't have touched Guber and Peters "with a 10-foot pole." Ross called these two men "shameless self-promoters," "profligate loose cannons," and generally larger-than-life "showmen" who spoke fluent hyperbole.[134] One observer close to the industry noted that Sony could not possibly accept the "madness" of Jon Peters.[135]

Be that as it may and setting aside the comments coming from Hollywood, to make sure that the inexperienced production duo of Guber and Peters would be able to concentrate on the creative aspects of producing hit movies while at the same time assuming ultimate responsibility for the performance of the studio, Schulhof told Guber to keep his hands off the day-to-day operations of the movie studio and to let his senior executives have autonomy in running the business.[136] Accordingly, the two hired several people that would run the studio for them, including Frank Price, Mike Medavoy, and Alan J. Levine, all of them veterans of the movie industry.

Frank Price, as we have seen, was a former head of Columbia and Universal Pictures. With Sony as the new overlords, Price was signed on by Guber and Peters as chairman of Columbia's film unit. During an earlier tenure at Columbia as studio head, Price had such hits as *Kramer vs. Kramer*, *Tootsie*, and *Gandhi*. During the 1950s Price had worked as a TV writer in Columbia's story department, and he later moved to Universal's TV unit. From 1984 to 1986, Price headed Universal's movie operations under the leadership of Wasserman and Sheinberg. Price later formed his own film company which he named Price Entertainment and which had ties with Tri-Star. Price had been described as a "dour, controlled, and buttoned down personality" who was not part of the Hollywood social scene and was surprisingly (for Hollywood, anyway) married to the same woman for 26 years.[137] From the descriptions of Guber and Peters, it may come as a surprise that Price was selected, and indeed later on they would admit that Price was not their first choice.[138] But given the fact that their new bosses back in Tokyo were essentially men in suits who were unaccustomed to the ponytail culture of Hollywood, the two may have felt a need to present a face of Columbia that was culturally similar to Sony—at least in outer appearances. As one executive put it, Price "has a track record, he's a very serious guy and

Peter and Jon needed someone like Frank Price to accommodate the Japanese."[139]

Mike Medavoy, a founder of Orion Pictures, was signed on as chairman of Columbia's Tri-Star Pictures Unit. Medavoy had spent 16 years as a senior vice president of production at United Artists. Born in Shanghai to Russian parents, Medavoy grew up in Chile and moved to the US in 1956. He graduated from UCLA and first became involved in the movie industry when he started delivering mail to Frank Price in the Universal mail room. In the 1970s Medavoy worked as an agent at the talent firm International Famous Agency, which had Jane Fonda, Steven Spielberg, and Francis Ford Coppola among its many clients.

Alan J. Levine was hired by Guber and Peters to become president of Columbia's film unit. A lawyer born in Los Angeles with law and business degrees from the University of Southern California, Levine was a partner in the entertainment law firm of Armstrong, Hirsch & Levine, which represented Guber and Peters. Levine grew up with the industry, with his grandfather a Hollywood talent agent, and his grandmother having worked in MGM's costume department.

Guber and Peters had Price, Levine, and Medavoy run the studio for them, or as Levine put it, "to ... help set the map, or help set the plan for the future."[140] From the background of the three there is nothing to suggest any incompetency or amateurism. All three had spent a considerable number of years in the movie entertainment industry, and while the senior management of Sony may not have been acquainted with their names, they were all certainly well known in the industry and had overall good reputations. Author Bernard Dick described the roster put together by Guber and Peters as "formidable."[141] Outwardly, there was nothing that would make Sony disagree with the appointments. For all practical purposes, it seemed to Sony's senior management, who was unfamiliar with the industry, that Guber and Peters had put in place the "right people for the right positions," a matter of supreme importance for Sony at the time.

Nevertheless, Guber and Peters cost Sony a lot of money. The Guber-Peters era was a costly one even before it actually began when the company paid US$200 million to the duo for their production company (which was US$60 million more than its market value) and paid US$300 to US$500 million to Warner Brothers to secure the release of the producers, who were under contract with the studio. Sony had also given Warner half ownership of Columbia (CBS) Records/Columbia House, which was the world's largest mail-order record club, and 10-year distribution rights to CPE's theatrical and TV movies for Warner's pay-TV service. Sony further gave up CPE's 35 percent stake in its Burbank Studios to Warner and agreed to move to the former MGM lot in Culver City that Warner had bought from the film studio Lorimar.[142] On top of these payments, Sony dished out US$2.75 million salaries each to Guber and Peters for five years, with annual cost-of-living adjustments, a share of studio profits, a US$50 million bonus pool, and 8.08 percent of any appreciation in the assessed value of CPE.[143]

It is clear that Sony wanted these two almost at all costs, which is not surprising since Sony was willing to pay what it took to get Columbia Pictures. Iwaki Ken, a former Executive Deputy President of the company, related to author John Nathan that Morita and the board "agreed that if we wanted the studio we would have to pay the price."[144] To the Sony employees in Tokyo at the time (myself included), getting such salaries and benefits was unheard of and unimaginable. The treatment afforded to Guber and Peters, however, was in retrospect a sign that Sony was going to allow a different pay and benefits scheme for its movie business and in effect tolerate the coexistence within the Sony Empire of a different set of values and practices which were in line more with those of the Hollywood movie industry than with those of its core consumer electronics business.

Driver no. 2: Sony's "Genghis Khan approach" to managing an entertainment empire

During the early years after its acquisition of Columbia Pictures in 1989, Sony took what I call the "Genghis Khan approach" to managing the studio. Genghis Khan, as we have seen, did not say much about the running of an empire and kept his mouth mostly shut on day-to-day matters such as the usage of language, traditions, and religions. So long as his conquered subjects paid taxes and tribute and participated in raids on other peoples as ordered and did not oppose Mongol rule, he and his cohorts were pretty much content to let his conquered subjects live as they pleased. Likewise, Sony took a similar approach, which could be described as hands-off. Sony stressed that no high level executives from the company were to be sent over to Columbia Pictures from Japan.[145] A Columbia Pictures television executive recalled one occasion when Ohga and several other Sony executives arrived for a tour of their television production operation. According to him, Ohga and his people were taken over to see the studio set of the TV comedy *Who's the Boss?*, but all they did while they were there was to look at the cameras and ask technical questions on the video tape being used.[146] Alan Levine, who was president of Columbia's film group at the time of the Sony acquisition, commented, "We don't anticipate, and have not experienced, any impact on our management and on our day-to-day running of the company."[147] When asked by the *Los Angeles Times* whether Levine and others in Columbia management needed to get approval from Japan on hiring decisions, Levine replied that approval wasn't needed; instead they were told by Sony to assemble the best management team at all levels of the studio and then state what they wanted to do.[148] A movie business executive in an interview with Edward Klein printed in *Vanity Fair* commented that nobody in Hollywood was dealing with the Japanese, who never showed up at the usual Hollywood events of dinner parties, screenings, birthday parties, or premieres. The executive added that most likely Sony did not have the vaguest idea of what was happening at their movie studio.[149]

For some people, however, Sony's stance was a bit of a puzzle. Peter Peterson, an outside member of the Sony board of directors from the investment firm the Blackstone Group, commented that he didn't understand what the fear was that was making the company passive in its stance towards its own studio.[150] Even Peter Guber at one point lamented the passiveness of Sony, claiming that Sony management was not committed to the studio.[151] Given how Sony had successfully managed its JV with CR, with CBS/Sony becoming the number one record company in Japan just after 10 years from its inception, however, their approach to management at CPE was perhaps not surprising. For the leaders of Sony, apart from implanting a new corporate identity to CPE by re-naming it Sony Pictures Entertainment (SPE), repeating the previous hands-off approach to managing a movie empire was the best way to ensure success.

A hands-off approach may have also been due to a view and awareness held by Sony executives that the acquisition of what was considered an icon of American culture by a Japanese company was whipping up anti-Japanese feelings in the US. Indeed, even the supposedly respectable magazine *Newsweek* was at the time succumbing to yellow journalism, hysterically claiming in bold letters on its US edition cover, along with an illustration of a kimono-clad Columbia Pictures icon, that the Japanese were "invading" Hollywood (at the same time opportunistically placing a considerably more level-headed headline on the cover of their Japanese-language edition, clearly intended not to offend Japanese audiences). Working on such fears, US congressman Leon Panetta introduced legislation that limited foreign ownership in the cultural and entertainment industries. Panetta stressed that the "domination" of the American entertainment and movie industry by foreign owners was not a "healthy" phenomenon.[152] Under such circumstances, it was prudent for Sony to stay low-key for the time being in managing its new acquisition. Morita promised to manage Columbia as an American company, which he admitted was the only way to reassure Americans that its acquisition by the Japanese was not counter to their interests.[153] In response to a reporter's question on whether Columbia would be allowed to make a movie that would be critical of the Japanese emperor Hirohito, Morita replied unequivocally that Sony would have no objections and if its studio management believed that the story was good, it would go right ahead and make the movie, though he added that he could not guarantee that the Japanese people or government would want to have it shown in Japan.[154]

The question for Sony, however, which in retrospect no one fully addressed within the company until the situation called for it, was: how far should Sony extend its hands-off approach to its movie business? Should it be almost completely hands-off in the day-to-day running of the business as was the case with CBS/Sony, as if it were in effect a passive investor or as if it were an absentee landlord like the Mongols, extracting tribute and taxes while leaving the running of the day-to-day lives of its conquered subjects to themselves? Or should the senior management of Sony be involved in managing the studio when some necessity and occasion arose?

The historical record shows that on the surface Sony was trying to establish a middle ground within a hands-off approach. Morita, it was clear, did not want to provoke and inflame American sensibilities by dictating what movies to make or not make or by meddling in the movie-making process. Yet, in a throwback to the days when Ohga became head of CBS/Sony and enforced a strict monitoring of expenses within the JV, some of the measures that Sony took suggest that the company was concerned with maintaining some form of financial discipline in the movie studio as well. Under Ohga's orders, all production budgets over US$40 million had to be approved by Schulhof, who as vice chairman of Sony's US operations was in charge of all of Sony's entertainment businesses. Furthermore, all national marketing campaigns, as well as any hiring and firing of executives at Columbia that would involve a large sum of money, could not be executed without Schulhof's approval.[155] As for the overall responsibility for the movie business, Schulhof, who reported directly to both Morita and Ohga, was positioned as the boss of Peter Guber.[156] While Sony originally toyed with the idea of setting up a steering committee consisting of Schulhof, Guber, and Yetnikoff with the responsibility of ostensibly running the business and of formalizing management control by Sony over Columbia, it was never realized. Sony did instead send into Columbia a mid-level Japanese employee of Sony whose role was to report on the new management team to his superiors in Tokyo.[157]

And so, in keeping with the spirit of tolerance practiced by Sony with its JV CBS/Sony and for pragmatic reasons that had to do with keeping the lid on xenophobia, with regard to its creative activity Columbia was to maintain its independence and Sony would be more of a passive investor, with some interest in ensuring financial discipline at the studio. As with the Mongols, who did not meddle in the cultural or religious affairs of their conquered subjects but simply made sure that taxes and tributes would be regularly paid up, Sony was to keep its mouth shut on the movie-making activities of the studio and see that its money was properly used and dividends kept pouring in.

Driver no. 3: the propensity for risk taking

Along with taking a Genghis Khan approach to management, there was a conspicuous propensity for Sony to take, or inordinately tolerate, risks associated with the spending activities of Guber and Peters. Sony gave a fairly free hand to Guber on using money for various projects, including spending extravagantly on overheads that ran from US$50 million to US$75 million more than other studios, and wooing and hiring with high pay friends such as Mark Canton from Warner Brothers to oversee the studio.[158] Huge severance packages were given to executives who were eventually pushed out by Guber. Frank Price and Mike Medavoy were reportedly given a settlement of about US$10 million each for leaving the studio.[159] Peters was given a settlement estimated at US$30 to US$50 million.[160] All this spending was done while Guber, in contrast to Wasserman and Sheinberg at the time (who released *Jurassic Park*, which clobbered *Last Action Hero*, in 1993), failed to develop a strong slate of successful movies and produced some bombs instead.

Despite what was going on in hiring and firing and spending, Sony hardly intervened. Medavoy and Price were fired by Guber. Mark Canton was hired by

Guber and came over from Warner Brothers to become chairman of Columbia Pictures. Tokyo did not influence any of these decisions. In reference to rumors at the time that Guber was intending to push out Price, Schulhof had no comment to make except to say to the *New York Times* that Sony Pictures was being managed by Peter Guber.[161] Even when Peters was suddenly ousted, it was Guber who ultimately decided to fire his partner, and not because of any pressure from Sony, despite the fact that Sony *must* have been aware of some of Peters' shenanigans, which were widely publicized and included using Sony corporate jets to pick up his girlfriend and putting his girlfriend and ex-wife on the Columbia payroll for US$250,000 each.[162] As for the money spent on severances that were done at the discretion of Guber, Morita waved off such concerns by commenting to the press, "That's always going on in Hollywood. It's no problem."[163] Ohga on his part defended the spending spree. In response to claims that Guber and Peters had caused a severe loss for Sony, Ohga countered that under the leadership of the pair, Sony had achieved the number one position in Hollywood for three consecutive years, and that such spending was necessary, citing for example the need to refurbish the elevators in the Sony Pictures building and renew the studio facilities, which according to Ohga were in a dilapidated state at the time of its acquisition.[164]

Aside from accepting the risks associated with the spending spree of Guber and Peters, Sony's propensity to take risks and stick it out with the studio was also demonstrated in its write-down for the studio, which centered on the goodwill, or excess value over its book value, of the acquisition price for its assets. In November 1994, Sony announced that as a result of poor box office results, executive resignations and rising costs, it was going to take a US$2.7 billion write-off.[165] An additional US$510 million for abandoned movie projects and contract settlements was written off as well, making the total loss approximately US$3.2 billion. To get some perspective on this amount, as described by journalist Edward Klein, US$3.2 billion would be equivalent to that of the production costs for six award-winning *Forrest Gump* movies made every month for a year.[166] Ohga defended the write-off, stating that for Sony to carry over costs such as goodwill value and depreciate them over 40 years would have been harmful to the company and to his successor. In a further comment aimed at putting a positive spin to the write-off, Ohga reminded the press about the losses which Mitsubishi was about to make on divesting Rockefeller Center, or the losses that Matsushita had made when they sold Universal.[167]

Not surprisingly, after the announcement of the write-off the company's stock price declined by 12 percent. At the time of the write-off, Sony also disclosed an additional US$510 million loss in operating income for the three-month period of July to September of 1994 because of the cancellation of movies in development, lawsuits, and termination fees to departing executives.[168] One might think that with such losses Sony would have called it quits, as did MEI with Universal. Instead, Sony stated that it had "no choice" but to sink even more money into the studios if it ever hoped to make a profit.[169]

Driver no. 4: limits to tolerance—the search for a middle way of tolerance

Various writers have touched on the cultural gap that existed between Japan and Hollywood. The *Washington Post* wrote concerning the troubles at MEI and Sony that according to certain observers of the industry, a common problem for these companies was this cultural gap, with the Japanese misunderstanding the fundamental hit-or-miss nature of the entertainment business.[170] Guber stated that Sony may have understood electronics, but they did not understand what the movie business essentially was: a "crappy business" that was determined by the fickle movie gods. As Guber saw it, the company needed to go out and buy more assets, such as a sports team, so as to get some leverage to go into cable broadcasting as Rupert Murdoch or Ted Turner were doing. Diversification of its movie entertainment business was necessary for growth. Despite his pleadings, however, Sony management would not hear of it, with Ohga telling Guber to "Make hits! Make hits!"[171] Ohga on his part became exasperated with Guber for reasons that resembled the concerns that MEI had voiced to Wasserman and Sheinberg at MCA: a perceived straying by the studio from what Sony (and MEI) had felt was their core business of making hit movies. For Ohga, Sony needed its movie studio to make films that could later be used as video software, not to have it waste time and money on a basketball or a volleyball team as Guber was proposing.[172]

In 1994, Peter Guber departed from SPE. Despite the mutual exasperation that hints at opposing outlooks on the entertainment business, and despite the views of various observers that the failure of the Guber–Peters era had at its origin a cultural cause, I argue that in the case of Sony (and unlike the situation at MEI-MCA), cultural differences or differences of understanding on what the entertainment business was all about were ultimately not a factor in the eventual replacement of Guber and the installment of a different management team. A case in point is the proposal of a theme park that Guber and Peters had envisioned, which according to them would enable the studio to compete more broadly with the likes of MCA (Universal Studios) and Disney. As Wasserman and Sheinberg did with their Japanese overlords at MEI, Guber and Peters pitched to Ohga an idea for a Sony theme park that would have theme-based attractions, rides, and displays showing the latest Sony technology and software contents. In contrast to the management of MEI, however, Ohga reportedly liked the idea, voicing concern only for the proposed location and costs.[173] There was no confrontation over the idea as there was between MEI and MCA over the latter's proposal of having a Universal Studios theme park in Japan. Given Ohga's personal experience as head of a music company, his reaction was not surprising. He had, after all, built CBS/Sony to make it the largest record company in Japan, a country with a wide variety of musical tastes, an extremely fickle population, and fads that constantly came and went. Under Ohga, CBS/Sony had branched out into other fields that involved its entertainment assets, such as a mail-order business, as well as areas that were unrelated such as cosmetics. Such experiences gave him an understanding of the entertainment business and of business diversification, which the MEI executives who were struggling with managing their studio lacked.

The reason for Sony's ejection of Guber was that even for a company that was willing to pay the price and take the associated risks of becoming a major player in Hollywood, there was a limit on how much the company would tolerate in giving a free hand to its management at the movie studio. This limit was determined by results rather than by different viewpoints stemming from cultural differences or lack of understanding of the entertainment business. As Ohga put it, although the studio released a series of successful films in its first two years, the number of hits became fewer over the years, costs ballooned as the studio became involved in extravagant movie projects, and the financial position of the studio deteriorated, leading him to undertake a sweeping restructuring of the studio that included replacing the studio heads.[174] Indeed, during the first two years of the Guber–Peters era more than US$1 billion was spent on revamping and refurbishing the studio facilities. Money was poured into costly movie projects which turned out to be bombs, such as *I'll Do Anything*, *Hudson Hawk*, and *Last Action Hero*. Market share, while recovering to 20 percent by 1992 from a low of 9 percent at the time of Sony's acquisition, fell again in 1994, putting SPE in last place in market share among the major Hollywood studios.[175] Only one movie, *Terminator 2: Judgment Day*, made by the struggling independent movie studio Carloco and distributed by Sony, was a notable hit from their era.[176] From 1989 to 1994, Sony poured a total of US$8 billion into Columbia, of which the bulk was spent not on making movies, but on hiring and firing executives using huge salaries and golden parachutes, bonus pools, remaking offices, and dining rooms described by the *New York Times* as "the sleekest in Hollywood."[177] During Guber's last year at SPE in 1994, of the 26 movies released in that year by the studio, 17 lost money, incurring a loss of US$150 million for the film studio.[178]

As the Mongols had extracted tribute and taxes from their conquered subjects while tolerating their traditions and religion and employing their people of talent, so it was that Sony would respect Hollywood culture and allow its day-to-day operations to be run by its studio people with the condition that it was making money. That is to say, Guber along with Schulhof and a host of other executives at SPE might not have been forced out despite presenting an expensive bill of costs to Sony, had they made money. For Sony, then, where the company failed was in getting the right people for the right positions who could deliver results. In this regard, according to the *New York Times*, Sony officials acknowledged that the company had made a wrong decision in choosing the people to run its studio.[179] In looking back at the Guber–Peters years, Frank Price summed up Sony's choice of Peters and Guber as equivalent to that of getting two hustlers who made money setting up pictures often made by other people, citing as an example the movie *Rain Man*, for which the duo received an Oscar. Price claimed that the pair were never around the movie set while it was being made, and dismissed the two as "outrageous promoters."[180]

One question that comes up out of all this is how could Sony have tolerated Guber and Peters as long as they did? Was it simply a manifestation of the tolerant culture of Sony at work? There will never be a definitive answer to this question. In a rambling interview with *Vanity Fair*, Schulhof replied that it was not part of Sony's culture to fire people but to accept people for their strengths and that accordingly it had been his desire, though to no avail, for Guber to change his behavior so that he could stay on.[181] An associate of Guber's, however, suggests that Schulhof, who was inexperienced in the movie business, was under the mind-control of Guber and would buy into anything that Guber had told him.[182] A Hollywood executive commented on the relationship between Guber and Schulhof, saying that Guber had Mickey, who had no experience in the entertainment business, "totally Svengalized."[183] A former Sony Pictures executive claims to have observed several times that Schulhof would just "melt" and become "mesmerized" in front of Guber.[184] It would seem from these comments that Schulhof had been taken by Guber and the allure of the entertainment world.[185] Indeed, Guber was known to have often entertained Schulhof at his Bel Air mansion. Guber would also fly with Schulhof at the controls of the Sony corporate jet to exclusive tourist spots in Asia and elsewhere outside the US.[186] But if Schulhof had been taken in by Guber and Peters or by the glitter of Hollywood, it was due more to inexperience and unfamiliarity with the ways of Hollywood than to naivety or incompetency. Frank Price commented that although Schulhof in his opinion knew nothing about the movie business, he nevertheless found him to be a "nice" and "certainly bright" man who seemed to have been doing a very good job of communicating what was going in Hollywood to the decision makers in Japan.[187] Rather amusingly, Peters on his part commented that although he and Guber had told Schulhof everything he wanted to know, Schulhof "didn't know what we were talking about."[188]

Another issue which prevented Schulhof from gaining more control over the studio business was that while claiming that Guber was not hands-on enough for managing the business, he himself did not want to get his hands busy with the details of a business and its execution. Part of the reason was an ingrained aversion to dealing with people who were involved with grunt-work. Ando Kunitake, who replaced Schulhof as head of the parts and service business of Sony in the US and later became president and COO of Sony Corporation, recalled that Schulhof was a hands-off manager who steered away from spending time at parts and service shops. According to Ando, Schulhof lacked the ability to talk to his people, who were mostly junior college graduates and could not make the business work.[189] Peter Peterson concurred with Ando that Schulhof was a hands-off guy but speculates that it was due more to a lack of experience as an operations person.[190]

Ohga may have been too trusting of the instincts and abilities of Schulhof, who was not only a subordinate business colleague but, according to Ohga in his own words, a person whom he had treated as "a younger brother" who shared the same hobbies and interests such as flying airplanes.[191] At one time when Schulhof wanted to appoint Jeff Sagansky, the former president of CBS

Entertainment (a division within CBS which is responsible for acquiring or developing entertainment programs for CBS's TV network), as head of the movie division at Sony Software with the role of being Schulhof's eyes and ears in Hollywood, and brought him over to Tokyo to get Ohga's approval, Ohga asked only two questions; one was to Schulhof asking him if he wanted Sagansky in Sony, and the other to Sagansky asking him whether he wanted to join Sony. No probing questions on Sagansky's prior experience in Hollywood were asked of either Schulhof or Sagansky. When both replied in the affirmative, Ohga gave his consent to the appointment.[192] No doubt such an account would make many Sony mid-level managers, who usually have to spend hours trying to get a particular proposal approved by their superiors, envious of Schulhof! If either Ohga or Schulhof had been aware of Sagansky's reputation, however, a more thorough probe might have taken place. A head of a major Hollywood studio who knew Sagansky commented that while he was a bright guy, he didn't have an understanding of the movie business and never grasped that the movie industry was different from television.[193]

A former Sony senior executive who was close to both Morita and Ohga saw a problem of language comprehension that may have contributed to excessive tolerance on the part of the Japanese executives towards Schulhof and other Westerners:

> Basically Morita's and Ohga's comprehension capabilities of the English language were not good. But as they did not want to be seen as incapable of understanding what was being said, they often went along with being swayed by the arguments of Westerners who would speak to them as though they were native English speakers. On the other hand, Schulhof was aware of the poor English language capabilities of the Japanese executives and what endeared him to Morita and Ohga was that he would speak English with a vocabulary and speed of delivery that was easy for them to understand. Schulhof was also extremely capable at buttering up to the two.[194]

In an interview with Nathan, Idei put some blame on Schulhof and other Americans working for Sony in one capacity or another for skillfully "working the generous entity called Sony."[195] There were reports that when Idei became president of Sony and began inspecting the movie studio operations, he was amazed at the "ridiculous" overhead, the offices in New York, and Los Angeles, the dining rooms, the planes, and found the management, the excesses, and the write-offs simply "appalling."[196] Idei was also incensed by the lucrative deal given to Guber by Schulhof after the former left the company: the setup of a US$275 million revolving fund by Sony to cover the overhead, salaries, and cost of movie making at Mandalay Entertainment, a production company created by Guber. What made the deal especially sweet for Guber was that he was given total autonomy to approve his own films without any interference from Sony— another grand example of Sony's generosity and tolerance.[197]

In 1995, Idei became chief operating officer (COO) of Sony and the successor to Ohga, who became chairman and CEO of the company. In both public and private Ohga said that he arrived at choosing Idei through a process of elimination, not from an evaluation of his achievements. Ohga admitted that Idei's track record didn't qualify him for COO. For one thing, he was not very successful as head of the company's consumer audio division, and he failed to move the company into the home computer business.[198] During his tenure at the helm of Sony as COO and later CEO, Idei's track record was mixed. On the one hand, at one point in his career he was considered one of the most admired executives in the world and praised for his intellectual savvy. He attempted to bring Sony into the digital age using such catch phrases as *Digital Dream Kids* and recognized and stressed the importance of developing electronic products that were network-capable for the Internet age. It was during his time as head of the company that Steve Jobs of Apple declared in 1999 in an interview with a Japanese journalist that the goal for his company was to become the Sony of the computer business. On the other hand, Idei was also lambasted for the poor performance of the company and along with Jurgen Schrempp of DaimlerChrysler was labeled as one of the worst managers in the world by *Business Week*. Former Sony employees attribute the origins of Sony's current troubles and declining performance as originating in the Idei years.[199] In retrospect, it seems from Ohga's statements that in true Sony tradition, the company had taken a big risk, as it did with employing Guber and Peters, in putting Idei at the helm of Sony.

Within this book, however, I will not go into a detailed analysis of the Idei era, of which much has been written during and since his departure. Judging his performance is perhaps the topic of another book or article. I argue, however, that Idei's appointment represented the beginning of a considerable change in Sony's management direction towards its movie studio. And to his credit, the changes made during Idei's time at the head of the company were the precursor to a healthy movie entertainment business for Sony. As Nathan put it, the stabilization of the movie studio, its conscious acceptance as part of the Sony group, and the disappearance of Hollywood's disdain for the outsider has to be considered a major achievement of Idei.[200]

No longer would the "generous entity" Sony remain a hands-off, passive investor. Under Idei's watch the management of Columbia changed dramatically. First to go was Schulhof in December 1995. As far as Ohga was concerned, "Mickey's era was over."[201] Along with the previously posed question as to why Sony tolerated Guber and Peters for as long as they did, a similar query can be raised as to why Ohga in particular was so trusting of Schulhof's sense of business even after it was known that things were going badly at SPE. There is no satisfactory answer to this question; suffice to say that there was a huge amount of mutual trust between the two that was built in part on similar hobbies such as flying airplanes and expensive clothes.[202] At one time, Schulhof arranged to have Ohga, who was formerly a professional opera singer, indulge in his music hobby for one night to conduct the Metropolitan Opera Orchestra in New York. On another occasion, Schulhof took Ohga on a shopping trip to buy a

painting to be displayed at Sony's global headquarters in Tokyo. It was a relationship that went beyond the bounds of business and became a friendship. Even
long after Schulhof had left Sony, he and his wife were invited to Ohga's home
for a private dinner with food cooked and served by Ohga himself.[203] Ohga remi-
nisced that if he asked Schulhof to look into something, he would immediately
come back with a detailed report and would master whatever subject was put
before him.[204] Morita and Ohga were also impressed by Schulhof's sense of
ambition. Ando Kunitake, former president of Sony Corporation, recalled that
Schulhof was very ambitious, and would only speak to those he considered bene-
ficial to him.[205] Schulhof was born in New York City to a Czech father and a
German mother. Both of them had fled Europe for the US with the rise of Hitler.
After having received a PhD from Brandeis in applied physics and doing a stint
at Columbia Records, Schulhof joined Sony's American subsidiary, the Sony
Corporation of America, where he caught the attention of Morita and became a
protégé of Morita and shortly after of Ohga. Schulhof's closeness with both
Morita and Ohga allowed him in many cases to bypass the Sony bureaucracy in
getting things done and to have immediate access to the two. As Schulhof put it,
that was the way Morita and Ohga wanted it. Schulhof maintains that to the very
end he was faithful and loyal to both of them.[206] Although there have been
instances in which Ibuka and Morita went out of their way to pluck someone
promising from the outside and make that person their protégé (the most notable
example being that of Ohga), no non-Japanese employee before him had risen as
high or amassed as much power as he had within the company. Not only did he
manage the acquisition of Columbia Records and Columbia Pictures, he was also
responsible for overseeing these newly acquired businesses and Sony's electronics business in the US and for managing the creation of businesses leading to the
synergies of the entertainment and electronics segments. It is to the credit of
Morita and Ohga and a reflection of Sony's culture of tolerance that they ele-
vated an outsider, and a Westerner to boot with no knowledge of Japanese, to
take on such important responsibilities.

Mark Canton, the head of Sony studios and another executive appointed by
his friend Guber to replace Frank Price, was ousted from his position in September 1996 after a string of box office failures including *The Cable Guy* and *The
Fan*, both movies which interestingly were about a deranged stalker. And of
course, *Last Action Hero* was also made under his watch. When Canton was
shown the way out, Sony had fallen to sixth place in market share, grossing
US$382.3 million on 29 pictures, while Disney in comparison released 31 pic-
tures and grossed US$849.4 million.[207] In place of Canton, Idei promoted Lucy
Fisher, Canton's former second-in-command whom he had met several times
and was impressed with.[208] Alan J. Levine, brought on board by Guber and
Peters, was the next major executive to leave in October 1996. Idei had nothing
but scorn for Levine, whom he described as a person who "thinks too much" and
is "always so nervous." Idei even derisively imitated in front of reporters the
way Levine had sounded on the phone.[209] Jeff Sagansky, vice president of Sony
Corporation of America, who was appointed by Schulhof to head the movie

division of Sony Software (which was the holding company for SPE), eventually left Sony in February 1998.

To replace Levine, Idei, after consulting with Peter Peterson and others in the business including Ovitz, Michael Eisner, and David Geffen, appointed a seasoned film studio executive, John Calley, to run Sony's movie studio. Speaking to the press, Idei said, "I have learned a lot. I've picked John Calley."[210] Calley had run the Warner Brothers film studio during the 1970s. Under his watch, the studio came out with such box office hits as *The Exorcist* and *Superman*. After his time at Warner, Calley retired rich at the relatively early age of 50, living the good life in his boat and sailing around the world, but later came back to work at Sony to coproduce *Postcards from the Edge* and *The Remains of the Day*, the latter of which received an Oscar nomination for best picture. Calley also had a stint after coming back from retirement of reviving the James Bond franchise, producing the hit movie *Goldeneye* at United Artists, where he also ran the studio as its president. For Sony, Calley was attractive because he had had a steady and productive career in the movie business that produced a string of successes at the box office. Furthermore, Calley was described by those who knew him as "a rational and sophisticated man entirely outside the Hollywood mold yet widely respected in the community."[211] Robert A. Daly, the cochairman of Warner Brothers who had known Calley for many years, commented upon hearing that Calley was in the running for the top position at SPE: "He's extremely bright; he has very good taste, and he gets along with talent very well. If John gets the job, he's a very good choice."[212] For Sony, the contrast in reputation between Calley and Guber and Peters could not have been sharper. Calley had also established a tight network of relationships with movie makers including Mike Nichols, John Boorman, Clint Eastwood, Sydney Pollack, and Stanley Kubrick.

For once it seemed Sony made the right choice in choosing its studio head. Luckily for Sony, the infatuation was mutual. Calley recounted after meeting with Idei that he became thrilled of the prospect of working with a company with an unlimited horizon and of meeting a person with a grasp on what he was talking about.[213] Although horror stories had been going around Hollywood concerning working for the Japanese, Calley claimed that a bigger cultural shock was in returning to a Hollywood in the early 1990s that seemed like something out of a George Orwell novel.[214]

Calley was officially appointed president and chief operating officer of SPE with a five-year contract immediately after Levine's departure in October 1996, with the responsibility of overseeing the operations of Columbia Pictures and Tri-Star Studios. Along with this appointment, Idei installed a Sony Corporation executive, Nozoe Masayuki, as executive vice president of the entertainment division of SPE reporting directly to Calley. Nozoe, an engineering graduate from Keio University, had previously worked for Idei in Tokyo. Nozoe had been living in the US for nine years after arriving in 1986, working out of Sony's electronics business headquarters in Park Ridge, New Jersey. He was head of consumer marketing for Sony's consumer electronics products and had developed a level of English competency that was passable enough to cope with fast-talking Hollywood. Although Nozoe had established relationships in Hollywood on account of his involvement with the promotion of the new disc-based video standard, the DVD, there was nothing in his career to date that suggested any sort of artistic insight on his part that would contribute to the creative aspects of the movie business. Rather, Nozoe was to serve as the eyes and ears for Idei. According to Calley, he had advised Idei to install a Japanese executive that had home office credibility.[215] As Calley put it, Nozoe was to make the relationship between Sony headquarters and SPE "flow more smoothly."[216] In addition to the various senior management changes, the appointment of Nozoe was another example of the parent company's getting involved in the management of the studio business. Calley recalls that thanks to the coaching by Nozoe, the movie studio was able for the first time to effectively communicate business plans to Tokyo headquarters using language and statistical methods familiar to the people in Tokyo. Nozoe hit it off well with his Hollywood colleagues, who were grateful for his coaching; the studio bought him a house in the Pacific Palisades.[217]

Although Sony headquarters through Nozoe was making its presence felt at SPE, its involvement was tempered with minimal participation in the creative aspects of the movie production business, which was going to continue to be run by tried and tested Hollywood executives. Aside from Nozoe, no other senior ranking executive from Japan was sent into the studio. Instead, Calley went ahead to install Amy Pascal, former head of Turner Pictures who had also previously worked at Columbia, as president of Columbia Pictures. Chris Lee, president of production, became head of Tri-Star.

With Calley at the helm and new management in place, performance at SPE gradually improved. In 1997, Calley's first year at SPE, the studio managed to climb to first place in market share from a dismal sixth in the previous year, riding on a success of box office hits such as *Jerry Maguire*, *My Best Friend's Wedding*, *Air Force One*, and *Men in Black*. Revenues jumped 47 percent over the previous year. In 1998 SPE slipped, with the studio dropping to third place in market share. *Godzilla*, a big-budget production costing more than US$100 million, failed to live up to expectations. But Calley could point out that the studio was now making money on every picture it was making.[218]

Having good and bad years was part of the Hollywood industry, and unless one had almost clairvoyant capabilities it was impossible to predict with certainty whether or not a movie would be a hit. For movie executives, their greatest fear was shortsightedness on the part of management, who would react by shuffling management with every drop of market share. In this regard, Sony's management involvement was tempered by headquarters' taking a long-term view. As Calley described Sony's attitude to the *New York Times*, "I think it's in their style that we don't have some maniac constantly coming over asking why we haven't fired everybody because a picture failed or a series cancelled."[219]

As SPE began to quietly rebuild itself under Calley's leadership and guidance from the parent company, in 1997 Idei hired Howard Stringer, a Welsh-American television broadcast executive, to take over Schulhof's position, which had been open since his departure. Stringer was named president of the Sony Corporation of America. The decision to bring in Stringer, who was a television broadcast executive with more than 30 years' experience in the industry producing such programs as *CBS Reports* and the *CBS Evening News with Dan Rather*, proved to be another success in Idei's efforts to stabilize the studio in the aftermath of the Guber–Peters debacle. Upon coming over to Sony, Stringer developed a personal rapport with Calley that provided a further anchor to stabilize the movie studio.[220] He made his physical presence felt at the studio by attending every Sony Pictures Hollywood premiere and attending various Hollywood award ceremonies such as the Golden Globe Awards and Academy Awards.[221]

Stringer, like Schulhof, does not speak Japanese, but he has shown the ability to go beyond cultural bounds and develop a rapport not only with Hollywood but also with the Japanese, especially with Idei. As Calley commented, "In my view, he was Idei's confidant in whatever degree you can become Idei's confidant. He's the only one I know of who can manage the Japanese and the showbizzers."[222] Noting Stringer's self-deprecating sense of humor and non-confrontational style of leadership and management, some Hollywood executives have joked that Stringer had more in common with the Japanese than the Welsh.[223] Dan Rather, former anchor and managing editor of the *CBS Evening News* and a friend of Stringer for more than 35 years, commented that Stringer "can explain each side to the other. Howard is a marvelous translator."[224] Jeffrey Katzenberg, one of the founders of DreamWorks SKG who had known Stringer for more than 20 years, had nothing but praise for Stringer which he related in the *New York Times*: "Howard has successfully bridged the cultural language between an international owner and entertainment company more successfully than anyone before."[225] Most importantly for a Sony, which wanted to maintain good relations with the prickly Hollywood community, Stringer had a close relationship with Hollywood stars, as Calley had noted.[226]

In 1998, Stringer was promoted to chairman and CEO of the Sony Corporation of America (SCA). Stringer reported directly to Idei. Calley, along with Thomas Mottola, the successor to Yetnikoff at Sony Music Entertainment (SME), reported to Stringer. A seven-member operating committee was set up within SPE which included Stringer, Rob Wiesenthal, a former investment banker hired by Stringer, John Calley, Joe Roth, a co-founder of Revolution Studios (in which Sony had a stake and whose films Sony distributed), and the vice chairmen/chairwoman of SPE: Jeff Blake, Yair Landau, and Amy Pascal.[227] The committee, which met weekly, was formed to review the studio's financing and costs. The setting up of this committee was a clear indication that aside from deciding senior management, Sony would also overcome its reluctance to actively get involved in certain areas of studio activity, particularly when pertaining to the use of money. As Idei put it, "We have been hesitant to interfere in CBS (Columbia) Records, but we will be less patient with Sony Pictures."[228]

Upon Calley's retirement in 2003, Stringer went outside Sony to hire Michael Lynton as Chairman and Chief Executive Officer of SPE. Amy Pascal, Vice

Chairman of SPE, was promoted to Chairwoman of the Motion Picture Group at SPE, with the responsibility for overseeing all of the films produced and distributed by SPE. It seems that Pascal, who had joined Columbia Pictures in 1996 having served as head of productions at Turner Pictures (and before that as executive at Columbia Pictures), was expected to succeed Calley. Indeed Pascal was reported to have been "virtually apoplectic" upon hearing that Lynton would be her boss.[229] Stringer admitted that Pascal had a right to argue about the decision. As he put it, "I had complete confidence in Amy with the movies. Amy had a pretty good argument for, 'Why are they bringing in this guy?' "[230] Nevertheless, Stringer felt that although he trusted Pascal as a movie picker, an executive would be needed to navigate the studio in the changing media environment, which was being increasingly shaped by new digital technologies, and to help globally expand the studio's operations.[231] Fortunately for Stringer and despite the protests from Pascal, an accommodation was eventually achieved which satisfied both Lynton and Pascal, with both accepting an equal footing and both reporting to Stringer. According to Lynton, a principle had to be observed between the two which stated that their relationship was to be "equal and open."[232]

Immediately before coming to Sony, Lynton was the chief executive of AOL Europe. Lynton had also served as president of Time Warner International, president of the Walt Disney Company's Hollywood Pictures, and chief executive of the book publisher Penguin Group. In these various positions, Lynton had a successful track record of producing a slate of money-making films as well as restructuring and turning around faltering businesses and making successful acquisitions. Although an American citizen, Lynton grew up in the Netherlands, became fluent in French, German, and Dutch, and received his university education at Harvard and Harvard Business School. As to why SPE was hiring the cosmopolitan Lynton, Idei told the press that Lynton's "diverse background will complement the talents of Amy Pascal, and together with Jeff Blake and Yair Landau they will form the most forward-thinking studio leadership in the industry."[233] Stringer added that Lynton's proven track record combined with his leadership skills would realize the transformation of SPE "into a 21st century entertainment company, and fully integrate its mission with the global strategy of Sony."[234] On his part, Lynton told the press, "I look forward to … maximize not only our creative opportunities, but also leverage all of Sony's technical strengths as we make Sony Pictures the standard bearer in the new era."[235] As these statements made to the press by Idei, Stringer, and Lynton suggest, Sony's management philosophy for its movie studio had gone from one end to another, starting off from the hands-off approach of the Guber–Peters era, with the parent company more of a passive bystander to events, to Sony taking the part of an active leader and driving the integration of the movie studio with Sony's corporate management framework and global strategy.

The coming on board of Lynton also led to what can be argued to be a change or modification in the culture of SPE that was felt in tangible ways by the SPE employees. As Lynton recalls, upon arriving at the studio he found the existence of such executive perks as a corporate dining room reserved for top executives and film stars. He also felt that the studio environment was one "in which people felt very reticent about sharing information, sometimes for personal reasons, and sometimes because they weren't in the same building."[236] The corporate dining room was eliminated, in effect doing away with one of the symbols that contributed to the hierarchical distance between employers and employees. To create an environment that would help facilitate teamwork and communication, a new cafeteria was built and a gym was opened for all SPE employees to use. The studio grounds were remade into a campus-style environment that projected an open and friendly atmosphere. By 2009, nearly five years after Lynton joined SPE, people around Hollywood commented that there was a noticeable improvement in the morale of the studio. Bryan Lourd, co-chairman of CAA, who often worked with Sony on movie projects, claimed that the new facilities had "enticed people to want to work there" and that the resulting stability at Sony was in contrast to the management upheavals at other studios such as Universal and Disney where top executives were ousted in 2009.[237]

Both Lynton and Pascal worked closely with Stringer and other Sony executives to align the strategies of the studio with those of the electronics division in Tokyo, which led to close collaboration on the development of new technologies such as Blu-Ray and 4K projectors and film. SPE and Sony also cooperated in developing 3D technologies leading to the production of 3D TVs and movies such as *Cloudy with a Chance of Meatballs*. Global cooperation between the two companies has also increased in countries and emerging markets such as India, where Sony and SPE worked closely to release the first ever Hollywood-produced Bollywood movie, made by SPE in 2007, and to open a film production education institute in India in 2011 with courses taught by staff from SPE working with Sony production equipment.

Despite the integration of strategies, the parent company management has not made any overt intervention in the studio's core business or in any creative aspects, such as which movies to make or not make. In this respect, the company has stayed true to the promise of Morita when the studio acquisition was made. In short, I argue that despite the modifications to SPE culture initiated by Lynton and SPE's integration within Sony's corporate strategic framework, the company has still continued to practice tolerance towards its acquired movie studio. I would, however, describe this tolerance as a tolerance with limits.

Most importantly for Sony, with the team of Stringer, Lynton, and Pascal at the helm of SPE, the company has not only stabilized but has also consecutively delivered on results for over nine consecutive years. With gross revenues contributing steadily to about 10 percent of total Sony revenue since 2002, SPE has become an integral and valuable part of the Sony portfolio. The company has also made impressive strides in its television business by serving over 435 million households in over 140 countries.[238] Of course, it is too early to tell where the business will end up for Sony in the coming years. But with steady performance over the past several years and stable management, for now at least Sony has been able to prove that a "Japanese" outsider can enter the closed world of Hollywood and succeed. This was no mean feat considering that even recently (2012) a Scottish female marketing executive at Walt Disney Studios who was hired from a New York marketing agency specializing in packaged goods was reported to have been in effect ousted by her movie business colleagues on account of her not being "one of them."[239]

Both Morita and Shima have passed away. In the Great Beyond or in the Halls of Valhalla what would Shima be telling Morita now? Would he be insisting that Morita had made a great mistake by buying Columbia Pictures? Indeed, what might all the people who were predicting that Sony would fail in Hollywood or have been criticizing the Japanese "invasion" of Hollywood be saying now?

Conclusion

While Sony did some backtracking in tolerating the autonomy of the studio by bringing it under the corporate strategic framework of the company and keeping a closer eye on its operations after Guber and Peters had departed, the fact that Sony did not send in a team of high-level executives from its electronics division to outright run the movie business, no matter how badly SPE had performed in the wake of Guber and Peters, is indicative of the tolerant nature of the company. Sony has also continued to demonstrate its capacity for tolerance by not interfering in the creative activities of the movie studio regarding the selection and production of movies. Furthermore, the company's acceptance of talented people from outside of Sony who were "insiders" of the industry, such as Calley, Pascal, and Lynton, to run its studio, is a major factor that has contributed to the duration of this seemingly odd-couple marriage and has allowed Sony to integrate itself as an "insider" of the Hollywood community. Under their watch and in contrast to the Guber-Peters years, the studio has produced a stream of hit movies and globally expanded operations while maintaining fiscal discipline, leading to a visible growth in revenues and contribution to Sony's profits.

Unlike what MEI had tried to do with MCA towards the end of their relationship, Sony in another show of tolerance did not attempt to have SPE conform to its own culture, nor did it attempt to change Hollywood culture. Instead, it set about neutralizing the impact of cultural differences between the two companies. Calley, for instance, used Nozoe to bridge the communication gap between Tokyo and Hollywood. Idei and Stringer worked to tie in Sony's corporate strategies with that of SPE's and encouraged more cooperation and contact between the electronics division and the entertainment businesses of movies and music.

All this goes to say that in the case of Sony's Hollywood Empire, tolerance does indeed matter: that is, it is the tolerance to use people based on their ability and not origin, to allow the acquired entity to largely run its own state of affairs, and to accept Hollywood culture as it is and not attempt to change it, all in all practices of tolerance which were similarly observed within the Mongol Empire. But at the same time it is a tolerance which is not unlimited but is tempered by the integration of the strategies of the movie studio with that of the corporate strategy of the parent company, which in effect has also become the basis for providing a common, superseding Sony corporate identity for its independent-minded Hollywood movie studio.

Postscript: the future

With an increasing number of competitors entering the consumer electronics market with innovative products and declining prices leading to commoditization for some devices, Sony is at this time of writing facing a tough moment in its history, as shown by lower rates of growth in its core electronics businesses and declining profit margins. While it is beyond the scope of this book to delve into the company's prospects for the future, I would instead like to humbly suggest as a former employee who still thinks fondly of the company that it may be worthwhile for Sony's management to reflect upon the cultural values that enabled the company to grow spectacularly as it did during the years of Ibuka and Morita, and to honestly appraise to what extent they are still observed in the company. From the examples of Sony's successes (with its past JV with CBS, its acquisitions of CR and CPE, and with releasing many trend-setting products), I argue that it was the following of the cultural principles established by Ibuka and Morita of emphasizing the abilities of the individual, having the right persons for the right positions, respecting the freedom to pursue one's goals and ideas, encouraging the free exchange of thoughts and ideas, and teamwork, that facilitated the company's past triumphs. In particular, the principle of having the right people for the right job regardless of where they came from, which coincides with what was observed by the Mongols in their global empire, was crucial in enabling Sony to make itself at one time a trend-setter in electronics. Aside from Kihara there were many other brilliant and highly individualistic engineers and managers that contributed to the success of the company. Many of these people were employees of Sony from the start of their careers, beginning right after their leaving school. But others came from other companies and institutions. Nakajima Heitaro was originally from the Japanese public broadcaster NHK and after coming over to Sony developed the company's digital recording technology and the CD format. Kikuchi Makoto, who was a scientist with the Japanese Ministry of International Trade and Industry (MITI), moved over to Sony to lead the company's efforts in improving CCD chip technology. Unoki Hajime came to Sony from a Mitsui-affiliated trading company and as head of the company's International Operations Group spearheaded from scratch Sony's global sales expansion in countries and territories such as China, Latin America, and the Middle East. Despite coming from the outside in the middle of their careers, such people rose up through the ranks in Sony like any other "home-bred" employee in accordance with their tangible achievements.

A company such as Sony may indulge in doing as many restructurings and reorganizations of the company as it wants to and spend millions in getting the management advice of outside consultants. But ultimately, whether it succeeds or not will depend on the quality of its people and the perspicacity of its management to, as the co-founder Morita had stressed, ensure that the right people are deployed in the right positions. That means respecting diversity when hiring people. Success will also depend on ensuring a fine balance between individualism and teamwork so that egos, jealousies and office politics do not get in the way of cooperation and collaboration.[240] The steady and profitable performance at SPE suggests that this principle of getting the right people for the right positions was ultimately observed in the movie entertainment business with Stringer, Calley, Pascal, and Lynton at the helm. On the other hand, Sony's rescent struggles to distinguish itself from its competitors in consumer electronics may indicate that this principle is not necessarily observed for some reason or another in other areas of the company.[241]

7   Conclusion

The impact of tolerance on empires and M&A

Tolerance is the one essential ingredient.... You can take it from me that the Queen [Elizabeth II] has the quality of tolerance in abundance.

Advice from the Duke of Edinburgh for a successful marriage[1]

The characteristics of "successful" empires

An empire, whether it is made up of nations or of businesses, is born when one distinct group of people takes over another. As it is the case in most empires that a hierarchical relationship of power exists between the conqueror and the conquered, the very act of taking over a people suggests that there is a possibility that an unequal relationship may arise, manifested in discriminatory differences in the rights and duties between those of the people of the empire builder and those of the people being taken over. Along with such inequality in power, economic disparity may occur. Inequality in relations may also show up in the disregard or disrespect that the empire builders holds for the culture of their conquered subjects, if the former have a self-image of superiority coming from their position as conquerors. If legal and political inequality and disregard for culture do occur, the subjugated people may perceive their status as inferior to that of their colonial masters, giving rise to discontent. The conquered subjects may also have feelings of humiliation if the conquerors do not recognize the merits of their culture. Instead of loyalty and sentiments of support and cooperation for the new colonial masters, mistrust and disloyalty may brew. The potential, then, for instability, rebellion, or non-cooperation of the conquered peoples becomes ripe, leading to the possibility of the empire's collapse unless the colonial masters take stern measures to keep their colonial subjects in line. As we have seen, in both the Philippines and Korea, measures for forcing submission to colonial rule including violent methods and deliberate acts of racial and economic discrimination did not for the most part develop the loyalty of the conquered subjects. Many Koreans and Filipinos persisted up to the very end of colonial rule to subvert or resist the efforts of their imperial masters to continue their rule over their colonial possessions. The Indian independence movement grew from Gandhi's public protests against discrimination towards Indians.

After decades of discriminatory treatment and marginalization, the Algerians rebelled against their French colonial masters and won their independence after a bloody war. Similarly in the world of business empires, the inability to establish equality of status and treatment between the business empire builder and the conquered enterprise, and the empire builder's lack of respect and understanding towards the culture of the conquered, have also led to cases where mutual trust, loyalty, cooperation, and ultimately the merger or acquisition itself collapsed, as we have seen with MEI's Hollywood empire, which lasted for only five years, and MEI's acquisition of Quasar, which ended up with lawsuits from dissatisfied American employees citing discrimination, and the disappearance of the Quasar brand.

In contrast, we have seen that within the long-continued and continuing empires of history and business, the coexistence of various cultures, practices, ethnicities, and beliefs were tolerated. Such was the case within the empires of the Mongols, Romans, and within the United Kingdom. MEI accepted the good business practices of Komori Kandenchi Seisakusho, which became the core group within MEI for driving its battery business, and tolerated the cultural independence of JVC such that the latter would maintain its own brand identity and management philosophies for more than 50 years within the MEI group of companies. Sony allowed its Hollywood studio creative independence with regard to movie making and the use of talented people who came from outside of Sony to run the studio. Within long-lasting empires, the people who were brought in or joined the empire enjoyed full or nearly full participation in the political process for co-running the empire. Africans, Syrians, Spaniards, and "barbarians" served as emperors in Rome. Scots and Welsh became prime ministers of the UK. In the example of the mega-merger of the six proto-VOC companies which lasted for two centuries, all of the companies received seats on the management board and participated in the management of the VOC. Matsushita Konosuke and MEI appointed Nakagawa Yasuharu, the president of Nakagawa Kikai, the refrigerator company that was acquired and absorbed by MEI, to become vice president of MEI, in effect making him the second-ranked person in MEI after Konosuke himself. Nakagawa Kikai became an integral part of the Matsushita Group that provided the company with valuable technical know-how and production capabilities for manufacturing refrigerators.

Judging from the examples herein of long- and short-lived global and business empires, a key to making an empire endure and for all of its people to prosper is to achieve the creation of a culture of equality by eradicating the differences of rights and duties between the conqueror and the conquered, and by recognizing, respecting, and accepting the merits of the conquered peoples' culture. This would mean making an empire a democracy—an oxymoronic concept if there ever was one—in order to survive. Indeed, the former Foreign Minister of the Soviet Union, Eduard Shevardnadze, noted that the collapse of the "socialist empire" of the USSR (1917–1991) less than a hundred years after its birth was sooner or later to be inevitable as it did not become democratized.[2]

To conclude, in all of the "successful" examples of empire that we have looked at, whether they are global or business empires, a common thread is the observance of tolerance of varying degrees by the imperial masters/M&A initiators, especially with regards to respecting cultural differences and removing major discriminatory differences in duties, rights, and privileges between the conqueror/acquirer and conquered/acquired. The consequence of the practice of tolerance is the cooperation and loyalty, if not the love, of the conquered subjects towards their imperial masters, which contributed to the stability and life of the empire.

Factors aside from tolerance

Admittedly though, tolerance is not the only factor that has had an impact on the life of an empire. From the examples of the VOC, Mongol Empire, MEI, Sony and others I suggest as follows other factors that may impact an empire.

The ability of empire builders to throw away pride and use the fruits of others

We have seen the extent to which the Mongols freely borrowed the technologies, culture, concepts, and ideas of other peoples without compunction if they saw benefit. Likewise the ancient Romans also enthusiastically adopted the customs and technologies of those who they ruled when they saw benefit to their use. A similar case of unabashed copying or borrowing in a business empire is Matsushita Konosuke's enthusiastic adoption of the best practices of other companies such as Philips, and the emulation of the product strategies of competitors such as Sony, which earned MEI the not-too-complimentary name of "Maneshita Denki" (Copycat Electric). Ibuka and Morita of Sony on their part vowed to come up with something new and different when they set up their company. But this determination did not prevent them from using technologies developed by other companies or research institutes, such as the transistor, or from adopting and emulating what they considered to be the best management practices of other companies.

In this day and age of countless court cases on patent infringement and copying, imitating the practices of others does not exactly present a reputable image. But in the past, even prominent individuals in history unabashedly copied others to gain the necessary inspiration to create new and original materials. A case in point is the German composer Johann Sebastian Bach. Although J.S. Bach comes across to us as a highly "original" thinking composer and a master of the art of fugue and counterpoint, his musical output of keyboard works, religious pieces, concertos and so forth were built upon many years of formidable study and literally copying other composers' works. An anecdote relates that the young Bach surreptitiously copied in the dark of night, using only the moon as his source of light, the manuscripts of other composers which were locked away by his older brother. At other times, Bach avidly transcribed the concertos of the

Venetian Antonio Vivaldi and other composers for the solo keyboard. And yet, out of all this copying and studying of other composers, Bach was able to create his own original works built upon the inspiration he had received from absorbing the knowledge of different styles and techniques. Thus, while Bach never set foot outside his native Germany, he laterally developed his own musical themes and content that reflected the fashionable "French" styles of dance music and the lyrical "Italian" style of concertos, and wrote masterworks for the organ and keyboard that reflected his study of the compositional techniques developed by past masters and his contemporaries.

In all of the above examples, a shortcoming or deficiency has led people to copy or emulate others, which may have involved the conscious or subconscious swallowing of pride. All too often, however, in the modern business world, there are companies and even nations too proud or arrogant to admit to their shortcomings or limitations. Indeed, in such cases they desperately try to develop technologies or competencies on their own even when they realize they haven't a chance due to a lack of manpower resources or simply a lack of know-how and ingenuity. Often, they cling to past successes as justification for going at it alone or not emulating others, even when they would stand a better chance of fighting against the competition by partnering with another company that can complement or augment resources. Henry Ford II's refusal to use a "Jap" engine in his cars, or the denial of US car companies for many years of the merits of the "lean production" methods of Japanese car companies, are typical examples where pride worked against rational business calculation.[3] In contrast to the situation with US car companies which had seen a drastic decline in market share on its own turf, owing largely to Japanese competition over several decades, the following example of the US conglomerate General Electric's (GE) acquisition and quick divesture of the US consumer electronics company RCA shows what happens when a business is able to swallow its pride.

GE's acquisition and divesture of RCA

The American industrial and financial conglomerate that we know today as GE was founded in 1892 as a result of a merger between the inventor Thomas Edison's Edison General Electric and the Thomas–Houston Electric Company led by investor Charles A. Coffin. Since its inception the company had on various occasions undertaken M&A as a means for business development, a recent major example being the purchase of MEI's former movie studio, Universal Pictures, from the French media conglomerate Vivendi in 2004 (GE later sold its majority interest in the studio to the American cable TV operator Comcast in 2011). Another major acquisition by GE was back in 1986, when the company re-acquired the consumer electronics company RCA and its radio and TV broadcast company NBC (RCA was originally founded in 1919 by GE to develop and sell radios but was later sold off in 1930). The following year, in a move that was meant to strengthen its medical business, GE acquired the medical imaging business of the French-government-owned electronics conglomerate Thomson in a swap for RCA's consumer electronics TV and radio business. At the time there was much criticism in the US directed towards GE, lambasting them for bowing to Japanese competition.[4] But by swallowing his pride as an American (after all, RCA had given birth to the TV industry, which was born in the US) GE CEO Jack Welch was able to engineer a deal that would allow his company to depart from the TV business, which was indeed being clobbered by the likes of Sony and MEI with no sign of a bottom-of-the-ninth-come-from-behind victory in sight, and at the same time enable GE to significantly bolster its European share of business for medical imaging equipment (in the US it was already number one) including CT scanners, x-ray devices, and magnetic resonance imaging (MRI) machines. The acquisition of Thomson's medical business had given GE a formidable chance to go after the number one medical business player in Europe, Siemens, and 25 years later GE is a major global player in the medical electronics and services industry.

So the lesson from past history is: To hell with pride—if at some point you realize that you haven't got a chance to beat 'em, join 'em, or do something else.

The ability of empire builders to use the right people for the right job

We have seen that one of the management principles which Ibuka and Morita had established for Sony was to ensure that the right persons were doing the right tasks. With this principle in mind, Sony had gone outside the company to hire Hollywood insiders to run its movie studio. Although the company in retrospect made the wrong choice initially, it nevertheless continued to follow through on its principle and eventually succeeded in stabilizing the studio with new, capable management who were veterans of the industry. During the establishment of the CBS/Sony JV, we have seen that its recruitment drive for hiring new employees did not place any limits on nationality, gender, age, or previous experience. People were hired from all over, and a little over 10 years from its start, the JV had become the largest music record company in Japan. Going back several centuries, we saw the unconcern which the VOC had towards a person's origin when it came to hiring people to man their ships, the diversity of the Heeren XVII membership, and also the VOC's ability to recruit and promote ruthless but nevertheless capable people such as Jan Coen. As for the Mongols, we have seen Genghis Khan choose his field commanders on the basis of ability rather than tribal origins, which I argue was a major reason for his success on the battlefield. And in their search for people to serve them for specific occupations or purposes, the Mongols had no scruples with regard to where people came from, their gender, their ethnicity or race, their religion, their language, their looks, tastes, or habits, so long as the people were capable and talented. As a result, the Mongol Empire became all the richer and more stable as it brought about the cross-fertilization of ideas and technologies leading to new inventions and innovations, new types of food and commodities, expansion in the exchange of goods, and new forms of art.

Modern examples of using the right persons for the right jobs

The practice of getting the right person for the right job regardless of their origin implies having the ability to get hold of or attract skilled talent wherever it may come from, which in effect entails the globalization of human resources for businesses and societies. In a parallel to the approach of the Mongols and others mentioned herein in getting capable people from all over, in the post-imperial era of the twentieth century and the early twenty-first, the US has done a remarkable job of attracting and assimilating half of the world's skilled immigrants, who were responsible for starting up a quarter of new venture-backed companies during the period 1990 to 2005.[5] Likewise Britain has seen an increase in the number of foreign entrepreneurs, who are lured to the UK by several factors; among them are a common language, attractive geography, cultural diversity, openness to foreigners, and enthusiasm for new ideas. For Emi Gal, a 23-year-old Romanian entrepreneur who set up a digital media company in London, London is practically the "center of the world" for people wanting to work in media and advertising.[6] German companies as well are making inroads in attracting talent from all over the world and strengthening their competitiveness as a result. The healthcare company Bayer, whose corporate headquarters is based in Germany, has its Diabetes Care business division headquarters based in the US. A multinational staff of North and South American, Chinese, Indian, Taiwanese, and European engineers work at this division to develop an array of products and services for diabetes patients around the world. The small number of German nationals in high positions within the division and the relatively large number of females in executive positions is suggestive of the unconcern of the German corporate leaders as to the nationality or gender of its employees and management when trying to find talented people. The Korean electronics conglomerate Samsung Electronics has been stepping up its efforts to headhunt and recruit first-rate Japanese engineers in particular by offering them salaries and perks that go beyond what they have been receiving at Japanese firms. Such efforts at diversity have borne fruit for the company in recent years, as shown in their stellar performance against Japanese competitors such as Sony and Panasonic. As Iizuka Tetsuya, president of Tokyo based THine Electronics Inc., points out, Samsung's strength is based on its philosophy of "attracting the best and the brightest."[7]

Using the right persons for the right jobs: the Japanese experience

As for the third largest economy in the world, Japan has done a relatively poor job in promoting diversity, whether it is in the company, research labs, universities, schools, or in politics. Before we even talk about the low level of globalization of human resources, it must be noted that the country to begin with lags behind most of the industrialized nations on gender equality, whether in wage differences or in appointing female executives at large Japanese firms or in the number of female politicians. In the 2009 Global Gender Index published by the

World Economic Forum, which benchmarks national gender gaps in political, economic, educational, and healthcare areas, Japan ranked 101 out of 134 countries, behind not only most of the Western industrialized nations but also the emerging economies of Russia (51st), China (60th), and Brazil (81st).[8] At the 100 largest employers in Japan, only 24 percent of the employees are female. In comparison, 52 percent are female at the 100 largest employers in the US.[9] Most Japanese companies report that only up to 10 percent of the managerial positions are held by women.[10] According to a survey conducted by the US-based NGO, Corporate Women Directors International (CWDI), only 1.4 percent of all corporate members of boards of directors in Japan are female, a low figure that is basically on par with such countries as Korea (1.5 percent) and Bahrain (1.0 percent) but slightly higher than Saudi Arabia (0.1 percent). In comparison, 44.2 percent of all board members in Norway are female, while the global average of 42 countries that were surveyed was at 8.8 percent.[11] The low profile of women in the Japanese workforce and in senior managerial positions is all the more surprising given that according to student performance data collected by the Program for International Student Assessment (PISA) of the OECD Japan, Japanese female students consistently outscored their male counterparts in every assessment category including reading literacy, mathematical literacy, scientific literacy, and problem-solving skills.[12] Genghis and his Mongol horde, who actively utilized women for all sorts of tasks, would have been bewildered by this underutilization of the smarter half of the population of Japan. Given, however, that Tokyo governor Ishihara Shintaro has stated that women who are not able to or no longer able to bear children are useless to society and that for them to continue living on is "pointless," this is perhaps not surprising.[13]

Conservative elements in Japanese society, however, may point out that even without the full participation of females in the workforce or skilled immigrant labor for that matter, at one time Japan became the second largest economy in the world and it is still the third largest. Indeed, politicians of a nationalist bent have in the past claimed that the strength of Japan lies in its homogeneity. For practical reasons, however, the promotion of diversity in Japan is becoming important not only for the purpose of sustaining growth, but in view of a rapidly falling birthrate[14] and what the former Japanese Ministry of International Trade and Industry (MITI) official Sakaya Taiichi calls "the disinterest and impotence (muyoku-mukiryoku) of the majority of the younger generation Japanese," who tend to avoid taking risks and prefer to settle for an uneventful life as a doctor or "salaryman."[15] Compounding the rise of these "disinterested and impotent" young Japanese whom the media and young disillusioned Japanese females have labeled "broccoli (or herbivorous) boys" (soshoku-kei danshi) is an increasingly insular mindset. According to a study conducted by Sangyo Noritsu University and published in the Japanese Ministry of Economics, Trade, and Industry's (METI) 2010 White Paper on trade and the economy, the number of employees who recently joined a Japanese company who had registered a desire to work outside of Japan declined by seven percentage points in 2007 compared to 2004. The same research showed that the number of employees who said they would refuse an overseas assignment increased by eight percentage points over the same period.[16] A more recent survey conducted by the Sanno Institute of Management verifies this earlier result. According to analysis carried out online in June 2010, which contacted 400 men and women between the ages of 18 and 26 who joined the workforce in April of the same year, 49 percent of the corporate recruits responded that they do not want to work overseas. Back in 2001, the corresponding figure was 29.2 percent.[17] In the latest survey, the major reasons given as to why the respondents do not desire to work outside of Japan were the great risks involved with working abroad and a lack of self-confidence in their abilities.[18]

The growing trend of insularity is not limited to new company recruits. The number of Japanese students doing post-secondary studies overseas declined over three consecutive years to just 75,156 in 2007. With regard to this trend, the Japanese daily *Mainichi Shinbun* had lamented that it would seem that ambition is missing from today's youth as they turn increasingly inward in outlook.[19] From my personal experience of many years as an interviewer for Japanese high school students who are applying for scholarships to study abroad, I have observed that while there has indeed been a gradual decline over the years in the number of students that have been applying, the greatest decrease has been in the number of male students. Female students have continued to apply in large numbers. That is to say, it seems that insularity is affecting male Japanese, while females tend to remain enthusiastic about the prospects of living and studying abroad. While I do not offer any reasons for this trend, a possible explanation for this is what Georgetown University professor Carroll Quigley observed was happening in middle-income families in the US after World War II: the development of strong ties between mothers and sons and the distant or competitive relationship that tended to develop between mothers and daughters, inducing mothers to hasten the growing up of daughters and have them leave the house quickly while delaying the social development of sons as a means of keeping them nearby for as long as possible.[20]

If current trends continue and Japan fails to revitalize its "disinterested and impotent young Japanese," Sakaiya fears that Japan will become the "last socialist state" to collapse.[21] These are serious words indeed, given that most Japanese companies who hire these "disinterested and impotent" young "broccoli boys" are run, according to Natsuno Takeshi of Keio University, by Japanese chief executives who, being immersed in traditional Japanese-style management and corporate culture characterized by seniority-based promotion and lifetime employment, are simply unable to deal with the global business environment.[22] The solution Natsuno proposes to this dire quagmire is strikingly reminiscent of what the Mongols did. That is, if Japanese companies are going to win in global competition, they will need to be flexible and multicultural in their outlook, which according to Natsuno means companies hiring people with diverse backgrounds and values, and promoting young people, non-Japanese, and women to senior executive posts.[23]

There are, however, divergent views. On the issue of a declining and aging population, the Japan-based management consultant James C. Abegglen points out that even with a declining population, the population of Japan in the middle of the twenty-first century will be at 100 million, which will still be considerably more than that of most other nations. Demand patterns will of course change with an aging population, but it is wage levels rather than total population which will ultimately determine the level of demand. For Abegglen, coping with a declining population, which will still be big anyway in the middle of the next century by large-scale immigration to Japan, "is nonsense" considering the costs involved in racial and cultural disputes such those which have erupted in Britain, the Netherlands, Germany, Italy, France, Denmark, etc.[24]

As for the practices of Japanese-style management, in contrast to Natsuno who sees it as a disadvantage in the age of globalization, Mitarai Fujio, CEO of the Japanese electronics company Canon, views it as the secret to his company's success. For him, the culture in Japan embodies the principle of lifetime employment, and he believes that conforming to this practice is a core competence of the company to help it survive global competition.[25] In an unintended jab at some Japanese companies such as Sony which have done much to introduce American-style corporate governance structures, complete with outside boards of directors and management oversight committees, Mitarai states that the "American" business practice in large companies of using outside executives has no function in Japan. As he sees it, "outsiders have no capacity to be able to make judgments concerning the internal affairs of the company."[26] On the other hand, the fact that an egregious case of corporate fraud that had seemingly been going on for decades at the Japanese medical device manufacturer Olympus, which rocked the Japanese business and financial community, was committed under the watch of an all-Japanese corporate board only to be internally exposed by the whistle-blowing activity of a sole non-Japanese (British) national on the Olympus board, is perhaps suggestive of the importance of hiring people of different backgrounds and values.

Regardless of the various arguments concerning the pros and cons of encouraging diversity through changing Japanese management styles or employing foreign nationals, there *have* been winds of change blowing even in laggard Japan as rural farming and fishing communities, universities, and IT-related industries have increasingly brought in Chinese and other foreign nationals.[27] Non-Japanese have even begun to hold positions as heads of departments at prestigious Japanese universities such as Hitotsubashi and Ritsumeikan. Japanese businesses that are global in scale are for the most part fully aware of the increasing challenges of globalization, a declining birthrate, and the sapping vitality of the native Japanese, and have begun what may seem extreme measures (for the Japanese, that is) to stimulate their Japanese employees by promoting diversity at the workplace. An example is the hiring of Lee Guanglin Samson, a 29-year-old Singaporean graduate of the National University of Singapore, who was hired by the electronics conglomerate Toshiba to work at the company's Corporate Software Engineering Center in the city of Kawasaki. Formerly it would have been impossible for Lee to work at Toshiba, as the company had a longstanding policy of only employing foreigners who had studied at

Japanese universities. According to Suzuki Seiichiro, head of Toshiba's personnel center, senior management, however, judged that a more global use of personnel was necessary to remain competitive, and hence decided that Japanese-language comprehension was not to be a requirement for employment, thus opening the way for people such as Lee to work in Japan. With this new employment direction, Toshiba plans to hire people who could become leaders of business divisions in 25 years, irrespective of national origin.[28] At Panasonic Electric Works Corporation (Panasonic Denko), Musaeva Feruza, a citizen of Uzbekistan, was hired by the company's personnel division in 2008. Part of the reason for hiring Musaeva, according to Yukioka Masayasu, head of the employment department in the company's personnel division, was that on account of shrinking housing starts in Japan fueled by a declining birthrate it was imperative to expand overseas and hence employ people with global skills. Yukioka believes that such hiring will help to promote the internationalization of the company.[29]

While progress towards encouraging diversity is in fits and starts, current developments in global business and trends in Japanese demographics and lifestyles suggest that more and more Japanese companies will eventually have to adopt policies that encourage diversity. This entails educating and training Japanese to enable them to work in a global work environment, and also bringing to Japan people of talent who will be able to augment and revitalize the native workforce. Aside from meeting the challenges in demographics and lifestyle changes, embracing diversity is important as it provides the opportunity for the Japanese to be regularly exposed to different ways of thinking, which according to some is linked with creativity. A case in point mentioned by Marc Tucker, the president of the US National Center on Education and the Economy, is that of the Renaissance inventor Leonardo Da Vinci who, by mastering the two different fields of art and science, was able to use the intellectual framework in one to nourish further creativity in the other. Tucker calls him a "great lateral thinker" that had the knowledge and mental ability to synthesize ideas and connect the dots necessary for the next intellectual breakthrough, which would not have been possible had he spent his whole life in an isolated intellectual silo with no stimulation from the outside.[30]

The Japanese have a long way to go in matching the Mongols for accepting diversity, but at least the process towards achieving it has begun among some of their companies.

The ability of empire builders to build a common identity/culture

As we have seen, Genghis Khan was able to keep his initial merger of the various Mongol tribes together primarily by his promise of booty through conquest. Fortunately for Genghis, he was able to deliver on his promise and the other tribes continued to follow him. Along with booty, however, came an empire of many different peoples and unprecedented challenges in keeping the empire together. The Mongols in this instance used a combination of the stick and carrot for ruling their conquered subjects: the former being that of brute military force and the strict enforcement of laws with harsh punishment for violations, and the latter being the incentives of riches, religious freedom, freedom of work, the guarantee of peace and stability, and the possibilities of advancement through one's abilities. In many cases, life under the Mongols improved. In short, the Mongol appeal for uniting their conquered subjects in one empire was based on practical considerations such as increased wealth and religious freedom, and not on offering any identity or sense of belonging to a common civilization to which the conquered peoples could relate. Without a common identity to unite the Mongols' conquered subjects, maintaining the empire in the end proved difficult. Over time the nomadic culture of the Mongols was ultimately pushed aside by the Mongols themselves in favor of the settled cultures of their conquered subjects, which facilitated the eventual disappearance of the Mongol Empire through assimilation. In contrast to the Mongols, both the Roman Empire and the United Kingdom were able to forge a superseding identity which the peoples of the subordinate cultures could identify with. Likewise, in the realm of business empires, we have seen that Sony and CBS through their joint venture of CBS/Sony were able to create a new, distinct culture that superseded those of the parent companies by allowing creative and managerial independence to exist in the new venture. The Heeren XVII of the VOC was able to create an identity that superseded the six original trading companies and made the VOC the focus of loyalty, thereby ensuring the support of all participants in the trading empire.

When an empire builder, however, is unable to create an overriding or superseding culture or gain support for its own culture, it may simply opt to forcibly impose its own culture without any regard or consideration of the culture and practices of the conquered entity. This could lead to resistance by the conquered people as a means to assert and preserve their identity. Such was the case with MEI's acquisition of MCA. MEI's inability to tolerate the ways of Hollywood and its failure to create an overriding culture that was acceptable to both MEI and the Hollywood studio in effect led to the rise of animosity and antagonism between the managements of both companies. The cases of the merger between the car companies Daimler-Benz and Chrysler and General Electric's (GE) acquisition of Nuovo Pignone are further examples of how a company might be successful or unsuccessful at building a new overriding culture after acquiring a new company.

The failed merger of "equals": Daimler-Benz and the Chrysler Corporation

In 1998 the car companies Daimler-Benz of Germany and Chrysler Corporation (Chrysler) of the US merged to form DaimlerChrysler. At the outset of the deal, management of both companies stressed that this was a "merger of equals." A dual chairmanship consisting of one person from each company was established for the merged company to cement this "equality." As the Daimler-Benz CEO put it, the union was "a merger of equals, a merger of growth, and a merger of unprecedented strength."[31] "Shareholder value" and "job creation" were other key words that were stressed at the time of the merger announcement.[32] The merger of a luxury car manufacturer (Daimler-Benz) with a mass-market brand manufacturer (Chrysler) was to result in the world's most profitable auto manufacturer as new economies of scale and scope, increased manufacturing expertise, and distribution reach were to be realized.

It soon became apparent, however, that the merger was in fact a takeover. From early on Daimler-Benz managers dominated in many of the discussions over positions and functions.[33] Several Chrysler executives left as they became frustrated with the management approaches used by the Germans. Less than a year after the merger was announced, the board of DaimlerChrysler consisted of nine former Daimler-Benz executives and only five former executives from Chrysler.[34] This number was further reduced to two just three years after the merger was concluded. In addition, with the resignation of former Chrysler CEO Robert Eaton from the position of co-chairman of the DaimlerChrysler board, Jurgen Schrempp of Daimler-Benz became the sole chairman of the board. In effect, the DaimlerChrysler management became "Daimlerized" at the expense of Chrysler management, with the implied message that Chrysler executives need not participate in the management of the merged entity. Daimler-Benz eventually showed its true intent when Schrempp stated in an interview with the British business newspaper *Financial Times* in 2000 that he had never intended a merger of equals and had always aimed to acquire Chrysler. Rather, he considered Chrysler to be a division of Daimler-Benz.[35] This statement was reported to have lowered morale among Chrysler employees and even to have created hostile feelings towards their German counterparts.[36] To add fuel to the fire of discontent for Chrysler employees, and in a move that uncannily recalls what MEI did at Quasar, the German Dieter Zetsche fired 26,000 Chrysler employees not long after he replaced James Holden as CEO of Chrysler (Zetsche later became CEO of DaimlerChrysler). The Germans also did little to hide their contempt of Chrysler cars, with some Daimler-Benz executives declaring that they "would never drive a Chrysler."[37] One Daimler executive was reported to have said that so long as he was responsible for the Mercedes-Benz brand, only over his "dead body" would there ever be a Chrysler car built in a Mercedes-Benz factory. For this to happen was simply "unthinkable."[38] Apparently, the Germans could not see or refused to see any positive aspects of the manufacturing culture of Chrysler. In response to such condescending attitudes, angry Chrysler managers and executives such as Chrysler vice chairman Bob Lutz responded by testily pointing out that Chrysler's Jeep Grand Cherokee outdid the Mercedes M-Class in customer satisfaction ratings.[39] All these integration measures and trading of insults added up to skepticism and distrust, which led to a breakdown in the integration process. Potential synergies that were touted at the time as justification for the merger, such as the creation of common engineering and design platforms and the implementation of a cohesive global brand architecture—none of this happened. Distrust also hampered efforts to neutralize the impact of culture.

There were even accusations of racism raised by the Americans towards the Germans, a situation reminiscent of what happened between the Japanese and Americans at Quasar.[40] As business consultant and author Michael Watkins put it, efforts to integrate the operations of Daimler and Chrysler collapsed as a result of conflict between the "cowboys" of Detroit and the "knights" of Stuttgart.[41] In 2007, Daimler-Benz called it quits and sold the Chrysler "division" to the investment fund American Cerberus Group for €5.5 billion.

General Electric and Nuovo Pignone

In 1994 General Electric (GE) acquired the Italian engine manufacturer Nuovo Pignone (NP) from the Italian state-owned oil and gas company, ENI. Although both GE and NP had technical competencies in engine manufacturing, the latter, like Thomson's medical business mentioned above, was part of a state-owned conglomerate subsidized by the government with a corporate culture shaped by political agendas. NP, which started out as a company named Pignone, was founded in 1842 in Florence Italy. The company became the producer of the world's first gas-powered combustion engine. In 1954, the Italian government agency responsible for developing hydrocarbons took over the company and renamed it Nuovo (New) Pignone. Under government ownership NP began developing electrical turbines, compressors, and pumps for energy-related industries. The high quality of its products and technologies and its competent production systems contributed to making the company a highly profitable business.[42]

Culturally, GE and NP were far apart. While according to one NP manager NP had a "relaxed" management style that placed no particular emphasis on measuring management performance or of having performance control mechanisms,[43] GE had a clearly defined management quality measurement system program—Six Sigma—that was implemented globally throughout the GE organization. Essentially a business philosophy that was first implemented by Motorola and later on by other technology companies such as Texas Instruments, Six Sigma is a management philosophy that involves using various managerial tools and techniques including statistical analysis to define, measure, improve, and control all aspects of business whether in production or operations. Now that it was a member of GE, Jack Welch could have rammed the "GE Way" down the throats of the Italians. But he didn't. Instead, he had his Italian vice chairman in charge of international operations, Paolo Fresco, a University of Genoa graduate, prevent the "colonization" of NP by having him appoint a president at NP whose main task was to keep the GE bureaucrats away.[44] GE systems and its culture would gradually be introduced, but the first priority was having the NP managers use GE resources to grow the business and understand the "GE Way." Accordingly, GE staff explained to the Italians that the merger process that was to be undertaken was one of integrating NP within GE, i.e., introducing GE management methods while respecting NP capabilities and promoting change rather than forcing it.[45] To this end, GE set up a massive organizational training program for NP employees that focused on the fundamentals of financial measurement while encouraging communication between accountants and engineers. While transforming the company, however, GE respected and accepted the technological capabilities of NP and accordingly conserved those practices of NP which were deemed as worth continuing.[46] The measures undertaken and the attitudes held by GE helped the NP employees to gradually change their way of thinking, build their support for GE's culture, and also develop a sense of loyalty to GE. The success of this acquisition is demonstrated by the fact that in 2012, almost 20 years after the acquisition, NP was still in operation as a highly profitable division of GE and was also a key training center for GE's European operations.

To conclude, the underlying message for empire builders from the experience of the Mongols and the other above examples is that while tolerance of diversity and other cultures facilitates the conquered peoples' acceptance of being taken over, the creation of a common identity which the conquered can relate to, whether it is a new superseding identity or the identity of the conqueror (if it is attractive enough to be accepted by the conquered), may serve as the cultural "glue" that holds the empire together and wins the loyalty of the conquered people.

The ability to show balance and flexibility in the practice of tolerance

While I have argued from the examples mentioned herein that the practice of tolerance has been a factor that has contributed in keeping an empire together whether it is of the Mongols or of Sony's movie empire, at the same time, too much tolerance may be fatal and may result in the loss of control by the acquirer/conqueror. Too much tolerance resulted in the Mongols being completely absorbed by the cultures of their conquered subjects and their eventual loss of identity as a coherent Mongol Empire. We have also seen that too much tolerance led to the screwing of Sony by the production team of Guber and Peters and its near loss of control of its movie studio.

The question then arises of how to create the "right" balance of tolerance. To this end, the Japanese immunologist Tada Tomio suggested looking at the workings of the immune system of animals as an analogy for a hint on the importance of balance in the level of tolerance and on how this could be achieved. According to Tada, vertebrate animals have developed two immune systems. In the most commonly known form, foreign bodies such as viruses that enter the body are destroyed by the body's immune system. In contrast, there is another form of behavior in the immune system where instead of destroying viruses that enter the body, the immune systems allows, or "tolerates" the virus to exist with other cells. The tolerant method is a logical outcome in the case when the immune system causes too much cell destruction by thoroughly going after and destroying infected cells. Excessive destruction of infected cells may result in fluminant hepatitis or liver failure, leading ultimately to death. But if before this happens the immune system becomes "tolerant," the immune system associates the identity of the infected cells with other cells and the existence of the virus causing the infection is tolerated. The destruction process of infected cells is terminated.

On the other hand, cancer viruses that are tolerated by the immune system and are accepted in other cells in the body still retain their original identity as a cancer virus. In this case the tolerance of the immune system allows the cancer virus to propagate within the cells in which it resides and eventually causes the cells to lose their own identity and become cancerous.[47]

As the immune system of animals suggests, striking a fine balance between too little and too much tolerance is no easy feat. Either too much or too little tolerance in the immune system of animals would lead to death. Likewise, in empires whether of the nation or of business, too little tolerance may result in dissatisfaction and the breakdown of loyalty leading to instability, while too much tolerance may bring about issues of control and identity. The key, then, is to be able to flexibly *adjust* the level of tolerance in accordance with the circumstances at hand—something which is admittedly easier said than done and is perhaps a form of know-how that can be garnered only through experience and from the study of history.

The ability of empire builders to show results

All of the successful empire builders mentioned above shared the ability to deliver results to their followers. The VOC promised the riches of spices and high shareholder returns which were delivered for decades and ensured continuing investment from shareholders, as well as providing a strong incentive for the six proto-VOC companies to stick together. Genghis promised and delivered booty, women, and booze to his unruly Mongol hordes in return for their support and cooperation if not their love. Matsushita Konosuke delivered to his acquired companies job security, increasing incomes, and prestige, which helped him convince his acquired employees of the benefits of the "Matsushita Way." Ohga Norio delivered on his promise in making the JV CBS/Sony the number one music record company in Japan in 10 years. After a rough start, Sony Pictures regained its footing and has prospered under the Sony umbrella and leadership. The Romans delivered to their imperial subjects the riches of the known world and the prestige that came from being a citizen of the Roman Empire. In contrast, the British, French, and American empires in India, Algeria, and the Philippines that in the end collapsed due to independence movements or lack of loyalty on the part of the colonial subjects failed to deliver prosperity to the majority of their subject peoples. The union of MEI and MCA largely failed to produce expected growth and synergies, which was a factor behind its dissolution. Likewise, the failure to realize the expected synergies leading to increased revenues and profits as originally planned was also a major reason behind the collapse of the merger of Daimler-Benz and Chrysler.

The ability of empire builders to demonstrate leadership

In some of the aforementioned examples, it can be argued that the demonstration of leadership by the empire builders was also a factor behind successful post-merger integration. This was seen when Matsushita Konosuke made personal efforts to teach his management principles to the employees of his newly acquired companies. In the case of CBS/Sony, there was no doubt that Ohga Norio was the driving force behind the post-JV integration process. Howard Stringer's active participation in various Sony-involved Hollywood events and his development of a close rapport with the heads of Sony's movie studio was another demonstration of leadership that contributed to the stabilization of the management of Sony Pictures. An additional example where leadership was critical in realizing the successful integration of two companies was in the merger between the US computer technology company Hewlett-Packard (HP) and the personal computer company Compaq.

Leadership at Hewlett-Packard (HP)

In 2002, HP acquired Compaq for US$19 billion. Putting aside the issue of whether this acquisition has turned out to be a long-term "success" for HP, executives who were involved in the merger process have pointed out that a critical component behind the integration *process* which they *did* consider to be a success was the commitment shown at the top of the organization, in particular by HP CEO Carly Fiorina, who was heavily involved from the beginning in the planning of the merger.[48] A 30-person integration team which came to be known as the "Clean Team" consisting of people from both companies was established to oversee the integration process. In stark contrast to what had happened at DaimlerChrysler and at Quasar, where in both cases the influence of the acquired enterprises were marginalized, Fiorina had instructed this team to ensure that the best assets of both companies would be used in the new combined entity of HP-Compaq. According to one Clean Team member, the team "objectively evaluated" an asset, kept whichever version, i.e., HP's or Compaq's, was considered better, and threw out the other.[49] In addition to the setting up of this team, Fiorina chose two of the most empowered people in *both* companies to lead in getting the day-to-day integration tasks completed, and built extensive relationships with management teams that ran the integration process.[50] And to eliminate a "we-versus-them" mentality among senior managers, Fiorina set up a "buddy system" whereby each senior executive from one company "adopted" a counterpart from another.[51] With these measures implemented under the leadership of Fiorina, the two companies undertook the process of integration which included a due diligence of each other's cultures and the adoption of the best practices of both companies.

The role of leaders in establishing culture

Hofstede observed that the values of the founders and key leaders of companies shape organizational or corporate culture. Likewise, for Edgar H. Schein, it is leadership that creates a particular culture that a group ends up with.[52] As Schein saw it, for leaders the only thing of real importance is to create, understand, and manage culture. At the same time, the ultimate demonstration of leadership was to destroy a culture when it was viewed as dysfunctional.[53] For Schein, therefore, culture and leadership were two sides of the same coin, with leaders creating cultures when they create groups and organizations. With the VOC, the dire circumstances surrounding the Dutch Republic, the sweeping intolerance of the Spanish, and the limited human resources of the Netherlands persuaded the collective leadership of the Herren XVII to set aside their differences and create a corporate culture that would be flexible and pragmatic enough to accept people from beyond the borders of the country to work in the VOC and accept the participation of all the proto-VOC companies, no matter how small, in the management of the new merged enterprise. Among the Mongols, the leadership of Genghis Khan and his successors such as Kublai set the tone of Mongol imperial policy, which espoused the acceptance of diversity and tolerance of other cultures. At MEI, the founder Konosuke Matsushita set forth his seven management principles and his policy of emulating and adapting the best practices of others, which served as the foundation for the success of M&A made under his watch. Ibuka and Morita set the cultural parameters of what kind of company the future Sony was to be: a company that promoted freedom and individualism and employed the best and the brightest regardless of origin. Such a culture was the driver behind the technological and marketing successes of Sony in its early years, its JV with CBS, and ultimately its acquisition of Columbia Pictures. In each of these cases, it was the leaders who defined and established the culture of the company or nation which would turn out to be conducive to creating a "successful" empire.

The shaping of a leader's views and behavioral traits

But if leaders create the culture of a nation or organization, what shapes the views and behavior of leaders? Hofstede argued that in order to understand the behavior of managers and leaders, it is necessary to understand attributes of their societies, such as what type of personalities are common in their country, what their country's literature and arts are like, and the mental software that was acquired during the first 10 years of their lives, which contains most of the basic values held by an individual.[54] Genghis Khan's harsh experience of treachery by blood relatives made him open to the idea of accepting people of diverse origins including defeated enemies and choosing his generals from other tribes. He also ensured that what he practiced was codified and passed down to his successors. Without this aspect of leadership, it could very well have been the case that the Mongol tribes after his death would have gone their own separate selfish ways. Later on, the formal education and instructions for respecting different cultures and religions given by Genghis' daughter-in-law Sorghagtani to her children including Kublai Khan would have an immense impact on the outlook of the Mongol rulers. They in turn guided the Mongol Empire into becoming a cosmopolitan empire that in many ways was at the forefront of human civilization in terms of technology, arts, religious tolerance, and the administering of justice.

With Ibuka Masaru, I have suggested that it was his experiences living under stifling Japanese ultra-nationalism and the influence of his liberal mentors that made him aware of the importance of tolerance and respecting the freedom of the individual. Morita Akio's tolerance in accepting the coexistence of different views and opinions within his company may have been inspired by his father, who respected his son's choice of going into a field that would entail breaking centuries of the family tradition of the eldest son heading the family sake-brewing business. As for Matsushita Konosuke, I argue that it was his humbling experiences with poverty and lack of education and social standing in a hierarchical society that made him consciously emulate those that he thought were superior to him in knowledge and ability, and drove him to establish a corporate culture that emphasized the practice of humility and modesty towards the customer.

In eighteenth- and nineteenth-century Europe and the US, the "enlightened" teachings of "scientific racism" contributed in spreading the ideology of white supremacy and the superiority of Western civilization among people such as Kipling, Theodore Roosevelt, and Churchill. It also served as justification for empire-building and the discriminatory treatment of colonial subjects. Yet although most of us today may find the views and attitude held by the empire builders towards their colonial subjects to be crude, repugnant, and inexcusable, they were probably for the most part not conscious of holding morally objectionable views, as the unequal, hierarchical relationship of races was during their time the accepted "reality." That is to say, Kipling, Roosevelt, etc., were all simply products of their time.

To conclude, the examples of Genghis and Kublai Khan, Matsushita, Ibuka, Morita, Theodore Roosevelt, and Churchill suggest that environment and education are key factors that shape a leader's views and with it the capacity for tolerance or proclivity towards intolerance. What will this mean for creating the future leaders of nations and businesses?

Creating global business empire leaders

The need for cultural intelligence

In various countries around the world there is a growing awareness of the need to meet the demands of globalization, or the integration of economies, societies, and cultures, from a human resources standpoint that calls for leaders who have intra-cultural communication skills. This includes the ability to speak foreign languages, in particular the current de facto global business language of English, and the flexibility and attitude of tolerance needed to work in and with different cultures. As Rollins College professors Ilan Alon and James M. Higgins put it, the managers of the twenty-first century will need to understand the cultural diversity of their working environments and workers around the world and adapt their leadership behaviors accordingly to the cultural variety existing in the global context.[55] When this is not realized, difficulties may occur. According to bankers and consultants involved with Chinese businesses, despite the global ambitions of the Chinese, Chinese companies lack certain necessary competencies for global expansion; among them is the managerial expertise and cultural sensitivity to build a truly multinational operation.[56] At an overseas plant owned by the Chinese appliance manufacturer Haier located in South Carolina, a Chinese manager was arousing resentment from his American employees because of his public berating of them for their mistakes, which is a common practice in China and other Asian countries such as Japan.[57]

In short, *cultural intelligence*, which author and business consultant Brooks Peterson defines as the aptitude to appropriately utilize various skills and abilities in a cross-cultural environment,[58] and to which I would add the ability to reject racism and tolerate the diversity of peoples and cultural values, will be required by future leaders, along with the other aspects of intelligence which are widely recognized such as rational and long-based verbal and quantitative intelligence (measured by traditional IQ tests) and emotional intelligence (EQ).[59] I argue that a recent case of a national leader having high levels of cultural intelligence is Abdurrahaman Wahid, better known as Gus Dur (1940–2009), the half-blind Islamic scholar and religious leader who took up the reins of government following the fall of President Suharto of Indonesia, having being elected to office in free elections. Gus Dur's greatest legacy was his leadership in promoting the principles of inclusiveness and tolerance. Towards the Chinese, he lifted discriminatory measures implemented for many decades in Indonesia such as the banning of the use of the Chinese language in public. He made sure that religious freedom prevailed in a country that was overwhelmingly Muslim. And he made great efforts to reconcile the demands of the country's Islamic religious leaders with the needs of a secular state.

For cultivating cultural intelligence, as we have seen with Genghis and Kublai Khan, Ibuka, Morita, Matsushita, and others, education is a key factor. Indeed, Alon and Higgins suggest that managers should be presented with cultural awareness case studies as well as given instruction on how appropriate cross-cultural behavior leads to the possibility of more satisfactory solutions. Global education initiatives should be sponsored.[60] To their suggestions, I would add that instruction should be given that aims at breaking down unfounded and biased conceptions of racial stereotypes. This is especially pertinent in light of advances made in our knowledge of genetics and human origin, thanks to programs such as the National Genographic Project conducted by the National Geographic Society and IBM, through which we now know that all of humanity shares a common ancestry originating in Africa. It makes it all the more imperative to put to rest for good the unfounded creed of "scientific racism" or notions of cultural superiority of one people over another based on biological determinism, which has been the basis of much racist thought, the driver of intolerance, and ultimately the destroyer of empires. Racism has been, and still is, a basis of discrimination in the workplace. Racism has also been a root cause of violent attacks against minorities and immigrants.

Rejecting racism and tolerating cultural diversity, however, is not simply a question of doing the right thing from a moral standpoint. As we have seen from the examples of empires that have lasted for centuries or decades on the world stage and in business, tolerance and the acceptance of diversity have led not only to the continuation but also to the prosperity of empires. For the imperial rulers such as the Mongols and the Romans, who tolerated diversity, enrichment came primarily through the cross-fertilization of ideas and technologies developed by different peoples. Enrichment also came as a result of social and political stability that was encouraged by the policies of tolerance, which allowed them to minimize costs of keeping the colonial subjects in line. Through such policies, the Mongols, who numbered less than a million, were able to rule over an empire of over one hundred million peoples. In certain provincial towns of the Roman Empire, Roman soldiers were rarely seen. From the experiences of these empires, there is thus a strong argument for the individual to reject racism and accept diversity from the standpoint of economic self-interest.

The need for language proficiency

Alon and Higgins also argue that in order to fully understand a culture, language proficiency is a must. As they see it, language lies at the base of establishing cultural understanding, intercultural communication, and possible immersion in a foreign culture.[61] From my own personal experience of having lived in Germany without being able to speak the German language, I fully concur. Indeed, had imperialists such as Thomas Macaulay (who we have seen admitted to having no knowledge of Sanskrit yet contemptuously brushed away Indian culture) understood something of the native languages of the Indian subcontinent, a different, more tolerant outlook towards native cultures might have developed.

We saw earlier the effect of language difficulties on the relationship between MEI and MCA. Language was also likely a factor that clouded the understanding of Sony senior management towards the situation at its Hollywood studio. Events from history and especially certain episodes concerning war and peace have also shown that the importance of language proficiency cannot be underestimated. A case in point was the language ability of Admiral Nomura Kichisaburo, who was appointed Japanese Ambassador to the United States in 1941. Although of affable and reputable character (as mentioned earlier, Matsushita had appointed Nomura as CEO of JVC after its acquisition by MEI), Nomura's command of the English language was not of the level that would be expected of a professional diplomat. Yet, despite this, Nomura was for some time a key participant in the fateful negotiations and talks between Japan and the US that began several months before the rupture of relations and the Japanese attack on Pearl Harbor. His language difficulties were further compounded by the fact that his main counterpart in negotiations with the US government was Secretary of State Cordell Hull, who spoke English with a heavy Tennessee drawl and a lisp to boot.[62] According to historian Lawrence James, at an international trade conference Hull was reported to have told his fellow delegates the need to conclude a "weccipwocal twade agweement pwogam to weduce tawiffs."[63] Nomura's bafflement at times by what Hull was saying, both because of his accent and lisp and because of Nomura's limited English-speaking abilities, led to a considerable amount of misinterpretation and misunderstanding between the two. This resulted in the loss of precious negotiation time for both countries and became additional fuel to the fire that burned down negotiations. Adding to the language difficulties of Nomura, the less than perfect mastery of the Japanese language by American code-breakers led to unintentionally poor translations of deciphered diplomatic mail sent between the Foreign Ministry in Tokyo and the Japanese Embassy in Washington during negotiations between Nomura and Hull; the translations differed widely in substance and tone from the original Japanese, which may have reinforced Washington's image of the Japanese as an amoral, reckless, fanatic people, since, according to one colorful translation (not written as such in the original Japanese), they were intent on "gambling the fate" of their land on the "throw of the die."[64]

In certain countries there is already an awareness of the importance of language as a key to understanding other cultures and preparing for globalization. In Indonesia, parents who in many cases have studied abroad are increasingly having their children attend schools in Indonesia where the primary language of instruction is English and not Indonesian. The mastery of English has also become linked with social standing.[65] Since 1997 Koreans have made the teaching of English compulsory from the third grade of primary school. English instruction has also begun to spread in nursery schools and kindergartens. In some Korean high schools, science classes are taught in English for those students who desire to later study abroad for university.[66] For the Korean government, which sees the goal of the country as becoming a financial and business hub for Northeast Asia, the teaching of English and increasing the number of proficient English speakers is a vital component for achieving this. But to some Koreans, the goal is lofty. Lee Won-il, the CEO of Allianz Global Investors Korea and a former member of the Korean government's financial hub committee, commented that while Korea has a highly skilled and educated labor force, the Koreans in his opinion compared to the people of Hong Kong and Singapore "do not speak English well," which is the nation's greatest handicap in striving to become a global finance and business center.[67] Despite the high hurdles, at least the Korean government starting with its president is showing leadership on the issue, which is driving not only changes in the Korean education system but is also influencing the global hiring and management practices of once insular-looking Korean companies. In 2008, the electronics manufacturer LG officially made English the common language within the company. All meetings are conducted primarily in English, and documents including email are written in English. Even company chauffeurs have received training to be able to converse in English. The *Dong A Ilbo* of Korea reports that such measures have doubled to tripled the number of non-Korean people wishing to apply to and enter LG. Likewise, LG's arch-rival Samsung announced that it intends to increase the number of foreigners working at its headquarters in Seoul from the current 800 to 2,000 by 2020.[68]

For many decades in Japan there has been a considerable drive among the public to improve English language skills, as the large number of language

schools and "how to" books being published attests. Despite this fever for learning English and going through in many cases six years of continuous and intensive English education, Japanese students score considerably lower than their
Chinese and Korean counterparts on the TOEIC (Test of English for International Communication) which is a widely administered test that measures
English fluency.[69] The low test scores may be responsible for the fact that,
according to a survey done in 2008 by the Benesse Education Research and
Development Center, only 21 percent of Japanese household students have ever
read an English language homepage on the Internet, or that only 18 percent of
Japanese students have ever had the experience of reading an English language
email. In comparison, the corresponding figures for Korean students were a
whopping 79 percent and 58 percent respectively.[70] Without wanting to show
signs of paranoia, I have often wondered whether the difficulties many Japanese
are facing in becoming proficient in the English language is the outcome of a
deliberate ploy on the part of the power-holders in Japan, who might find it an
inconvenience for the Japanese hoi polloi to communicate freely in English. Proficiency in another language and especially English means access to a far greater
range and amount of additional knowledge and ways of thinking, perhaps too
much from the point of view of those who want to control the masses by keeping
them as ignorant as possible. This brings to mind the famous dictum of Kong Zi
(Confucius) in his *Analects*: "The people should do as they are told. There is no
need for them to understand *why*" (Yorashimu beshi. Shirashimu bekarazu.).
There have been movements, however, coming from the private sector that may
be a catalyst for more serious efforts to master English. Two fast-growing companies, Fast Retailing Corporation, makers of the Uniqlo brand of clothes, and
Rakuten Inc., an online shopping and Internet services company, have both
announced that English is to be their official language, even in their Japanese
offices.[71] When asked his reasons for making this decision, Mikitani Hiroshi, the
chairman and CEO of Rakuten, told the Japanese daily *Asahi Shinbun* that the
many international gatherings of the company are, as a matter of unavoidable
fact, conducted in English, as it the most commonly used language of different
nationalities; it would thus be necessary for his Japanese employees to "tran-
scend borders" and have the ability to impart their knowledge in English to their
colleagues in the US or China, which he feels is vital for the company's global
growth. Mikitani lamented that this was not the case at the moment with his
Japanese engineers, who were not able to participate in discussions at these gatherings as they could not speak and even in some cases read English.[72] Whether
this drastic (for the non-native English speaking Japanese, that is) policy of Fast
Retailing and Rakuten will succeed is difficult to assess, given the mediocre
level of English of many Japanese graduates and the considerable amount of
opposition there may be from those who are unable to speak English. I previously worked on a project to make it mandatory for all employees working at the
Sony Corporation's global headquarters to take the TOEIC exams which test
English proficiency. Although the president and COO of the company agreed to
the proposal and was ready to sign off on it, lower level executives balked at the

idea, and the proposal was quashed. One executive told me off in a rather threatening tone, "I am definitely NOT going to take this exam even if you find a way to force me to do it!" Mikitani at Rakuten, however, is adamant that this policy of making English the official language for his company is to succeed. He warns his Japanese employees, "No English, no job!"[73]

The global leadership challenges for Japan

Genghis Khan and his descendants, and more recently Gus Dur of Indonesia have shown that leadership from the top of society is essential in driving through the process of globalization and the practice of tolerance, particularly with regard to respecting diversity. While we have mentioned earlier the relatively dismal state of diversity in the Japanese workplace, in all fairness to the Japanese government, it *has* started to act on developing programs to promote the globalization of Japanese society. For example, to further ease the entry of foreign workers into Japan, the Japanese government has begun formulating guidelines to allow the preferential entry of skilled professional workers such as researchers, doctors, lawyers, and entrepreneurs based on a point system similar to those introduced in Canada and the UK.[74] But progress in Japan towards this end seems to come only in fits and starts. A case in point is the program to allow Indonesians work as nurses in Japan, where the number of Japanese nurses has been dwindling over the years. Despite its initiation and much publicity attached to it, the government is making it almost impossible, except for a few who have a natural talent in learning languages even relatively late in life, to pass the qualification exams, which must be taken in Japanese regardless of the applicant's knowledge and capabilities in nursing.[75] The terminology and written kanji characters used in the exams are even difficult for native Japanese speakers.[76] In such circumstances, it does not seem clear whether the Japanese government is truly enthusiastic about the prospects of having Indonesian nurses work in Japan or is just paying lip-service to the concept of globalization. If the government were truly serious about welcoming Indonesians, it would make sense for them to explore ways to make the qualification process consider language difficulties while maintaining the required standards for passing.

In considering the ambiguous posture of the powers-that-be in Japan, I argue that the problem facing the country is the *quality* of its leaders, with a *lack* of leadership in driving the process of the globalization of Japanese society. Politicians who hold or have held high positions in the government, such as prime ministers and governors, have previously made without compunction and with conviction statements that go contrary to the spirit of globalization, tolerance, and diversity. Former Prime Minister Nakasone Yasuhiro, one of the more memorable Japanese prime ministers of recent times, on one occasion insinuated to his fellow parliamentarians that Japan is an "intelligent society" with average scores much higher than those of countries such as the US where there are "many blacks, Puerto Ricans, and Mexicans."[77] Aside from blaming blacks and other minorities for pulling down the educational performance of US students and taking a swipe at the diversity of the US population, which he apparently sees as a national weakness, Nakasone referred to the Japanese as a people of single ethnicity, a "mono-racial society," apparently forgetting about or ignoring the indigenous Ainu, the not insignificant number of Koreans, Taiwanese, and Chinese who became naturalized Japanese citizens, or the people of Okinawa who before being conquered by Japan had their own independent kingdom that developed separately from mainland Japan. Nakasone also seemed to have had a memory lapse with regards to the ethnic diversity of his own country in its early history. In the *Nihon Shoki*, a chronicle of the history of Japan written around 720 by officials of the Japanese imperial court, there is an account of a large number of people including priests and laymen from the Korean kingdom of Pakeche coming to Japan in 663 as immigrants and actually being helped by the imperial court to settle in the country.[78] Some of the Koreans, such as the daughter of the Pakeche king Muroyong, married into the Imperial Family, as Emperor Akihito has reminded Japanese citizens.[79] The *Nihon Shoki* also mentions a large number of Chinese families who came to Japan and were immediately included in the local population registers, suggesting that they were also welcomed to the country.[80] As the British scholar W.G. Aston, who translated the *Nihon Shoki* into English, observed and concluded, the various accounts in that ancient text are an indication that the people of Japan, far from being mono-racial, are actually a mixed "race."[81] And in fact, Aston's conclusion has been substantiated by recent DNA testing, which has shown that many present-day Japanese share the same haplotype of genes with the Koreans and Chinese (including, as mentioned in the preface, this author).

Along with Nakasone, another former prime minister, Aso Taro, forgot about the diverse origins of the Japanese and the existence of other ethnicities in the country when in a speech he described Japan as having "one nation, one culture, and one race. There is no other nation (that has such characteristics)," a statement reminiscent of the Nazi slogan, "ein Volk, ein Reich, ein Führer," and which attracted the admiring attention of the Norwegian anti-immigration, anti-multiculturalism, mass murderer Anders Behring Breivik. In his 1,500 page manifesto posted online, Breivik expressed a desire to meet with Aso and commended Japan as a "model country" for not allowing many immigrants into the country.[82] Aso also put his foot into his mouth concerning certain minorities in Japan. According to Kamei Hisaoki, a member of the Japanese parliament, in response to the possibility that Nonaka Hiromu (a well-respected politician within the Liberal Democratic Party and a descendant of an outcaste group in Japan) might become the next head of the party and prime minister, Aso was heard to remark, "Are we really going to let those people take over the leadership of Japan?"[83]

Nakasone and Aso were not the only prominent politicians to hold views that smacked of racism and xenophobia. A former Minister of the Ministry of Finance, Watanabe Michio of the Liberal Democratic Party, remarked in 1988 that while the Japanese "would escape into the night or commit suicide" rather than fall into debt, blacks would use credit cards to run up debts and then go into bankruptcy to avoid paying them.[84] A former trade minister in the Japanese government, Hiranuma Takeo, criticized a Diet member Renho by attacking not her stance or policies but by pointing out instead that she was not originally born a Japanese citizen but was later naturalized.[85] Tokyo Governor and former minister of state Ishihara Shintaro back in 2000 made the claim that atrocious crimes have repeatedly been made by the "sangokujin" (a term for former Korean, Chinese, and Taiwanese colonials that has a derogatory connotation) and foreigners who have illegally entered Japan, and warned his fellow countrymen to expect them to riot in the event of a major disaster.[86] In making such a statement, Ishihara identified foreigners, including those who have lived in Japan for long periods such as ethnic Koreans and Chinese, as a potential source of danger, while conveniently ignoring the fact that the vast majority of crimes in Japan are committed daily by Japanese.

The contrast between such views with the legacy of inclusiveness practiced by Gus Dur in Indonesia could not be greater. If these statements had been made by people on the lunatic fringe, while not acceptable, they could at least be ignored. Unfortunately, however, they were for the most part made by supposedly the cream of the crop, or, if you will, the leaders of Japanese society, including former prime ministers and ministers of state, who were educated at the top universities of Japan. If we concur with Hofstede and Schein that culture comes from the top of an organization, it is perhaps not a mystery with leaders such as those mentioned above as to why the drive for globalization in Japan is in fits and starts.

It is to be hoped that future generations of Japanese will become more sensitive to cultural and ethnic diversity and will also realize that being praised as a "model country" by a racist mass murderer such as Breivik is not something to be proud of. To this end, it is further to be hoped that Japan's insular education system will come to grips with the challenges of globalization and transform itself into a system that is able to turn out global citizens who are relevant and can tolerate working with anyone and anywhere. This means not only being able to speak and communicate in a foreign language fluently but also having cross-cultural awareness and tolerance. As Alon and Higgins pointed out in their study on global leadership, the challenges and changes facing societies as a result of globalization make it essential for global leaders to be culturally attuned and emotionally sensitive.[87] Future global leaders will need to understand, appreciate, and at times adapt to different ways of thinking and be able to respond and interact in a culturally sensitive manner. Perhaps what Japan and other societies struggling to globalize their workforces need is someone with the perspicacity and foresight of Kublai Khan's mother Sorghagtani, to teach the Japanese and others a thing or two about tolerance.

The future of cultural diversity

Creating an empire that has the tolerance to accept cultural diversity means having a leadership that is tolerant of such diversity and has the ability to implement policies that support this. As Hofstede put it, "The basic values of a multinational business organization are determined by the nationality and personality of its founders and later significant leaders."[88] Leaders, however, are created, not born. Schein argued that it is cultures, or cultural norms, that will determine the parameters of leadership and ultimately who will or will not be a leader of a nation or organization.[89] Hofstede on his part stated that it is the environment which a leader has grown up in and the basic values that were acquired during the first 10 years of life that shape the views of a leader.[90] That is to say, from the observations of Schein and Hofstede, leaders create cultures and cultures create leaders, ad infinitum. Assuming this is true, in order to have globally minded and culturally tolerant leaders, a culture that accepts cultural diversity may have to be created to begin with. In this regard, I argue that as education is at the core of all societies as an instrument for molding a national culture, our education systems and programs will need to be tailored to meet the challenges of working in a culturally diverse world and at the same time instruct people in understanding the importance and benefits of tolerating different views and opinions through dialogue.

Aside from designing such an education system, concrete measures to enforce tolerance may also be needed, such as enacting laws that eliminate all forms of discrimination and promote equal opportunity for the advancement of all individuals within a society regardless of origin and gender. A case in point is the law enacted in Norway in 2006 that made it mandatory for all major companies to have females comprise more than 40 percent of its board members. The law stipulated that unless companies comply with this law, they would be delisted from the stock exchange market. Although Norwegian companies protested vigorously against the enactment of the law, claiming that such a quota system would deprive Norwegian companies their discretionary powers in personnel management and their international competitiveness, the Norwegian government nevertheless stuck to its guns, stating that if it were left solely to the companies to achieve this numerical target (of 40 percent), even if a hundred years passed, this goal would not be reached.[91] Five years have passed since the implementation of this law, and according to a survey conducted by the Confederation of Norwegian Business and Industry (NHO), most companies have responded positively to the impact of the law, with comments that cite an increase in women directors leading to an improvement in risk management and in labor relations and human resources management.[92] It may sound like a contradiction, but this is one example that suggests from a legal standpoint the need of having zero-tolerance of intolerance in order to enforce tolerance.

Admittedly, practicing tolerance and accepting cultural diversity is not the only way to run an empire. An empire builder may choose a more intolerant and at times destructive manner of ruling an empire by completely eradicating the influence of other cultures and their peoples, which in an egregious way would also neutralize or eliminate the xenophobic impact of two or more cultures coming together. This is what the European colonizers successfully did in Australia by exterminating the Tasmanians, what the European colonialists and

Americans did to several Native American tribes, and what the Germans came perilously close to doing with the Jews and other peoples not to their liking. This is what the Norwegian Anders Behring Breivik attempted to embark upon when he killed 76 people in racially motivated bomb and gun attacks in Norway. In the arena of business empires, MEI tried to eliminate American managerial influence in Quasar, which led to a costly discrimination lawsuit for MEI. Likewise, Daimler-Benz attempted to eliminate Chrysler's American management and influence from DaimlerChrysler. This gave rise to feelings of hostility from the Americans which was a factor that drove the breakdown of the joint venture.

It seems from just looking at the above examples that attempting to completely eliminate the influence of other cultures except for one's own may not be a peaceful or viable way of running an empire, be it that of a nation or a business. Furthermore, in this day and age of possible nuclear annihilation, attempting to eradicate another culture through violent means is probably not recommendable. The scientist Jarred Diamond suggested that another more peaceful way to essentially neutralize the impact of the xenophobia of humans towards other cultures is to reduce human cultural diversity or create cultural homogeneity.[93] In certain ways this is increasingly becoming a reality with TV, the Internet, a growing global urban middle class, and the widespread exchange of peoples from all over. Whether Diamond's suggestion would lead to further sparks in human creativity, however, is a question. After all, many of the inventions, innovations, and ideas produced throughout human history, as in the case of J.S. Bach and his music mentioned above, have been a result of the interactions of peoples and ideas from different cultures. Cultural homogeneity or the loss of cultural diversity, then, may make the world a more boring place to live in. In a sequence from the Monty Python movie *And Now for Something Completely Different*, an accountant goes to a vocational guidance counselor to find an opportunity that would help him achieve his dream of becoming a lion tamer. When asked by the bewildered counselor why on earth he wants to switch from being an accountant to become a lion tamer, the accountant replies with his eyes fanatically gleaming that he wants to live, to have excitement, to experience thrills and danger, unlike in accounting, which he has been doing all his life, and which he finds "boring, boring, boring, and dull, dull, dull." To which the counselor replies in a matter-of-fact manner that accounting should be the right job for him, since personality tests show him to be "an appallingly dull and boring person." Since the accountant would have a better chance of staying alive by remaining in the "boring" world of accounting (with no offense to accountants) than by making a personal cultural change to become a lion-tamer, so it is that the rise of cultural homogeneity and possible boredom may not be a bad price to pay to ensure the survival of the human race.

This book has focused on examining M&A and empires and the similarities between successful empires of world history and of business. In this final chapter, I have talked about the importance of certain principles: accepting diversity, leadership in promoting diversity, and education in molding culturally sensitive leaders. In short, this book has gone way beyond a discussion on M&A

to become a book on the future shape of societies. However, in order not to disappoint those ambitious business empire builders who may have wanted insight on succeeding in M&A after reading this book, I will suggest the following seven principles to keep in mind (aside from doing the usual due diligence, financial and strategic assessments), drawn from the aforementioned examples in history and business:

- Respect the employees you are acquiring and show recognition of their achievements.
- Treat the employees you are acquiring as equals with your own employees.
- Keep the employees you are acquiring on the basis of the "right person for the right job."
- Actively adopt and implement within your company those aspects and methods of the acquired company, including its culture, which may be considered useful and superior to your own.
- Do not force your own culture upon the acquired employees—work towards building up support and understanding of your culture.
- Include the employees being acquired in every stage of the integration process on the basis of using the right people for the right positions.
- Be able to show positive results that you can point to as a consequence of the M&A.

Notes

Preface

1 Test conducted by the National Genographic Project, a DNA-mapping research project undertaken jointly by National Geographic and IBM.
2 Ogi, Masamichi, *Panasonic ga Sanyo o baishu suru honto no riyu* [The Real Reason Why Panasonic Acquired Sanyo], Ark Shuppan, 2009, p. 348.
3 Ibid., p. 336.
4 Chua, Amy, *Day of Empire*, Doubleday, 2007, p. xxi.

1 Introduction

1 Legge, James, *The Chinese Classics* vol. ii: *The Works of Mencius, Trubner and Co.*, 1861, p. 50, online, available http://books.google.am/books?id=SUxkAAAAMAAJ& printsec=frontcover&hl=hy&source=gbs_ge_ summary_r&cad=0#v=onepage&q&f=false (accessed March 21, 2010).
2 Machiavelli, Nicolo, *The Prince* (1515), translated by Marriott, W.K., 1908, online, available www.constitution.org/mac/prince03.htm (accessed June 11, 2010).
3 Tucker, Irwin St. John, *A History of Imperialism*, Rand School of Social Science, 1920, p. 5.
4 Benson, A.C., *Land of Hope and Glory*, 1902, online, available www.fordham.edu/halsall/mod/rulebritannia.asp#Land of Hope and Glory (accessed February 14, 2012).
5 Ferguson, Niall, *Empire*, Penguin Books, 2004, pp. xiii–xiv.
6 Ibid., p. xvi.
7 Smil, Vaclav, *Why America is Not a New Rome*, The MIT Press, 2010, pp. 17, 24, 42.
8 Ibid., p. 45.
9 Howe, Stephen, *Empire: A Very Short Introduction*, Oxford University Press, 2002, p. 30.
10 Doyle, Michael, *Empires*, Cornell University Press, 1986, p. 51.
11 Ibid., p. 23.
12 McCarthy, Thomas, *Race, Empire, and the Idea of Human Development*, Cambridge University Press, 2009, p. 3.
13 Hardt, Michael, Negri, Antonio, *Empire*, Harvard University Press, 2000, p. xv.
14 Ibid., p. 51; McCarthy, op. cit., p. 3.
15 Howe, op. cit., p. 29.
16 Micklethwait, John, Wooldridge, Adrian, *The Company*, The Modern Library, 2005, p. 27.
17 Mankiewicz, Herman J., Welles, Orson, *Citizen Kane*, screenplay, online, available www.dailyscript.com/scripts/citizenkane.html (accessed June 5, 2010).
18 Wharton School of the University of Pennsylvania, Why Do So Many Mergers Fail? *Knowledge@Wharton*, March 30, 2005, online, available http://knowledge.wharton.upenn.edu/article.cfm?articleid=1137 (accessed June 5, 2010).

19 Porter, Michael E., From Competitive Advantage to Corporate Strategy, *Harvard Business Review*, vol. lxv, no. 3, 1987, pp. 43–59.

20 T. Mallikarjunappa, Panduranaga Nayak, Why do Mergers and Acquisitions Quite Often Fail? *AIMS International*, vol. i, no. 1, January 2007, pp. 53–69, online, available www.aims-international.org/aimsijm/abstracts/1–1–4-a.pdf (accessed June 5, 2010).

21 Wharton School, op. cit.

22 Paton, Nic, Nine out of 10 M&As Fail to Deliver, Management Issues Ltd., March 26, 2007, online, available www.management-issues.com/2007/3/26/research/nine-out-of-10-mas-fail-to-deliver.asp (accessed June 5, 2010).

23 Terjesen, Siri, Mergers & Acquisitions: Patterns, Motives, and Strategic Fit, *QFINANCE*, Thomson Financial, Bain & Company, online, available www.qfinance.com/contentFiles/QF02/glus0fcl/12/0/mergers-and-acquisitions-patterns-motives-and-strategic-fit.pdf (accessed April 3, 2010).

24 Ibid.

25 Ibid.

26 Reuters, FACTBOX: China's Outbound M&A in 2009 and the Past Decade, January 20, 2010, online, available www.reuters.com/article/2010/01/20/us-davos-china-deals-factbox-idUSTRE60J46K20100120 (accessed January 31, 2010).

27 Armed with a Strong Yen, *The Economist*, December 17, 2011.

28 Pursche, Bill, Do Most Mergers Really Fail?, *First Call Advisors*, 2001, online, available www.firstcalladvisors.com/files/DoMostMergersReallyFail_v6.pdf (accessed May 8, 2010).

29 Mercer, *The Impact of Culture on M&A*, Mercer Ltd., 2009, p. 2, online, available www.mmc.com/views/Mercer_impactCultureM&ATransactions.pdf (accessed May 9, 2010).

30 Ibid., p. 2.

31 Deloitte, *Japanese Outbound M&A: Targeting Global Growth in Volatile Times*, Deloitte Touche Tohmatsu, May 2009, online, available www.tohmatsu.com/assets/Dcom-Japan/Local%20Assets/Documents/knowledge/fas-pdf/jp_k_fas_tran001_en_231009.pdf (accessed June 12, 2010).

32 Hofstede, Geert, Hofstede, Gert Jan, *Cultures and Organizations*, McGraw Hill, 2005, p. 4.

33 Schein, Edgar H., *Organizational Culture and Leadership*, John Wiley & Sons, 2004, p. 17.

34 Chua, Amy, *Day of Empire*, Doubleday, 2007, p. xxi.

35 Hofstede, Hofstede, op. cit., p. 175.

2 An overview of empires

1 Fukuyama, Francis, *The End of History and the Last Man*, Free Press, 2006, p. xvi; Hegel, Georg W.F., *The Philosophy of Right*, 1820, translated by T.M. Knox, Encyclopaedia Britannica, 1982, p. 66.

2 Marx, Karl, *Manifesto of the Communist Party*, 1848, Marxist Internet Archive, 2010, p. 14, online, available www.marxists.org/archive/marx/works/download/pdf/Manifesto.pdf (accessed May 3, 2010).

3 Caprio, Mark E., *Japanese Assimilation Policies in Korea, 1910–1945*, University of Washington Press, 2009, p. 29.

4 Kiger, Patrick J., Chew. Spit. Repeat. The Movie Industry Consumes Carpetbagging Investors Like Prime-Cut Steak. What's the Appeal of Being Eaten Alive?, *Los Angeles Times*, February 29, 2004.

5 Howorth, Sir Henry Hoyle, *History of the Mongols*, Longmans, Green, and Co., 1876, p. 110.

6 Gill, Anton, *Ruling Passions: Sex, Race and Empire*, BBC Books, 1995, p. 37.

7 Diamond, Jarred, *The Third Chimpanzee*, Harper Perennial, 1993, p. 220.

8 Marx, op. cit., p. 17.

9 Ibid., p. 16.

10 Hobson, John A., *Imperialism*, George Allen & Unwin, 1954, reprinted in Williams, Phil, Goldstein, Donald, Shafritz, Jay, *Classic Readings of International Relations*, second edition, Harcourt Brace, 1999, p. 60.

11 Ibid., p. 61.

12 Lenin, V.I., *Imperialism, The Highest Stage of Capitalism*, Lenin Internet Archive, 2005, p. 265, online, available www.marxists.org/archive/lenin/works/1916/imp-hsc/ch07.htm (accessed May 3, 2010).

13 Howe, Stephen, *Empire: A Very Short Introduction*, Oxford University Press, 2002, p. 24.

14 Seeley, Sir John Robert, *The Expansion of England*, Findlay, Roberts Brothers, 1883, p. 8, online, available http://books.google.com/books?id=Zsm3TLe1cAUC&pg=PA37&hl=ja&source=gbs_toc_r&cad=4#v=onepage&q&f=false (accessed May 1, 2010).

15 Ibid., p. 9.

16 Beasley, W.G., *Japanese Imperialism: 1868–1945*, Clarendon Press, 1991, pp. 12–13.

17 Morgenthau, Hans J., *Politics Among Nations*, McGraw-Hill Inc., 1985, pp. 31–85.

18 Rusling, James, Interview with President William McKinley, *The Christian Advocate*, 1903, online, available http://historymatters.gmu.edu/d/5575/ (accessed May 1, 2010).

19 Macaulay, Thomas, *Minute on Education*, Bureau of Education, February 2, 1835, online, available www.columbia.edu/itc/mealac/pritchett/00generallinks/macaulay/txt_minute_education_1835.html (accessed February 11, 2010).

20 Kant, Immanuel, *Idea of a Universal History on a Cosmopolitical Plan*, translated by Thomas de Qunicey, 1824, online, available http://en.wikisource.org/wiki/Idea_of_a_Universal_History_on_a_Cosmopolitical_Plan (accessed November 6, 2010).

21 Macaulay, op. cit.

22 Roosevelt, Theodore, The Strenuous Life, April 10, 1899, speech to the Hamilton Club, Chicago, online, available www.theodore-roosevelt.com/trspeeches.html (accessed February 11, 2010).

23 Jacques, Martin, *When China Rules the World*, Penguin Press, 2009, p. 238.

24 Hirata, Atsutane, Kodo Taii, in Tsunoda, Ryusaku, De Bary, W.M., Keene, Donald (eds), *Sources of Japanese Tradition*, vol. ii, Columbia University Press, 1958, p. 39.

25 Ibid., pp. 42–43.

26 Jacques, op. cit., p. 246.

27 Chua, Amy, *Day of Empire*, Doubleday, 2007, p. 67.

28 Jacques, op. cit., p. 246.

29 Rattansi, Ali, *Racism: A Very Short Introduction*, Oxford University Press, 2007, p. 18.

30 Montesquieu, Jean Jacques, *The Spirit of Laws*, translated by Thomas Nugent, G. Bell & Sons, Ltd., 1914, book xv-5, online, available www.constitution.org/cm/sol.htm (accessed June 21, 2010).

31 Hume, David, *Of National Characters*, 1742, online, available www.econlib.org/library/LFBooks/Hume/hmMPL21.html#Part I, Essay XXI, OF NATIONAL CHARACTERS (accessed June 21, 2010).

32 Henning, Joseph M., *Outposts of Civilization*, New York University Press, 2000, p. 12.

33 Lauren, Paul Gordon, *Power and Prejudice*, Westview Press, 1996, p. 36.

34 Henning, op. cit., p. 12.

35 Lauren, op. cit., p. 37.

36 Bradley, James, *The Imperial Cruise*, Little, Brown and Company, 2009, p. 132.

37 Howe, op. cit., p. 87.

38 Roosevelt, Theodore, *The Winning of the West*, vol. iii, chapter 2, online, available www.gutenberg.org/files/11943/11943–8.txt (accessed May 3, 2010).

39 Ibid.

40 Roosevelt, Theodore, speech, January 1886, online, available www.bluecorncomics.com/roosvelt.htm (accessed November 25, 2011).

41 Duus, Peter, *The Abacus and the Sword*, University of California Press, 1995, p. 414.

42 Ibid.

43 Ibid., pp. 414–415.

44 Jacques, op. cit., p. 250.

45 Rattansi, op. cit.

46 Bradley, op. cit., pp. 185–186.

47 Ibid., p. 188.

48 LaFeber, Walter, *The Clash*, W.W. Norton & Company, 1997, p. 44.

49 Bradley, op. cit., p. 188.

50 Ibid., pp. 185–186.

51 Ibid., pp. 227, 231.

52 Tsunoda, De Bary, Keene, op. cit., p. 207.

53 James, Lawrence, *The Rise & Fall of the British Empire*, Abacus, 2001, p. 460.

54 Ibid.

55 Ienaga, Saburo, *The Pacific War 1931–1945*, Pantheon Asia Library, 1978, p. 6.

56 Okubo, Maki, Ex-soldier Regrets Atrocities, *Asahi Shinbun*, August 18, 2010.

57 Kamenka, Eugene (ed.), *The Portable Karl Marx*, Viking Penguin Inc, 1983, p. 353.

58 Ibid.

59 Ibid.

60 Hibbert, Christopher, *The Great Mutiny: India 1857*, Penguin Books, 1980, p. 318.

61 Proclamation by the Queen in Council to the Princes, Chiefs, and Peoples of India, 1858, online, available http://en.wikisource.org/wiki/Queen_Victoria's_Proclamation (accessed February 11, 2010).

62 Lauren, op. cit., 1996, p. 62.

63 Hari, Johann, Reconciling Churchill's Brutal Side, *International Herald Tribune*, August 14–15, 2010.

64 Ibid.

65 British and Indian, Yet Neither, *International Herald Tribune*, August 14–15, 2010.

66 Hibbert, op. cit., p. 391.

67 Horne, Gerald, *Race War!* New York University Press, 2004, p. 18.

68 Ibid., p. 17.

69 Ibid.

70 Ibid., p. 21.

71 Ibid., pp. 28–29.

72 Kipling, Rudyard, *Sea to Sea: Letters of Travel*, Doubleday Page & Company, 1913, pp. 283–285.

73 Horne, op. cit., p. 63.

74 Ibid., p. 72.

75 Ibid., p. 141.

76 Ibid., p. 142.

77 Ibid., p. 143.

78 Ibid., p. 298.

79 Said, Edward W., *Culture and Imperialism*, Vintage Books, 1994, p. 182.

80 Ibid., p. 183.

81 Ibid., pp. 182–183.

82 Shepard, Todd, *The Invention of Decolonization*, Cornell University Press, 2006, p. 34.

83 Diamond, op. cit., p. 300.
84 Ibid., pp. 180, 267.
85 Ibid., pp. 288, 300.
86 Duus, op. cit., p. 204.
87 Ibid., pp. 198, 220.
88 Ienaga, op. cit., pp. 7–8.
89 Ibid., p. 8.
90 Cummings, Bruce, *Korea's Place in the Sun*, Norton, 2005, p. 153.
91 Caprio, Mark E., *Japanese Assimilation Policies in Colonial Korea, 1910–1945*, University of Washington Press, 2009, p. 110.
92 Ibid., p. 151.
93 Ibid., pp. 103–104.
94 Duus, op. cit., p. 398.
95 Caprio, op. cit., p. 109.
96 Ibid., p. 207.
97 Atkins, E. Taylor, *Primitive Selves*, University of California Press, 2010, pp. 33–34.
98 Caprio, op. cit., p. 197.
99 Bix, Herbert P., *Hirohito and the Making of Modern Japan*, Harper Collins, 2000, p. 140; Ienaga, op. cit., p. 8.
100 Forced to be Loyal Subjects of Japan, *Asahi Shinbun*, January 4, 2008.
101 Ibid.
102 Korean girls 'Enslaved' in Wartime Japan, *Asahi Shinbun*, July 31–August 1, 2010.
103 Itoh, Mayumi, *The Globalization of Japan*, St. Martin's Press, 2000, p. 86.
104 Cummings, op. cit., p. 141.
105 Ibid., p. 148.
106 Japan-South Korea Ties/South Korea Aiming High/Seeks to be World Leader as Economic Strength Increases, *Yomiuri Shinbun*, August 29, 2010, online, available www.yomiuri.co.jp/dy/world/T100828001946.htm (accessed May 3, 2010).
107 Cummings, op. cit., p. 148.
108 Ibid., pp. 167, 169.
109 Ibid., p. 160.
110 Atkins, op. cit., p. 30.
111 Caprio, op. cit., p. 209.
112 Cose, Ellis, Yellow-Peril Journalism, *Time Magazine*, November 27, 1989.
113 Halberstam, David, *The Reckoning*, Avon, 1986, p. 544.
114 Ferguson, Niall, *The Ascent of Money*, Penguin Books, 2009, p. 31.
115 Micklethwait, John, Wooldridge, Adrian, *The Company*, The Modern Library, 2005, p. 4.
116 Moore, Karl, Lewis, David, *Foundations of Corporate Empire*, Financial Times/ Prentice Hall, 2000, pp. 97–98.
117 Micklethwait, Wooldridge, op. cit., p. 4.
118 Ibid., p. 98.
119 Ibid., p. 4.
120 Ibid., p. 12.
121 Hutcheson, James Olan, The End of a 1,400-Year-Old Business, *BusinessWeek*, April 16, 2007.
122 Moore, Lewis, op. cit., p. 169.
123 Micklethwait, Wooldridge, op. cit., pp. 7–8.
124 Ibid., p. 8.
125 Baigent, Michael, Leight, Richard, Lincoln, Henry, *Holy Blood, Holy Grail*, Dell Publishing Co., 1983, pp. 47–48.
126 Marrs, Jim, *Rule of Secrecy*, Perennial, 2001, p. 286.
127 Micklethwait, Wooldridge, op. cit., p. 9.
128 Ibid.

129 Terjesen, Siri, Patterns, Mergers & Acquisitions: Motives, and Strategic Fit, *QFI-NANCE*, Thomson Financial, Bain & Company, online, available www.qfinance.com/contentFiles/QF02/glus0fcl/12/0/mergers-and-acquisitions-patterns-motives-and-strategic-fit.pdf (accessed April 1, 2010).
130 Chandler, Alfred D., *Strategy and Structure*, Doubleday & Company, 1962, p. 22.
131 Micklethwait, Wooldridge, op. cit., pp. 20–21.
132 Besanko, David, Dranove, David, Shanley, Mark, Schaefer, Scott, *Economics of Strategy*, John Wiley & Sons, 2000, p. 52.
133 Chandler, op. cit., pp. 40–41.
134 Ibid., pp. 35, 40–41.
135 Duncan, William, Ten Important Lessons from the History of Mergers & Acquisitions, Ezinearticles.com, online, available http://ezinearticles.com/?Ten-Important-Lessons-From-the-History-of-Mergers-and-Acquisitions&id=1486559 (accessed February 11, 2010).
136 Harvard Business School, *Our History*, online, available www.hbs.edu/about/history.html (accessed May 1, 2010).
137 Chandler, op. cit., p. 28.
138 Besanko *et al.*, op. cit., p. 54.
139 Ibid., p. 54.
140 Armed with a Strong Yen, *The Economist*, December 17, 2011.

3 A seafaring empire

1 Gaastra, F.S., *VOC Organization, Toward a New Age of Partnership (TANAP)*, National Archives of the Netherlands, online, available www.tanap.net/content/voc/organization/organization_intro.htm#intro (accessed January 10, 2010).
2 Ibid.
3 Ibid.; Landes, David, *The Wealth and Poverty of Nations*, Little, Brown and Company, 1998, p. 148.
4 Landes, op. cit., p. 146; Ferguson, Niall, *The Ascent of Money*, Penguin Books, 2009, p. 134.
5 Findlay, Robert, O'Rourke, Kevin, *Power and Plenty*, Princeton University Press, 2007, p. 183.
6 Neal, Larry, *Venture Shares of the Dutch East India Company*, Yale University, 2003, p. 9.
7 A Taste of Adventure, *The Economist*, December 17, 1998, online, available www.economist.com/node/179810 (accessed January 10, 2010); Bernstein, William J., *A Splendid Exchange*, Grove Press, 2008, p. 235.
8 Ferguson, op. cit., p. 137.
9 Ibid., p. 137.
10 Bernstein, William J., *A Splendid Exchange*, Grove Press, 2008, p. 224.
11 Ibid., p. 222.
12 Ibid., p. 223.
13 Landes, op. cit., p. 137.
14 Chua, Amy, *Day of Empire*, Doubleday, 2007, p. 145.
15 Ibid., p. 145.
16 Ibid., p. 147.
17 Oliver J. Thatcher (ed.), *The Library of Original Sources* (Milwaukee: University Research Extension Co., 1907), vol. v: *9th to 16th Centuries*, pp. 189–197, online, available www.age-of-the-sage.org/history/dutch_independence_1581.html (accessed January 10, 2010).
18 Findlay, O'Rourke, op. cit., p. 177.
19 Bernstein, op. cit., p. 218.
20 Nakano, Tsuneo, *Kabushikikaisha to kigyotochi: sono rekishiteki kosatsu* [The

Corporation and Corporate Governance: A Historical Overview], University of Kobe School of Management, 2002, p. 7, online, available www.b.kobe-u.ac.jp/resource/br/pdf/no. 48.pdf (accessed January 10, 2010); Dillen, J.G., Poitras, Geoffrey, Majithia, Asha, *Isaac Le Maire and the Early Trading in Dutch East India Company Shares, Pioneers of Financial Economics*: vol. i, p. 47, online, available www.sfu.ca/~poitras/ch2_lemaire.pdf (accessed February 11, 2010).

21 Dillen, Poitras, Majithia, op. cit., p. 47.
22 Nakano, op. cit., p. 7.
23 Ibid., pp. 7–8.
24 Ibid.
25 Ibid.
26 Dillen, Poitras, Majithia, op. cit., p. 47.
27 Nakano, op. cit., p. 7.
28 Ibid., p. 47.
29 De Jongh, Matthijs, *Shareholder Activists Avant La Lettre: The Complaining Share-holders in the Dutch East India Company*, Research Department of the Supreme Court of the Netherlands, September 29, 2008, online, available http://papers.ssrn.com/sol3/papers.cfm?abstract_id=1275305 (accessed March 21, 2010).
30 Nakano, op. cit., p. 10.
31 Ibid.
32 Ibid., pp. 10–11.
33 Ibid., p. 11.
34 Ibid., p. 10.
35 Ibid., p. 9.
36 Ibid., p. 9; De Jongh, op. cit.
37 Nakano, op. cit., p. 10.
38 Ibid., p. 8.
39 Reynders, Peter, *A Translation of the Charter of the Dutch East India Company*, Australasian Hydrographic Society, online, available www.australiaonthemap.org.au/voc-charter/ (accessed March 21, 2010).
40 Bernstein, op. cit., p. 220.
41 Boxer, C.R., *The Dutch Seafaring Empire*, Penguin, 1978, p. 26.
42 Bernstein, op. cit., p. 220.
43 Reynders, op. cit.
44 Ferguson, op. cit., p. 130; Bernstein, op. cit., p. 224.
45 Bernstein, op. cit., p. 224.
46 Ferguson, op. cit., p. 130.
47 Dillen, Poitras, Majithia, op. cit., p. 51.
48 Ibid.
49 Reynders, op. cit.
50 Dillen, Poitras, Majithia, op. cit., p. 51.
51 Crump, Thomas, *The History of the Dutch East Indies Company*, Gresham College, 2006, online, available www.gresham.ac.uk/print/1977 (accessed April 29, 2010).
52 Chua, op. cit., p. 155.
53 Ibid.; Neal, op. cit., p. 6.
54 Neal, op. cit., p. 8.
55 Chua, op. cit., p. 154.
56 Ibid., p. 155.
57 Ferguson, op. cit., p. 132.
58 Ibid.
59 Gaastra, op. cit.
60 Ibid.
61 Ibid.
62 Gaastra, op. cit.

63 Brujin, Iris D.R., *The Health Care Organization of the Dutch East India Company at Home*, The Society for the Social History of Medicine, 1994, p. 364.

64 Ibid., p. 364.

65 Ibid.

66 Ibid.

67 Gaastra, op. cit.

68 Ibid.; Cook, Harold J., *Matters of Exchange*, Yale University Press, 2007, p. 65.

69 Reynders, op. cit.

70 Gaastra, op. cit.

71 Ferguson, op. cit., p. 134.

72 Ibid.

73 Ibid., p. 134; Nakano, op. cit., p. 16.

74 Nakano, op. cit., p. 16.

75 Reynders, op. cit.

76 Cotterell, Arthur, *Western Power in Asia*, Wiley, 2010, p. 62.

77 Bernstein, op. cit., pp. 232–233.

78 Boxer, op. cit., p. 273.

79 Ibid., p. 313.

80 Ferguson, op. cit., p. 136.

81 Landes, op. cit., p. 146.

82 Bernstein, op. cit., p. 234.

83 Fernandez-Armesto, Felipe, *Millennium*, Black Swan, 1995, p. 311.

84 MacCulloch, Diarmaid, *Reformation*, Penguin Books, 2004, pp. 370–371.

85 Cotterell, op. cit., p. 56.

86 Chua, op. cit., p. 155.

87 Ibid.

88 Gaastra, op. cit.

89 Dillen, Poitras, Majithia, op. cit., p. 45.

90 Ibid., p. 47.

91 Bernstein, op. cit., p. 235.

92 Ibid.

93 Cotterell, op. cit., p. 59.

94 Bernstein, op. cit., p. 228.

95 A Taste of Adventure, *The Economist*, op. cit.

96 Ibid.

97 Ibid.

98 Cook, op. cit., p. 186.

99 Ibid., p. 184.

100 Ibid., p. 183.

101 Bernstein, op. cit., p. 228.

102 Brown, Stephen R., *Merchant Kings*, Douglas and McIntyre, 2009, p. 2.

103 Boxer, op. cit., p. 261.

104 Cook, op. cit., p. 149.

105 Brown, op. cit., p. 11.

106 Ibid., p. 12.

107 Ferguson, op. cit., p. 132.

108 Cook, op. cit., pp. 183–184.

109 Oostindie, Gert J., Squaring the Circle, *KITLV*, 2003, online, available www.kitlv-journals.nl/index.php/btlv/article/viewFile/3110/3871 (accessed May 3, 2010).

110 Cook, op. cit., p. 189.

111 Ibid., p. 188.

112 Livinginindonesia.info, *Chinese-Indonesians, Massacre of 1740*, online, available http://livinginindonesia.info/item/chinese-indonesians/ (accessed May 3, 2010).

113 Ibid.

114 Fernandez-Armesto, op. cit., p. 299.
115 Livinginindonesia.info, op. cit.
116 Cook, op. cit., p. 182.
117 Cotterell, op. cit., p. 59.
118 Massarella, Derek, *A World Elsewhere*, Yale University Press, 1990, pp. 237–242.
119 Boxer, op. cit., p. 267; Bernstein, op. cit., p. 234.
120 Massarella, op. cit., p. 234.
121 Ibid.
122 Ibid.
123 Landes, op. cit., p. 144.
124 Cook, op. cit., p. 178.
125 Bruijn, Iris D.R., op. cit., p. 371.
126 Cook, op. cit., p. 178.
127 Ibid.
128 Landes, op. cit., p. 145.
129 Chua, op. cit., pp. 159, 162.
130 Cook, op. cit., p. 184.
131 Hofstede, Geert, Hofstede, Gert Jan, *Cultures and Organizations*, McGraw Hill, 2005, p. 199.
132 Lauren, Paul Gordon, *Power and Prejudice*, Westview Press, 1996, p. 214.

4 The Mongols and the practice of tolerance

1 Rossabi, Morris, Women of the Mongol Court, lecture at Denver Art Museum transcribed by Roupp, Heidi, online, available www.woodrow.org/teachers/world-history/teaching/mongol/women.html (accessed December 24, 2011); Turchin, Peter, Adams, Jonathan M., Hall, Thomas D., East–West Orientation of Historical Empires and Modern States, *Journal of World-Systems Research*, vol. xii, December 11, 2006, pp. 219–229.
2 Weatherford, Jack, *Genghis Khan and the Making of the Modern World*, Three Rivers Press, 2004, p. xx.
3 Kahn, Paul (adapted by), *The Secret History of the Mongols*, Cheng & Tsui Company, 1998, p. 3.
4 Ibid., p. 6.
5 Ratchnevsky, Paul, *Genghis Khan: His Life and Legacy*, Blackwell Publishing, 1991, p. 14.
6 Mayell, Hilary, Ghenghis Khan a Prolific Lover, DNA Data Implies, *National Geographic News*, February 14, 2003.
7 Ibid.
8 Ratchnevsky, op. cit., p. 164.
9 Polo, Marco, *The Travels of Marco Polo*, Wordsworth Classics of World Literature, 1997, pp. 95–96.
10 Cheng, Baoweng, Tang, Wenru, He, Li, Dong, Yongli, Lu, Jing, Lei, Yunping, Yu, Haijing, Zhang, Jiali, Xiao, Chunjie, *Genetic Imprint of the Mongol: Signal From Phylogeographic Analysis of Mitochondrial DNA*, The Japan Society of Human Genetics and Springer, 2008, online, available www.springerlink.com/content/m4w480281v26t357/fulltext.pdf (accessed June 6, 2010).
11 Lane, George, *Daily Life in the Mongol Empire*, Hackett, 2006, p. 165.
12 Ratchnevsky, op. cit., pp. 1, 85.
13 Carpini, Friar Giovanni DiPlano, *The Story of the Mongols whom we Call the Tartars*, Branden Publishing Company, 1996 (originally written in 1252), p. 39.
14 Ibid., p. 51.
15 Lane, op. cit., p. 35.

16 Friar William of Rubruck, *The Journey of William of Rubruck to the Eastern Parts of the World*, London, Hakluyt Society, 1900, pp. 74–75.

17 Polo, op. cit., p. 95.

18 Ibid., pp. 135, 169.

19 Carpini, op. cit., p. 51.

20 Ibid., pp. 51, 54.

21 Weatherford, op. cit., pp. 239–240.

22 Lane, op. cit., p. viii.

23 Voltaire, *The Orphan of China*, vol. viii of *The Dramatic Works* Part I (Merope, Olympia, The Orphan of China, Brutus), translated by William F. Fleming, E.R. Dumont, 1901, online, available http://oll.libertyfund.org/?option=com_staticxt&staticfile=show.php%3Ftitle=2187&chapter=201388&layout=html&Itemid =27 (accessed December 24, 2011).

24 Montesquieu, *The Spirit of Laws*, translated by Thomas Nugent, G. Bell & Sons, 1914, book xviii-20, online, available www.constitution.org/cm/sol.htm (accessed December 24, 2011).

25 Ibid., book xvii-6.

26 Ratchnevsky, op. cit., p. 212.

27 Talbott, Strobe, *The Great Experiment*, Simon & Schuster, 2008, p. 63.

28 Ibid., p. 64.

29 Ratchnevsky, op. cit., p. 212.

30 Man, John, *Genghis Khan*, Bantam Books, 2005, p. 312; Lane, op. cit., pp. 164–165.

31 The 2,000-Year-Old Businessman, *Fortune*, June 14, 2010.

32 Chambers, James, *The Devil's Horsemen*, Atheneum, New York, 1979, p. 73.

33 Ibid., p. 76.

34 Ibid., p. 93.

35 Ibid., p. 71.

36 One can learn about this particular Mongol practice at the Mongol Invasion Memorial Museum in Fukuoka, Japan.

37 Bartlett, W.B., *The Mongols*, Amberley, 2010, p. 197; Who Goes to the Gallows, *The Economist*, January 28–February 3, 2002.

38 Morgan, David, *The Mongols*, Basil Blackwell, 1986, p. 57.

39 Ibid., p. 15; Kahn, op. cit., p. 141.

40 Weatherford, op. cit., p. 14.

41 Ratchnevsky, op. cit., p. 12.

42 Carpini, op. cit., p. 37.

43 Weatherford, op. cit., p. 13; Chua, Amy, *Day of Empire*, Doubleday, 2007, p. 91.

44 Kahn, op. cit., p. 82.

45 Morgan, op. cit., p. 28.

46 Kahn, op. cit., p. 96.

47 Ibid., p. 101.

48 Gabriel, Richard A., *Genghis Khan's Greatest General: Subotai the Valiant*, University of Oklahoma Press, 2006, p. 31.

49 Ibid., p. 171.

50 Ibid.

51 Gabriel, op. cit., p. 49.

52 Columbia University, *The Mongols in World History*, pp. 7–8, online, available http://afe.eeasia.columbia.edu/mongols/ (accessed May 3, 2010).

53 Ratchnevsky, op. cit., p. 89.

54 Columbia University, op. cit., pp. 7–8.

55 Ibid., p. 50.

56 Polo, op. cit., p. 5.

57 Chambers, op. cit., p. 10.

58 Man, op. cit., p. 193.

59 Chambers, op. cit., p. 12.
60 Ibid., p. 17.
61 Morgan, D.O., The Great Yasa of Chingiz Khan and Mongol Law in the Ilkhanate, *Bulletin of the School of Oriental and African Studies*, vol. xlix, no. 1, 1986. p. 170.
62 Ratchnevsky, op. cit., p. 160.
63 Ibid., p. 72.
64 Polo, op. cit., p. 92.
65 Bartlett, op. cit., p. 197.
66 Polo, op. cit., pp. 122–123.
67 Ibid.
68 Polo, op. cit., p. 6.
69 Rossabi, op. cit., p. 123.
70 Ibid.
71 Weatherford, op. cit., p. xix.
72 Polo, op. cit., p. 121.
73 Ibid., pp. 232–233.
74 Weatherford, op. cit., p. xxiii.
75 Man, op. cit., p. 183.
76 Chambers, op. cit., p. 63.
77 Man, op. cit., p. 183.
78 Ibid., pp. 200, 203–204.
79 Diamond, Jarred, *The Third Chimpanzee*, Harper Perennial, 1993, p. 283.
80 Ibid., p. 281.
81 Bradley, James, *The Imperial Cruise*, Little Brown and Company, 2009, p. 127; Luzviminda, Francisco, *The First Vietnam: The US–Philippine War of 1899*, 1973, online, available www.historyisaweapon.com/defcon1/franciscofirstvietnam.html (accessed February 11, 2010).
82 Johnson, Chalmers, *The Sorrows of Empire*, Metropolitan Books, 2004, p. 43.
83 LaFeber, Walter, *The Clash*, W.W. Norton & Company, 1997, p. 62.
84 Chua, op. cit., pp. 282–283.
85 Ferguson, Niall, *The War of the World*, Penguin/Allen Lane, 2006, p. lxviii.
86 Ferguson does mention the American experience in the Philippines in another book about the American Empire (*Colossus*, Penguin Books, 2004, pp. 48–52).
87 Cotterell, Arthur, *Western Power in Asia*, Wiley, 2010, pp. 150, 210.
88 Kramer, Paul A., Race-Making and Colonial Violence in the U.S. Empire: The Philippine–American War as Race War, *Diplomatic History*, vol. xxx, no. 2, April 2006, pp. 181–182; Wolff, Leon, *Little Brown Brother*, History Book Club, 1961, p. 190.
89 Kramer, op. cit., p. 185.
90 Zinn, Howard, *A People's History of the United States*, Harper Perennial, 1995, p. 306.
91 Miller, Stuart Creighton, *Benevolent Assimilation*, Yale University Press, 1982, p. 88.
92 Zinn, op. cit., p. 307.
93 Miller, op. cit., p. 89.
94 Ibid., p. 307.
95 Luzviminda, op. cit.
96 Bradley, op. cit., p. 106.
97 Luzviminda, op. cit.
98 Wolff, op. cit., p. 306.
99 Ibid., p. 307.
100 Ibid.
101 Zinn, op. cit., p. 308.
102 Bradley, op. cit., p. 106.
103 Luzviminda, op. cit.

104 Zinn, op. cit., p. 308.
105 Kahn, op. cit., p. 65.
106 Bradley, op. cit., p. 123; Zinn, op. cit., p. 308.
107 Bradley, op. cit., pp. 107–108.
108 Kramer, Paul A., The Water Cure, *The New Yorker*, February 25, 2008, online, available   www.newyorker.com/reporting/2008/02/25/080225fa_fact_kramer (accessed May 3, 2010).
109 Weatherford, op. cit., p. 201.
110 Kramer, Paul A., Race-Making and Colonial Violence in the U.S. Empire, *Diplomatic History*, vol. xxx, no. 2, April 2006, p. 192.
111 Wolff, op. cit., p. 305.
112 Kramer, Race-Making, op. cit., pp. 202–203.
113 Ibid., p. 193.
114 Zinn, op. cit., p. 307.
115 Kramer, Race-Making, op. cit., p. 203.
116 Luzviminda, op. cit.
117 Bradley, op. cit., p. 125.
118 Zinn, op. cit., p. 306.
119 Kramer, Race-Making, p. 207.
120 Roosevelt, Theodore, *Expansion of the White Races*, January 18, 1909, online, available   www.humanitiesweb.org/human.php?s=h&p=c&a=p&ID=23051   (accessed November 28, 2011).
121 Horne, Gerald, *Race War!* New York University Press, 2004, p. 124.
122 Wolff, op. cit., p. 339.
123 Horne, op. cit., p. 298.
124 Miller, op. cit., pp. 264–265.
125 Man, op. cit., p. 201.
126 Bartlett, op. cit., p. 186.
127 Weatherford, Jack, *The Secret History of the Mongol Queens*, Crown Publishers, 2010, p. 120.
128 Ibid., pp. 303–304.
129 Chambers, op. cit., p. 110.
130 Rossabi, op. cit., p. 169.
131 Ibid., pp. 166–167.
132 Ibid., p. 171.
133 Man, op. cit., pp. 200, 230–231.
134 Morgan, *The Mongols*, op. cit., pp. 108–110.
135 Rossabi, op. cit., p. 172.
136 Weatherford, 2010, op. cit., p. 115.
137 Chambers, op. cit., p. 71.
138 Polo, op. cit., pp. 105–106.
139 Lane, op. cit., p. 230.
140 Ibid., p. 232.
141 Man, op. cit., p. 41.
142 Lane, op. cit., p. 170.
143 Ibid., pp. 174–177.
144 Rossabi, op. cit., pp. 119–185.
145 May, Timothy (commentary), *Great Yasa of Chinggis Khan*, online, available www. milestonedocuments.com/documents/view/great-yasa-of-chinggis-khan   (accessed June 7, 2010).
146 May, op. cit.
147 Ratchnevsky, op. cit., p. 148.
148 Ibid., p. 66.
149 Ibid., p. 148.

150 Ibid., p. 150.
151 Kahn, op. cit., pp. 118–119.
152 Ratchnevsky, op. cit., p. 149.
153 Talbott, op. cit., p. 47.
154 Gibbon, Edward, *The Decline and Fall of the Roman Empire*, Encyclopaedia Britannica Inc., 1982 (first published 1776–1788), p. 14.
155 Polk, William R., *Neighbors and Strangers*, University of Chicago Press, 1997, p. 89.
156 Gibbon, op. cit., p. 4.
157 Polk, op. cit., p. 89.
158 Forbes, Steve, Prevas, John, *Power Ambition Glory*, Crown Business, 2009, p. 195.
159 Gibbon, op. cit., pp. 12–13.
160 Ibid., p. 14.
161 Forbes, Prevas, op. cit., p. 195.
162 Gibbon, op. cit., p. 15.
163 Ibid., p. 18.
164 Talbott, op. cit., p. 47.
165 Doyle, Michael, *Empires*, Cornell University Press, 1986, p. 97.
166 Talbott, op. cit., p. 47.
167 Chua, op. cit., pp. 121–124.
168 Ratchnevsky, op. cit., p. 209.
169 Ibid., pp. 208–209.
170 Lane, op. cit., p. 26.
171 Bartlett, op. cit., p. 218.
172 Weatherford, 2010, op. cit., p. 130.

5 Matsushita's movie entertainment empire

1 Kageyama, Yuri, Green at the Heart of Panasonic's Bid for Sanyo, AP News, November 17, 2008.
2 Sanger, David E., Tanii-san Goes Fishing in Hollywood, *New York Times*, November 25, 1990.
3 Matsushita, Konosuke, *Monono mikata, kangaekata* [The Way to Look at Things and Think], PHP Books, 1986, pp. 106–110.
4 Ibid., p. 112.
5 Morikawa, Hidemasa, *A History of Top Management in Japan*, Oxford University Press, 2001, p. 146.
6 Matsushita, 1986, op. cit., p. 212.
7 Ibid., p. 212.
8 Ibid., p. 213.
9 Ibid.
10 Ibid.
11 Ibid.
12 Matsushita, Konosuke, *Watashi no ikikata, kangaekata* [My Way of Life, My Way of Thinking], Nihon Tosho Center, 2008, pp. 222–227.
13 Panasonic, *History of Panasonic*, online, available http://panasonic.co.jp/history/chronicle/1931–02.html (accessed June 12, 2010).
14 Matsushita, 2008, op. cit., pp. 230–232.
15 Panasonic, op. cit.
16 Matsushita, 1986, op. cit., p. 233.
17 Ibid., pp. 239–240.
18 Ibid., p. 242.
19 Ogi, Masamichi, *Panasonic ga Sanyo o baishu suru honto no riyu* [The Real Reason Why Panasonic Acquired Sanyo], Ark Shuppan 2009, p. 140.

20 Ibid.
21 Matsushita, 1986, op. cit., pp. 241–242.
22 Yoshino, M.Y., Endo, Yukihiro, *Transformation of Matsushita Electric Industries, Co., Ltd. 2005 (A)*, Harvard Business School, 2005, p. 1.
23 Ibid., p. 14.
24 McInerney, Francis, *Panasonic, The Largest Corporate Restructuring in History*, St. Martin's Press, 2007, p. 35.
25 Matsushita, Konosuke, Sakaya, Taiichi, *Matsushita Konosuke keiei kaisoroku* [The Management Recollections of Matsushita Konosuke], President-sha, 2007, p. 305; Tokushu denki okoku no genso [The False Vision of the Japanese Electronics Kingdom], *Shukan Diamond*, July 22, 2006, p. 40.
26 Yoshino, Endo, op. cit., p. 2.
27 McInerney, op. cit., p. 35.
28 Yoshino, Endo, op. cit., p. 2.
29 Morikawa, op. cit., p. 149.
30 Matsushita, Sakaya, op. cit., pp. 142–163.
31 Matsushita, Konosuke, *Keiei no ketsudan* [The Decision of Management], PHP Books, 2007, p. 90.
32 Ibid., p. 88.
33 Ogi, op. cit., p. 141.
34 Matsushita, Konosuke, *Sunao no kokoro ni narutame ni* [Developing an Honest Mind], PHP Books, 2005, pp. 34–35.
35 Matsushita, 2007, op. cit., p. 102.
36 Ibid., p. 103.
37 Ibid., pp. 103–104.
38 Ibid., p. 104.
39 Matsushita, Konosuke, *Jinji mangekyo* [A Kaleidescope of Human Affairs], PHP Books, 1977, p. 66.
40 Ibid., p. 68.
41 Ibid., p. 66.
42 Ibid., p. 68.
43 Ogi, op. cit., p. 159.
44 Ibid., p. 162.
45 Panasonic would spin off JVC in 2008.
46 Onishi, Hiroshi, *Panasonic sokojikara no himitsu* [The Secret of Panasonic's Inner Strength], Jitsugyo no Nihon sha, 2008, pp. 104–105.
47 Ogi, op. cit., p. 168.
48 Morikawa, op. cit., p. 149.
49 Mathes, Tom, Leclerc, Louis, interviews with former Quasar employees, online, available www.bcit-broadcast.com/monash/matsushita.pbs (accessed March 21, 2010).
50 Matsushita Guilty of Discriminating Against Americans, *Chicago Tribune*, December 12, 1990.
51 Ibid.
52 Ibid.
53 Mathes, Leclerc, op. cit.
54 Ibid.
55 Ibid.
56 Ibid.
57 Ibid.
58 Ibid.
59 Ibid.
60 Ibid.
61 Matsushita, Konosuke, *Yume o sodateru* [Cultivating One's Dreams], PHP Shuppan, 1998, p. 58.

62 Griffin, Nancy, Masters, Kim, *Hit & Run*, Touchstone, 1996, p. 245.

63 A Tough Innovative Superagent Emerges as King of the Hollywood Deal, *People Magazine*, December 31, 1990.

64 Ibid.

65 McDougal, Dennis, *The Last Mogul*, Dacapo, 2001, p. 481.

66 Ibid.; also Fabrikant, Geraldine, Pollack, Andrew, MCA's Impatience with Wary Parent, *New York Times*, November 4, 1994.

67 Deady, Tim, Japan Hardware Giants wants MCA for its Software, *Los Angeles Business Journal*, October 1, 1990.

68 Soft ga migaku Matsushita AV kakumei [The Matsushita AV Revolution Enhanced by Software], *Nikkei Business*, January 14, 1991.

69 Ibid.

70 Anonymous, Shitteiru tsumori, bangai, Hirata Masaharu [The Hirata Masaharu You May Have Thought You Knew], online, available www.geocities.co.jp/outdoors/3447/page128.html (accessed April 29, 2010); Takeuchi, Kazumasa, Takeda, Kenny, *Matsushita denki* [Matsushita Electric], Baru Shuppan, 2005, p. 77.

71 Anonymous, op. cit.

72 Matsushita no miezaru kiki "kamisama" o koerarenu hitobito [The Unforeseen Risk for Matsushita—The Poeple that Cannot Exceed "God"], *Nikkei Business*, August 25, 1997.

73 Jidai no leader, Tanii Akio, Matsushita denki sangyo shacho [The Leader of Our Times, Tanii Akio, President of Matsushita Electric], *Nikkei Business*, March 26, 1990.

74 Takeuchi, Takeda, op. cit., p. 81.

75 *Nikkei Business*, op. cit., 3/26/90.

76 *Nikkei Business*, op. cit., 1/14/91.

77 Ibid.

78 *Nikkei Business*, op. cit., 3/26/90.

79 *Nikkei Business*, op. cit., 1/14/91.

80 Ibid.

81 Ibid.

82 *Nikkei Business*, op. cit., 8/25/97.

83 Interview with Panasonic employee, September 2010.

84 Interview with Panasonic employee, August 2010.

85 Takeuchi, Takeda, op. cit., p. 192.

86 Interview with Panasonic employee, October 2009.

87 *Nikkei Business*, op. cit., 3/26/90.

88 Takeuchi, Takeda, op. cit., p. 183.

89 *Nikkei Business*, op. cit., 1/14/91.

90 Interview with Panasonic executive in September 2010.

91 *Nikkei Business*, op. cit., 1/14/91.

92 Fabrikant, Geraldine, Chairman Holds Key to MCA's Sale, *New York Times*, October 1, 1990.

93 Fabrikant, Geraldine, MCA Turns Hand to Acquisitions, *New York Times*, February 9, 1987.

94 McDougal, op. cit., p. 481.

95 Ibid.

96 Sanger, op. cit.

97 *Nikkei Business*, op. cit., 8/25/97.

98 Sanger, op. cit.

99 Ibid.

100 Ibid.

101 Fortgang, Ron S., Lax, David A., Sebenius, James K., *Negotiating the Spirit of the Deal—The Ingredients of a Deal Disaster*, Harvard Business School, March 3, 2003,

online, available http://hbswk.hbs.edu/archive/3353.html (accessed March 21, 2010).
102 McDougal, op. cit., p. 482.
103 Ibid., pp. 485–486.
104 Ibid., p. 483.
105 Ibid., p. 484.
106 Ibid., p. 482; Fabrikant, Geraldine, Who Gets What from MCA Deal, *New York Times*, December 1, 1990.
107 Fabrikant, 12/1/90, op. cit.
108 McDougal, op. cit., p. 482.
109 Fabrikant, 12/1/90, op. cit.
110 Ibid.
111 McDougal, op. cit., p. 484.
112 Ibid., p. 482.
113 Ibid.
114 Fabrikant, 12/1/90, op. cit.
115 Ibid.
116 Dick, Bernard F., *City of Dreams: The Making and Remaking of Universal Pictures*, The University Press of Kentucky, 1997, pp. 193–194.
117 PR Newswire, Matsushita and MCA Transition Fact Sheet, November 26, 1990.
118 PR Newswire, Matsushita Electric Industry Company Ltd. Statement Reaffirms Position on Creative Independence at MCA, November 29, 1990.
119 Dick, op. cit., pp. 193–194.
120 Citron, Alan, Helm, Leslie, Matsushita Plays a Low-Key Role at MCA for Now, *Los Angeles Times*, November 17, 1991.
121 McDougal, op. cit., p. 487.
122 Ibid.
123 Ibid.
124 Citron, Helm, 11/17/91, op. cit.
125 McDougal, op. cit., p. 487.
126 Ibid., p. 486.
127 Glover, Kara, Sony Matsushita Takes Hands-off Stance at their U.S. Film Studios, *Los Angeles Business Journal*, July 13, 1992.
128 Citron, Helm, 11/17/91, op. cit.
129 Citron, Helm, 11/17/91, op. cit.
130 Glover, op. cit., 7/13/92.
131 Citron, Helm, op. cit., 11/17/91.
132 Glover, op. cit.
133 Citron, Helm, 11/17/91, op. cit.
134 Ibid.
135 Ibid.
136 McDougal, op. cit., p. 495.
137 Fabrikant, Geraldine, The Osaka Decision, *New York Times*, May 3, 1992.
138 Ibid.
139 Ibid.
140 Ibid.
141 Ibid.
142 Ibid.
143 Ibid.
144 Ibid.
145 McDougal, op. cit., p. 495.
146 Fabrikant, 5/3/92, op. cit.
147 Ibid.
148 Ibid.

149 Ibid.
150 McDougal, op. cit., p. 485.
151 Ibid.
152 WuDunn, Sheryl, For Matsushita, Life Without MCA Probably Means a Return to Nuts and Bolts, *New York Times*, April 8, 1995.
153 Kiger, Patrick J., Chew. Spit. Repeat. The Movie Industry Consumes Carpetbagging Investors Like Prime-Cut Steak. What's the Appeal of Being Eaten Alive?, *Los Angeles Times*, February 29, 2004.
154 Fabrikant, 5/3/92, op. cit.
155 Glover, 7/13/92, op. cit.
156 *Nikkei Business*, 8/25/97, op. cit.
157 Glover, 7/13/92, op. cit.
158 Fabrikant, 5/3/92, op. cit.
159 Ibid.
160 Ibid.
161 McDougal, op. cit., pp. 494–495.
162 Takeuchi, Takeda, op. cit., p. 82.
163 McDougal, op. cit., pp. 494–495.
164 Ibid., p. 495.
165 Zokuzoku kinyujikenbo "kihon o wasreboso shita keiri" [The Accounting Department that Forgot the Basics and Just Went Wild], *Asahi Shinbun*, July 2, 1997; Court Sentences Onoue to 12 Years for Fraud, *The Japan Times*, March 2, 1998.
166 *Asahi Shinbun*, 7/2/97, op. cit.
167 Ibid.
168 Matsushita's Urgent Quest for Leadership, *BusinessWeek*, March 8, 1993.
169 Yoshino, Endo, op. cit., p. 5.
170 Ogi, op. cit., pp. 317–318.
171 Morikawa, op. cit., p. 151.
172 Ogi, op. cit., pp. 319–320.
173 Ibid., p. 319.
174 Ibid.
175 Yoshino, Endo, op. cit., p. 6.
176 *Asahi Shinbun*, 7/2/97, op. cit.
177 Ibid.
178 *Nikkei Business*, 1/14/91, op. cit.
179 Citron, Alan, Helm, Leslie, Leader of MCA Buyout Talks is Demoted, *Los Angeles Times*, March 25, 1992.
180 *Nikkei Business*, 8/25/97, op. cit.
181 Dick, op. cit., p. 196.
182 Brull, Steven, Matsushita Chief Rethinks the Winning Formula, *New York Times*, November 8, 1993; Management Tradition be Damned, *BusinessWeek*, October 21, 1994.
183 *BusinessWeek*, 10/21/94, op. cit.
184 Masters, Kim, Squaring Off Over a Hollywood Empire; Japanese Owners Meeting with U.S. Moguls Seeking to Set MCA's Course, *Washington Post*, October 19, 1994.
185 *Asahi Shinbun*, 7/2/97, op. cit.
186 Citron, Helm, 3/25/92, op. cit.
187 *Nikkei Business*, 8/25/97, op. cit; Anonymous, op. cit.
188 Anonymous, op. cit.
189 *Nikkei Business*, 1/14/91, op. cit.
190 Takeuchi, Takeda, op. cit., p. 89.
191 Masters, op. cit; *Nikkei Business*, 8/25/97, op. cit.
192 Dick, op. cit., p. 198.
193 Fabrikant, Pollack, 11/4/94, op. cit.

194 Ibid.
195 Dick, op. cit., p. 199.
196 Fabrikant, Pollack, 11/4/94, op. cit.
197 Brull, op. cit.
198 Ibid.
199 Fabrikant, Pollack, 11/4/94, op. cit.
200 Masters, op. cit.
201 Fabrikant, Geraldine, At a Crossroads, MCA Executives Plan to Confront Their Bosses, *New York Times*, October 13, 1994.
202 Fabrikant, Pollack, 11/4/94, op. cit.
203 McDougal, op. cit., p. 500.
204 Ibid.
205 Fabrikant, Pollack., 11/4/94, op. cit.
206 Ibid.
207 Masters, op. cit.
208 Takeuchi, Takeda, op. cit., p. 83.
209 Fabrikant, Pollack, 11/4/94, op. cit.
210 Ibid.
211 Ibid.
212 Ibid.
213 Masters, op. cit.
214 McDougal, op. cit., p. 501.
215 Weinraub, Bernard, Hollywood Giants Team Up to Create Major Movie Studio, *New York Times*, October 13, 1994.
216 Pollack, Andrew, For MCA's Japanese Parent No Signs Yet of Letting Go, *New York Times*, October 14, 1994.
217 Masters, op. cit.
218 Fabrikant, Geraldine, MCA Chiefs Fail to Sway Matsushita, *New York Times*, October 20, 1994.
219 Ibid.
220 Ibid.
221 Ibid.
222 Ibid.
223 McDougal, op. cit., p. 501.
224 Ibid., p. 501.
225 Sterngold, James, Seagram Heads for Hollywood: The Tensions; a Marriage not Made in Heaven, *New York Times*, April 7, 1995.
226 Bates, James, Matsushita Moves to Patch Rift with MCA, *Los Angeles Times*, November 18, 1994.
227 Ibid.
228 *Nikkei Business*, 8/25/97, op. cit.
229 Dick, op. cit., p. 201.
230 Ibid., p. 205.
231 Ibid., p. 197.
232 Ibid.
233 McDougal, op. cit., p. 499.
234 Ibid.
235 Ibid.
236 Sterngold, James, The MCA Sale: The Glittering Prize: Seagram Deal Buys Glamour and a Cash Cow Called Music, *New York Times*, April 10, 1995.
237 Dick, op. cit., p. 201.
238 Ibid., p. 212.
239 McDougal, op. cit., p. 506.
240 Ibid.

241 Ibid.
242 Ibid., p. 507.
243 McDougal, op. cit., p. 508.
244 McDougal, op. cit., p. 507.
245 Pollack, Andrew, Industry Changes Led to Sale, *New York Times*, 4/12/95.
246 Fabrikant, Geraldine, Pollack, Andrew, Company News; Matsushita Is Said to Be Eager To Sell Off Its MCA Division, *New York Times*, April 1, 1995; PR Newswire, Matsushita and MCA transition fact sheet—includes information on intention to sell Yosemite Park and Curry Company, November 26, 1990.
247 Business Wire, Matsushita Sells 80% of MCA to Seagram for $5.7 Billion, Company will Remain a Minority Partner, April 9, 1995.
248 *Nikkei Business*, 8/25/97, op. cit.
249 Pollack, 4/12/95, op. cit.
250 Ibid.
251 Ibid.
252 MCA's Not so Excellent Adventure, *New York Times*, April 16, 1995.
253 Sanger, op. cit.
254 Ibid.
255 Takeuchi, Takeda, op. cit., p. 84.
256 Panasonic Corporate IR website, online, available http://panasonic.net/ir/ (accessed June 20, 2010).
257 McInerney, op. cit., p. 146.
258 Yoshida, Reiji, Takahara, Kanako, Matsushita Gives Way to Panasonic, *The Japan Times*, October 1, 2008.
259 Panasonic Corporate IR website, op. cit.
260 Ogi, op. cit., p. 336.
261 Ibid.
262 Yoshino, Endo, op. cit.
263 McInerney, op. cit., p. 147.
264 Panasonic Corporation, Matsushita denki kabushikikaisha, kojin to kaisha ni WIN-WIN no kankei o motarasu jinzai ikusei o suishin [Matsushita Electric, the Development of Human Resources that Results in a Win–Win Situation for the Individual and the Company], PRoVISION, no. 46, Summer 2005, online, available www-06.ibm.com/ibm/jp/provision/no46/pdf/46_interview2.pdf (accessed June 6, 2010).
265 Ibid.
266 Panasonic Corporation website, online, available http://panasonic.net/csr/employee/div/ (accessed June 6, 2010).

6 Sony's movie entertainment empire

1 Klein, Edward, A Yen for Hollywood, *Vanity Fair*, September 1991, pp. 242–243.
2 Ginsberg, Steve, Are Japanese Planning Pullout from Hollywood?, *Los Angeles Business Journal*, February 14, 1994.
3 Griffin, Nancy, Masters, Kim, *Hit & Run*, Touchstone, 1996, p. 308.
4 Nathan, John, *Sony: The Private Life*, HarperCollins, 1999, p. 232.
5 Finkelstein, Sydney, Why Smart Executives Fail: Four Case Histories of How People Learn the Wrong Lessons from History, *Business History*, vol. xlviii, no. 2, April 2006, p. 161.
6 Ibid.
7 Arango, Tim, Sony's Version of Tracy and Hepburn, *New York Times*, October 25, 2009.
8 Bruner, Robert F., *Deals From Hell*, John Wiley & Sons, 2005, p. 163.
9 Sony Company History website, online, available www.sony.net/SonyInfo/CorporateInfo/History/prospectus.html (accessed August 1, 2010).

10 Ibid.
11 Yoshino, M.Y., Endo, Yukihiro, *Transformation of Matsushita Electric Industries, Co., Ltd. 2005 (A)*, Harvard Business School, 2005.
12 Ibid.
13 Morita Akio, *Made in Japan*, Dutton, 1986, p. 146.
14 Ibid., pp. 147–8.
15 Sony Company History website, op. cit.
16 Kobayashi, Shunichi, *Sony o tsukutta otoko: Ibuka Masaru* [The Man who Built Sony: Ibuka Masaru], Wakku Kabushikaisha, 2002, p. 62.
17 Ibuka, Masaru, *"Sony" sozo e no michi* [The Road to the Birth of "Sony"], Graph sha, 2003, p. 88.
18 Ibid., p. 31.
19 Kobayashi, op. cit., p. 74.
20 Ibuka, op. cit., p. 88.
21 Ibid., p. 86.
22 Ibid., p. 80.
23 Ibid., p. 88.
24 Kobayashi, op. cit., p. 142.
25 Ibid., p. 142.
26 Ibid., p. 140.
27 Ibid., p. 142.
28 Tsunoda, Ryusaku, De Bary, William Theodore, Keene, Donald, *Sources of Japanese Tradition*, vol. ii, *Fundamentals of our National Policy*, Columbia University Press, 1964, p. 280.
29 Shinmin no Michi [The Way of the Subjects], online, available www.worldfuture-fund.org/wffmaster/Reading/Japanese%20Documents/wayofthesubjectsnew.html (accessed February 11 2010).
30 Samuels, Richard J., *Machiavelli's Children*, Cornell University Press, 2003, p. 127.
31 Ibid.
32 Tsunoda, De Bary, Keene, op. cit., p. 167.
33 Ibid.
34 Ibid., pp. 167–168.
35 Samuels, op. cit., p. 127.
36 Pyle, Kenneth B., *Japan Rising*, The Century Foundation, 2007, p. 122.
37 Samuels, op. cit., pp. 128–131.
38 Ibid.
39 Kobayashi, op. cit., p. 75.
40 Morita, op. cit., p. 146.
41 Ibid., p. 147.
42 Ibid., p. 146.
43 Klein, 9/91, op. cit., p. 202.
44 Sony no hatten o sasaeta gijutsusha Kihara Nobuo san no jiyu sozo [Kihara Nobuo—The Engineer Who with his Free Thinking Drove Sony's Development], *Shukan Shincho*, March 3, 2011.
45 Nippon Columbia website, online, available http://columbia.jp/company/corporate/history/index.html (accessed April 29, 2010).
46 Sony Corporate Website, Company History, chapter 22, CBS/Sony Records is Established in First Round of Capital Deregulation, online, available www.sony.net/SonyInfo/CorporateInfo/History/SonyHistory/2–22.html (accessed May 1, 2010).
47 Nathan, op. cit., p. 97.
48 Ibid.
49 Sony Corporate Website, op. cit., chapter 22.
50 Nathan, op. cit., p. 97.
51 Sony Corporate Website, op. cit., chapter 22.

52 Ohga, Norio, *Doing It Our Way*, International House of Japan, 2008, p. 49.
53 Nathan, op. cit., p. 97.
54 Griffin, Masters, op. cit., p. 179.
55 Ibid.
56 Ohga, op. cit., p. 49.
57 Ibid., p. 52.
58 Sony Corporate Website, op. cit., chapter 22.
59 Ohga, op. cit., p. 53.
60 Ibid., pp. 54–55.
61 Ibid., pp. 53–54.
62 Sano, Tsuneo, *Sony, shirarezaru seicho monogatari* [Sony: The Unknown Story of its Growth], Mainichi Shinbunsha, 2007, p. 29.
63 Ibid., p. 30.
64 Ibid.
65 Interview with former Sony executive.
66 Ohga, op. cit., p. 54.
67 Sony Corporate Website, op. cit., chapter 22.
68 Ibid.
69 Ibid.
70 Ohga, op. cit., p. 61.
71 Kester, W. Carl, *Japanese Takeovers*, Harvard Business School, 1991, p. 122.
72 Griffin, Masters, op. cit., p. 180.
73 Ohga, op. cit., p. 86.
74 Ibid., pp. 86–87; Nathan, op. cit., p. 172.
75 Ohga, op. cit., p. 87.
76 Ibid., p. 59.
77 Ibid., p. 56.
78 Ibid., p. 57.
79 Ibid., pp. 57–58.
80 Sony Corporate Website, op. cit., chapter 22.
81 Ibid.
82 Griffin, Masters, op. cit., p. 186.
83 Ohga, op. cit., p. 89.
84 Dick, Bernard F. (ed.), *Columbia Pictures*, University of Kentucky Press, 2010, pp. 6–7.
85 Ibid., p. 23.
86 Ibid., p. 22; Harvard Business School, *Being There: Sony Corporation and Columbia Pictures*, December 8, 1994.
87 Dick (ed.), op. cit., p. 36.
88 Ibid.
89 Ibid., p. 38.
90 Dick (ed.), op. cit., p. 36.
91 For Coke's Peter Sealey, Hollywood is It, *BusinessWeek*, March 15, 1993.
92 Ibid.
93 Sealey, Peter, Entertainment o kirisute gyomukiki ni tokka seyo [Cut Off Entertainment and Concentrate on the Core Business], *Nikkei biztech*, June 26, 2005.
94 Dick (ed.), op. cit., p. 37.
95 Ibid., p. 39.
96 *BusinessWeek*, 3/15/93, op. cit.
97 Sealey, 6/26/05, op. cit.
98 Ibid.
99 Cieply, Michael, Citron, Alan, A Virtually 'Empty' Vault, *Los Angeles Times*, April 15, 1990.
100 Dick (ed.), op. cit., p. 38.

101 Ibid., p. 39.
102 Ibid.
103 Columbia Pictures Firing Told, *Los Angeles Times*, December 10, 1987.
104 Bruner, op. cit., p. 156.
105 Cieply, Michael, Benesch, Connie, Aftershocks of Cutback at Columbia Pictures: The Company and Its Ex-Employees Are Still Trying to Come to Terms with Dismissal Process, *Los Angeles Times*, February 13, 1988.
106 Harvard Business School, op. cit., December 8, 1994.
107 Bruner, op. cit., p. 156.
108 Cieply, Citron, op. cit.
109 Sony Wishes Upon a Star, *New York Times*, November 22, 1989.
110 Bruner, op. cit., p. 150.
111 Griffin, Masters, op. cit., p. 184.
112 Perry, Nancy J., Kirsch, Sandra L., Will Sony Make it in Hollywood?, *Fortune*, September 9, 1991.
113 Sanger, David E., Sony's Norio Ohga: Building Smaller, Buying Bigger, *New York Times*, February 18, 1990.
114 Nathan, op. cit., p. 186.
115 Sanger, David E., Sony Has High Hopes for Columbia Pictures, *New York Times*, September 28, 1989.
116 Nathan, op. cit., p. 190.
117 Griffin, Masters, op. cit., p. 199.
118 Ibid., p. 175.
119 Ibid.
120 Klein, 9/91, op. cit.
121 Griffin, Masters, op. cit., p. 199.
122 Klein, 9/91, op. cit, p. 243.
123 Nathan, op. cit., pp. 298–299.
124 Klein, 9/91, op. cit, p. 243.
125 Nathan, op. cit., p. 191.
126 Klein, 9/91, op. cit, p. 243.
127 Nathan, op. cit., p. 191.
128 Shah, Diane, K., The Producers, *New York Times*, October 22, 1989.
129 Griffin, Masters, op. cit., p. 224; Nathan, op. cit., pp. 196–197.
130 Nathan, op. cit., p. 200.
131 Shah, op. cit.
132 Ibid.
133 Ibid.
134 Bruner, op. cit., p. 155.
135 Nathan, op. cit., p. 227.
136 Weinraub, Bernard, Fabrikant, Geraldine, Sony is Overhauling its Film Studios, *New York Times*, January 11, 1995.
137 Weinraub, Bernard, At Columbia Pictures, Turmoil Over Top Job Yields a Peak at Power, *New York Times*, September 23, 1991.
138 Dutka, Elaine, Into the Frying Pan, *Los Angeles Times*, November 10, 1991.
139 Weinraub, op. cit.
140 Cieply, Citron, op. cit.
141 Dick (ed.), op. cit., p. 56.
142 Ibid.
143 Harvard Business School, 12/8/94, op. cit.; *New York Times*, 11/22/89, op. cit.
144 Nathan, op. cit., p. 190.
145 Glover, Kara, Sony Matsushita Take Hands-off Stance at their U.S. Film Studios, *Los Angeles Business Journal*, July 13, 1992; Griffin, Masters, op. cit., p. 272.
146 Ibid., p. 336.

147 Cieply, Citron, op. cit.
148 Ibid.
149 Klein, 9/91, op. cit., p. 244.
150 Nathan, op. cit., p. 231.
151 Ibid., p. 227.
152 Harvard Business School, 12/8/94, op. cit.
153 Nathan, op. cit., p. 217.
154 Ibid.
155 Ibid., p. 223.
156 Ibid.
157 Griffin, Masters, op. cit., p. 272; Klein, 9/91, op. cit.
158 Weinraub, Bernard, Sony Mulls a Public Sale of Entertainment Assets, *New York Times*, November 20, 1996.
159 Weinraub, Bernard, Turmoil and Indecision at Sony's Film Studios, *New York Times*, October 24, 1994.
160 Griffin, Masters, op. cit., p. 302.
161 Weinraub, 9/23/91, op. cit.
162 Klein, 9/91, op. cit.
163 Griffin, Masters, op. cit., p. 320.
164 Ibid., pp. 460–461.
165 Sterngold, James, Sony, Struggling, Takes a Huge Loss on Movie Studios, *New York Times*, November 18, 1994.
166 Klein, Edward, The Lost Tycoon, *Vanity Fair*, May 1995, p. 67.
167 Nathan, op. cit., p. 239.
168 Sterngold, op. cit.
169 Ibid.
170 Farhi, Paul, MCA, Sony: Why Mergers Didn't Work; Cultural Gap Between Japan, Hollywood Cited, *Washington Post*, April 8, 1995.
171 Nathan, op. cit., pp. 234–235.
172 Ibid., p. 234.
173 Griffin, Masters, op. cit., pp. 274–275.
174 Ohga, op. cit., p. 99.
175 Sterngold, op. cit.
176 Box Office, online, data available http://boxofficemojo.com (accessed May 15 2010).
177 Weinraub, 10/24/94, op. cit.
178 Brownell, Andrew, *Sony Pictures Entertainment*, Tuck School of Business at Dartmouth, 2000.
179 Weinraub, 11/20/96, op. cit.
180 Klein, 5/95, op. cit, p. 68.
181 Ibid., p. 55.
182 Griffin, Masters, op. cit., p. 341.
183 Klein, 5/95, op. cit, p. 62.
184 Griffin, Masters, op. cit., p. 410.
185 Ibid.
186 Klein, 5/95, op. cit, p. 62.
187 Ibid., p. 68.
188 Ibid., p. 70.
189 Nathan, op. cit., p. 165.
190 Ibid., p. 254.
191 Ibid., p. 171, 306.
192 Weinraub, Fabrikant, 1/11/95, op. cit.
193 Klein, 5/95, op. cit, p. 74.
194 From interview with former senior executive of Sony Corporation.

195 Nathan, op. cit., p. 298.
196 Weinraub, Bernard, Behind Sony Ouster, One Excess Too Many, *New York Times*, December 7, 1995.
197 Ibid.
198 Nathan, op. cit., p. 287.
199 Yame Sony ni ki-ke! yametenao Sony o aisuru yame Sony tachino kuge [Listen to Those Who Quit Sony! The Recommendations of Those Who Quit Sony But Who Still Love the Company], *Shukan Diamond*, February 12, 2011. According to the magazine, all of the former Sony employees interviewed remarked that Sony started to become "out of order" from the mid 1990s, i.e., when Idei took the helm of the company.
200 Nathan, op. cit., p. 312.
201 Ibid., p. 306.
202 Klein, 5/95, op. cit., p. 50.
203 Former Sony executive comment.
204 Nathan, op. cit., p. 170.
205 Ibid., p. 166.
206 Ibid., p. 306.
207 Griffin, Masters, op. cit., p. 457.
208 Weinraub, Bernard, Sony Ousts The Chairman of its Studios, *New York Times*, September 14, 1996.
209 Bates, James, Eller, Claudia, Sony Ousts the Head of Entertainment Unit, *Los Angeles Times*, October 3, 1996.
210 Weinraub, 11/20/96, op. cit.
211 Nathan, op. cit., p. 310.
212 Weinraub, Bernard, Sony Says Studio Head Has Resigned, *New York Times*, October 3, 1996.
213 Nathan, op. cit., pp. 310–311.
214 Fabrikant, Geraldine, A Strong Debut Helps, as a New Chief Tackles Sony's Movie Problems, *New York Times*, May 26, 1997.
215 Nathan, op. cit., p. 311.
216 Weinraub, Bernard, Sony Names Its New Team to Run Studio Operations, *New York Times*, October 9, 1996.
217 Nathan, op. cit., pp. 311–312.
218 Ibid., p. 312.
219 Lyman, Rick, President of Columbia Pictures Promoted, *New York Times*, December 16, 1999.
220 Nathan, op. cit., p. 314.
221 Holson, Laura M., The Affable Ax Wielder at Sony, *New York Times*, May 4, 2003.
222 Manly, Lorne, Sorkin, Andrew Ross, At Sony, Diplomacy Trumps Technology, *New York Times*, March 8, 2005.
223 Holson, op. cit., 5/4/03.
224 Manly, Sorkin, op. cit.
225 Holson, op. cit., 5/4/03.
226 Manly, Sorkin, op. cit.
227 Holson, Laura M., Sony is Looking to Cut Costs at Its Movie Division, *New York Times*, April 18, 2003.
228 Nathan, op. cit., p. 308.
229 Arango, Tim, op. cit.
230 Ibid.
231 Ibid.
232 Ibid.
233 Sony corporate press release, December 10, 2003, online, available www.sony.com/SCA (accessed April 29, 2010).

234 Ibid.
235 Ibid.
236 Arango, Tim, op. cit.
237 Ibid.
238 Sony Corporate Website, business update meeting: Entertainment and BRIC's, online, available www.sony.net/SonyInfo/Ir.ino (accessed May 3, 2010).
239 Barnes, Brooks, Disney's Marketing Chief the Latest Casualty of an Insular Movie Industry, *International Herald Tribune*, January 10, 2012.
240 Sony Struggles to Regain Reputation for Innovation, *International Herald Tribune*, May 24, 2011. According to Tsujino Koichiro, a former engineer at Sony who led the company's development of its PC laptop business and left Sony in 2006 to head Google's Japanese business unit, Sony's problems were due to "failures of corporate governance and petty jealousies that ... crushed what had been a creative atmosphere like the one at Google.".
241 Voices for Change Grow in a Corporate Japan Seen as Sluggish and Hermetic, *International Herald Tribune*, November 24, 2011. According to Amagai Satoshi, a former Sony executive, rather than being led by innovators Sony was now in the grips of accountants—a development that was partly responsible for Amagai's decision to call it quits after working for over 30 years and set up his own technology venture.

7 Conclusion: The impact of tolerance on empires and M&A

1 Ninety Gaffes in Ninety Years, *Independent*, May 28, 2011.
2 Jinsokuna joho kokai hissu [Immediate Disclosure of Information is a Must], *Nihon Keizai Shinbun*, April 19, 2011.
3 Appleby, Joyce, *The Relentless Revolution*, Norton, 2010, p. 340.
4 Welch, Jack, *Straight From the Gut*, Business Plus, 2003, p. 184.
5 Brooks, David, Relax. America's Future is Exceedingly Bright, *International Herald Tribune*, April 7, 2010.
6 Foreign Entrepreneurs Increasingly Find a Home in Britain, *International Herald Tribune*, January 15, 2010.
7 Morishita, Kae, Headhunting in Japan Put Samsung on the Path to Greatness, *Asahi Shinbun*, August 13, 2010.
8 Fukasaku, Yukiko, Gender Equality & Economic Growth in Japan, *Japan Spotlight*, Japan Economic Foundation, May/June 2010, p. 16.
9 Ibid., p. 17.
10 Ibid.
11 Atsumi, Naoki, Shokuba no tayosei kiki ni tsuyoku [Diversity in the Workplace Leads to Strength Against Risks, *Nihon Keizai Shinbun*, August 12, 2011.
12 Shinotsuka, Eiko, Use Women Effectively as Human Resources in Japanese Economy, *Japan Spotlight*, Japan Economic Foundation, May/June 2010, p. 6.
13 Ishihara Could be Spiked With His Own Barbs, *The Japan Times*, November 10, 2002.
14 Staying on the Fast Track, *Fortune*, July 26, 2010. Latest figures show that by 2050, 40 percent of the population of Japan will be over 65.
15 Sakaiya, Taichi, Manzoku kojo e uchibenkei haise [Eliminate the Inward-Looking Stance to Achieve a Higher Level of Satisfaction], *Nihon Keizai Shinbun*, January 4, 2008.
16 Global jin umu kyoiku o [Education for the Global Person], *Nihon Keizai Shinbun*, July 25, 2010.
17 Half of New Hires Fret Work Overseas, *Asahi Shinbun*, August 16, 2010.
18 Ibid.
19 Fewer Japanese Students Studying Abroad a Cause for Concern, *Mainichi Shinbun*, June 7, 2010.
20 Quigley, Carroll, *Tragedy and Hope*, The Macmillan Company, 1966, p. 1260.

21 Sakaiya, op. cit.
22 Reshape 'Galapagos' Cellphones for the World, *Asahi Shinbun*, July 21, 2010.
23 Ibid.
24 Abegglen, James C., *21st Century Japanese Management*, Palgrave Macmillan, 2006, pp. 68–69.
25 Ibid., p. 144.
26 Ibid., p. 145.
27 Chinese Influx Poses Profound Policy Challenges, *Asahi Shinbun*, June 22, 2010.
28 Japanese Firms Adopt a Global Appearance, *Asahi Shinbun*, April 6, 2010.
29 Ibid.
30 Friedman, Thomas L., Broadway and the Mosque, *International Herald Tribune*, August 5, 2010.
31 Finkelstein, Sydney, *The DaimlerChrysler Merger*, Tuck School of Business at Dartmouth, 2002.
32 Kuhlmann, Torsten, Dowling, Peter J., Daimler Chrysler: A Case Study of a Cross-Border Merger, in Stahl, Gunter K., Mendenhall, Mark E. (eds), *Mergers and Acquisitions*, Stanford Business Books, 2005, p. 354.
33 St. Jean, Dianne C., *DaimlerChrysler Merger: The Quest to Create "One Company"*, Babson College, 2004, p. 14.
34 Rottig, Daniel, Successfully Managing International Mergers and Acquisitions: A Descriptive Framework, *The Journal of the AIB-SE*, 2007, p. 110.
35 BBC News, Daimler Boss Denies Takeover Plan, December 9, 2003, online, available http://news.bbc.co.uk/2/hi/business/3305249.stm (accessed June 7, 2010).
36 Rottig, op. cit., p. 110.
37 Finkelstein, op. cit.
38 Terjesen, Siri, Mergers and Acquisitions: Patterns, Motives, and Strategic Fit, *QFinance*, online, available www.qfinance.com/contentFiles/QF02/glus0fcl/12/0/mergers-and-acquisitions-patterns-motives-and-strategic-fit.pdf (accessed June 7, 2010).
39 Finkelstein, op. cit.
40 Paul, Herbert, *DaimlerChrsyler: Lessons in Post-Merger Integration*, University of Applied Sciences Mainz, 2003, p. 252.
41 Watkins, Michael, Why DaimlerChrysler Never Got into Gear, *Harvard Business Review*, online, available http://blogs.hbr.org/watkins/2007/05/why_the_daimler-chrysler_merger.html (accessed June 11, 2010).
42 Busco, Cristiano, Riccaboni, Angelo, Scapens, Robert W., *When Culture Matters: Processes of Organizational Learning and Transformation*, Society of Organizational Learning and the Massachusetts Institute of Technology, 2002, p. 43.
43 Ibid., pp. 44–45.
44 Bower, Joseph L., *Not All M&A Are Alike–and That Matters*, Harvard Business School Publishing, 2001, p. 99.
45 Busco, Riccaboni, Scapens, op. cit., p. 44.
46 Ibid., p. 50.
47 Tada Tomio, Yamamori Tetsuo, Ningen no ikikata [The Way of Life for Humans], Bunshun Nesco, 2000, pp. 109–113.
48 Stanford Graduate School of Business, HP and Compaq Combined, in Search of Scale and Scope, July 15, 2004, p. 13.
49 Ibid., pp. 14–15.
50 Ibid., p. 13.
51 Ibid., pp. 13–14.
52 Schein, Edgar H., *Organizational Culture and Leadership*, John Wiley & Sons, 2004, p. 86.
53 Ibid., p. 11.
54 Hofstede, Geert, Hofstede, Gert Jan, *Cultures and Organizations*, McGrawHill, 2005, p. 286.

55 Alon, Ilan, Higgins, James M., *Global Leadership Success Through Emotional and Cultural Intelligences*, Indiana University Kelley School of Business, 2005, p. 506.
56 Big Obstacles to China's Ambitions, *International Herald Tribune*, January 21, 2010.
57 American made ... Chinese Owned, *Fortune*, May 24, 2010.
58 Alon, Higgins, op. cit., p. 506.
59 Ibid., p. 503.
60 Ibid., p. 507.
61 Ibid., p. 508.
62 Moore, Fredrick, *With Japan's Leaders*, New York, Scribner, 1942, pp. 170–171.
63 James, Lawrence, *The Rise & Fall of the British Empire*, Abacus, 2001, p. 479.
64 Gaimusho, Nihon gaiko bunsho gekan [Japanese Diplomatic Documents], *Gaimusho*, 1990, p. 6; Shaffer, Ralph E., *Toward Pearl Harbor*, Markus Wiener Publishing, Inc., 1991.
65 Embracing a Linguistic Interloper, *International Herald Tribune*, July 27, 2010.
66 *Nihon Keizai Shinbun*, 7/25/10, op. cit.
67 M&A to Power Korea's Future Growth, *The Korea Times*, June 8, 2009.
68 *Nihon Keizai Shinbun.*, 7/25/10, op. cit.
69 Keizai Koho Center, *Japan: An International Comparison, 2010*, December 28, 2009. Japanese students had an average test score of 457. In comparison, Chinese students scored 573, and Korean students 535.
70 *Nihon Keizai Shinbun.*, 7/25/10, op. cit.
71 Maeda, Masataka, *Uniqlo, Rakuten Make Official Language English*, Japan Center for Economic Research, July 15, 2010.
72 Future Success Translates into English, *Asahi Shinbun*, July 24–25, 2010.
73 Ibid.
74 Immigration Policy to Favor Wealthy, Skilled, *Asahi Shinbun*, January 21, 2010.
75 Taizai encho taishosha no 6 wari ga kikoku, Indonesia jin kangoshi koho [60 Percent of Indonesian Nurse Candidates who Prolong their Stay in Japan Go Back to Indonesia], *Asahi Shinbun*, August 2, 2011. Of the first 104 nursing candidates from Indonesia who came to Japan, only 15 were able to pass the national nursing qualification examinations.
76 Lower Language Barrier for Caregivers from Overseas, *The Daily Yomiuri*, January 30, 2012.
77 Nakasone's World Class Blunder, *Time Magazine*, October 6, 1986.
78 Aston, W.G. (translation), *Nihongi*, Charles E. Tuttle Company, Inc., 1980, vol. ii, p. 285.
79 Emperor's Remark Pours Fuel on Ethnic Hot Potato, *The Japan Times*, March 11, 2002.
80 Ibid., pp. 38–39.
81 Ibid., p. 38.
82 Aso Says Japan is Nation of One Race, *The Japan Times*, October 18, 2005; Norway Attack: Killer Praises Japan as Model Country, *The Telegraph*, July 26, 2011, online, available www.telegraph.co.uk/news/worldnews/europe/norway (accessed July 30, 2011).
83 Japan's Outsiders Waiting to Break In, *International Herald Tribune*, January 17–18, 2009.
84 Racist Remark Show Japanese Badly In Need of Attitude Change, *SunSentinel*, August 22, 1988, online, available http://articles.sun-sentinel.com/1988-08-22/news/8802180385_1_american-black-leaders-japanese-black-mannequins (accessed July 30, 2011).
85 Ex-minister Hiranuma Says Renho Not Originally Japanese, *Kyodo News*, January 18, 2010, online, available www.japantoday.com/category/politics/view/ex-minister-hiranuma-says-lawmaker-renho-not-originally-japanese (accessed July 1, 2010).
86 Ishihara Says Use of 'Sangokujin' Inappropriate, *Kyodo News*, April 24, 2000, online,

available   http://findarticles.com/p/articles/mi_m0XPQ/is_2000_April_24/ai_61968881/ (accessed July 1, 2010).

87 Alon, Higgins, op. cit., p. 510.

88 Hofstede, Geert, Hofstede, Gert Jan, *Cultures and Organizations*, McGraw Hill, 2005, p. 286.

89 Schein, Edgar H., *Organizational Culture and Leadership*, John Wiley & Sons, 2004, p. 22.

90 Hofstede, Hofstede, op. cit., pp. 284–286.

91 Atsumi, Naoki, Shokuba no tayosei kiki ni tsuyoku [Diversity in the Workplace Leads to Strength Against Risks], August 12, 2011.

92 Ibid.

93 Diamond, Jarred, *The Third Chimpanzee*, Harper Perennial, 1993, p. 234.

Suggested further reading

Abegglen, James C., *21st Century Japanese Management*, Palgrave Macmillan, 2006.

Appleby, Joyce, *The Relentless Revolution*, Norton, 2010.

Atkins, E. Taylor, *Primitive Selves*, University of California Press, 2010.

Bartlett, W.B., *The Mongols*, Amberley, 2010.

Beasley, W.G., *Japanese Imperialism: 1868–1945*, Clarendon Press, 1991.

Bernstein, William J., *A Splendid Exchange*, Grove Press, 2008.

Besanko, David, Dranove, David, Shanley, Mark, Schaefer, Scott, *Economics of Strategy*, John Wiley & Sons, 2000.

Bix, Herbert P., *Hirohito and the Making of Modern Japan*, Harper Collins, 2000.

Boxer, C.R., *The Dutch Seafaring Empire*, Penguin, 1978.

Bradley, James, *The Imperial Cruise*, Little, Brown and Company, 2009.

Brown, Stephen R., *Merchant Kings*, Douglas and McIntyre, 2009.

Brownell, Andrew, *Sony Pictures Entertainment*, Tuck School of Business at Dartmouth, 2000.

Bruner, Robert F., *Deals From Hell*, John Wiley & Sons, 2005.

Caprio, Mark E., *Japanese Assimilation Policies in Colonial Korea, 1910–1945*, University of Washington Press, 2009.

Carpini, Friar Giovanni DiPlano, *The Story of the Mongols whom we Call the Tartars*, Branden Publishing Company, 1996 (originally written in 1252).

Chambers, James, *The Devil's Horsemen*, Atheneum, New York, 1979.

Chandler, Alfred D., *Strategy and Structure*, Doubleday & Company, 1962.

Chua, Amy, *Day of Empire*, Doubleday, 2007.

Cook, Harold J., *Matters of Exchange*, Yale University Press, 2007.

Cotterell, Arthur, *Western Power in Asia*, Wiley, 2010.

Diamond, Jarred, *The Third Chimpanzee*, Harper Perennial, 1993.

Dick, Bernard F., *City of Dreams: The Making and Remaking of Universal Pictures*, The University Press of Kentucky, 1997.

Dick, Bernard F. (editor), *Columbia Pictures*, University of Kentucky Press, 2010.

Doyle, Michael, *Empires*, Cornell University Press, 1986.

Duus, Peter, *The Abacus and the Sword*, University of California Press, 1995.

Esthus, Raymond A., *Theodore Roosevelt and Japan*, University of Washington Press, 1966.

Ferguson, Niall, *Colossus*, Penguin Books, 2004.

Ferguson, Niall, *The War of the World*, Penguin/Allen Lane, 2006.

Ferguson, Niall, *The Ascent of Money*, Penguin Books, 2009.

Fernandez-Armesto, Felipe, *Millennium*, Black Swan, 1995.

Findlay, Robert, O'Rourke, Kevin, *Power and Plenty*, Princeton University Press, 2007.

Forbes, Steve, Prevas, John, *Power Ambition Glory*, Crown Business 2009.

Fukuyama, Francis, *The End of History and the Last Man*, Free Press, 2006.

Gabriel, Richard A., *Genghis Khan's Greatest General: Subotai the Valiant*, University of Oklahoma Press, 2006.

Gibbon, Edward, *The Decline and Fall of the Roman Empire*, Encyclopaedia Britannica Inc., 1982 (first published 1776–1788).

Gill, Anton, *Ruling Passions: Sex, Race and Empire*, BBC Books, 1995.

Griffin, Nancy, Masters, Kim, *Hit & Run*, Touchstone, 1996.

Halberstam, David, *The Reckoning*, Avon, 1986.

Hardt, Michael, Negri, Antonio, *Empire*, Harvard University Press, 2000.

Hibbert, Christopher, *The Great Mutiny: India 1857*, Penguin Books, 1980.

Hofstede, Geert, Hofstede, Gert Jan, *Cultures and Organizations*, McGraw Hill, 2005.

Horne, Gerald, *Race War!* New York University Press, 2004.

Howe, Stephen, *Empire: A Very Short Introduction*, Oxford University Press, 2002.

Howorth, Sir Henry Hoyle, *History of the Mongols*, Longmans, Green, and Co., 1876.

Ibuka, Masaru, *"Sony" sozo e no michi* [The Road to the Birth of "Sony"], Graph sha, 2003.

Ienaga, Saburo, *The Pacific War 1931–1945*, Pantheon Asia Library, 1978.

Itoh, Mayumi, *The Globalization of Japan*, St. Martin's Press, 2000.

Jacques, Martin, *When China Rules the World*, Penguin Press, 2009.

James, Lawrence, *The Rise & Fall of the British Empire*, Abacus, 2001.

Johnson, Chalmers, *The Sorrows of Empire*, Metropolitan Books, 2004.

Kahn, Paul (adaptation), *The Secret History of the Mongols*, Cheng & Tsui Company, 1998.

Kamenka, Eugene (editor), *The Portable Karl Marx*, Viking Penguin Inc, 1983.

Keizai Koho Center, *Japan: An International Comparison, 2010*, December 28, 2009.

Kester, W. Carl, *Japanese Takeovers*, Harvard Business School, 1991.

Kobayashi, Shunichi, *Sony o tsukutta otoko: Ibuka Masaru* [The Man who Built Sony: Ibuka Masaru], Wakku Kabushiki Kaisha, 2002.

LaFeber, Walter, *The Clash*, W.W. Norton & Company, 1997.

Landes, David, *The Wealth and Poverty of Nations*, Little, Brown and Company, 1998.

Lane, George, *Daily Life in the Mongol Empire*, Hackett, 2006.

Lauren, Paul Gordon, *Power and Prejudice*, Westview Press, 1996.

MacCulloch, Diarmaid, *Reformation*, Penguin Books, 2004.

Man, John, *Genghis Khan*, Bantam Books, 2005.

Massarella, Derek, *A World Elsewhere*, Yale University Press, 1990.

Matsushita, Konosuke, *Jinji mangekyo* [A Kaleidoscope of Human Affairs], PHP Books, 1977.

Matsushita, Konosuke, *Monono mikata, kangaekata* [The Way to Look at Things and Think], PHP Books, 1986.

Matsushita, Konosuke, *Yume o sodateru* [Cultivating One's Dreams], PHP Shuppan, 1998.

Matsushita, Konosuke, *Sunao no kokoro ni narutame ni* [Developing an Honest Mind], PHP Books, 2005.

Matsushita, Konosuke, *Keiei no ketsudan* [The Decision of Management], PHP Books, 2007.

Matsushita, Konosuke, *Watashi no ikikata, kangaekata* [My Way of Life, My Way of Thinking], Nihon Tosho Center, 2008.

Matsushita, Konosuke, Sakaya, Taiichi, *Matsushita Konosuke keiei kaisoroku* [The Management Recollections of Matsushita Konosuke], President-sha, 2007.

McCarthy, Thomas, *Race, Empire, and the Idea of Human Development*, Cambridge University Press, 2009.

McDougal, Dennis, *The Last Mogul*, Dacapo, 2001.

McInerney, Francis, *Panasonic, The Largest Corporate Restructuring in History*, St. Martin's Press, 2007.

Micklethwait, John, Wooldridge, Adrian, *The Company*, The Modern Library, 2005.

Miller, Stuart Creighton, *Benevolent Assimilation*, Yale University Press, 1982.

Moore, Karl, Lewis, David, *Foundations of Corporate Empire*, Financial Times/Prentice Hall, 2000.

Morgan, David, *The Mongols*, Basil Blackwell, 1986.

Morgenthau, Hans J., *Politics Among Nations*, McGraw-Hill Inc., 1985.

Morikawa, Hidemasa, *A History of Top Management in Japan*, Oxford University Press, 2001.

Morita, Akio, *Made in Japan*, Dutton, 1986.

Nathan, John, *Sony: The Private Life*, HarperCollins, 1999.

Ogi, Masamichi, *Panasonic ga Sanyo o baishu suru honto no riyu* [The Real Reason Why Panasonic Acquired Sanyo], Ark Shuppan, 2009.

Ohga, Norio, *Doing It Our Way*, International House of Japan, 2008.

Onishi, Hiroshi, *Panasonic sokojikara no himitsu* [The Secret of Panasonic's Inner Strength], Jitsugyo no Nihon sha, 2008.

Polo, Marco, *The Travels of Marco Polo*, Wordsworth Classics of World Literature, 1997.

Pyle, Kenneth B., *Japan Rising*, The Century Foundation, 2007.

Quigley, Carroll, *Tragedy and Hope*, The Macmillan Company, 1966.

Ratchnevsky, Paul, *Genghis Khan: His Life and Legacy*, Blackwell Publishing, 1991.

Rattansi, Ali, *Racism: A Very Short Introduction*, Oxford University Press, 2007.

Samuels, Richard J., *Machiavelli's Children*, Cornell University Press, 2003.

Schein, Edgar H., *Organizational Culture and Leadership*, John Wiley & Sons, 2004.

Shepard, Todd, *The Invention of Decolonization*, Cornell University Press, 2006.

Smil, Vaclav, *Why America is Not a New Rome*, The MIT Press, 2010.

Takeuchi, Kazumasa, Takeda, Kenny, *Matsushita denki* [Matsushita Electric], Baru Shuppan, 2005.

Talbott, Strobe, *The Great Experiment*, Simon & Schuster, 2008.

Weatherford, Jack, *Genghis Khan and the Making of the Modern World*, Three Rivers Press, 2004.

Weatherford, Jack, *The Secret History of the Mongol Queens*, Crown Publishers, 2010.

Welch, Jack, *Straight From the Gut*, Business Plus, 2003.

Wolff, Leon, *Little Brown Brother*, History Book Club, 1961.

Zinn, Howard, *A People's History of the United States*, Harper Perennial, 1995.

Index